The Pub Crawler's Guide to Montana's Small Town Taverns

The Pub Crawler's Guide to Montana's Small Town Taverns

A Field Guide to 365 Taverns in Montana's Smallest Communities.

Doug Ardary

Pub Crawler Promotions
Helena, Montana

ISBN 0-9655981-0-1

Library of Congress Catalog Card Number 96-93006

ACKNOWLEDGEMENTS

I wish to thank all the tavern owners, bartenders, and other individuals who provided their valuable time and information for this book. The kindness and enthusiasm you've shown not only fueled my interest in the project, it kept me going through some very trying moments. This note of gratitude extends to everyone I dealt with at the Montana Liquor Division, especially Adam Brooks, who was always very patient and cooperative when I showed up at his desk.

I would like to offer a special note of appreciation to Ron "Dak" Rea for his outstanding efforts in developing the conceptual design for the book cover. Only a true pub crawler like Dak could create such a masterpiece.

And finally, I owe a very deep debt of gratitude to my wife, Chris, for her never-ending support and encouragement.

This book is dedicated in memory of Chris Hoyt and Jeff "Flint" Fleming; two great friends who checked out early in life for that big tavern in the sky.

TABLE OF CONTENTS

PREFACE

INTRODUCTION

How It All Began • The Selection Criteria; Science or Voodoo? • Becoming a Professional Drinker • Tavern Tours and Olympia Beer • Book Organization and Format • Accuracy of the Information (Another Badly Worded Disclaimer) • Using the Book • Ghost Bars

COUNTY MAP OF MONTANA

ORDER FORM

PREFACE

You probably haven't been waiting all your life for someone to write a book about small town taverns in Montana, but here it is anyhow. I hope you get as much enjoyment out of reading the book as I got out of writing it. During my extensive travels through Big Sky Country, I met others who had considered the notion but never followed through on their idea. I also discovered I was not the first to write about Saloons in Montana. *Watering Hole, A User's Guide to Montana Bars* was published by Montana Magazine in 1980. Joan Melcher authored the book, and Nik Carpenter did an admirable job with the illustrations. A handful of the 365 bars included in *The Pub Crawler's Guide to Montana's Small Town Taverns* are described in "Watering Hole". I also stumbled upon a magazine, of sorts, that was published on an annual basis during the early 1990s. *Montana Watering Holes, A Connoisseur's Guide to Montana's Most Notable Saloons* is no longer in circulation, but the primary purpose of the publication appears to have been advertisement.

Unlike my predecessors, my goal was not to "go in search of the perfect Montana bar", nor was it to sell advertisements and discount coupons. I simply reached a point in my life where I needed to get away from a tedious desk job and do something meaningful. What to do took some thought, but the moment I considered writing a guidebook to small town taverns in Montana, I realized there was no turning back. To me, the idea was perfect. With the exception of my family, there have probably been no greater influences on my life than small communities, taverns, and the great state of Montana. I had no previous creative writing experience, but considering the subject matter, I figured I could struggle through the task. If nothing else, I would gain a great deal of personal satisfaction by writing the book.

I'll be the first to admit I am not an accomplished writer. My education and work experience are of a scientific nature, and us "beakerheads" aren't known for our writing skills. Hell, some of us don't even know how to structure a sentence, and I'm certain I will receive some criticism on this and other important aspects of creative writing. I could have secured the services of a professional editor, but I chose not to simply because I couldn't afford to. You see, I not only authored the book; I published it as well. My funds were dwindling at a rapid rate by the time I was ready to have the book printed, and the editing portion of my budged was funneled into the newly created "Save an Author from Starving Relief Fund".

Assuming you can overlook the grammatical errors and my primitive writing style, I believe you will enjoy reading The Pub Crawler's Guide to Montana's Small Town Taverns. The final product was over two years in the making. My initial task of determining precisely which bars to include in the book turned out to be no easy job. A complete description of the criteria I used is included in the Introduction section, but the general criteria was to only write about those places with a full liquor license that are in or near communities with a population of 500 or less. Personal judgement was employed in some cases, especially in the western part of the state, but I eventually ended up with 365 saloons. This number was arrived at partly as a matter of coincidence and partly because of last minute additions.

You will undoubtedly notice there is only one page of information about each bar. Some of the places I've written about could easily be the subject of an entire book, but I chose the one page format so as not to show favoritism toward one establishment over another. The summary information at the top of each page is quite brief, but it may help you decide whether you want to stop at a particular bar. For instance, if you are looking for a place to eat, you can quickly find out which bars in the area serve food and what types of food are available. I honestly don't know how useful this information will be, but I hope it is helpful. The three of four paragraphs of text are intended to give the reader information about each bar's location, physical appearance, history, and distinguishing characteristics. I apologize for using redundant terms throughout the book, but there's only so many ways you can describe "a straight wooden bar with a brass foot rail". "Unbent, tightly compacted cellulose fixture containing a copper/zinc-alloyed tubular structure attached to its base" seems a bit ridiculous.

Well folks, here it is; the most comprehensive guidebook of its kind. I sincerely hope there will be future Pub Crawler books, but only time will tell. Performing the research has been one of the most rewarding experiences of my life. I met the greatest people in the world during my travels, and you will too when you visit the places I've written about. Montana's scenic beauty is nothing short of spectacular, but the people are what make the Treasure State so special. Long time residents of Big Sky Country are well aware of this; however, most people who visit Montana never get a true feel for the lifestyle. If you want to discover what truly makes Montana "The Last Best Place", get off the beaten path and meet the people. 365 places where you can do just that are described in this book.

INTRODUCTION

How It All Began

The idea for this book struck me suddenly and forcefully on October 28, 1994. The only reason I remember the date is I wrote it down, assuming I might one day want to reminisce about the moment that changed my life. Whether the change would be for better or worse, I didn't know, but I sensed a change was imminent. I can't say for sure how this crazy idea entered my mind. I'm not about to blame God for the inspiring moment, but some force greater than man embedded the notion deep into my thoughts. Perhaps it was an Artesian speaking from the bottle of Olympia Beer I was enjoying with my lunch. It certainly wouldn't have been the first time Olympia Beer had influenced my decision making process, and it undoubtedly wouldn't be the last. Powerful motivational forces, which only people who drink heavily and often can understand, occasionally inspire me to exhibit unconventional behavior. More times than not, I attribute these strange inspirations to the Artesians, the friendly creatures who own the wells where the Olympia Brewery gets its brewing water. It seems the Artesians have a warped sense of humor, and they derive great pleasure from watching people drive on the sidewalk, fall off barstools, and sleep in their own vomit. I may never know for sure whether the Artesians planted the idea for the book in my mind, but it sure sounds like something they would do.

Regardless of who or where the idea came from, it ignited an insuppressible chain reaction in my normally dormant brain. You see, I had spent years training my brain to look busy but do nothing, and this sudden flurry of activity inside my cranium caused me considerable alarm. I eventually realized the only way to get my beloved lazy brain back was to pursue the uninvited notion and write the book. Up to that point, I was miserably but gainfully employed. I realized writing the book would mean throwing away a secure career to embark on a risky escapade, but I was willing to make the sacrifice to get my old brain back.

I waited until the following April to quit my job at the Idaho National Engineering Laboratory and pursue my new mission full time. Several factors influenced my timing, the greatest being I knew my employer would soon be downsizing, and I might be entitled to severance pay if I held out long enough. As luck would have it, I qualified for the severance package. The problem of funding my research was at least partially solved, and I happily moved on.

The Selection Criteria; Science or Voodoo?

Before quitting my job, I had carefully conceived a strategy for writing the book. My fondness for small towns, Montana, and taverns naturally led to the general subject matter, but which taverns to include became somewhat of a dilemma. The overall size of the book and the format used to present the information became the two primary factors in determining the number of bars I would write about.

I decided a book of approximately 400 pages would be appropriate. Introductory material, appendices, and probably a whole bunch of disclaimer statements would occupy several chapters, leaving about 350 pages to devote to the bars. After careful consideration, I figured one page of information about each bar would suffice. After all, I had no business writing a book in the first place, so why pressure myself into writing more than I had to?

Narrowing the field to 350 bars took a little help from the U.S. Census Bureau and the Montana Liquor Division. While studying the list of licensed establishments, I discovered approximately 400 taverns were located in and around towns with a population of 500 or less, at least according to 1990 census figures. Thus, my definition for **small town** became **a community with 500 or fewer permanent residents, as reported in the 1990 census.** Several of the towns I've written about have grown dramatically in recent years (Frenchtown and Montana City are just two that come to mind), but I decided to stick with the 1990 census data to avoid confusion.

Now that small town was defined, I proceeded to develop some additional criteria to further narrow the field. For the sake of consistency, I chose to exclude places that do not have a full liquor license. I also excluded bars that are open only during the summer tourist season and establishments that are located in what I consider to be tourist towns or resort communities. This was perhaps my most difficult and controversial decision, but I'm hoping to make these establishments the subject of a future book. Among the small towns I consider to fit the category of tourist towns and resort communities are Virginia City, Big Sky, Cooke City, and Silver Gate. I also did not write about bars at golf courses, bowling alleys, ski areas, or other places where the bar is only an incidental part of the business. Fraternal organizations, such as American Legions and VFWs, were evaluated on a case-by-case basis, but only those open to the general public were considered. Quite honestly, I did not visit every bar in the state that is operated by a fraternal organization, so I undoubtedly missed a few. I wish to apologize to those places in advance. And finally, there was some subjective selection. As the research phase of my project was coming to a close, I realized there could be 365 bars in the book—one for every day of the year—if a couple of places that met most, but not all, the criteria were added. In the end, I decided to make it an even 365.

Now for my first disclaimer: I made every reasonable effort to include in the book all bars that meet the criteria described above. I'm only human (I've been informed on several occasions this is more so by default than personality), and us humans have a remarkable way of sometimes overlooking the obvious. If you know of a bar I missed, it's due to one of several reasons. The first would be I just plain blew it and didn't know the bar was there. Another possibility is the bar wasn't in operation while I was doing my research. A couple of places went out of business completely between the times I started and completed the project, and there were also some bars that had closed indefinitely. I didn't feel comfortable writing about a place that may or may not reopen. In what came as a surprise to me, a few bar owners specifically requested I not include their business in the book. A couple of others were so openly uncooperative that I took the hint and left them alone.

Becoming a Professional Drinker

My first official tavern tour, which is how I refer to the time I spend traveling across Montana interviewing people, taking notes, and drinking on Company time, began in July, 1996. I still lived in Idaho Falls at the time, so I packed the essential travel gear—some clothes, a sleeping bag, cooler, and beer money—and headed north. The Kirby Saloon was my first stop. I learned about ex-professional wrestler Bronc Bristol (the man who established the business), drank an Oly or two, and whizzed on some ice cubes in what may be the world's most unique urinal before heading off to Alzada. My first night on the road was spent at a gravel pile outside Ekalaka. I'd never been to Ekalaka before, and I was quite impressed with the caliber of people I met. My enthusiasm, as well as my bladder, grew with each tavern I visited. I certainly contributed my fair share to dust suppression in Eastern Montana during that first trip. I visited twenty-eight saloons in six days before heading back to Idaho Falls to regroup. There was definitely no stopping me now.

Although my second tavern tour didn't get under way until September, I kept a steady schedule through the fall, winter and spring. I moved to Helena in October to be closer to my work. Sleeping in my truck became increasingly uncomfortable as the temperatures dropped, but I wasn't about to abandon my quest. I visited several saloons that are haunted, several more that are housed in old bank buildings, and a few that aren't exactly the safest places in the world to drink a beer. There were timed team toilet races in Tumbleweed, a free bed-n-breakfast at the Northway Bar in Sunburst, a tatoo parlor in Alzada's Stoneville Saloon, pig races in Bearcreek, the world's largest pile of beer cans at the Jimtown Bar, and the open air toilets at Ingomar's Jersey Lilly. Loggers bars, Indian bars, and even a skydivers bar made the seemingly endless journey pass quickly. I met thousands of people, made hundreds of friends, and had the time of my life. I traded stories with a couple named Antelope and Bert at Pony, met the legendary Pat Merva in Stockett, and posed for a quick pencil sketch for Vernon LaBoy at the Lone Tree Bar in Box Elder. I can only think of a handful of negative experiences along the way, but there were a few.

My first encounter with the law occurred in April, 1996 at the Lozeau Retreat Tavern. I was gathering information at the bar when two officers from the Mineral County Sheriff's Department approached me and asked if I would step outside with them. I resisted my initial urge to scream "I didn't do nuthin', man, I was framed" and followed the officers out the door. The men in blue informed me I was a suspect in a string of casino burglaries in Central Montana. I had completed a tavern tour in that part of the state a few weeks earlier, and by mere coincidence, several of the bars were burglarized within a couple of days of my visits. Apparently, the investigating officer believed I was using the book as a front to gain information about the bars and later return to rob them. Word of my alleged evil ploy quickly spread throughout the state. Unfortunately, I seemed to be the last person to hear the news.

I did my best to convince the deputies in Lozeau it was merely coincidental that I had been asking detailed questions about the bars just days before they were robbed, but their faces reeked of skepticism as they listened to my statements. Perhaps it was my beady and bloodshot eyes that caused them such anguish. I politely agreed when the officers requested to search my truck for evidence. As the search proceeded, another deputy and a trainee pulled into the parking lot to assist. I was quite fascinated with all the attention I was receiving, especially when I discovered Mineral County had dispatched half its entire force of deputies to apprehend me. I was also impressed at the thorough manner in which the men searched my vehicle. The officers went as far as to carefully examine the contents of a box of Fruit Loops in the cab of my pickup. I had no idea what they were looking for, but they apparently didn't find it. The kind officers released me without as much as threatening me with a rubber hose or mentioning I would be wise to never show my wretched face in their county again.

My second direct encounter with the law took place a full nine months later. Between encounters, I learned the Lewis and Clark County Sheriff's Department had been asking about me at the bar across the road from where I live. The bartender knew me well, and she had no trouble convincing the deputies I was too stupid to pull off the burglaries. Her story was so convincing the deputies didn't even bother contacting me directly. Anyhow; back to my second encounter...I was making a return visit to the bars in Central Montana in November, 1996 (I make a second visit so the bar owners have an opportunity to comment on my draft write-ups before the book goes to print). As I was driving along, I couldn't help but notice a Chouteau County Sheriff's Department car following me from a distance. This seemed odd, especially since I was in Judith Basin County at the time. Within minutes, two more cars joined the "chase". I pulled to the side of the road and found myself surrounded by officers from the Chouteau County Sheriff's Department, the Judith Basin County Sheriff's Department, and the Montana Highway Patrol. Another interrogation and vehicle search commenced, and although there were no Fruit Loops involved this time, the search was quite thorough. Once again, no incriminating evidence was uncovered. By the time it was over, the officers informed me I was no longer a suspect in the case. I never found out if the real thieves were ever apprehended, but at least I haven't been bothered by any sheriff's deputies lately.

Tavern Tours and Olympia Beer

I never kept track of the number of Olympia Beers I consumed during my journeys, and I probably can't count that high anyhow. I just love a cold Oly, which makes my job that much more enjoyable. Certain people criticize my choice of beverage, but that doesn't bother me. I am a proud Oly drinker, and I hope to go to my grave with a six pack by my side. What does bother me is most younger people don't drink Oly, and the people who have enjoyed the beer for decades seem to be dying off at alarming rates. I can't recall the number of times during my travels when I walked into a bar and asked for an Olympia Beer, only to have the bartender tell me "we don't stock Olympia anymore; our last Oly drinker died a few months ago". I find this quite disturbing, not because I knew the people who passed away, but because the number of places that stock Olympia Beer seems to be dwindling at a rapid pace.

I am not receiving any sort of compensation from the Olympia Brewery or the Pabst Brewing Company for promoting their product. In fact, I'm certain they've never heard of me. My reason for mentioning the subject is to let all you Oly drinkers out there know something must be done if we hope to see the brand ten years from now. I don't believe Pabst has done enough to promote Olympia since they bought the company, and that has certainly had an impact on sales. We can't control Pabst, but we can encourage others to try Oly. It doesn't get near the promotion the national brands get, but I honestly believe Olympia is just as good or better than any beer on the market.

OK, I'll start with the encouraging words, and the rest of you join in. If you've never tried Olympia Beer, do yourself a favor and order an Oly the next time you're at the bar. If you live in a state where Oly isn't available, keep the brand in mind when you travel to the Northwest. I can't promise an encounter with the Artesians, but if you drink enough of their product, something out of the ordinary is bound to happen. I must admit I never actually saw the Artesians while I was on my tavern tours, but I could sense their presence every step of the way.

Book Organization and Format

Now that my sermon about Olympia Beer is over, I should explain the manner in which the book is organized and formatted. A mountain of information was gathered during my many tavern tours, and it eventually came time to put it in print. Developing a consistent format for presenting the information and selecting a suitable method of organizing the material turned out to be no simple assignment. Deciding exactly what to write and where to place it in the final document kept me awake through the night on several occasions. The final format was chosen as a result of an extensive trial and error process, but sleep deprivation may have been the determining factor in my decision about organizing the material.

The format is consistent throughout the book. Every page has a summary section at the top, followed by three or four paragraphs of text. Most of the summary information is self-explanatory, but two categories may cause some confusion. The **"BEER"** category describes the types of beers available at a particular establishment, but nothing is mentioned about liquor. Do not interpret this to mean liquor isn't available at the bar. Every bar in the book sells liquor, so

I didn't bother writing the obvious. The other category that may cause confusion is **"AMUSEMENT"**. Please understand *pool* does not mean a swimming pool; it refers to a pool table.

There were basically two methods I could have used to organize the material; geographically or alphabetically. I chose alphabetically, with the primary consideration being the county in which a bar resides. The heading at the top of each page shows the county where the bar is located. For instance, bars in Beaverhead County appear first in the book because *Beaverhead* is alphabetically the first county in Montana. Within each county, the name of every community is sorted alphabetically. As an example, the Buffalo Lodge at Clark Canyon is on page 1, because for the purposes of this book, *Clark Canyon* is alphabetically the first community in Beaverhead County. The name of the community where a bar resides is highlighted in bold lettering toward the upper right hand corner of each page to make it easier to see. For towns with more than one bar, the bars are listed in alphabetical order according to the name of the business. For instance, of the two bars in Lima, the Club Bar and Motel appears before the Peat Bar and Restaurant.

There are a few cases where a particular bar is one or two pages out of alphabetical order. This was done intentionally in limited circumstances so the corresponding photograph would be visible along with the text describing the bar.

For those of you who have no idea where most counties in Montana are located, a map has been provided on the pages immediately preceding the first page of text. I realize the map alone will be of limited value. Readers are encouraged to refer to a road map or atlas to find the exact location of a county or town mentioned in the book.

Two indices follow the text. Index A is organized alphabetically by town, and Index B is organized alphabetically by the name of the bar. If you want to know where to look in the text for information about all the bars in a particular community, find the community in Index A and refer to the corresponding page numbers. If you know the name of a particular bar you're interested in reading about, simply find the name of the bar in Index B and refer to the corresponding page number.

Accuracy of the Information (Another Badly Worded Disclaimer)

I am not a historian, partly because I do not wear bow ties, but mostly because I have no formal training or education in the profession. With this in mind, please realize I cannot guarantee the complete accuracy of every piece of information in the book. A lot of what's been written is based solely on discussions with bar owners, bartenders, and long time residents of the communities. Where possible, dates and events were verified through records at the Montana Liquor Division, newspaper articles, photographs, and other written materials. I went the extra mile (actually, it was more like 10,000 miles) by having the bar owners review and comment on my preliminary stories. In the few cases where the bar owners weren't available,

I tried to have someone familiar with the business complete the review. This required more time and expense at a point when both time and money were running low, but it proved to be an invaluable step in the process.

Another thing to keep in mind is the book describes the bars as they existed at a certain point in time. The bar business is not a stable business, and things tend to change rapidly. Owners, hours of operation, and even the names of the bars change periodically, so please don't send me a letter bomb if a particular place I've written about doesn't meet your expectations. I did the best job I could to create a quality product.

Using the Book

Some of my harshest critics claim the best way to use this book is to keep it in the bathroom and use the pages as an emergency supply of toilet paper. I strongly disagree with this approach because the ink could run and cause a nasty infection. This will not only result in a great deal of personal discomfort, it may create an embarrassing moment between you and your proctologist.

I really don't care how you use the book, as long as you buy it, but I will offer a suggestion (no, the suggestion has nothing to do with Olympia Beer). Pick out a few of the places you've read about and visit them. Once you get started, you may find it difficult to stop until you've been to every saloon in the book. After all, reading about something can be informative and entertaining, but it's always better when you can say "I've been there". If you are fortunate enough to live in Montana, it's a simple matter of firing up the family truckster and taking a drive. A little planning may be required for people who live out of state, but the experience will be well worth the effort. I'm not suggesting you spend your entire family vacation at saloons, but I believe any trip to Montana would be more enjoyable if, along the way, you take some time and meet the people. After all, people are what really make Montana so spectacular, and you can normally find these wonderful folks at the local tavern.

Some people will use the book as a genuine travel guide, and others will simply find it a source of entertainment. Some of the more serious pub crawlers I've talked to actually plan on documenting their travels in the book. The way to do this is to carry the book into each tavern and have the bartender sign and date the corresponding page. The heading line makes a great signature line, but there is also room for a name and date at the bottom of each page. One bar owner has even stated he will buy a free drink for anyone who brings a copy of this book into his bar. I won't disclose the bar owner's identity here, but you can find it in the text.

Ghost Bars

As I mentioned earlier, the bar business is not a stable business. It's possible, if not likely, some of the establishments I've written about will be closed by the time you visit them. There is no way of knowing how many saloons have come and gone in Montana over the years. Many bars had a relatively short existence, and a few have survived for well over 100 years. During my travels, I was told of several notorious ghost bars across the state. Some had been out of business for decades, and some had just closed within the past couple of years. Places like the Shawmut Bar in Shawmut, the Silver Slipper in Maxville, and the Polar Bar in Polaris are a few that come to mind.

For some people, losing a bar is like losing a loved one. A new bar can be built to replace the old one, but the character of the old place can never be reclaimed. I suppose that's why people hate to see certain taverns close their doors. I some cases, the liquor license is revoked but the bar survives. The Polar Bar is one such example. The primitive building still stands proud alongside the road, and the people of Polaris continue to use the facility as a BYOB club. It's a marvelous way of preserving the past without having to deal with the bureaucratic restrictions of the modern world.

In the spirit of ghost bars everywhere, I salute the people of Polaris for refusing to stand by idly while their beloved Polar Bar is destroyed. It is people like this who will ensure the small town tavern as we know it continues to thrive in Montana.

The Polar Bar in Polaris; One of Montana's "living" ghost bars.

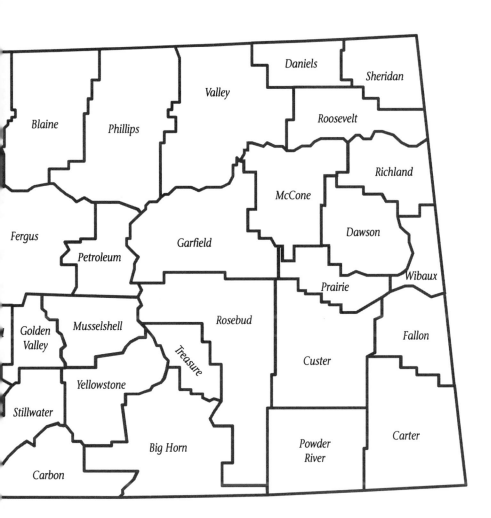

BUFFALO LODGE

OWNERS: Marty and Mike Heard

LOCATION: **Clark Canyon Reservoir**

HOURS: Open 11:30 a.m. Daily (Summer)
Open 11:30 a.m. Weekends (Winter)
Open 3:30 p.m. Weekdays (Winter)

PHONE: 406-683-5535

BEER: Domestics; Imports; Microbrews

HAPPY HOUR: No

GAMBLING: Video Poker/Keno

AMUSEMENT: Pool; Darts; Video Games; Horseshoes

LIVE MUSIC: Occasionally

FOOD: Full Menu Restaurant

The Buffalo Lodge stands approximately 1/4 mile east of the Clark Canyon Reservoir Interchange (exit 44) off Interstate 15. The barroom, a game room, and a dining room are all housed in the ground-level floor of the building which overlooks the lake. Barroom customers have their choice of two separate bars; one facing the west wall and another facing the south wall. About the only difference between the two is the bar facing the south wall has a top made from an old shuffleboard table. Some enormous mounted trout are on display throughout the barroom. Most of the fish hanging from the wall were taken locally from either the Beaverhead River or Clark Canyon Reservoir.

The business was established as a cafe and tourist cabins in the community of Armstead. Fire destroyed the original buildings in January, 1947. A rebuilding effort quickly commenced, and the business reopened as the Buffalo Lodge later that same year. Construction on the Clark Canyon Dam began in 1963, and the owner of the lodge was notified he would have to vacate because Armstead would soon be under water. The building was eventually moved to its present location, and it finally reopened in 1966. The existing game room was added soon after the lodge was moved to the property, but the dining room wasn't built until 1990.

Marty and Mike Heard have owned the Buffalo Lodge since January, 1994. They've entertained visitors from all over the world who stopped by based recommendations from friends and relatives. The lodge is in a premier outdoor recreation area, so it's no surprise they get a lot of business from hunters and fishermen. It's not uncommon to see people tying flies in the barroom, and sportsmen frequently call the lodge to get the latest information on local hunting and fishing conditions. The Buffalo Lodge is also an excellent dining establishment. They offer an extensive dinner menu featuring hand-selected cuts of beef and exceptional seafood. Four different cuts of prime rib are available, and either lobster or king crab is usually the featured dinner special on Friday evenings.

RED ROCK INN

OWNER: Bus Lahrem

HOURS: 5:00 p.m. to Closing Daily

HAPPY HOUR: No

GAMBLING: No

LIVE MUSIC: No

LOCATION: Main Street, **Dell**

PHONE: 406-276-3501

BEER: Domestics; Imports; Microbrews

AMUSEMENT: No

FOOD: Full Menu Restaurant

The Red Rock Inn is on Main Street in Dell. Although the building is over 100 years old, extensive renovations have recently been completed on the entire facility. The barroom, a lobby, and two separate dining rooms are housed in the first floor of the building, and seven hotel rooms are in the second floor. Each room is tastefully decorated in a different theme derived from the history of the local area. Oak woodwork has been installed to preserve the natural beauty of the building's interior, and where possible, the original furnishings and structural components were left intact. The antique wooden bar, back bar, and liquor cabinet that were installed in the building in 1913 are still in place today.

The business was established in 1895 as the C&D House, a lodging facility for Red Rock Stage Company hands. The C&D House was eventually opened to the public and renamed the Dell Hotel. The hotel has seen its share of colorful guests over the years, and I'm told that somewhere along the line, the building became haunted. The ghost is believed to be the spirit of "Jimmy Joe", a former hotel cook who was shot and killed in a neighboring bar. Jimmy Joe often makes his presence known by leaving an imprint on the bed in the Railroad Room. The friendly spirit has also been credited with playing harmless pranks on employees at the Inn.

Bus Lahrem bought the Dell Hotel in 1994 and transformed it into the Red Rock Inn. Private baths were added to all the hotel rooms, and dinner guests now have their choice of atmosphere. The Victorian Dining Room is more formal, with an open floor plan, carpeting, and traditional decor. The Livery Stable Dining Room has wooden privacy booths, the original pine flooring, and various antiques on display. The restaurant opens every day except Monday at 5:00 p.m. from June through hunting season. Meals are available only on weekends through the winter. The bar has no set hours, so don't be surprised if there's a "Closed" sign in the window when you arrive. All you have to do is knock on the door, and assuming someone's at the Inn, they will open the bar for you. One last thing...the entire facility is smoke free, so you have to go outside to light up.

BIG HOLE RIVER INN

OWNER: Mike Martin

HOURS: 10:00 a.m. to Closing Daily

HAPPY HOUR: 6:00 to 8:00 Tuesdays

GAMBLING: Video Poker/Keno; Shake-A-Day

LIVE MUSIC: Occasionally

LOCATION: Highway 43, **Dewey**

PHONE: 406-832-3103

BEER: Domestics; Imports

AMUSEMENT: Pool; Darts; Video Game

FOOD: Chicken; Pasties

The Big Hole River Inn is housed in a two story wooden structure on the south side of Highway 43 in Dewey. The barroom resides in the ground-level floor, and several sleeping rooms are available upstairs. The building is over 100 years old, but it's been maintained in excellent condition. The original hardwood flooring is still intact, and the wooden bar and hand-crafted back bar along the east wall of the barroom are the same pieces that were installed when the business first opened.

A barroom has always been housed in the first floor of the building, but it's rather obvious the second story was once used as a brothel. The configuration of the small sleeping rooms surrounding a waiting area in the center of the floor leave little doubt as to the purpose of the architecture. Fred and Martha Hummel bought the business in 1928. They converted the old bedrooms into legitimate sleeping rooms, and the Dewey Bar and Hotel remained in the Hummel family for the next sixty years. Ruth E. May managed the business from 1967 until 1988. I'm told the Dewey Bar became known as "The Home of the Clean Johns" during Ruth's tenure because the rest room floors were so clean you could eat off them. The Dewey Bar was sold in 1988, and the new owner changed the name to the Big Hole River Inn. Mike Martin began leasing the bar in 1989, and he has since purchased the business.

The Big Hole River Inn is a very friendly tavern that caters to the residents of the surrounding communities. People from as far away as Butte, Anaconda, and Dillon are the regular customers, and everyone takes a personal interest in everyone else's well being. If you have too much to drink, the bartender will typically take your keys and insist you spend the night in one of the recently renovated rooms upstairs. As a service to the community, Mike holds benefits for local charities at the bar. He also an exceptional hunter's barbecue every fall when people from all over the country converge on the Big Hole Valley to hunt for trophy elk. Visiting fishermen and snowmobilers also frequent the Big Hole River Inn, but you will typically find a local crowd on hand.

ELK LAKE RESORT

OWNERS: Wayne Schofield/Nancy Loper

LOCATION: Elk Lake

HOURS: 8:00 a.m. to Closing Daily

PHONE: 406-276-3282

HAPPY HOUR: No

BEER: Domestics; Imports

GAMBLING: No

AMUSEMENT: Pool; Volleyball; Horseshoes

LIVE MUSIC: No

FOOD: Full Menu Restaurant

The Elk Lake Resort is forty miles west of West Yellowstone on the northeast edge of the Red Rock Lakes National Wildlife Refuge. To get there, take the Red Rock Pass Road (the gravel road between Monida, Montana and Henry's Lake in Idaho) to the Elk Lake Road and turn north. Drive approximately seven miles to the end of the road and you will see the resort on your right. The barroom resides in the ground-level floor of a two story wooden lodge. The Mallard Room (dining room) and the Great Room (lobby) are also housed in the first floor of the building. The second floor is a private residence, but six cabins are available for guest lodging. Boats can also be rented at the resort.

The Elk Lake Resort is operated under a special use permit from the National Forest Service. The land was homesteaded in 1876, but as time passed, the owners began operating it as a seasonal fishing resort. In recent years, snowmobiling has become so popular in the area that the resort now stays open year round. Because of its remote location and scenic surroundings, the Elk Lake Resort has become a very popular destination resort as well as a daytime stopover point.

Wayne Schofield and Nancy Loper bought the Elk Lake Resort in May, 1996, and they've done a fantastic job promoting the resort's remote location, rustic lodging facilities, and informal atmosphere. Commercial power is not available, so electricity is supplied through generators and a battery system. A backup propane lighting system has also been installed in each cabin, and wood burning stoves and down comforters ensure the guests get a comfortable night's sleep. The cabins are usually booked in advance, so be sure to call ahead for reservations if you plan on staying the night. The informal setting in the lodge is naturally inviting for people who want to kick back, relax and unwind with a few drinks or a good meal. Whether you're looking for a place to spend a week, a day, or just a few hours, the Elk Lake Resort offers everything you need, plus some. Seclusion, outstanding scenery, great fishing, and a snowmobiler's paradise are just a few of the many attractions.

GROGAN'S GLEN BAR

OWNER: Joe Grogan

HOURS: 9:00 a.m. to Closing Daily

HAPPY HOUR: No

GAMBLING: Video Poker/Keno

LIVE MUSIC: Occasionally

LOCATION: Highway 91, **Glen**

PHONE: 406-835-3861

BEER: Domestics; Microbrews

AMUSEMENT: Pool; Darts; Foosball; Horseshoes

FOOD: Bar Snacks

Grogan's Glen Bar is housed in a log structure on Highway 91 in Glen. The barroom has an L-shaped bar with a brass foot along the east wall, a few tables spread throughout the room, and plenty of open floor space. The facility is modern, yet rustic, with a covered wooden deck spanning the length of the front side of the building. The flooring is comprised entirely of 3/4-inch Tennessee Oak boards, and the vaulted ceiling is made from unstained pine lumber. The interior decor is sparse, but a stuffed moose head hangs from the north wall, and a stuffed elk head hangs from the south wall. The wood burning stove in the southwest corner is not only decorative, it's the building's main source of heat.

The bar's history dates back to 1879, shortly after Glen had been founded as a railroad stop. The original business, which consisted of a mercantile store, saloon, and hotel, operated out of a building that stood just south of the present-day Glen Bar. A lady who was a known madam owned the hotel for several years, so it's very likely a few dollars were passed under the sheets during the hotel's early years of operation. Prohibition didn't force the saloon out of business, but it did cause the barroom to become mobile. Bootlegged booze that was distilled in the nearby hills was sold from the old hotel building, but the location of the barroom constantly changed to keep the local authorities confused. The original bar, store, and hotel building was destroyed by fire in 1988. The log structure that now stands on the property was erected 1989.

Joe Grogan has owned the Glen Bar since 1948. Joe operates your basic drinker's tavern, but the customers are always courteous and well-mannered. A steady local crowd keeps the place going throughout the year, and fishermen from all over the world stop in during the summer months. Blue ribbon trout fishing is as close as the Big Hole River that nearly runs through Joe's back yard. Joe keeps a supply of hand-tied flies on stock at the bar, and people commonly call for a report on the river conditions. Hell, even if the fishing is bad, you can always hook into a cold beer at Grogan's Glen Bar.

JACKSON HOT SPRINGS

OWNERS: Peterson Family		**LOCATION:**	Main Street, **Jackson**
HOURS: 8:00 a.m. to Closing Daily		**PHONE:**	406-834-3151
HAPPY HOUR: No		**BEER:**	Drafts; Domestics; Imports; Microbrews
GAMBLING: Video Poker/Keno		**AMUSEMENT:**	Pool; Shuffleboard; Pinball; Video Games
LIVE MUSIC: Twice Monthly		**FOOD:**	Full Menu Restaurant

Jackson Hot Springs is on the east side of Main Street (Route 278) in Jackson. A huge barroom is housed in the main lodge, a two story log building with a beautiful oak interior. The mezzanine surrounding the barroom/lounge area has several trophy-sized big game head and antler mounts hanging beneath the wooden railing. A horseshoe-shaped bar stands along the south wall of the barroom, and several tables are lined against the interior walls surrounding the spacious dance floor. A massive stone fireplace rises from the floor against the east wall, accentuating the rustic atmosphere in the lodge.

Lewis and Clark had lunch on the site of the natural hot springs on July 7, 1806. The grounds underwent gradual development over time, and the first saloon was built at the hot springs around the turn of the 20th century. In 1950, a local ranch hand who had married an heir to the Proctor and Gamble fortune built a lodge called the Diamond Bar Inn. The couple eventually divorced, but the man stayed on and ran the lodge. The terms of the divorce settlement were apparently vague, because I've been told that after the man died, one of his sons claimed rights to half the Diamond Bar Inn. The lodge was literally cut down the middle, and half of the building was moved to Dillon and renovated into a house. The other half of the lodge was simply left standing on its foundation. The east side of the present-day lodge was eventually added to replace the "missing piece" of the original building. The springs have since been developed into a 30 x 75 foot pool on the north side of the main lodge.

Aside from the barroom and hot pool, Jackson Hot Springs has eating, lodging, and camping facilities. The full service restaurant features cowboy gourmet cooking, which means you will get homemade meals prepared from only the freshest ingredients. The lunch and dinner menus are created on a daily basis, and prime rib is the featured dinner item on Saturday evenings. Lodging facilities include twenty recently remodeled cabins and a four-plex apartment, and RV spaces and tent sites are also available.

ROSE'S CANTINA

OWNERS: Doug and Jennifer Kirby

HOURS: 9:00 a.m. to Closing Daily

HAPPY HOUR: No

GAMBLING: Video Poker/Keno; Shake-A-Day

LIVE MUSIC: Occasionally

LOCATION: Main Street, **Jackson**

PHONE: 406-834-3100

BEER: Drafts; Domestics; Microbrews

AMUSEMENT: Pool; Pinball

FOOD: Full Menu Restaurant

Rose's Cantina is on Main Street (Route 278) in Jackson. A covered wooden deck spans the length of the front side of the building, and a couple of log benches are just outside the main entrance on the deck. The barroom is relatively large. A straight bar with a brass foot rail faces the south wall in the front portion of the room, and several tables are spread across the floor. The light fixtures hanging from the ceiling are fashioned from old wagon wheels, providing a unique, yet functional, method of illuminating the barroom.

The history of the business is somewhat vague, but the people I spoke with believed the bar probably opened in the early 1900s. Hurley's Place was the name of the business when the first liquor license was issued in 1937. The name was changed to the Jackson Pool Hall in 1940, the Wagon Wheel Club in 1951, and finally to Rose's Bar 1978. The original saloon was destroyed by fire in 1969. I'm told there were plenty of bullet holes in the walls and ceiling of the old building, so apparently there were some pretty wild times in Jackson. The existing structure is an old schoolhouse that was moved from Dillon. The decorative tin ceiling that was installed when the schoolhouse was built in the early 1900s is still intact in the east side of the barroom.

Doug and Jennifer Kirby have owned Rose's Cantina since June, 1994. Doug and Jennifer operate a friendly establishment where people gather to relax and have fun. The fun sometimes gets a little out of hand, but there's never any trouble at the bar. People have, on occasion, ridden horses into the crowded barroom, so be prepared for just about anything. Rose's Cantina enjoys a steady local crowd throughout the year. Visiting skiers, snowmobilers, fishermen, and hunters also stop in. Hunting season is always the busiest time of the year at the bar. Big game is plentiful in the area, and the hunters stop in for meals and drinks after a long day in the forest. If it's a meal you're after, be sure to try the ranch burger. Paul Harvey once commented in a broadcast that the best burger he's ever eaten came from Rose's Cantina in Wisdom, Montana.

THE CLUB BAR AND MOTEL

OWNERS: Howard and Barb Young

HOURS: 9:30 a.m. to Closing Daily

HAPPY HOUR: No

GAMBLING: Video Poker/Keno

LIVE MUSIC: Occasionally

LOCATION: S. Broadway Street, **Lima**

PHONE: 406-276-9996

BEER: Domestics

AMUSEMENT: Pool; Horseshoes

FOOD: Grill Items

The Club Bar and Motel is on South Broadway Street in Lima. The barroom is actually a multi-functional facility that serves as a motel lobby, community library, piano lounge, and tavern. The working part of the barroom is in the rear, where the bar stands. The L-shaped bar has a wooden top that is covered with coins arranged in the shapes of brands from local ranches, people's names, and initials. Approximately 600 hats and 300 posters cover the barroom walls and ceiling, and God only knows how many old beer cans, beer bottles, and books line the shelves toward the front of the barroom. The antique piano near the main entrance was made in 1906, and the cash register behind the bar was manufactured in 1904. Both the till and the piano are in perfect working condition.

The business was established in 1948. The bar originally operated out of the south side of the building, and a restaurant was housed in the north side. Nobody has ever been shot at the Club Bar, but evidence of past gunfire is visible in the barroom. One of the Indians pictured in the framed "Attack on the Overland Stage" print hanging from the barroom wall has a bullet hole in his rear end. Nobody today seems to know how the hole got there, but it's a real bullet hole. The existing bar top has a history of its own. The original bar top was damaged during the Challis earthquake in 1986, so boards from the old Lima High School Gymnasium floor were used to replace the damaged item. After the boards were installed, several hundred coins were glued in place and covered with a coat of polyurethane.

Howard and Barb Young have owned the Club Bar and Motel since 1979. Howard and Barb promote a friendly atmosphere in the barroom, and they cater to the needs of the local community. Of the two bars in Lima, the Club seems to attract the older crowd. Visiting hunters, fishermen, and tourists also find their way to the Club Bar and Motel during the summer and fall. As a community service, Howard and Barb serve a free Thanksgiving Day Dinner every year. Between 50 and 150 people attend the event, and everyone gets plenty to eat. They also serve excellent food off the grill. The buffalo burgers are the house specialty, and homemade soups and chili are usually available during the winter.

PEAT BAR AND STEAK HOUSE

OWNER: Dan Caplis

HOURS: 3:00 p.m. to Closing Weekdays
1:00 p.m. to Closing Weekends

HAPPY HOUR: 5:00 to 6:00 Mon - Fri

GAMBLING: Video Poker/Keno

LIVE MUSIC: Occasionally

LOCATION: 1 Broadway Street, **Lima**

PHONE: 406-276-9967

BEER: Drafts; Domestics;
Imports; Microbrews

AMUSEMENT: Pool; Darts

FOOD: Full Menu Steak House

The Peat Bar and Steak House, home of the "Cook Your Own Steak", is at 1 Broadway Street in Lima. The bar and steak house occupy the ground-level floor of the old Peat Hotel building, a two story structure with a pink stucco exterior. The spacious barroom has a straight wooden bar and an antique back bar against the north wall. Several tables are spread throughout the room, and an open pit gas grill with an exhaust hood overhead is near the middle of the floor.

The Peat Hotel was built by Johnnie Peat in 1889 when the railroad came through what was then the town of Spring Hill. Arriving in Spring Hill meant a shift change for the railroad hands. The workers who got off the train stayed at the hotel until they were due back on the job the following day. The hotel lobby, a drug store, barber shop, lunch counter and saloon were all housed in the first floor in the early years. There was never any insulation in the building while the hotel was in operation, and I'm told the rooms got so cold that a couple of people actually froze to death while they were sleeping. The hotel closed in the mid 1960s, so nobody has frozen to death in recent years.

Dan Caplis has owned the Peat Bar and Steak House since 1985. Dan's "cook your own steak" policy enables him to serve good food at reasonable prices, and the customers have nobody to blame but themselves if their steak isn't prepared the way they ordered it. The side dishes are prepared in the kitchen, but you have to personally attend to your steak while it cooks over the open pit grill. Interestingly enough, a lot of people actually prefer this method over having someone else prepare their steak.

Most of the customers at the Peat Bar and Steak House are residents of Lima and the surrounding communities, but visiting hunters join the locals at the bar during the fall. The barroom also gets busy during the town's annual 4th of July barbecue. The Lima Volunteer Fire Department sponsors the barbecue during the day, and the bar has live music on the nights of July 3 and 4. It sometimes gets elbow-to-elbow in the barroom, but it's usually a very friendly crowd.

GRASSHOPPER INN

OWNER: Mike Baer	**LOCATION:** Polaris Road, **Polaris**
HOURS: 8:00 a.m. to Closing Daily	**PHONE:** 406-834-3456
HAPPY HOUR: No	**BEER:** Domestics; Microbrews
GAMBLING: Video Poker/Keno	**AMUSEMENT:** Pool; Video Games; Foosball; Volleyball
LIVE MUSIC: Occasionally	**FOOD:** Full Menu Restaurant

The Grasshopper Inn is ten miles north of Route 278 on the Polaris Road. The bar and restaurant are housed in the main floor of the lodge, and a game room is in the basement. The vaulted wooden ceiling, hardwood flooring, and large stone fireplace in the middle of the room create a very comfortable atmosphere. Brands from local ranches have been burned into the ceiling rafters, and the name of the owner of each mark is written on a piece of leather that hangs below the brand. The oldest registered brand in Montana is among the marks on the rafters.

The Grasshopper Inn was built in 1971. There's not a lot of history to the business, but I'm told the antique hutch in the barroom originally resided in a local whorehouse. Allegedly, a valley rancher purchased the hutch as a surprise anniversary gift for his wife, but he was forced to get rid of it when his wife discovered where he bought it. There's also a story behind the beautiful oak bar, back bar, and liquor cabinet. The three matching pieces were allegedly built in England in the late 1800s, shipped around Cape Horn to San Francisco, and transported overland by team and wagon to the Bannock Hotel. The bar, back bar, and liquor cabinet also spent time in a tavern in Dillon before being restored to their original condition and moved to the Grasshopper Inn. A brass foot rail is attached to the base of the antique bar, and the original beveled mirror is still intact on the hand-crafted back bar.

Mike Baer has owned the Grasshopper Inn since December, 1995. Local residents provide a steady business throughout the year, and the surrounding mountains draw people to the area for the exceptional hunting, fishing, skiing, snowmobiling, and rock digging opportunities. A local group known as the Grasshopper Coffee Club meets at the bar every morning at 8:00 to start their day. Each member has their own coffee mug with their name on it hanging from the wall. The restaurant serves breakfast, lunch, and dinner daily, and meal specials are offered on weekends. Ten modern motel units are available for overnight lodging, and the Grasshopper Inn has the only gas available in the Grasshopper Valley.

ANTLERS SALOON

OWNER: Kristie Held		**LOCATION:**	Main Street, **Wisdom**
HOURS: 9:00 a.m. to Closing Daily		**PHONE:**	406-689-9393
HAPPY HOUR: 5:00 to 6:00 Mon - Fri		**BEER:**	Drafts; Domestics; Imports
GAMBLING: Video Poker/Keno		**AMUSEMENT:**	Pool; Darts
LIVE MUSIC: Occasionally		**FOOD:**	Homemade Pizza

The Antlers Saloon is on Main Street in Wisdom. The building's wooden exterior and covered boardwalk are reminiscent of a scene from an old west movie, and the interior is rustic as well. The L-shaped wooden bar has a log foot rail and a thick top that was made by cutting a plank from the middle of a tree trunk. A wooden leaning rail stands in the middle of the room, and a spacious dance floor is in the west side of the building. The interior decor consists of antique pistols, big game head mounts, and various types of antlers hanging from the walls.

The business was established as the Elk Club in 1934, but the name was changed to the Antler Bar in 1954. There's not a lot in the way of unique history to report, but I'm told the barroom once served as a makeshift dental office. Several years back, a man entered the barroom complaining of an aching tooth. A local forest service employee who had been hitting the bottle pretty hard that day offered to extract the tooth and save the guy a trip to the dentist. The man initially declined the offer, but he eventually got all liquored up and agreed to the procedure. Amazingly enough, the forest service employee exercised great care and precision while removing the tooth. The only problem was he pulled the wrong tooth, so the man still ended up going to the dentist to have one tooth removed and one replaced.

Dentistry is no longer performed in the barroom, but there's no lack of entertainment. Kristie Held bought the saloon in February, 1995, and she keeps things plenty lively. There's a steady local crowd throughout the year, and hunting season always brings hoards of new faces to Wisdom. Fishermen, skiers, and snowmobilers also stop in, and everyone gets along just fine. Kristie hosts a barbecue and pot luck dinner every Memorial Day Weekend, and the place gets busy during the annual Wisdom Gun Show and the annual Cow Pasture Open Golf Tournament that's held in a neighboring cow pasture every year in August. There's not much call for part time dentists at the Antlers Saloon anymore, but be sure to bring your cow chip wedge if you plan on playing in the golf tournament.

FETTY'S BAR AND CAFE

OWNERS: Randy and Julie Spoon		**LOCATION:**	Main Street, **Wisdom**
HOURS: 8:00 a.m. to Closing Daily		**PHONE:**	406-689-3260
HAPPY HOUR: 5:00 to 6:00 Mon - Fri		**BEER:**	Drafts; Domestics; Imports; Microbrews
GAMBLING:	Video Poker/Keno; Shake-A-Day	**AMUSEMENT:**	Pool
LIVE MUSIC: Occasionally		**FOOD:**	Full Menu Cafe

Fetty's Bar and Cafe is on the north side of Main Street in Wisdom. The barroom resides in the west side of the building, and the cafe is in the east side. A sliding partition has been installed at the center of the hardwood floor under the peak of the vaulted ceiling to provide separation between the two areas. Opening the partition is a convenient way to temporarily expand the barroom on dance nights or other special occasions.

Fetty's Bar and Cafe was established by R. C. Fetty in 1932. The business thrived during the Great Depression because of Mr. Fetty's innovative approach to credit management. Fetty was quick to establish a line of credit for men who came to town looking for work, even though they were flat broke. Mr. Fetty would give people food and drinks when they first arrived in Wisdom, and then find them jobs on local ranches. When the ranch hands got paid, they would come to town to pay off their debt. More often than not, the customers ran up another tab in the bar before heading back to the ranch, so they always owed Mr. Fetty money. This kept people coming back to the bar every month to spend their wages.

R. C. Fetty passed away in 1965. There have only been three other owners since then, the latest being Randy and Julie Spoon, who bought the business in 1991. Things are fairly calm at the bar these days, but there have been some tense moments over the years. I'm told Mr. Fetty's house blackjack dealer was once nearly killed for dealing cards off the bottom of the deck, and on another occasion, a man was shot in the stomach while arguing with a fellow ranch hand. Other shots have been fired inside the barroom. The bullet holes are still visible in the floor, but only one person has had the misfortune of getting struck by a bullet.

If you want large portions of food at reasonable prices, Fetty's is the place you're looking for. Omelettes are the breakfast specialty, and the burgers are an excellent choice for lunch or dinner. The bar stocks approximately 75 different kinds of beer through the summer, so you're sure to find a brand you like. Whether you want a meal, a drink, or just some coffee for the road, Fetty's has what you need.

12

H BAR J SALOON AND CAFE

OWNERS: Charlie Beck/Randy Bathrick

HOURS: 11:00 a.m. to Closing Daily

HAPPY HOUR: No

GAMBLING: Video Poker/Keno; Shake-A-Day

LIVE MUSIC: Approximately Twice Monthly

LOCATION: Highway 43, **Wise River**

PHONE: 406-832-9292

BEER: Domestics; Imports

AMUSEMENT: Pool

FOOD: Full Menu Cafe

The H Bar J Saloon and Cafe is in Wise River at the junction of Highway 43 and the Wise River Road. The saloon operates out of the east side of the building, and a relatively small cafe is in the west side. There are no tables in the barroom, but plenty of seating is available at the straight wooden bar that spans almost the entire length of the south wall. Overnight camping spaces and a few full RV hookups are available outside the building, and propane is available if your tank runs dry.

The H Bar J Saloon and Cafe was established in 1961 by Herschel and Jean Wells. They obtained the liquor license from the old One Horse Bar in Wise River, moved the business into a new building, and changed the name to the H Bar J Bar and Cafe. The H bar J is normally a very peaceful place, but a non-fatal shooting occurred in the barroom during the early 1980s. If you know where to look, you can still see the mark where the bullet ricocheted off the top of the bar after exiting a man's body.

Charlie Beck and Randy Bathrick bought the H Bar J in January, 1994. The bar and cafe are in a premier outdoor recreation area, so the customer base is split between local residents and visiting outdoors enthusiasts. The H Bar J is an excellent place to coordinate any type of outdoor activity in the Big Hole Valley. Trophy elk hunting, blue ribbon trout fishing, and outstanding terrain for snowmobiling and cross country skiing are within a few minutes drive. Crystal Park, a popular digging site for amateur rock jocks, is also within twenty miles of town. The folks at the H Bar J will assist with vehicle shuttles for float trips on the Big Hole River, and they can coordinate guided fishing trips with local outfitters.

Cafe hours are 7:00 a.m. to 10:00 p.m. daily in the summer, but the cafe is open only on weekends through the winter. Steaks are the house specialty, and homemade pies and sack lunches are available if you want to get something to go. The Wise River Road is a designated National Scenic Byway through the Pioneer Mountains, so travelers can stock up at the H Bar J before taking a drive over the mountain. A soothing plunge at Elkhorn Hot Springs awaits on the other side.

WISE RIVER CLUB

OWNER: Chester Pearce   **LOCATION:** Highway 43, **Wise River**

HOURS: 8:00 a.m. to 2:00 a.m. Daily   **PHONE:** 406-832-3258

HAPPY HOUR: None   **BEER:** Drafts; Domestics

GAMBLING: Video Poker/Keno;   **AMUSEMENT:** Pool; Shuffleboard;
Shake-A-Day   Video Games; Horseshoes

LIVE MUSIC: Every 2nd Weekend (Summers)   **FOOD:** Full Menu Restaurant

The Wise River Club is on the north side of Highway 43 in Wise River. The entire business consists of the bar, a restaurant, seven hotel rooms, six cabins, and an RV park. The barroom is relatively large, with a beautiful river rock fireplace in the middle of the floor. An antique cherry wood back bar which has been restored to near-original condition stands against the east wall behind a long wooden bar. The antlers on the barroom ceiling all came from a single bull elk. The elk lived for twenty-two years in a corral across the highway from the Wise River Club, and the owners collected the antlers every spring when they dropped.

The history of the Wise River Club dates back to 1890 when the Wise River Hotel first opened. Although you wouldn't know it today, the Wise River area was once a booming mining community. The hotel, a saloon, and a restaurant operated out of the original two story building. The saloon was eventually relocated into a log structure that was moved to the property and attached to the west side of the hotel. Over the years, the barroom has at least doubled in size. The back bar was built in the late 1800s, but it's a recent addition to the Wise River Club. The back bar was moved here from the Butte VFW in 1995.

Chester Pearce bought the Wise River Club in July, 1995. Some wild moments have occurred in the barroom over the past 100 years, but Chester now keeps things pretty well under control. There's a steady local crowd at the bar and restaurant, and plenty of hunters, fishermen, snowmobilers, and tourists stop by for food, drinks, and lodging. Everything served in the restaurant is homemade, and everything is excellent. Daily lunch specials are offered, and they prepare a fantastic steak sandwich. Outdoor barbecues are held every Memorial Day, 4th of July, and Labor Day. Chester also throws one hell of a New Year's Eve Party, and he has live music every other weekend through the summer. The Wise River Club has so much to offer that even city slickers will enjoy their visit to one of Montana's premier outdoor recreation areas. The Wise River Club is a wonderful place to stop while traveling through the spectacular Big Hole Valley.

14

The Big Hole Valley's Wise River Club.
The business was established as the Wise River Hotel in 1890.

THOMPSON'S CORNER

OWNER: Don Thompson

LOCATION: Highway 43, **Wise River**

HOURS: 9:00 a.m. to Closing Daily

PHONE: 406-832-3171

HAPPY HOUR: No

BEER: Domestics

GAMBLING: Video Poker

AMUSEMENT: Pool

LIVE MUSIC: No

FOOD: Grill Items

Thompson's Corner is on the banks of the Big Hole River between Dewey and Wise River on Highway 43. The log structure stands on the north side of the road approximately three miles east of the community of Wise River. The barroom is relatively small, and seating space is limited to the stools at the straight wooden bar along the north wall. The barroom's log walls, tongue-and-groove woodwork, and a wood burning stove create a rustic appearance and a comfortable atmosphere.

The business was founded as a beer parlor and cafe in the late 1940s by Liz Patterson, the daughter of Montana's Lieutenant Governor at the time. Liz's father owned the property, and he was using his political influence to promote the development of the Elkhorn Mine near Elkhorn Hot Springs. Patterson's Corner became Thompson's Corner in 1959 when Don Thompson bought the business. Don obtained a full liquor license from the old Pipe Organ Lodge south of Dillon in 1965. He also built an addition onto west end of the building and installed indoor rest rooms at that time. Prior to the rest rooms being added, customers went outside behind a tree to relieve themselves. Don says it's a good thing he installed the rest rooms, because a couple of years after people quit using the tree for a privacy shelter, somebody drove through the parking lot and knocked the tree over with their vehicle. Don also says he used to bring his newborn calves into the barroom to keep them warm, but he hasn't done this for several years. Apparently, the State Health Department frowns on such practices.

Thompson's Corner is a local tavern where people of all ages gather to relax and socialize. There's always a friendly crowd on hand, so you don't have to worry about fights or rude behavior. The majority of Don's customers either live in the Big Hole Valley or Butte, but visiting hunters and fishermen stop in from time to time. Because of the bar's proximity to the Big Hole River, fishermen commonly pull their boats to shore at Thompson's Corner and have lunch and a few beers before heading on down stream. There's no developed boat ramp on the property, but people don't seem to mind climbing up the bank to get to the bar.

KIRBY SALOON

OWNERS: Dick and Delores Roebling

HOURS: 10:00 a.m. to 2:00 a.m. Daily

HAPPY HOUR: No

GAMBLING: Video Poker/Keno; Shake-A-Day

LIVE MUSIC: Occasionally

LOCATION: Route 314, **Kirby**

PHONE: 406-757-2233

BEER: Domestics

AMUSEMENT: Pool

FOOD: Bar Snacks

The Kirby Saloon is on Route 314 in Kirby. If you have a road map that's been printed in recent years, it probably won't include Kirby because the local post office pulled out a few years ago. To get there, drive 14-1/2 miles south of Busby or 20 miles north of Decker on Route 314. The saloon is housed in a stone and brick structure that stands behind several pine trees on the west side of the road. The brick walls inside the barroom are sparsely decorated with a few painted animal skulls and beer signs. A dance floor, which serves as a storage area most of the time, is in the south end of the building behind the bar. The urinal in the men's room may be a one-of-a-kind fixture. It's basically a concrete shower stall with ice cubes covering the floor. Aside from its practical application, the urinal provides endless hours of entertainment for guys who enjoy watching ice cubes melt while they empty their bladders.

The Kirby Saloon was established by an ex-professional wrestler named Bronc Bristol in 1973. Bronc bought the general store that stood on the property, made an addition to the building, and opened the bar. The original building was destroyed by fire in 1975, so the brick structure was erected and the bar reopened about a year later. Dick and Delores Roebling purchased the business in 1987. Prior to that, confrontations among patrons, some of which involved guns and knives, were rather common. Dick assured me these incidents quickly halted when he and Delores took over. Aside from Dick's "misbehave and you're outta-here" management style, the remoteness of the bar in itself is a deterrent to fighting. You don't just walk across the street to another tavern after being 86'd from the Kirby Saloon because the next nearest bar is about thirty-five miles away.

The regular crowd at the Kirby Saloon is made up of local ranchers, loggers, miners, and Native Americans from the neighboring Reservations. Tourists provide a boost to the business during the summer months, but it's mostly a local crowd. The Kirby Saloon is a nice place with a quiet atmosphere, so be sure to stop in and say Hi to Dick and Delores if you're ever in the area. Also, please sign the guest book before you leave.

SPRING CREEK BAR AND CAFE

OWNERS: John and Roberta Myrstol   **LOCATION:** Sarpy

HOURS: 11:00 a.m. to Closing Mon-Fri   **PHONE:** 406-342-5414
Noon to Closing Sat-Sun

HAPPY HOUR: No   **BEER:** Domestics

GAMBLING: Video Poker/Keno;   **AMUSEMENT:** Pool; Darts
Shake-A-Day

LIVE MUSIC: Occasionally   **FOOD:** Full Menu Cafe

The Spring Creek Bar and Cafe is in the community of Sarpy, which is twenty-five miles East of Hardin on Route 384. Sarpy is another one of those places you won't find on your road map, but it certainly exists. The bar and cafe are housed in a building that stands just north of Route 384. The bar is in the west side of the building, and a dining area resides in the east side. The entire facility has recently been remodeled, so everything is modern and well-maintained.

Jim and Betty Romine established the business in 1973. Construction activities had recently begun in support of a large open pit coal mine in the area, and Jim and Betty figured the construction workers and miners would need a place to eat and drink. Business was so good during the first five years that people were literally lined out the door waiting to buy beer. Although the boom days are long gone, local loggers, farmers, ranchers, and miners now provide a steady clientele. John and Roberta Myrstol bought the Spring Creek Bar and Cafe in November, 1995. There haven't been a lot of changes since the business first opened, but John and Roberta made some upgrades to the building and started serving a prime rib dinner on Saturday evenings. The prime rib dinner has become so popular that you need reservations just to get in the door.

The Spring Creek Bar and Cafe serves as a community center for the Sarpy area, which unofficially runs east and west from Colstrip to Hardin and north and south from Interstate 94 to Highway 212. Several planned gatherings take place at the bar each year, but impromptu parties seem to develop more often than the planned functions. You never know when or why these parties start, but they're always a lot of fun. Aside from the local crowd, foreign businessmen who visit the nearby coal mine occasionally visit the bar to conduct business meetings and have lunch. Some of these visitors, especially the Japanese, inadvertently provide hours of free entertainment to the locals because of their excited behavior and seemingly uncontrollable use of 35mm cameras.

CLEVELAND BAR

OWNER: Nick Faber   **LOCATION:** Cleveland

HOURS: 10:00 a.m. to Closing Mon-Fri   **PHONE:** 406-357-3440
9:00 a.m. to Closing Sat-Sun

HAPPY HOUR: No   **BEER:** Domestics

GAMBLING: Video Poker/Keno   **AMUSEMENT:** Pool; Darts;
Video Game

LIVE MUSIC: Occasionally   **FOOD:** Full Menu Grill

The Cleveland Bar is twenty-five miles south of Chinook in the community of Cleveland. Cleveland doesn't appear on some road maps, so the best directions I can offer is to take Route 240 out of Chinook and drive south until you come to the T in the road where the pavement ends. Turn right at the T, and you will see the bar on the right-hand side of the road. Don't plan on taking your dog or horse into the barroom; there's a hand written sign on the door forbidding dogs and horses. I was informed by the manager that the sign was placed there out of necessity, not for humor. An antique wooden bar and matching back bar stand along the west wall of the barroom. The three stuffed birds (two owls and one golden eagle) perched on top of the back bar are over sixty years old. Two archways separate the main barroom from the game room. The markings painted above the archways represent authentic brands from local ranches.

The bar's origin dates back to 1889 when a saloon opened in a settlement which is now referred to as Old Cleveland. Allegedly, the Cleveland Bar is the fourth oldest saloon in Montana. The bar and back bar that stand in the barroom today were installed in the original saloon when it first opened. In the early part of the 20th century, the saloon was moved into a hotel building in New Cleveland, a settlement located approximately 1/2 mile west of Old Cleveland. The saloon operated out of the hotel building until about 1960 when it was moved across the road to its present location. Nick Faber, a local rancher who already owned the property surrounding the bar, bought the business in January, 1993.

The regular customers at the Cleveland Bar are residents of Cleveland and the surrounding area. Business is steady throughout the year, but it picks up considerably during hunting season, on dance nights, and during the annual Rocky Mountain Oyster feed at the end of the summer. The people here are friendly and courteous, even to strangers who happen to wander in. An occasional fight may break out in the barroom from time to time, but it's usually settled without causing any harm to the building contents or innocent bystanders.

PLAINSMAN BAR

OWNERS: Lou and Linda Suddarth

HOURS: Noon to Closing Tue-Sun
4:00 p.m. to Closing Monday

HAPPY HOUR: No

GAMBLING: Video Poker/Keno

LIVE MUSIC: No

LOCATION: Highway 2, **Lohman**

PHONE: 406-357-4113

BEER: Drafts; Domestics

AMUSEMENT: Pool; Darts; Foosball;
Pinball; Horseshoes

FOOD: Grill Items

The Plainsman Bar is housed in a steel-sided structure that stands on the south side of Highway 2 just west of Lohman. There's a big "Plainsman Bar" sign in front of the building so you don't mistake it for a heavy equipment repair shop. The exterior is nothing elaborate, but once inside, you will find a modern facility that is very clean and well-maintained. The spacious barroom has a straight bar along the east wall, and several tables are spread throughout the room. The walls are finished in modern wood paneling, carpeting covers the floors, and various artifacts hang from the walls as decorations. Painted plates, beer steins, antlers, and antique tools are just a few of the items hanging from the barroom walls. If you happen to collect belt buckles, be sure to check out the belt buckle collection behind the bar. I normally don't get too excited about belt buckles, but they've got some very interesting pieces on display.

The Plainsman Bar was established in 1977. During the first few years, the business was promoted as a lounge, steak house and entertainment emporium. Bobby Bare, Ferlin Husky, and Little Jimmy Dickens are just a few of the big name entertainers who have played and sang at the Plainsman Bar. The live entertainment was eventually discontinued completely, and the number of items available on the dinner menu was reduced substantially. You can still get an excellent steak, hamburger, or steak sandwich, but don't expect a seven course meal.

Lou and Linda Suddarth bought the Plainsman Bar in October, 1992. They promote a friendly atmosphere where entire families can gather to enjoy a quiet evening out together. Local residents keep the bar going throughout the year, and travelers passing by on Highway 2 stop in occasionally. Aside from the food, there's plenty of games to keep the kids occupied while the adults drink and socialize. Lou and Linda usually have a few pieces of locally-crafted artwork in the display case at the north end of the bar. They make great souvenirs, and you don't even have to leave the bar to do your shopping.

GLENN'S BORDER BAR

OWNERS: Glenn and Marilyn Hutton

HOURS: 9:30 a.m. to 2:00 a.m. Daily

HAPPY HOUR: No

GAMBLING: Video Poker/Keno; Live Poker

LIVE MUSIC: No

LOCATION: Main Street, **Turner**

PHONE: 406-379-8241

BEER: Domestics

AMUSEMENT: Pool; Darts; Video Games

FOOD: Grill Items; Soups; Frozen Pizza

Glenn's Border Bar is on Main Street in Turner. Being that a man named Glenn owns the business and Turner is only twelve miles from the Canadian border, it's obvious how the bar got its name. About fifteen people can be seated at the straight bar along the north wall of the barroom, and several more can rest comfortably in the booths that line the south wall. If you prefer standing, there's plenty of open floor space.

Glenn Hutton established Glenn's Border Bar in 1959. Glenn started the business in another building on Turner's Main Street, but he moved the bar in 1968. The building that now houses Glenn's Border Bar had been home to Turner's Mint Bar since 1929. Glenn bought out the old Mint Bar 1966, spent two years making upgrades and renovations to the facility, and finally moved his Border Bar into the building in 1968.

The customers at Glenn's Border Bar are relatively peaceful these days, but Glenn says there were some exciting moments at the old bar. One day, an angry lady entered the barroom with a loaded gun and demanded "her money". Apparently, the gal had lost a substantial amount of change at the poker table earlier that day, and she was determined to recoup what she felt was rightfully hers. Fortunately, the people in the bar were able to calm the gal down and talk her into leaving without the money and without shooting anyone. In another episode involving a loaded weapon, the outcome was less fortunate. One of Glenn's bartenders was sleeping on a cot behind the bar late one night when two men broke in through the front door. One thing led to another, and the startled bartender fired a shotgun in the direction of the other men. The intruders quickly fled the scene, but one of them later died from the shotgun pellets that were lodged in his neck.

The rowdy days may be a thing of the past, but you will still find plenty of excitement at Glenn's Border Bar. The regular customers are a friendly bunch who make you feel at home. Glenn tells me the place used to be quite popular among the Canadians, but he doesn't get near as much business from his neighbors to the north as he used to. That's fine with Glenn, however, because his regular customers keep him plenty busy.

THE SPA

OWNERS: Howard and Loma Miller

HOURS: 10:00 to Closing, Daily

HAPPY HOUR: No

GAMBLING: Video Poker/Keno

LIVE MUSIC: Occasionally

LOCATION: Highway 2, **Zurich**

PHONE: 406-357-4222

BEER: Domestics

AMUSEMENT: Pool; Video Games

FOOD: Broiled Sandwiches; Frozen Pizza

The Spa is just west of Zurich on the south side of Highway 2. The sign out front is badly faded, but the bar isn't hard to recognize. Just look for the large green building with neon signs in the front windows. The spacious barroom has a straight bar along the west wall, and a large game room resides in the east side of the building. There's plenty of open floor space, and several booths are available if you'd rather not sit on a barstool. They still use ice in the urinals at the Spa, so the male customers can always look forward to creating mini ice avalanches when they visit the men's room. It's a cheap form of entertainment, but at least you don't have to flush before you go back to the bar.

The Spa's history dates back to the early 1900s when the bar first opened in downtown Zurich. The barroom occupied half the building at that time, and a mercantile store operated out of the other side. The prohibition years came and went without any real impact on the saloon business in Zurich. A lot of booze was bootlegged across the Canadian border in those days, and the Spa was one of the places where people could always get it. The building was moved to its present location in 1942. The new highway had just been completed, and the owner wanted to make his business as visible as possible to passing motorists. The mercantile store went out of business in 1954, so the barroom expanded into the rest of the building. The Spa now occupies the entire ground-level floor.

Howard and Loma Miller have owned the Spa since 1984. They promote a friendly atmosphere at the bar, and the customers are typically well-behaved. There's usually not an overabundance of excitement in the barroom, but it's a great place to meet people and relax with a few drinks. With the exception of visiting hunters, virtually all the customers are residents of Zurich and the surrounding farming and ranching communities. For some reason, the Spa doesn't seem to attract travelers. I guess that's their loss, because I've always found it a pleasure to visit the friendly folks at the Spa.

DEEP CREEK RESTAURANT AND LOUNGE

OWNERS: Rose and Leon Henke

LOCATION: Highway 12, **Deep Creek**

HOURS: Noon to Closing Sat-Sun
4:00 p.m. to Closing Tue-Fri

PHONE: 406-266-5346

HAPPY HOUR: No

BEER: Domestics; Imports; Microbrews

GAMBLING: No

AMUSEMENT: Pool; Darts

LIVE MUSIC: Occasionally

FOOD: Full Menu Restaurant

The Deep Creek Restaurant and Lounge is twelve miles east of Townsend on Highway 12. The 4,000 square foot peeled log structure stands along the highway, but the natural surroundings provide a secluded setting. A wooden pedestrian bridge crosses the creek between the west parking lot and the building, and a covered wooden deck spans the length of the south and west walls. Log posts support the ceiling, and the log walls are beautifully trimmed with natural wood. The barroom has a long bar with a wooden foot rail. The solid bar top was made by cutting a thick plank from the center of a tree trunk. A few wooden tables are spread throughout the room, and various big game head mounts hang from the walls. A huge stone fireplace rises from the floor in the southwest corner of the spacious dining room, enhancing the building's rustic charm.

The Deep Creek Bar was established in 1927. A large framed painting of the original building hangs from the north wall of the present-day dining room. The original building was destroyed by fire in 1960, so a new structure was built across the creek to the east. The business moved back across Deep Creek when construction on a new log structure was completed in 1989. Rose and Leon Henke bought the business in December, 1996. They were just getting started when I last visited Deep Creek, but things seemed to be going well for the new owners. The interior decor was quite sparse at that time, but plans were in place to finish the interior in a Montana-Alaska motif.

The Deep Creek Restaurant and Lounge has the appearance of a formal establishment, but Leon assured me the atmosphere is informal and everyone is welcome. In fact, hunting and fishing stories are always allowed, if not encouraged, at the Deep Creek Restaurant and Lounge. The dinner menu features steaks, Alaskan seafood, and Italian dishes. Specialty meals, such as vegetarian dishes, can be prepared on request. An extensive wine list and a large selection of imported, microbrewed, and domestic beers are available. A Sunday champagne brunch is served occasionally through the summer, and dinner specials are offered on a daily basis.

BUNKHOUSE BAR

OWNERS: Rodger and Bonnie Vetter

HOURS: 10:00 a.m. to 2:00 a.m. Daily

HAPPY HOUR: No

GAMBLING: Video Poker/Keno; Shake-A-Day

LIVE MUSIC: Occasionally

LOCATION: Highway 287, **Toston**

PHONE: 406-266-5302

BEER: Drafts; Domestics; Microbrews

AMUSEMENT: Pool; Horseshoes

FOOD: Grill Items; Fresh Pizza

The Bunkhouse Bar is on Highway 287 in Toston. An L-shaped bar faces the west wall of the barroom, a few small tables are spread across the floor, and a stone fireplace rises from the floor against the north wall. The smaller back room is used primarily as a game room. The interior walls are covered with wood, in one form or another, and the exterior is part log and part wood siding. An outdoor bar and beer garden have recently been added, and several RV parking spaces with full hookups are available if you want to spend the night in your motor home.

The Bunkhouse Bar was established in 1955. Bunkhouse was selected as the name for the business because the building was originally used as a bunkhouse and survey office at the Keating Gold Mine near Radersburg. The smaller room on the east end of the building was added a year or two after the bar first opened. The room was actually a sleeping barracks that was moved to Toston from Fort Harrison.

Rodger and Bonnie Vetter bought the Bunkhouse Bar in March, 1994. They promote a friendly atmosphere where people can gather without having to worry about being bothered by rude or obnoxious customers. Local trade keeps the Bunkhouse going throughout the year, and travelers, hunters, and fishermen stop in during the summer and fall. There's even a few regular customers who commonly drive forty miles one way from Helena simply because they enjoy the friendly atmosphere at the Bunkhouse Bar.

About twice a year, the Bunkhouse hosts a Bartender Appreciation Day. People who normally come to the bar as customers take two hour shifts as bartenders throughout the day while the regular bartenders sit on the other side of the plank and bark out orders. Both the customers and the bartenders have a great time, and the customers learn first hand what it's like to be on the other side of the plank. The Bunkhouse also hosts a branding party after calving season ends each spring, and they hold several outdoor barbecues during the summer. Regardless of whether they're having a special party or not, you're sure to enjoy your visit to Toston's Bunkhouse Bar.

SILOS INN LOUNGE AND SUPPER CLUB

OWNERS: Charlie and Faith Arnold

LOCATION: Highway 287, 7 Miles North of **Townsend**

HOURS: 11:00 a.m. to Closing Daily

PHONE: 406-266-5622

HAPPY HOUR: No

BEER: Drafts; Domestics; Imports; Microbrews

GAMBLING: Video Poker/Keno; Shake-A-Day

AMUSEMENT: Darts; Horseshoes

LIVE MUSIC: Occasionally

FOOD: Full Menu Restaurant

The Silos Inn Lounge and Supper Club is seven miles north of Townsend on Highway 287. The wooden structure has a covered boardwalk that spans the entire length of the west side of the building. The barroom is housed in the south side of the ground-level floor, a dining room is in the north side, and a banquet room is in the basement. The plate glass windows in the east wall afford the barroom and dining room guests a spectacular view of Canyon Ferry Reservoir. The comfortable atmosphere in the dining room is enhanced by an antique wood stove that stands just inside the main entrance and a modern wood pellet stove in the northeast corner. The barroom decor isn't elaborate, but a large elk skin and a mountain lion pelt, with the head still intact, hang from the walls.

The Silos Inn was established in 1984. The business was named for the two brick silos that stand near the property. The silos were built in the early 1900s by A. B. Cook, a stockman who came to the area to raise purebred cattle. The brick silos, a rare sight today, have become a local landmark. Charlie and Faith Arnold bought the Silos Inn Lounge and Supper Club in January, 1996, and they continue to operate it today.

The customers at the Silos Inn are a mix of local residents and visiting tourists and outdoors enthusiasts. Visitors from all over the world have stopped in for meals and drinks. The Silos Inn has an extensive dinner menu featuring steaks and seafood. The restaurant has become quite noted for its prime rib, and dinner specials are offered on weekends. With its banquet facilities, the Silos Inn has also become a very popular spot for private gatherings and holiday parties.

To create a competitive spirit among their customers, Charlie and Faith sponsor a weekly Biggest Fish Contest at the bar, with the winner receiving a free dinner. If your fish doesn't quite measure up to the competition, you can always sit back and enjoy the wonderful view from the bar. Antelope, deer, moose, and osprey are often seen in the fields between the Silos Inn and Canyon Ferry Reservoir.

WINSTON BAR

OWNER: Dale Smith

HOURS: Noon to Closing Daily

HAPPY HOUR: No

GAMBLING: Video Poker/Keno; Shake-A-Day

LIVE MUSIC: No

LOCATION: Highway 287, **Winston**

PHONE: 406-227-3301

BEER: Drafts; Domestics; Microbrews

AMUSEMENT: Pool; Darts; Pinball; Horseshoes

FOOD: Bar Snacks

The Winston Bar is on Highway 287 in Winston. A straight wooden bar faces the north wall of the barroom, two buddy bars stand in the middle of the floor, and a wood burning stove is in one corner. The adjoining room has a separate bar and a small bandstand, but it's used primarily as a game room. If you prefer drinking outdoors, a wooden deck spans the length of the east side of the building. Over 1,000 currency bills are stapled to the ceiling above the bar, spelling out a message that can only be read with a mirror. If you don't have a mirror but are willing to donate a signed dollar bill, the bartender will gladly read you the message.

The Winston Bar was established under unusual circumstances in 1948. A store once operated out of a two story log building across the road from where the bar now stands, but I'm told a fierce wind lifted the entire second story from the building, roof intact, and gently dropped it to the ground. Since it was virtually undamaged, the second story of the store was moved across the road, placed on a foundation, and renovated into the Winston Bar. The original bar was destroyed by fire in 1983. After the smoke cleared, the north side of the existing steel-sided structure was erected, and the bar reopened. Dale Smith bought the Winston Bar in June, 1991. Dale added a dance hall onto the south side of the building a couple of years later, but he ended up using the space for a game room because he always lost money when he held dances at the bar.

Although the Winston Bar is in a premier outdoor recreation area, it's basically a local tavern. A few visiting hunters and fishermen stop in throughout the year, but it's not a place that attracts tourists. The customers are always friendly, unless you count the time a former bar owner's girlfriend shot holes in the ceiling during a fit of rage. Dale treats his customers well, and he holds several special events during the year. A "Ling Ding" fishing tournament and cookout, the bar's anniversary party, a turkey bowling tournament, and a White Elephant Christmas Party are some of the more interesting annual events held at the Winston Bar.

BEARCREEK SALOON

OWNERS: Pits and Lynn DeArmond

LOCATION: Highway 308, **Bearcreek**

HOURS: 2:00 p.m. to Closing Thurs-Sun

PHONE: 406-446-3481

HAPPY HOUR: No

BEER: Domestics; Imports

GAMBLING: Video Poker/Keno;
Live Pig Races

AMUSEMENT: Live Pig Races

LIVE MUSIC: No

FOOD: Mexican Restaurant

Pig Races! That's right, swine on the track and hundreds of crazed human spectators screaming and cheering for the little critters to run like the wind. That's precisely what you'll find every weekend at the Bearcreek Saloon. The saloon is on Highway 308 in Bearcreek, and it's definitely a place you have to see to believe. The barroom is housed in the east side of the building, a dining room and the Mini Downs Piglet Raceway are in the west side, and the world famous Bearcreek Downs Track is in the yard out back. Wagering on horses is fairly common, but the Bearcreek Saloon is the only place I know of where you can bet on an animal that oinks to win a foot race against its peers.

The pig races are a relatively recent addition at the saloon, which opened in 1904. The beautiful antique bar and back bar in the building today were hand-crafted from European Walnut and installed when the saloon first opened. The barroom initially resided in the west side of the building, and a grocery store and meat market were in the east side. The center wall was eventually removed, and the barroom was expanded. Pits and Lynn DeArmond brought pig racing to Bearcreek after they bought the saloon in 1982. The betting booth in the south side of the barroom is an antique postal counter that came from the old Washoe Post Office, and the stage railing around the Mini Downs Track was once an alter rail in a church.

The pigs run on Friday, Saturday, and Sunday. The outdoor track is used in the summer, and piglets race on the indoor mini track during the winter. All profits from the pig races are donated to a scholarship fund. To date, over $28,000 in scholarships have been awarded. People from all fifty states and countless countries have been to the Bearcreek Saloon, but the pigs aren't the only attraction. Excellent Mexican food is served Thursday through Sunday beginning at 5:00 p.m. If you plan on visiting the Bearcreek Saloon, take note that the business is closed from September 15 through the first of December and from mid April through the weekend before Memorial Day. Both the owners and the pigs take a break from their grueling schedules before gearing up for the following season.

BELFRY BAR

OWNER: Cordell Stern

HOURS: Noon to Closing Daily

HAPPY HOUR: No

GAMBLING: Video Poker/Keno; Live Poker

LIVE MUSIC: No

LOCATION: Broadway Street, **Belfry**

PHONE: 406-664-3245

BEER: Domestics; Imports

AMUSEMENT: Pool

FOOD: Grill Items

The Belfry Bar is housed in a wooden structure on the south side of Broadway Street in Belfry. The building looks much the same today as it did when it was built in the 1920s. Glass brick surrounds the top and both sides of the front door, the decorative tin ceiling is intact, and the original hardwood floor is still in place. A long bar faces the west wall of the barroom, and a wooden pew and a potbellied stove are against the opposite wall. A sofa and an old barber's chair are in the middle of the barroom floor. A complete collection of old Olympia Beer plaques hangs from the barroom walls along with several old Rainier Beer signs. The only thing I saw that was new when I visited the Belfry Bar was a Labrador Retriever puppy playfully romping around the barroom.

The Belfry Bar was established in 1937. The building was a grocery store and meat market prior to the bar moving in. The murals on the wall behind the bar were painted by Chuck Davis in 1960. Chuck the Whittler, as he was known, was a multi-talented artist who was better known for his wood carvings than his paintings. I'm told Chuck never painted anything on canvas because he didn't want other people selling and profiting from his works. Cordell Stern has owned the bar since 1991, but the business has been in his family since 1962. Cordell says he bought the old barber's chair from a former customer, partly to pay off the man's bar tab. Most of the money went toward financing the man's move from town, but paying off the bar tab is usually the part of the story that gets repeated.

As you enter the barroom, you will probably notice a lot of dollar bills stuck to the ceiling. First time visitors at the Belfry Bar often wrap a signed dollar bill around their billfold, stick a wad of chewing gum to the dollar, and throw the billfold against the ceiling. If your aim is true, the billfold hits the ceiling gum-side up. The bill should stick, but your wallet will fall to the floor. If you're a gambler, you may want to save that dollar for the poker table. Live poker is played every Friday, Saturday, and Sunday, and the games are so popular that people from as far away as Billings and Cody, Wyoming commonly participate.

SILVER TIP BAR

OWNERS: Bob and Jean Roberts **LOCATION:** Broadway Street, **Belfry**

HOURS: 3:00 p.m. to Closing Daily **PHONE:** No Phone

HAPPY HOUR: No **BEER:** Domestics

GAMBLING: Video Poker/Keno **AMUSEMENT:** Pool

LIVE MUSIC: No **FOOD:** Homemade Pizza

The Silver Tip Bar is on Broadway Street in Belfry. A beautiful antique bar, back bar, and liquor cabinet stand along the east wall of the barroom. The back bar, which is over 100 years old, has stained glass panels on both ends and a large mirror in the middle. Three booths are lined against the west wall in the front portion of the room, and a wooden candy counter stands at the north end of the bar. The building is by no means new, but the facility is very clean and well-maintained. The tongue-and-groove pine woodwork on the interior walls helps create a rustic appearance and a comfortable atmosphere.

The Silver Tip Bar was established in 1946. Bob and Jean Roberts have owned the business since 1982, but they had the bar up for sale when I last visited Belfry in December, 1996. There's usually a friendly, well-mannered crowd on hand. The last real excitement at the Silver Tip Bar occurred in the late 1980s when a vehicle was driven part way through the front of the building. Apparently, the driver was in a bit of an alcoholic haze, and she didn't locate the brake pedal in time to prevent the car from crashing through the wall.

The Silver Tip Bar enjoys a steady local clientele throughout the year. Tourists, fishermen, and hunters provide a boost to the business during the summer and fall, and people from Northcentral Wyoming commonly stop in to play the video gambling machines. A lot of bikers also stop while traveling to or from the annual Biker's Rally in Sturgis, South Dakota. The atmosphere in the barroom is usually quiet and relaxed, but things can get a bit wild during Belfry's annual Pioneer Day Celebration in mid August. The two bars in Belfry team up to sponsor a street dance for the festival, and the customers sometimes over-celebrate.

Bob and Jean don't have a formal happy hour, but they always keep their drink prices at a very reasonable level. To show appreciation for their customers, Bob and Jean also host an occasional outdoor barbecue during the summer. If you're a pizza lover, you have to try the homemade pizza at the Silver Tip Bar. After one bite, you will understand why the pizzas are so popular among the people of Belfry.

EDGAR BAR

OWNERS: Matt and JoAnn Specht

HOURS: 11:30 a.m. to Closing Daily

HAPPY HOUR: No

GAMBLING: Video Poker/Keno; Shake-A-Day

LIVE MUSIC: No

LOCATION: Main Street, **Edgar**

PHONE: 406-962-9868

BEER: Domestics; Microbrews

AMUSEMENT: Pool

FOOD: Frozen Pizza

The Edgar bar is housed in a brick structure on the north side of Main Street in Edgar. The building is over 100 years old, but the barroom is very clean and well-maintained. The relatively small barroom has a beautiful pine ceiling supported by solid wooden beams. A straight bar faces the north wall, and a couple of tables are spread across the floor toward the front part of the room. There's not a lot of fancy decorations in the barroom, but some nice antique signs and figurines are displayed at various locations throughout the room.

The business was established as the Bright Spot in 1936, but the name was changed to the Edgar Bar in 1941. Matt and Joanne Specht bought the Edgar Bar in August, 1994. During their first several months, JoAnn and Matt spent a considerable amount of time cleaning and upgrading the old barroom. Layers of smoke, dirt, and dust covered everything in the building, so new materials and a lot of elbow grease were used to make the place look respectable. New carpeting and front windows were installed, the bar top was repainted and covered with eight coats of polyurethane, a modern central heat and air system was installed, fresh paint was applied throughout, and countless hours of scrubbing took place. Matt and Joanne now have an immaculate barroom that's very neat and free of clutter.

The Edgar Bar is a friendly tavern where people gather to relax and unwind. Most of the customers are local residents, but travelers stop in occasionally. A unique aspect about the Edgar Bar is the fact that smoking is prohibited inside the barroom. The owners don't have anything against smokers, but JoAnn is allergic to tobacco smoke. Since she usually spends her entire day at the bar, the smoke could have a serious impact on her health. The smoke-free environment is also appreciated by non-smoking customers, especially since the place is so small. Matt and Joanne don't run a happy hour, but they always keep their drink prices at a reasonable level. In fact, the price on just about everything at the Edgar Bar is reasonable. This is one of the few places where you can still play a game of pool for 25 cents.

BUFFALO CHIP SALOON

OWNERS: Bob and Patty Rogers

LOCATION: 102 W. River, **Fromberg**

HOURS: 10:00 a.m. to 2:00 a.m. Daily

PHONE: 406-668-7642

HAPPY HOUR: No

BEER: Domestics

GAMBLING: Video Poker/Keno; Shake-A-Day

AMUSEMENT: Pool; Darts; Video Game

LIVE MUSIC: Karaoke Music Monthly

FOOD: Full Menu Cafe

The Buffalo Chip Saloon is at 102 West River Street in Fromberg. A spacious barroom resides in the north side of the building, and a smaller game room is in the south side. An L-shaped bar spans the length of the west wall. The rough cut boards covering the interior walls and heavy wooden doors with buffalo head cutouts in them add to the building's rustic charm. The brands displayed on the barroom walls are authentic brands from local ranches.

The business was established in 1938 as the Nu Modern Club in the nearby town of Bridger. The name was changed to the Silva Inn when the bar was moved to Fromberg in 1942. The bar also operated under the names Al's Tavern, the Mint Bar, and Miller's Inn between 1945 and the mid 1980s when it became the Buffalo Chip Saloon. I'm told knife fights were a fairly common occurrence at Miller's Inn. Allegedly, the number of knife fights was directly proportional to the number of migrant farm workers who happened to be in the bar at any given time. These days, however, the Buffalo Chip Saloon is a very friendly place where trouble rarely starts.

Bob and Patty Rogers bought the business in January, 1994. Their slogan, Come As A Stranger, Leave As A Friend, is an accurate description of the kind of treatment you can expect at the Buffalo Chip Saloon. Fresh pizzas and burgers are served at the bar, and daily lunch and dinner specials are also offered. Hand-breaded chicken fried steaks are featured every Friday, and prime rib is the special on Saturdays. No matter what you order, you always get a generous portion of food at a very reasonable price, and the quality of the food is outstanding.

Bob and Patty promote a family-oriented atmosphere at the Buffalo Chip Saloon, and their customers are typically very friendly and well-mannered. A cash drawing is held every Wednesday evening, and the saloon also hosts an annual Rocky Mountain Oyster feed on the second weekend of June. This "Festival of Testicles" has become quite popular in recent years, and the souvenir T-shirts that are made for the annual event have been shipped to people from as far away as New York.

LITTLE COWBOY BAR AND MUSEUM

OWNER: Shirley Smith

LOCATION: W. River St., **Fromberg**

HOURS: 8:00 a.m. to 2:00 a.m. Daily

PHONE: 406-668-9502

HAPPY HOUR: No

BEER: Drafts; Domestics

GAMBLING: Video Poker/Keno; Shake-A-Day

AMUSEMENT: Darts

LIVE MUSIC: No

FOOD: Frozen Pizza

The Little Cowboy Bar and Museum is on West River Street in Fromberg, just off Highway 310. It's not hard to recognize the place, especially since there are dozens of brands from local ranches painted on the exterior of the building near the front entrance. A moderate-sized barroom resides in the front portion of the building. A wood burning stove stands in the corner just inside the main entrance, and numerous framed pictures and various other forms of memorabilia line the walls. A small storage room in the middle of the building separates the barroom from Fromberg's own Little Cowboy Museum. The museum contains hundreds of interesting artifacts pertaining to Fromberg, residents of the community, and the farming and ranching lifestyle of the people who live in the area.

The bar was built in 1946. Hank's Bar was the name of the original business, but the name was changed to the Little Cowboy Bar when Shirley Smith bought the business in 1972. Shirley's love for the western life is very evident. Most of the photographs on the barroom walls are of champion rodeo cowboys or rodeo participants. Shirley opened the Little Cowboy Museum in 1992. Several of the items in the museum are things Shirley has collected over the years, but most were donated by local residents. The items on display include pictures of Fromberg and local citizens, various documents, antique farm implements and household items, weapons, animal bones, artwork, belt buckles, and other items too numerous to mention. There's even a wooden Indian complete with head dress that came from a tack shop in Frannie, Wyoming.

The majority of the customers at the Little Cowboy Bar are local residents, but travelers passing through the area stop in occasionally. Things sometimes get a bit rowdy in the barroom, but there's normally a friendly crowd on hand. If you get a chance to visit the Little Cowboy Bar and Museum, spend some time looking around and talking to Shirley. You can also buy locally crafted gifts at the bar which Shirley's daughter, Val, makes. It's not very often you find a museum in a saloon, so be sure to stop at the Little Cowboy Bar and Museum the next time you're in Fromberg.

BROWN BEAR INN

OWNER: Jim White

HOURS: 10:00 a.m. to 2:00 a.m. Daily

HAPPY HOUR: 4:30 to 6:30 Daily

GAMBLING: Video Poker/Keno

LIVE MUSIC: Occasionally

LOCATION: 2 N. 1st Street, **Roberts**

PHONE: 406-445-2318

BEER: Drafts; Domestics; Imports; Microbrews

AMUSEMENT: Pool; Darts

FOOD: Full Menu Steak House

The Brown Bear Inn is on 1st Street in Roberts. Although the building technically houses both a barroom and dining room, there is no physical separation between the two. A straight wooden bar stands along the east wall just outside the kitchen, and the dining room tables occupy most of the remaining floor space. The small casino area just inside the front entrance is partially petitioned-off from the bar and dining room. The interior of the building is modern and well-maintained. Carpeting covers the floor, except for a small tiled area immediately around the bar, and tongue-and-groove wood trim runs about half way up the walls. Each window has a set of wooden shutters with bear paw cut-outs in them. Most of the framed artwork hanging from the walls was done by Bill Rains, an artist from Billings.

The history of the Brown Bear Inn dates back to 1933 when Batt Bertolino's Beer Parlor was built. The name of the bar became the New Deal in 1935, in reference to President Franklin D. Roosevelt's administration. The business changed hands three times between 1990 and 1995. The interior of the structure was completely renovated in 1992 when the name of the business became the Brown Bear Inn. I'm told that when the renovations were completed and the Inn reopened, live bears were brought into the building as a promotional event. The live critters are gone, but two bear skin rugs still hang from the back wall of the barroom. Jim White currently owns the Brown Bear Inn, but Stephanie Ramirez manages the day-to-day operations.

There's usually a local crowd at the bar, but the dining room draws people from all over the region, as well as visiting skiers and tourists. A surprisingly high number of foreigners also stop at the Brown Bear Inn for meals. The customers are typically friendly, so you don't have to worry about rude or obnoxious behavior. The kitchen is open from 11:00 a.m. to 11:00 p.m. seven days a week, and you can always count on getting excellent prime rib and steaks. All cuts of meat served at the Brown Bear Inn are hand-selected and cut fresh daily.

LOST VILLAGE BAR

OWNER: Mike Smith

HOURS: 10:00 a.m. to 2:00 a.m. Daily

HAPPY HOUR: No

GAMBLING: Video Poker/Keno

LIVE MUSIC: Occasionally

LOCATION: Highway 212, **Roberts**

PHONE: 406-445-9993

BEER: Drafts; Domestics

AMUSEMENT: Pool; Darts; Pinball; Video Games

FOOD: Pizza; Soup; Sandwiches

The Lost Village Bar is on Highway 212 in Roberts. The main part of the barroom and a small casino area are housed in the front portion of the building, and a game room is in the back. Large red and black square tiles cover the barroom ceiling, so be prepared to see a giant checkerboard if you get drunk and fall over on your back. Fortunately, they don't have any giant checkers that drop from the ceiling, so you don't have to be in a hurry to get back on your feet. Several sets of antlers are mounted to the wooden awning above bar. The antique back bar against the south wall was built in the early 1900's. The back bar was shipped via steamboat up the Missouri River to Montana, where it was off-loaded and transported overland to Roberts by team and wagon. The beautiful hand-carved wood has embedded stained glass and an arched mirror.

The bar originally stood on Main Street in Roberts, but the building was moved to its present location in 1945. As amazing as it may sound, virtually no interruption in service occurred during the move. In the early morning hours, the building was jacked up, placed on skids, and hauled part of the way to its final destination. The bar opened just long enough to serve some customers, and the building was then pulled the rest of the way to its final destination and placed on a pre-constructed foundation. Concrete block steps were placed in front of the door, and the bar was back in business. The entire move was completed in one morning, and the customers didn't even have to wait until the move was completed to be served. Some years later, the barroom expanded into part of a motel that stood beside the building. The present-day game room now occupies this part of the building.

Mike Smith has owned the Lost Village Bar since August, 1996. Most of his customers are local residents, but tourists and hunters also stop in. Fresh pizza, homemade soup, and hot sandwiches are served every day, and the prime rib sandwich special on Thursdays has become a local favorite. Good food, a nice atmosphere, and friendly people are basically what you'll find at the Lost Village Bar. What more could you ask for?

FORT ROCKVALE RESTAURANT AND CASINO

OWNER: Melanie Hurley

HOURS: 11:00 a.m. to Closing Daily

HAPPY HOUR: 5:00 to 7:00 Daily

GAMBLING: Video Poker/Keno; Shake-A-Day

LIVE MUSIC: Weekly During the Summer

LOCATION: Highway 212, **Rockvale**

PHONE: 406-962-3963

BEER: Domestics; Imports; Microbrews

AMUSEMENT: Pool; Darts

FOOD: Full Menu Restaurant

The Fort Rockvale Restaurant and Casino is at the junction of Highways 212 and 310 in Rockvale. The building houses a spacious barroom, a casino area, and a separate dining room. Extensive renovations were recently completed, so the entire facility is very modern. The rustic barroom is finished primarily in unstained rough cut wood, and fresh wallpaper and paint have been applied in the dining room. A straight wooden bar faces the west wall of the barroom, a big-screen TV stands in the middle of the floor, and a large dance floor and a raised wooden bandstand are in the south side of the room. Several tables are available, so there's plenty of seating.

The history of the Fort Rockvale Restaurant and Casino dates back to 1947 when the Rockvale Store obtained a retail beer license. The name of the business was changed to Rockvale Village in 1951, Rockvale Enterprises in 1954, and the Rockvale Bar and Cafe in 1956. A company called Fort Clarkvale, Inc. owned the business in 1971 when the name was changed to the Fort Rockvale Bar and Cafe.

Melanie Hurley has owned the Fort Rockvale Restaurant and Casino since 1992. Melanie invested a lot of time and money into building renovations, and her efforts have paid off. Residents of Rockvale and the surrounding communities support the business, but the primary source of revenue at the Fort Rockvale Restaurant and Casino are people from Billings and Northern Wyoming. Travelers also stop in to eat, drink, or gamble before trudging on to their destination. There's usually a quiet, relaxed atmosphere in the barroom, but things get going on the weekends during the summer when live bands perform at the bar.

Restaurant hours are 7:00 a.m. to 10:00 p.m. during the summer, but the winter hours vary. Daily lunch and dinner specials are offered throughout the week, and they have a good selection of menu items to choose from. If you happen to be passing through the area, the Fort Rockvale Restaurant and Casino is a good place to stop for food, drinks, or relaxation. It's easy to find, and you're certain to enjoy your visit.

GRIZZLY BAR

OWNERS: Linda and Clifford Espeland

HOURS: 11:00 a.m. to 2:00 a.m. Daily

HAPPY HOUR: No

GAMBLING: Video Poker/Keno

LIVE MUSIC: No

LOCATION: Main Street, **Roscoe**

PHONE: 406-328-6789

BEER: Drafts; Domestics; Imports; Microbrews

AMUSEMENT: None

FOOD: Full Menu Restaurant

The Grizzly Bar is on Main Street in Roscoe, a town of about fifty permanent residents at the foot of the scenic Beartooth Mountains. The business is more of a dining establishment than a drinking establishment, but it's a great place to visit. A relatively small barroom is toward the back of the building. Log barstools stand at the straight wooden bar, and hardwood flooring surrounds the bar area. A huge stone fireplace on the opposite side of the room enhances the rustic atmosphere. If you prefer the great outdoors, a large concrete deck and an adjacent beer garden, complete with its own bar, are just outside.

The business had its humble beginnings in 1939 when Sam Stokke built the Horseshoe Inn. The original barroom had a horseshoe-shaped bar in the front of the room and a dance hall in the rear. The Horseshoe Inn became the Grizzly Bar in the late 1960's. A massive stone fireplace was added to the front of the building, and a large bear figure was mounted above the main entrance. Linda Espeland bought the business in 1981, and she and her husband, Clifford, operate it today.

The Grizzly Bar gets some business from local residents, but it relies heavily on the tourist trade during the summer months and skiers in the winter. People from all over Southcentral Montana and Northcentral Wyoming also stop at the Grizzly Bar throughout the year, primarily for the fine dining. The lunch and dinner menus feature everything from hamburgers to seafood. Excellent steaks and seafood entrees are available, and the prime rib is nothing less than superb. In 1989, the Grizzly Bar received the Montana Beef Council's award for outstanding beef. With credentials like this, you know you're going to get a great meal.

Along with the bar and restaurant, Linda and Clifford own Papa's and Granny's Guest House, which is located in the former Rosebud Trading Company Building across the street from the bar. If you're looking for a unique lodging experience, Papa's and Granny's offers a quiet place to get away from it all. The guest house can sleep up to four people, and it's the only lodging available in Roscoe.

EL RANCHO INN

OWNERS: Henry and Sally Rodriguez

HOURS: 11:00 a.m. to 2:00 a.m. Daily

HAPPY HOUR: 4:00 to 6:00 Mon - Fri

GAMBLING: Video Poker/Keno

LIVE MUSIC: Occasionally

LOCATION: Highway 212, **Silesia**

PHONE: 406-962-3251

BEER: Drafts; Domestics; Imports; Microbrews

AMUSEMENT: Pool; Darts

FOOD: Full Menu Restaurant

The El Rancho Inn is on Highway 212 in Silesia. The building's not actually "on" the highway, but be careful, because the front door is only a few short steps away from the road. The barroom occupies the east side of the building, and the dining room resides in the west side. If you prefer eating outdoors, seating is available on the concrete patio out back. The interior decor consists of framed posters and pictures, wood carvings, porcelain figurines, and colorful ponchos and sombreros. A large set of Texas Longhorns is mounted above the archway separating the barroom from the dining room, and several antique lamps, derringers, and bronze statuettes are on display behind the custom-built bar. The place is heavily decorated, but it doesn't appear cluttered.

The bar's history dates back to 1945 when an automobile service station was renovated into the Longhorn Bar. I'm not sure why, but a stool that was once used in the service station is still in the barroom today. The Longhorn was a mainstay in Silesia until Henry and Sally Rodriguez bought the business in 1975. Henry and Sally did some renovations of their own and changed the name of the business to the El Rancho Inn. The Longhorn is said to have been a pretty rowdy place, but Henry and Sally have made the El Rancho a very friendly, family-oriented business.

The bar does a pretty fair trade, but the El Rancho Inn has acquired an outstanding reputation because of the authentic Mexican food served in the restaurant. Everything is made fresh from scratch, and everything is delicious. Sally operated a restaurant in Laurel over twenty years ago, and a lot of the same customers she served in Laurel now drive to Silesia for Mexican Food. I guess that proves people are willing to go out of their way for good food and good service. If you don't care for Mexican food, traditional American dishes are available. The El Rancho Inn also serves some of the best margaritas you'll find anywhere, and they stock a wide assortment of beers. For a unique dining experience, the El Rancho Inn can't be beat. It's also a wonderful place to stop if you just want to relax with a cold beer or a margarita.

STONEVILLE SALOON

OWNERS: Diane Turko & Rob Peterson

HOURS: 11:00 a.m. to Midnight Daily

HAPPY HOUR: No

GAMBLING: Video Poker/Keno

LIVE MUSIC: Occasionally

LOCATION: Highway 212, **Alzada**

PHONE: 406-828-4404
FAX: 406-828-4454

BEER: Domestics

AMUSEMENT: Pool; Pinball; Horseshoes

FOOD: Full Menu Cafe

The Stoneville Saloon is on Highway 212 in Alzada. Their slogan, Cheap Drinks, Lousy Food, sets the tone of the place before you ever set foot in the door. The barroom is tastefully decorated in a manner that would put any teenager's room to shame. Crushed peanut shells cover the floor, various posters, pictures, license plates, and antiques hang from the walls and ceiling, and a wooden stage which serves as a bandstand and tattoo parlor stands in the middle of the floor. The antique wooden bar and back bar were built in the mid 1800s. Both pieces were originally installed in the Deadwood Gulch Saloon in Deadwood, South Dakota, but they somehow ended up in Alzada after prohibition ended.

Diane Turko and Rob Peterson bought what was the Alzada Bar and Cafe in 1991 and transformed it into the Stoneville Saloon. Since there's not much of a local population, Diane and Rob primarily cater to people who are visiting or passing through the area. The Stoneville Saloon is a popular spot during the annual biker's rally in Sturgis, South Dakota. Each year, thousands of bikers make the sixty mile trip to Alzada to buy drinks and souvenir T-shirts or just party and spend the night. Customers can park overnight for free, and hot showers are available. There's also hunting and fishing licenses and ammunition for sale at the bar.

Contrary to the "Lousy Food" slogan, excellent meals are served in the cafe. "Fartless chili" and "nitro buffalo wings" are available for those who prefer a spicy meal, and Rob has even installed seat belts on the toilets in case you experience digestive problems. If you don't care for spicy food, the hamburgers are terrific, and free peanuts in the shell are given out in the bar every evening at 9:00.

Among its many attributes, the Stoneville Saloon serves as a tattoo parlor. Diane is the artist, and she performs high quality custom tattoo work. Walk-ins are accepted, but appointments are recommended because Diane's time is very limited. Custom artwork can be faxed to Diane prior to your appointment so she is prepared when you arrive.

VALLEY INN BAR AND CAFE

OWNER: Kay Nelson

HOURS: 2:00 p.m. to Closing Daily

HAPPY HOUR: No

GAMBLING: Video Poker/Keno; Shake-A-Day

LIVE MUSIC: No

LOCATION: Highway 212, **Alzada**

PHONE: 406-828-4551

BEER: Domestics

AMUSEMENT: Pool; Pinball

FOOD: Full Menu Cafe

The Valley Inn Bar and Cafe is on the south side of Highway 212 in Alzada. The barroom resides in the west side of the building, and a full service cafe is in the east side. Tongue-and-groove boards cover the interior walls throughout the entire building, creating a comfortable atmosphere for both the barroom and dining room guests. A straight wooden bar with a brass foot rail stands in front of an antique wooden back bar against the south wall of the barroom. The barstools stand on a bare concrete floor, but carpeting has been installed in the north side of the room under the card tables and pool table. Besides being a great bar and cafe, the Valley Inn sells the only gasoline along Highway 212 between Broadus, Montana and Belle Fourche, South Dakota.

The Valley Inn was established in 1939. The business originally operated out of a building to the west the present-day bar and cafe, but Gene and Carley Brimmer moved the business to its present location in 1983. The move was required because the original structure was about to collapse. Gene passed away in October, 1994, so Carley substantially reduced the hours of operation until she found a buyer for the business. Kay Nelson took over in August, 1995, and she now has the Valley Inn Bar and Cafe back in full operation.

Contrary to the management philosophy at Alzada's Stoneville Saloon, the Valley Inn primarily caters to local residents. A few travelers, hunters, and tourists stop in throughout the year, but the Valley Inn is basically operated as a neighborhood bar and cafe. People commonly stop by during the evenings to play cards, and a pitch tournament is held at the bar every Friday night. Members of the local roping club also stop at the Valley Inn on Thursday evenings during the summer after their weekly roping sessions. Breakfast, lunch, and dinner are served on a daily basis from 6:00 a.m. until 9:00 p.m., and lunch specials are offered throughout the week. Although Kay has owned the Valley Inn Bar and Cafe for a relatively short period of time, she seems to be doing a great job with her new business.

BUCKHORN BAR

OWNER: Skeet Hedges

HOURS: 8:00 a.m. to 2:00 a.m. Daily

HAPPY HOUR: No

GAMBLING: Video Poker/Keno

LIVE MUSIC: No

LOCATION: Main Street, **Ekalaka**

PHONE: 406-775-6503

BEER: Drafts; Domestics

AMUSEMENT: Darts; Foosball

FOOD: Bar Snacks

The Buckhorn Bar is on the west side of Main Street in Ekalaka. The building is relatively old, but the entire barroom has recently undergone extensive renovations. Tongue-and-groove cedar boards cover three walls, new tile flooring and ceiling panels have been added, and a new formica bar top was installed. There's even a brand new front door surrounded by stones set in mortar on the wall facing Main Street. The old stucco finish on the front of the building was still in place when I last visited, but plans were in place to install a modern wooden front in the spring of 1997. The barroom is relatively small, but a long bar spans nearly the entire length of the north wall, and a few tables are available along the south wall if you can't find an empty barstool.

The Buckhorn Bar was established in 1933. The bar originally operated out of a building that stood one block north of the present-day structure, but it moved in 1957. I'm told the original building had deteriorated to the point where it was no longer safe for occupancy. A man named Bud Kelstrom owned and operated the Buckhorn Bar from the mid 1960s until his death in 1994. There wasn't much interest in the bar among Bud's family, so the business basically sat idle until a buyer was found. Skeet Hedges bought the Buckhorn Bar in July, 1995, but he didn't open for business until the renovations were completed in March of 1996. Skeet had previously owned the Old Stand Bar in Ekalaka, so he is no newcomer to the bar business.

Although the barroom has been given a much needed facelift, Skeet still manages the place as it's always been managed; a quiet tavern with a friendly atmosphere. The residents of Ekalaka seem to drift from bar to bar when they're out on the town, so Skeet's customers are basically the same people that frequent Ekalaka's other two saloons. Which bar attracts the most people at any given time is more dependent on luck than strategic planning on the part of the bar owner. The Buckhorn Bar is too small for live music, but Skeet plans on adding an outdoor beer garden with a bandstand in the spring of 1997. I'm sure that will make visiting the Buckhorn Bar an even more enjoyable experience.

NEW LIFE BAR

OWNER: Vivian Mackay

HOURS: 9:00 a.m. to 2:00 a.m. Daily

HAPPY HOUR: No

GAMBLING: Video Poker/Keno

LIVE MUSIC No

LOCATION: Main Street, **Ekalaka**

PHONE: 406-775-6723

BEER: Drafts; Domestics

AMUSEMENT: Pool; Video Games; Skeeball

FOOD: Frozen Pizza; Toasted Garlic Cheese Bread

The New Life Bar is on Main Street in Ekalaka. The spacious barroom has a straight bar facing the south wall, a couple of small tables and wooden booths spread throughout the room, and plenty of open floor space. There's an old safe in the back of the barroom, but it serves no useful purpose for the business. I'm told the safe was left at the bar several years ago by a local rancher, but he never came back to claim it. The safe has now become a permanent fixture in the barroom.

The history of the New Life Bar dates back to 1934 when the Pastime Cigar Store obtained a retail beer license. The name of the business was changed to the New Life Bar when the business moved across Main Street to its present location in 1935. Previous to becoming a tavern, the building housed an automobile service station. Vivian Mackay bought the New Life Bar in 1975, and it didn't take her long to learn first hand that a service station formerly operated out of the building. One day while working in the bar, Vivian accidently fell into the old service pit the mechanics used when working under the vehicles. Vivian decided a barroom was no place for a service pit, and she had the pit covered soon after emerging from its oily depths. I'm not aware of anyone else ever falling into the pit, but I think Vivian did the right thing by covering the hole.

I've never met a friendlier bunch of people than the folks I met at the New Life Bar in Ekalaka. The locals have a special way of making strangers feel welcome, and they're not shy about including you in on their conversations. When I first visited the New Life Bar, I quickly discovered it's common for people to buy rounds of drinks for their friends. I didn't know a single person in town the first time I walked into the New Life Bar, but I had plenty of friends by the time I crawled out later that night. Vivian treats her customers well and keeps her drink prices at a reasonable level. There's no formal happy hour at the New Life Bar, but everyone always seems to be happy. You may have to crawl home when the bar closes, but you'll crawl home with a smile on your face.

OLD STAND BAR

OWNERS: Tammy and Gene Martens

HOURS: 8:00 a.m. to 2:00 a.m. Daily

HAPPY HOUR: 5:30 to 6:30 Mon - Fri
(Winter Months Only)

GAMBLING: Video Poker/Keno;
Shake-A-Day; Live Poker

LIVE MUSIC: Occasionally

LOCATION: Main Street, **Ekalaka**

PHONE: 406-775-6661

BEER: Drafts; Domestics;
Imports

AMUSEMENT: Pool; Darts

FOOD: Full Menu Restaurant

The Old Stand Bar is on the west side of Main Street in Ekalaka. The barroom resides in the front part of the building, and a restaurant is in the rear. A horseshoe-shaped bar with a log elbow rail stands in the middle of the barroom, and several tables are available if all the barstools are taken. The facility is very clean and well-maintained, and the people are as friendly as they come.

The Old Stand Bar was established in 1889. The Old Stand wasn't the first tavern in town, but if not for a saloon, Ekalaka may never have been founded. An inscription on a wooden marker along Route 7 just north of town provides a summary of Ekalaka's birth. Back in the late 1800s, a buffalo hunter decided he could make a better living selling whiskey than trading buffalo hides. As the man and his wagon load of whiskey headed west, the wagon became bogged down, so he unloaded the whiskey and set up a plank on two barrels. "Hell", he said, "any place in Montana is a good place for a saloon." The saloon prospered and the town of Ekalaka grew up around it. The Old Stand officially became a pool hall and soda fountain during prohibition, but bootlegged booze that was distilled in the nearby hills was sold to known customers. The bar has been destroyed by fire on three different occasions, but it was rebuilt each time. The latest fire occurred in 1982 when the business was housed in a building on the vacant lot just south of where it stands today.

Tammy and Gene Martens bought the Old Stand Bar and adjoining B&B Grill in January, 1995. The grill opens at 10:00 a.m. daily, and some of the best steaks in Montana are served here. They also offer an awesome prime rib dinner on the first Friday of each month. Card games are popular in the barroom, especially during the winter months. The games commonly last from opening until closing time. At the Old Stand Bar, people go out of their way to make strangers feel at home. I can almost guarantee you will never met a friendlier bunch of people anywhere in the world than you will in Ekalaka, and the Old Stand Bar is the perfect place to meet them.

MISSOURI INN

OWNER: Bud Osterman

HOURS: 6:00 a.m. to 11:00 p.m. Daily

HAPPY HOUR: No

GAMBLING: Video Poker/Keno

LIVE MUSIC: Occasionally

LOCATION: Old Highway 91, **Cascade**

PHONE: 406-468-9884

BEER: Drafts; Domestics

AMUSEMENT: None

FOOD: Full Menu Cafe

The Missouri Inn is ten miles south of Cascade on old Highway 91. It's a 2-1/2 mile drive south of exit 247 and a 2-1/2 mile drive north of exit 244 off Interstate 15. The entire business consists of the bar, a cafe, campground, and public laundry and shower facilities. The main building houses a moderate-sized barroom, two dining rooms, and one of the largest painted saw blade collections in Montana. Approximately 145 saw blades painted with western and outdoor scenes hang from the interior walls. A few painted animal bones, frying pans, shovels, and plates, hang amongst the painted saw blades. All the artwork was done by local artists. The campground offers nine full RV hookups and fifteen overnight parking spaces without hookups. One of the best developed boat access ramps on the Missouri River is just across the road.

The Missouri Inn may never have been built if it weren't for a greedy landlord who was leasing a bar to the man who eventually built the Missouri Inn. Business was good, but the rent kept rising as business increased. The man who leased the bar finally told the building owner where he could stick his lease and started building a place of his own. The Missouri Inn opened in 1942, and the rest is history. Although the business has changed hands five times since first opening, it's still going strong today.

Bud Osterman bought the Missouri Inn in 1981. Bud promotes a family-oriented atmosphere where people of all ages are welcome. Although they can't serve alcohol until 8:00 a.m., the doors open at 6:00 every morning for coffee and breakfast. The Hawaiian Ham breakfast is excellent, and a great sirloin roast is available for dinner. From May through November, the majority of Bud's business comes from visiting tourists, hunters, and fishermen. Local residents are the main customers during the remaining five months. Bud says about 80% of his business comes from people who are forty years old and over, which probably reflects the high number of retired people who live in, and travel to, the area. Whether you're looking for a place to spend the entire summer or just a couple of hours, the Missouri Inn has what you're looking for.

CENTERVILLE BAR

OWNERS: Dennis and Joan Yatsko

HOURS: 8:00 a.m. to 2:00 a.m. Daily

HAPPY HOUR: 5:00 to 7:00 Mon - Fri

GAMBLING: Video Poker/Keno; Shake-A-Day

LIVE MUSIC: Occasionally

LOCATION: Route 227, **Centerville**

PHONE: 406-736-9188

BEER: Drafts; Domestics

AMUSEMENT: Pool; Horseshoes; Volleyball

FOOD: Broiled Foods

The Centerville Bar is on the west side of Route 227 in Centerville. The stone and mortar structure houses a barroom in the ground-level floor, and unless things have changed recently, the second story is used as a foundry to make bronze statuettes. A straight bar faces the south wall of the barroom, and a couple of tables are spread throughout the room. If you prefer drinking outdoors, a covered concrete patio is attached to the north side of the building. There's also a large concrete stage and an open beer garden and dance arena to the north of the deck. The outdoor tap system comes in handy during the summer months when live bands play on the outdoor stage.

The Centerville Bar has been around longer than anyone I spoke with could remember, probably since the late 1800s. As far as anyone knows, the business has never changed locations over its 100 year history. The building's interior has been gutted by fire on two different occasions, but the heat and smoke caused no damage to the two foot thick stone walls. The latest fire occurred in 1977. The blaze destroyed several hand-painted murals on the barroom walls, but like the previous fire, it didn't cause a bit of structural damage. The smoke and water damage was repaired in a relatively short period of time, and the Centerville Bar was back in business.

Dennis and Joan Yatsko have owned the Centerville Bar since 1963. Most of their business comes in the form of local trade, but tourists wander into the barroom on occasion. There's usually an adult crowd on hand, but kids sometimes stop by to eat or shoot pool. The broiled burgers are excellent, and pigs in a blanket are available every Saturday. There's no charge to use the pool table from 6:00 p.m. until closing every Tuesday, so you can sharpen your billiard skills without going broke. Dennis and Joan operate the bar in a community-minded manner. They sponsor an annual party to raise scholarship money for a student at the local high school. The scholarship is in memory of Dennis and Joan's oldest son, who was killed in a logging accident some years ago.

DEARBORN COUNTRY INN

OWNERS: Bob and Bill Montanye

LOCATION: Dearborn

HOURS: 11:00 a.m. to 2:00 a.m. Summer
Winter Hours Vary

PHONE: 406-468-2838

HAPPY HOUR: No

BEER: Drafts; Domestics; Imports; Microbrews

GAMBLING: Video Poker/Keno; Shake-A-Day

AMUSEMENT: Pool; Darts; Horseshoes

LIVE MUSIC: Approximately Monthly

FOOD: Full Menu Restaurant

The Dearborn Country Inn is just off the Dearborn Interchange (exit 240) on Interstate 15. The log and frame structure houses a spacious barroom in the west side and a separate dining room in the east side. The building's interior is beautifully finished in logs and natural wood, and a huge stone fireplace stands between the barroom and the dining room.

The business was established as the 7-9 Saloon in 1975. The saloon operated out of the old Warsaw Schoolhouse, which had been moved to the area a couple of years earlier for filming of the movie *Thunderbolt and Lightfoot*. In the movie, the schoolhouse stood at the rest area just south of the Dearborn Exit. After filming was completed, the schoolhouse was moved to the bottom of the hill and renovated into a tavern. The 7-9 Saloon was destroyed by fire in 1976. A metal building was erected, and the business reopened in 1977 under the name Dearborn Steak House and Lounge. Unfortunately, the metal building burned to the ground in 1979. Construction on the present-day structure was completed in 1981, and thus far, it hasn't gone up in flames.

The Dearborn Inn gets its share of tourists, fishermen, and hunters during the summer and fall, but a colorful bunch of local residents keeps the place going throughout the year. Several years ago, one of the locals rode a horse into the crowded building and wasn't able to get the critter out until after it soiled the barroom floor. I won't mention who was on the horse, but if you want a detailed account of the event, ask for Hank. There was another instance a few years back where several of the bar patrons disassembled the steering column on an automobile in the parking lot. They were attempting to perform a diagnostic process to determine why their friend couldn't get the ignition switch to turn with his car key. Nobody, including the man who couldn't get the car to start, realized they were tearing apart someone else's car until the real owner walked out of the barroom and started screaming profanities. I guess it can be quite embarrassing when two cars in the same parking lot look so much alike.

45

TWO J'S TAVERN

OWNER: Diane Coulter

HOURS: 1:00 p.m. to Closing Daily

HAPPY HOUR: No

GAMBLING: Video Poker/Keno; Shake-A-Day

LIVE MUSIC: Occasionally

LOCATION: 13453 Hwy 200, **Fort Shaw**

PHONE: No Phone

BEER: Domestics

AMUSEMENT: Pool; Darts; Pinball; Bumper Pool; Video Games

FOOD: Frozen Pizza; Snacks

The Two J's Tavern is housed in a log structure just east of Fort Shaw on the north side of Highway 200. The barroom has a rustic appearance and a comfortable atmosphere. The log walls, wooden ceiling, and wood burning stove add to the building's charm. The spacious game room in the east side of the building has a brick fireplace against the east wall. An L-shaped bar with a wooden awning above it faces the north wall of the barroom, and a lone wooden buddy bar stands in the middle of the floor. The painting hanging from the barroom wall was done by Bill Rogne, a local artist who passed away a few years ago.

Jim and Julia (two J's) Tenney established the business in 1946. The original barroom was only about 1/2 the size it is today, and there was no game room on the east end of the building. During the summer of 1976, the south wall was caved in when a truckload of drunks drove their vehicle into it. Apparently, the men were on their way home from the Augusta Rodeo and decided to stop for a drink. The men were so intoxicated when they arrived the bartender wouldn't serve them, so they rammed the front of the building with their pickup truck. After caving in the wall, the men drove to Great Falls where they were apprehended by the authorities and taken to jail. Things didn't work out so well for the guys in the pickup truck, but the barroom got bigger when the damaged wall was repaired. The bar owner decided he might as well add some floor space as long as he had to fix the wall anyhow, so he built an addition on the south end of the building. The game room was added a couple of years later, and now there's plenty of room inside the building.

The Two J's Tavern is a friendly place where people of all ages gather to socialize with friends and neighbors. Business is pretty steady throughout the year, and the bar always gets busy during the annual broomstick rodeo that's held during the first weekend of May. Contestants ride broomsticks instead of horses in events such as roping, barrel racing, and egg races. A dinner, auction, and live music are all part of the event, and all the proceeds are donated to the local seniors rodeo.

CABIN SALOON

OWNER: Dave Obresley

LOCATION: Highway 89, 4 Miles north of **Monarch**

HOURS: 10:00 a.m. to Closing Thur-Tue Closed Wednesdays

PHONE: 406-738-4331

HAPPY HOUR: None

BEER: Drafts; Domestics

GAMBLING: Video Poker/Keno

AMUSEMENT: Darts

LIVE MUSIC: Occasionally

FOOD: Grill Items

The Cabin Saloon is approximately four miles north of Monarch on Highway 89. The cinder block building houses a moderate-sized barroom, a sunken casino area, and a small game room. A small handcrafted back bar stands against the south wall of the barroom. The back bar originally resided in the Tent Saloon in Alder Gulch, but nobody seems to know how or when it made its way to the Cabin Saloon.

The Cabin Saloon was built in 1982. Dave Obresley bought the bar in 1985, and he continues to operate it today. Dave has affectionately become known as Uncle Grumpy among the regulars customers. Dave is a man of few words and even fewer facial expressions, but he's actually a pretty nice guy once you get to know him. Getting to know Dave can be a bit of a challenge, however, so don't be offended if he appears less than thrilled to serve you. It's just Dave's way of welcoming his guests.

There's normally a local crowd on hand at the bar, but hunters, fishermen, and snowmobilers also stop in. Dave doesn't necessarily cater to bikers, but the Cabin Saloon is a popular rest stop for people on their way to and from the annual biker's rally in Sturgis, South Dakota. Dave runs a simple business where common people come to drink. He doesn't care much for kids in the barroom, and he hates yuppies, preppies, and hoards of skiers. If you fancy blended drinks, imported beer, and service with a smile, go somewhere else. Dave prefers real people with real lives.

Dave may not always be in a festive mood, but his customers are usually friendly. Unruly guests get to meet Max the bouncer, a 120 pound chap with four legs and a collar. With five TVs, the Cabin Saloon has become a popular place for people to watch televised sporting events. If you get hungry while watching the game, the Uncle Grumpy's New York Steak Sandwich comes highly recommended. People from all over the United States have stopped in to get one. A couple of Dave's Bloody Marys or Long Island Iced Teas are great for washing down the sandwich, as long as you don't have to drive. You can also try your luck in Uncle Grumpy's Silver Mine Casino. Perhaps you'll win enough money to buy Max a beer.

CUB'S DEN BAR AND CASINO

OWNERS: Larry and Sherry Davis

HOURS: 11:00 a.m. to Closing Wed-Mon
Closed Tuesdays

HAPPY HOUR: No

GAMBLING: Video Poker/Keno;
Shake-A-Day

LIVE MUSIC: Occasionally

LOCATION: Highway 89, **Monarch**

PHONE: 406-236-5922

BEER: Drafts; Domestics;
Imports; Microbrews

AMUSEMENT: Pool; Horseshoes;
Video Game

FOOD: Full Menu Restaurant

The Cub's Den is on the west side of Highway 89 in Monarch. The entire business consists of the bar, self service gas, a convenience store, restaurant, and a motel. A curved bar faces the south wall of the barroom, and a huge stone fireplace rises from the floor against the north wall. Branched tree trunks support a wooden awning above the bar, providing a natural-looking environment for the two full mount bear cubs on the awning. If you're a nature lover, you can take your drink and head for the elevated wooden deck outside the sliding glass doors. A formal dining room is housed in the adjacent room to the south of the barroom.

The Cub's Den first opened in 1949, but the original building was destroyed by fire in 1966. Upon completion of a new building in 1967, the bar and restaurant reopened. Larry and Sherry Davis bought the Cub's Den in 1992. They added the convenience store that same year and built the motel in 1993. Larry spent nine years managing the College Finals Rodeo in Bozeman and five years managing the National Finals Rodeo in Las Vegas prior to buying the Cub's Den. The framed photographs that hang above the bar are all National Rodeo Champions that Larry has known over the years.

Although the bar and restaurant are closed Tuesdays, the convenience store and motel are open seven days a week. The fifteen motel rooms surround a beautiful indoor pool, hot tub, and sauna. The rooms are very modern, and the rates are very reasonable. The restaurant features a very complete dinner menu. Spaghetti with homemade sauce, two pound rib steaks, and cajun catfish are just a few of the items available.

Larry and Sherry promote a family-oriented atmosphere at the Cub's Den. Drunks and abusive language aren't tolerated, and Larry isn't shy about asking rude customers to leave. The Davis' host several annual events at the bar, including a Jazz Festival, pig roast, Halloween dance, and Christmas tree trimming party. Sherry says she just puts decorations out on the tables for the tree trimming party and lets the customers put them up. That way, nobody can complain about how they look.

LAZY DOE

OWNER: Darvin Johnson   **LOCATION:** Highway 89, **Monarch**

HOURS: 8:00 a.m. to Closing Tue-Sun Closed Mondays   **PHONE:** 406-236-9949

HAPPY HOUR: No   **BEER:** Domestics

GAMBLING: Video Poker/Keno   **AMUSEMENT:** Pool; Darts

LIVE MUSIC Occasionally   **FOOD:** Full Menu Restaurant

The Lazy Doe approximately two miles south of Monarch on Highway 89. The log structure houses a spacious barroom in the west side and a smaller dining room in the east side. The main barroom has an L-shaped bar facing the west wall. A couple of small tables are spread throughout the room if you prefer sitting away from the bar, and additional seating is available in the room off the north end of the main barroom. The interior walls are mostly covered with unstained wood, which provides a rustic appearance and a comfortable atmosphere.

The business was established as Geis' Tavern and Cabins in 1938. A bar and restaurant were housed in the main building, and tourist cabins were rented out on the property to the west. New owners took over the business in 1956 and changed the name to the Lazy Doe. The cabins were sold off individually, so lodging is no longer available. An addition was built on the north side of the barroom during the mid 1980s. Buck's Addition, as the room is now known, was named after a farmer from Geraldine. Apparently, Buck once stated he drank enough at the Lazy Doe to pay for the addition, so a wooden sign was placed above the entrance to make people aware of his contribution.

Darvin Johnson has owned the Lazy Doe since 1970. The business is in a prime recreational area, so Darvin's customers come from all over the world. Summer is the busiest season at the Lazy Doe, but plenty of skiers and snowmobilers stop by in the winter. No matter what time of year it is, you will find a very friendly crowd on hand. Dining room hours are 5:00 p.m. to 9:00 p.m. Tuesday through Saturday and 3:00 p.m. until 9:00 p.m. on Sundays. Items on the lunch menu are available any time, and Darvin says the Johnson Burgers are probably his best seller in the restaurant. As a show of appreciation for his customers, Darvin hosts a Christmas party each December and a birthday party every year on June 1. Free food and drinks are provided, and the turnout is very good. The Lazy Doe is a great bar and restaurant in a scenic location. Whether you're just passing through the area or staying for a while, it's worth your time to stop in.

BOB'S BAR

OWNERS: Tony and Sherry Juntunen

LOCATION: Highway 89, **Neihart**

HOURS: 11:00 a.m. to Closing Daily

PHONE: 406-236-5955

HAPPY HOUR: No

BEER: Drafts; Domestics

GAMBLING: Video Poker/Keno; Shake-A-Day

AMUSEMENT: Pool; Darts

LIVE MUSIC: Occasionally

FOOD: Full Menu Restaurant

Bob's Bar is on the west side of Highway 89 in Neihart. The barroom and a restaurant reside in the north side of the building, and a ten unit motel is attached to the south side. The spacious barroom has a straight wooden bar facing the south wall, and a few tables are spread throughout the room. A large dining room is adjacent to, but separate from, the barroom. The bar and restaurant were recently rebuilt, so everything is very modern and well-maintained.

Bob's Bar was established by Bob O'Connor in 1946. The business operated out of a small wooden building that stood on the property until 1995. Tony and Sherry Juntunen bought Bob's Bar in 1982. They built a motel next door to the bar in 1988, and on Labor Day, 1995, they destroyed the original bar building and began construction on a new facility. While construction was in progress, the bar operated out of the small area at the top of the stairs leading from the dining room. This area is now used as a motel lounge, private party area, and passageway between the motel and the bar and restaurant. The new bar and dining room officially opened for business in January, 1996.

There's not much history to the new bar, but Tony said he had to repair several bullet holes in the old barroom ceiling when he and Sherry first bought the place. The holes had appeared several years earlier when three men became enraged over an uncooperative juke box. I don't know whether shooting the ceiling solved their problem, but at least they didn't shoot the bartender. You won't find any bullet holes in the ceiling of the new barroom. Today's customers are friendly, low keyed types who don't normally carry loaded pistols.

Because Bob's Bar is located in a premier outdoor recreation area, a lot of the customers are travelers and recreationists. The Little Belt Mountains surrounding Neihart are a popular get-away for hunters, fishermen, snowmobilers, skiers, and hikers. After a hard day in the hills, there's nothing like relaxing in a warm bar with a cold beer. Bob's Bar is the perfect place to do this.

MINER'S BAR

OWNERS: Cathy and Steve Loucks

LOCATION: Corner of Church & Main, **Sand Coulee**

HOURS: Noon to 2:00 a.m. Wed-Sun
Closed Mondays

PHONE: 406-736-5644

HAPPY HOUR: 5:00 to 7:00 Mon - Fri

BEER: Drafts; Domestics

GAMBLING: Video Poker/Keno; Shake-A-Day

AMUSEMENT: Pool; Darts; Horseshoes

LIVE MUSIC: No

FOOD: Grill Items

The Miner's Bar is at the corner of Church and Main Streets in Sand Coulee. I have yet to see a single street sign in Sand Coulee, but the local directions for finding the bar is "it's beside the post office". The barroom resides in the west side of the building, and a vacant mercantile store occupies the east side. The front portion of the barroom is adjoined by a smaller game room, which has a parachute suspended from the ceiling above the pool table. When I last visited the Miner's Bar, plans were in place to expand the barroom into the vacated mercantile store.

During the early 1900s, a livery stable and blacksmith shop operated out of the part of the building that now houses the barroom. The livery stable and blacksmith shop closed down in the early 1930s, so a saloon was opened. The antique wooden bar, back bar, and liquor cabinet in the barroom today made their way to Fort Benton via steamboat up the Missouri River. A team and wagon then hauled the pieces overland to Sand Coulee. The oil paintings on the barroom walls were painted during the 1930s by a local man who traded the artwork for drinks. I'm told the man spent most of his adult life painting, drinking, and sleeping under a tree. Cathy and Steve Loucks have been operating the Miner's Bar since September, 1993. They managed the business for a couple of years before purchasing the bar in 1995.

The Miner's Bar is a great party place where people unwind and let loose. Cathy and Steve serve excellent 1/2 pound burgers, so you don't have to interrupt your drinking if you work up an appetite. There's typically a friendly crowd on hand, but fights break out from time to time. The scuffles are usually between people from Great Falls and people from "The Coulee", so you don't have to worry about becoming involved as long as you mind your own business. Steve says that for some reason, people seem to enjoy stripping off their clothes in the barroom. It's happened on more than one occasion, but Steve can't explain why this occurs. My guess is it has something to do with alcohol intake.

AMERICAN BAR

OWNER: Brian Guisti	**LOCATION:**	6 Front Street, **Stockett**
HOURS: 8:00 a.m. to Closing Daily	**PHONE:**	406-736-5601
HAPPY HOUR: No	**BEER:**	Drafts; Domestics
GAMBLING: Video Poker	**AMUSEMENT:**	Pool; Pinball; Shuffleboard
LIVE MUSIC: No	**FOOD:**	Sandwiches; Grill Items

The American Bar is at 6 Front Street in Stockett. I've been in barrooms all over Montana, but this is one place that has a character all its own. The brown and lime green paint on the interior walls might seem a bit unsightly, but the colors nicely compliment the stuffed two headed calf that stands on top of the antique phone booth in the back of the room. The antique wooden bar and back bar are both quite valuable, but they could stand to be refinished. Another thing that makes the American Bar unique is that it may be the only tavern in Montana that has a permanently reserved barstool for a customer. *Smitty's Corner* is the name on the wooden sign that hangs above the west end of the bar. The end stool is always reserved for Smitty, a long-time customer who has all but taken up residency at his designated seat.

The American Bar was established in 1916. The prohibition era started in 1920, but I'm told it didn't have much effect on the sale of booze from this establishment. The Guisti family bought into the bar in 1938, and the business has been in the same family ever since. Brian Guisti is the present owner, but Pat Merva is the senior employee behind the bar. Pat has over fifty years of bartending experience, and he still tends bar nearly every day. Pat's bartending career has been so successful that he has been inducted into the National Bartender's Hall Of Fame. On most days, you can find Pat serving Smitty a cold draft at the American Bar. No matter how many taverns you visit, I doubt you will ever find a closer bartender-customer relationship than Pat and Smitty have formed.

The American Bar is a family-oriented place where people of all ages are welcome. Most of the customers are local residents, and the people are friendly and open to conversation. If you arrive with an appetite, fresh sandwiches piled high with shaved meat are the house specialty. The barroom can get quite crowded, but there's usually a calm crowd on hand. The last real excitement occurred on Thanksgiving weekend in 1995 when a lady drove her vehicle part way through the building. The hole in the wall has been repaired, but the shuffleboard table may never be the same.

Pat Merva at the American Bar in Stockett.

**Pat's fifty plus years of bartending have earned
him a spot in the National Bartenders Hall of Fame.**

WOOF'S (USC)

OWNER: Kenny Wolf

HOURS: Noon to 2:00 a.m. Wed-Mon
Closed Tuesdays

HAPPY HOUR: 6:00 to 7:00 Mon - Fri

GAMBLING: Video Poker/Keno

LIVE MUSIC: Occasionally

LOCATION: 532 East Hunter Rd.,
Sand Coulee

PHONE: 406-736-5104

BEER: Drafts; Domestics

AMUSEMENT: Pool; Darts; Horseshoes;
Video Games

FOOD: Frozen Pizza

Woof's Bar is on East Hunter Road in Sand Coulee. I don't know when or why Woof's unofficially became the University of Sand Coulee (USC), but a large *University of Sand Coulee (USC); Dean Woof Presiding* sign is posted on the north side of the building. A smaller sign above the front entrance reads *USC Registrars Office*, and the sign above the back exit reads *USC Dropouts*. Besides the USC propaganda, there are some nice oil paintings on the barroom walls. The paintings were done by a local man who traded artwork for drinks during the 1930s. I'm told the artist basically lived under a nearby tree the majority of his adult life.

The business was established as the Centerville Beer Hall in 1934. The Centerville Beer Hall was destroyed by fire in 1936, so the business moved to Sand Coulee and became the Sand Coulee Beer Hall. Allegedly, the people of Sand Coulee sacrificed their community center so the beer hall could open. I'm told a group of local miners jacked up the old community center building, placed logs under it, and then attached ropes to the structure and pulled it across town. The community center was never replaced, but the bar has been going strong ever since. Kenny Wolf bought the business in 1978, and he continues to operate it today.

The customers at Woof's are a friendly, fun loving bunch who drink lots of beer and lots of schnapps. The customers are allowed to let loose and have fun, as long as it's kept at a somewhat reasonable level. The tire marks on the barroom floor provide some indication that people enjoy themselves at Woof's. It seems like every time the marks are about to wear off, someone rides their Harley in to lay a new set of tracks. The bar hosts an annual New Year party, but the party is always held at the end of January. They do this because January is usually such a lousy month in Sand Coulee that people like to celebrate its passing. Woof's also has free pool every day of the week, and the bar can be rented out for private parties for a reasonable price and a reasonable cause. Whatever the reason, Woof's is a place where you're sure to have a great time.

BOB AND ETHEL'S RAMBLE INN

OWNERS: Bob and Ethel McBurney

HOURS: 10:00 a.m. to 2:00 a.m. Daily

HAPPY HOUR: Promotional Cards

GAMBLING: Video Poker/Keno; Shake-A-Day

LIVE MUSIC: Karaoke Occasionally

LOCATION: 13899 Hwy 200, **Sun River**

PHONE: 406-264-9435

BEER: Drafts; Domestics

AMUSEMENT: Pool

FOOD: Bar Snacks

Bob and Ethel's Ramble Inn is approximately one mile east of Sun River on Highway 200. A straight bar faces the west wall of the barroom, and a couple of tables are spread across the floor. Several amusing bumper stickers and signs, some dating back as far as 1966, hang from the wall behind the bar. The east wall of the barroom is home to the Ramble Inn's brassiere collection. Over the past several years, more than thirty women have sacrificed the bra off their back (so to speak) to add to the growing collection of brassieres at the Ramble Inn. Some of the bras are signed by their former owners, and some hang from the wall with no identifying marks other than the size.

The bar's history dates back to the early 1900s when a building that served as a stage stop, saloon, dance hall, restaurant, and sleeping rooms stood on the property. The original building was destroyed by fire in 1942, but another structure was soon erected, and the Ramble Inn was back in business. In 1979, fire once again destroyed the Ramble Inn. A double-wide trailer was moved onto the property 1981, and the bar has been operating out of the trailer ever since.

Bob and Ethel McBurney bought the Ramble Inn in 1990. They run a family-oriented business where people can drink in peace. The customers are friendly and fun loving. After all, having a good time is a prerequisite for visiting the Ramble Inn. A lot of first time visitors stop in to see the brassiere collection that they've heard about from friends. There's no official happy hour, but Bob and Ethyl hand out promotional cards at the beginning of each month that entitle people to one free drink per day with the purchase of the same drink. That way, everyone gets a reduced price on drinks, not just those who happen to be there at a certain time. Bob and Ethel also host several special events throughout the year, including a chili cookoff, a St. Patrick's Day party, an Old Time Fiddlers Jamboree, a pig roast, and a fund raiser for a local person or family in need. Bob and Ethel's Ramble Inn is a fun place with a great bunch of people. It's well worth the stop if you're in the area.

GINGER'S SALOON

OWNER: Ginger Hanser

HOURS: 11:00 a.m. to 2:00 a.m. Daily

HAPPY HOUR: 4:30 to 6:00 Mon - Fri

GAMBLING: Video Poker/Keno; Live Poker; Shake-A-Day

LIVE MUSIC: Approximately Monthly

LOCATION: 13837 Hwy 200, **Sun River**

PHONE: 406-264-5405

BEER: Drafts; Domestics

AMUSEMENT: Pool

FOOD: Full Menu Cafe

Ginger's Saloon is on Highway 200 in Sun River. The building houses a barroom, cafe, and a dance hall. Various antiques are on display throughout the building, and some very interesting photographs, murals, and paintings hang from the walls in the dance hall. The decorative tin ceiling and floating hardwood floor that were installed in the dance hall in the 1920s are still intact. The floating dance floor is one of the few of its kind left in the United States. Springs were installed under the wooden slats so the floor would "float" as people moved across it.

A building called Murray Hall originally stood on the property, but it was destroyed by fire in 1920. After the smoke cleared, a dance hall called the Sun River Lodge was built from stone and mortar. A wood-framed addition was added onto the west side of the dance hall a few years later. The addition initially housed a supper hall and living quarters, but the supper hall became a beer parlor when prohibition ended. The existing barroom on the east side of the building was once the B. A. Robertson Store. The building was moved across the road and renovated into a saloon a few years after the beer parlor opened. The dance hall customers then had their choice of two places to buy alcohol. Early pictures show a space between the dance hall and saloon, but they were eventually connected together. Louie Pinocci owned the business from 1971 until 1989. Louie is credited with saving the old building because he basically restored the entire facility during his eighteen years at the bar. The bar and back bar that now stand in the barroom and the small bar and beautiful antique back bar in the dance hall were installed during Louie's tenure.

Ginger Hanser bought what was the Covered Wagon Bar in May, 1996 and changed the name to Ginger's Saloon. Most of Ginger's customers are from the Sun River Valley, so she operates the business in a community-minded manner. Pinochle is a popular afternoon pastime at the bar, and Ginger lets people use the dance hall for private parties at no charge. Besides owning the bar, Ginger operates an antique shop out of the building. She has some very unique items, so you really should stop in and see them.

TRACY BAR

OWNERS: Dan Griffin

HOURS: 11:30 a.m. to Closing Mon-Fri
8:00 a.m. to Closing Sat-Sun

HAPPY HOUR: 5:00 to 6:00 Mon - Wed

GAMBLING: Video Poker/Keno

LIVE MUSIC: Occasionally

LOCATION: Route 227, **Tracy**

PHONE: 406-736-9189

BEER: Drafts; Domestics

AMUSEMENT: Pool; Darts; Horseshoes;
Video Games

FOOD: Full Menu Grill

The Tracy Bar is on Route 227 in Tracy. The barroom has a straight bar facing the south wall, and plenty of tables are available if all the barstools are occupied. The unique thing about the Tracy Bar is the business is operated as a memorial to military veterans. Photographs of World War II Veterans from Tracy are on display on the east wall, and several interesting military hats that were donated by local residents line the shelf behind the bar. An authentic West Point Ceremonial Cap and a CPO Hat from World War II are among the many hats on display. The antique piano in the corner of the room still gets played from time to time by some of the customers. I'm told the piano is so old that it was transported from Chicago to Tracy by team and wagon.

The Tracy bar was built in 1947. The construction phase of the project entailed moving two railroad boxcars onto the property and joining the open ends together. The liquor license was obtained from Morlacci's Bar, which formerly resided in a brick building a couple of blocks to the east. The old Morlacci's Bar building is still standing, but it now houses an antique shop. A renovation project was completed at the Tracy Bar in 1950. A sloped roof and siding were added to the building, and outhouses were installed on the grounds. Believe it or not, indoor plumbing wasn't available at the Tracy Bar until 1960. The name of the business was changed to the E-Zee Bar in 1974, but it was changed back to the Tracy Bar in 1987.

Dan Griffin bought the business in July, 1996. Dan started the military theme at the bar, and he also expanded the menu. Lunch and dinner are served daily, and breakfast is available from 8:00 a.m. until 1:00 p.m. on Saturday and Sunday. An assortment of menu items are available throughout the week, and the dinner special on Wednesdays is prime rib. Besides the prepared food, Dan also sells fresh eggs, milk, butter, and bread. If you happen to be vacationing in the area, the Tracy Bar has three full RV hookups outside the building. There's no better place to spend the night than the back yard of a bar.

GRIFFIN'S VILLAGE INN

OWNERS: Dan and Karen Griffin

LOCATION: Frontage Road, **Ulm**

HOURS: 4:00 p.m. to 10:00 p.m. Mon-Thur
4:00 p.m. to 11:00 p.m. Fri/Sat
3:00 p.m. to 10:00 p.m. Sunday

PHONE: 406-866-3241

HAPPY HOUR: No

BEER: Drafts; Domestics; Microbrews

GAMBLING: Video Poker/Keno

AMUSEMENT: None

LIVE MUSIC: No

FOOD: Full Menu Supper Club

Griffin's Village Inn is on the Frontage Road just north of the Ulm Interchange (exit 270) off Interstate 15. The building houses two separate dining areas, a banquet room, and a barroom. The open floor plan is laid out so that the barroom in the middle of the building provides separation between the two dining areas. A stained glass awning that was hand-crafted in Ireland hangs from the brick fireplace on the north wall, and a stone fireplace rises from the floor against the west wall in the banquet room. A horseshoe-shaped bar with a brass foot rail faces the north wall of the barroom, and several painted plates hang from the wall behind the bar.

The Village Inn started out as a small tavern in 1953. The building has been expanded several times since then, and a supper club eventually became part of the business. Dan and Karen Griffin bought the Village Inn in July, 1994. They spent a good portion of their first year upgrading the building. The building renovations were eventually completed, and the Village Inn is now a very modern facility.

When you visit Griffin's Village Inn for the first time, don't expect to find a smoky barroom environment. The business is more of a supper club than a bar, and the fine dining draws people who want a good meal, not people who want to spit tobacco juice on the floor. The dinner menu features steaks and seafood. Lobster, king crab legs, and prime rib are the house specialties. The lobster comes in several different sizes, and every item on the menu is available daily. The Village Inn also has a good selection of wines and microbrewed beers to help wash down your meal.

The majority of the customers at Griffin's Village Inn are from the Great Falls area. People traveling along Interstate 15 also stop in, and they've even had celebrities in the barroom. I'm told Clint Eastwood, Jeff Bridges, and George Kennedy frequented the Village Inn during filming of the movie *Thunderbolt and Lightfoot*. Regardless of who's there, you can always count on a good meal and a good time at Griffin's Village Inn. It's a wonderful place to enjoy a great meal.

ULM BAR

OWNERS: Earl Cereck
LOCATION: Ulm/Cascade Road, **Ulm**

HOURS: 10:00 a.m. to Closing Daily
PHONE: None

HAPPY HOUR: No
BEER: Drafts; Domestics; Microbrews

GAMBLING: Video Poker/Keno
AMUSEMENT: Pool; Darts; Pinball; Horseshoes

LIVE MUSIC: Occasionally
FOOD: Homemade Pizza

The Ulm Bar is on the old Ulm-Cascade Highway in Ulm. To get there from Interstate 15, take the Ulm Interchange (exit 270) and turn east at the bottom of the off ramp. You will see the bar on your left as you drive through town. A spacious barroom occupies the entire ground-level floor of the building. Plenty of seating is available at the straight wooden bar along the east wall, and several tables are available if you prefer some privacy. The large rattlesnake skin hanging behind the bar is from a snake killed in Texas, but the mounted big horn ram's head, moose antlers, and grizzly bear paw casts are from animals taken in Montana.

The Ulm Bar was built around the turn of the 20th century. Frank Ball now owns the building and lives in the second floor, but Earl Cereck owns the liquor license. Frank's grandfather established the business as a saloon and stage stop. The original building was quite small compared to the size it is today. Numerous additions have been made over the years, and the bar has shared space with several other businesses at one time or another. Besides the stage stop, a post office, general store, and hotel have all operated out of the building. The other businesses have all come and gone, but the bar is still going strong after nearly 100 years of operation. Charlie Russell would be glad to know this if he were still alive, because he liked to stop at the Ulm Bar when he traveled between Cascade and Great Falls.

Earl Recently installed a pizza parlor in the bar, but he still operates the place as a neighborhood tavern. Local residents provide a steady business throughout the year, and hunters, fishermen, and tourists stop by during the summer and fall. Earl says he occasionally receives postcards from people in Ulm, Germany who have visited the bar in past years. For some reason, the Ulm Bar seems to be a place where people want to be remembered. Hundreds of names, messages, and drawings cover the barroom ceiling. There's really not much room left to write on the ceiling, but you can always be remembered by buying a round for the house.

DOMINICK'S

OWNERS: Vic and Kathy Fatz

HOURS: 10:00 a.m. to 2:00 a.m. Daily

HAPPY HOUR: No

GAMBLING: Video Poker/Keno

LIVE MUSIC: Occasionally

LOCATION: Highway 87, **Carter**

PHONE: 406-734-9214

BEER: Drafts; Domestics; Imports; Microbrews

AMUSEMENT: Darts

FOOD: Full Menu Restaurant

Dominick's Bar is on the west side of Highway 87 at the Carter turn-off. A moderate-sized barroom is in the south side of the building, and the Gobbler Inn Restaurant occupies the north side. The business started out as the Carter Beer Parlor in 1935. The bar was originally housed in a building on Main Street in Carter, but it moved to its present location in 1941. Poker games were very popular at the bar during its early years of operation. It's rumored that a substantial amount of real estate changed hands during the many high-stake games.

Vic and Kathy Fatz bought Dominick's in 1981. They promote a friendly atmosphere, and their customers are courteous and well-mannered. Vic and Kathy enjoy a steady local trade, and travelers passing through the area stop in frequently. A lot of people from the Hi-Line even make the drive to Carter to enjoy the good food and friendly environment. The Gobbler Inn Restaurant is open from 11:30 a.m. until 9:00 p.m. daily, and they serve excellent lunches and dinners. Homemade potato chips are the house specialty, and they're available with any meal.

Vic and Kathy treat their guests well, but the man who previously owned the bar was so rude that one of his customers assassinated him. Allegedly, the former owner was the type of person who frequently lost control of his temper and maybe said some things or threatened to shoot someone he shouldn't have. Early one evening, he and a customer got into a verbal confrontation, and the angry customer stormed out the door. Apparently, the two men had a history of problems with each other, so things didn't seem all that unusual to the other bar patrons at the time. Just before closing time, a loud gunshot echoed through the barroom, and the bar owner dropped over dead beside the juke box. It turns out the angry customer had returned to the bar and shot his nemesis from outside the building through a window. I'm told very few people who knew the men were surprised with the news, and even fewer were remorseful. The man who did the shooting was convicted of the crime, but he got off relatively easy, as he was sentenced to only a few years in prison.

MIKES BAR AND CAFE

OWNER: Georgianna Rowland

HOURS: Noon to 2:00 a.m. Tue-Sun
Closed Mondays

HAPPY HOUR: 5:30 to 7:00 Tue - Thur

GAMBLING: Video Poker/Keno

LIVE MUSIC: No

LOCATION: Main Street, **Geraldine**

PHONE: 406-737-4541

BEER: Drafts; Domestics

AMUSEMENT: Pool

FOOD: Full Menu Cafe

Mike's Bar and Cafe is on Main Street in Geraldine. Although the bar and cafe are housed in the same building, they are physically separated from each other. As you face the building from Main Street, the barroom is through the door on the right and the cafe is through the door on the left. The barroom has a fairly long bar facing the west wall, and a couple of tables are available if you prefer sitting away from the bar. The antique liquor cabinet that stands behind the bar originally resided in Gerald's Bar in Great Falls. Some years ago, the liquor cabinet was shipped to Mike's Bar and Cafe from Square Butte without suffering any damage to the original glass or beautiful wood finish.

The business has undergone several changes in ownership and location since it was established the 1920s. The building that now houses the barroom was originally used as a blacksmith shop in the nearby community of Square Butte. Somewhere along the line, the structure was moved to Geraldine and renovated into a saloon. The cafe didn't become part of the building until the mid 1960s when an addition was made to the bar.

Georgianna Rowland has owned Mike's Bar and Cafe since 1983. Georgianna primarily caters to the local residents of Geraldine and the surrounding communities, but everyone is welcome at the bar. Although the barroom is closed on Mondays, the cafe is open from 10:30 a.m. until 8:30 p.m. daily. The Mike's Best Sandwich comes highly recommended, and prime rib is the featured dinner item every Tuesday. Daily lunch specials are also available in the cafe.

Like most small town taverns, you never know when a crowd will gather at Mike's. It's as likely to be crowded at 2:00 on a weekday afternoon as it is during a weekend evening. One thing you can normally count on is the daily pinochle game that gets going in the barroom during the weekday afternoons. Aside from that, it's pretty much up to the beer gods when people will show up. The customers here are friendly, so you don't have to worry about getting into too much trouble. Just sit back, relax, and enjoy your visit to Mike's Bar and Cafe.

RUSTY'S BAR AND GRILL

OWNER: Marty Clark		**LOCATION:**	Main Street, **Geraldine**
HOURS: 11:00 a.m. to Closing Daily		**PHONE:**	406-737-4549
HAPPY HOUR: No		**BEER:**	Drafts; Domestics
GAMBLING: Video Poker		**AMUSEMENT:**	Pool
LIVE MUSIC: Occasionally		**FOOD:**	Full Menu Grill

Rusty's Bar and Grill is housed in the ground-level floor of a two story cinder block building on Main Street in Geraldine. The main barroom in the front portion of the building is adjoined by a smaller game room and reading area in the rear. The decorative tin ceiling that was installed when the structure was built in 1914 is still in place today. A curved bar is to your right as you enter the barroom from Main Street, and a few tables are available if you prefer sitting away from the bar.

The building that now houses Rusty's Bar and Grill was originally a department store. An automobile service station also operated out of the building before Rusty's Bar moved in. The bar was established as the Double R Bar in 1934 by Roscoe Peet and Rusty Slowey. Rusty took over complete control of the business in 1935 and changed the name to Slowey's Place. The name of the business changed to Rusty's Bar in 1938, and the bar moved to its present location in 1945.

Marty Clark bought the business in August, 1995. Although Marty is a relatively new bar owner, she had tended bar at Rusty's for the previous eight years. When Marty bought the business, over 500 clocks covered the barroom walls and ceiling. Marty said it made the place look like a junk store, so she ousted the clocks in favor of bare walls. Her customers don't don't seem to miss the time pieces a bit. The friendly, fun loving people at Rusty's entertain themselves by pulling practical jokes on one another and planning future parties.

If you're a big eater, Rusty's serves a huge SOB Burger (yes, SOB stands for what you think it stands for). The burgers range in size from 1/4 pound all the way up to a full pound, and if that's not enough, you can order the SOB as a side dish with a daily lunch special. Marty also serves a great Bloody Mary that will either help you conquer a hangover or start you on your way to achieving one. While you're at the bar, be sure to get a Rusty's Bar and Grill Gone to Wee Wee Card. These unique business cards have a pull-out tab that you can insert in the opening of your drink container to let people know not to mess with your drink or your barstool while you're in the rest room.

HIGHWOOD BAR

OWNERS: Susie & JohnPatrick Sprinkle

LOCATION: Broadway St., **Highwood**

HOURS: Noon to Closing Daily

PHONE: 406-733-2951

HAPPY HOUR: No

BEER: Domestics; Microbrews

GAMBLING: Video Poker/Keno; Shake-A-Day

AMUSEMENT: Pool

LIVE MUSIC: Occasionally

FOOD: Burgers; Sandwiches

The Highwood Bar is on Broadway Street in Highwood. A beautiful antique oak bar and back bar stand along the east wall of the barroom, and several tables are spread across the floor. The bar and back bar are nearly 100 years old, but they have been maintained in immaculate condition. The old Greyhound Bus that's normally parked on the east side of the building is sometimes used as sleeping quarters by customers who have had too much to drink. The bus also comes in handy for recruiting customers on slow days, and it makes a great party bus.

The business was established in 1943 when Elmo Davison opened a bar in the Highwood Hotel, which stood on the lot just east of the present-day bar. Rumor has it Elmo and his wife were roused from their sleep one morning by the sound of a gunshot and the sight of their bed exploding. It turns out a man who was downstairs swamping out the barroom accidently discharged Elmo's 270 caliber rifle into the ceiling, which also happened to be the floor of Elmo's bedroom. The bullet went through the box springs and mattress, right between Elmo and his wife. Bed stuffing and springs flew everywhere, but nobody was struck. About all Elmo had to say to the man was "if that would have happened twenty years ago, you would have killed us both". The hotel was torn down in 1990, so the old Highwood Youth Center was moved to the property and renovated into a tavern.

Susie Sprinkle bought the Highwood Bar in January, 1993, and her brother, John, soon came to help run the business. It's interesting to note one of the pony tails hanging from the bull horns behind the bar belonged to John when he first came to town. A local man offered John forty dollars to cut it off, so John now proudly displays his forty dollar pony tail beside a donkey's tail that also hangs from the horns. As a show of appreciation to their customers, Susie and John host several parties at the bar during the year, including a Tom and Jerry Party around Christmas. They have also started selling George Dickel #12 Tennessee Sipping Whiskey. Susie tells me the drink has become so popular that the Highwood Bar is now the biggest seller of Dickel #12 in Montana.

ACE HIGH CASINO

OWNER: Bud Heidlebaugh		**LOCATION:**	Highway 87, **Loma**
HOURS: Noon to 2:00 a.m. Daily		**PHONE:**	406-739-4220
HAPPY HOUR: 6:00 to 7:00 Daily		**BEER:**	Drafts; Domestics
GAMBLING: Video Poker/Keno		**AMUSEMENT:**	Pool; Darts; Horseshoes; Video Games
LIVE MUSIC: Occasionally		**FOOD:**	Steaks; Sandwiches

The Ace High Casino is housed in a double-wide modular building on the east side of Highway 87 in Loma. A straight bar stands near the south end of the barroom, and a couple of tables are available if all the barstools are occupied. It's surprisingly roomy for a modular building, and the facility is kept clean and well-maintained.

Bud Heidlebaugh opened the Ace High Casino in 1988. Bud had retired from the aerial photography business a couple of years earlier, so he decided to renovate his former office building into a tavern. After the initial renovations were completed, Bud began the tedious process of entertaining inspectors from various state agencies to get permission to open the bar. It seemed none of the inspectors quite knew what they wanted, but they all wanted something different done to the building. After several frustrating months, Bud was finally granted permission to open the bar. The way Bud tells it, he made so many upgrades that a helicopter could land on the building and not even dent the roof. The bar initially operated under a beer and wine license, but Bud was able to obtain a full liquor license in 1991.

The customers at the Ace High Casino are mostly either residents of Loma and the surrounding communities or travelers who stop in while passing through the area. Waylon Jennings even stopped by late one evening a few years ago while he was on his way to a performance at the Sleeping Buffalo Resort near Saco. You will usually find a quiet, friendly crowd in the bar. On those rare occasions when differences between customers can't be settled verbally, they get settled outside in the parking lot instead of inside the barroom. If you're not feeling particularly amicable when you arrive at the bar, try one of Bud's Ace High Specials. The tasty drink contains a variety of liquors and mixers, and it's all but guaranteed to improve your disposition. If it's food you're after, try the homemade soup or one of the hot dishes cooked in an air oven. The Ace High Casino serves a great six ounce sirloin steak for only $5.95, so you don't need a lot of money to enjoy a good meal.

PEPPER POT TAVERN

OWNERS: Tom and Barb Evans   **LOCATION:** Highway 87, **Loma**

HOURS: 11:00 a.m. to 2:00 a.m. Daily   **PHONE:** 406-739-4325

HAPPY HOUR: 6:00 to 7:00 Mon - Fri   **BEER:** Drafts; Domestics

GAMBLING: Video Poker/Keno   **AMUSEMENT:** Pool; Darts

LIVE MUSIC: Occasionally   **FOOD:** Full Menu Cafe

The Pepper Pot Tavern is on the east side of Highway 87 in Loma. Because of the tavern's close proximity to the road, you shouldn't have any trouble spotting it while driving through town. An arched bar with a glass brick front faces the south wall in the front part of the barroom. The back portion of the room is fairly open, with a lone pool table in the middle of the floor.

I'm told the Pepper Pot Tavern was issued the first liquor license in Chouteau County after prohibition ended. It was all just a technicality, however, because bootlegged whiskey had been sold from the building during the prohibition years. The bar was originally housed in a two story structure that stood a block east of the present-day tavern. The barroom occupied the ground-level floor, and the second story was used as a dance hall. In 1947, the business was moved to be more visible to passing motorists. Since the move, the Pepper Pot has had only four owners, the most recent being Tom and Barb Evans who bought the business in 1979. The bar was for sale the last time I visited Loma, so Tom and Barb may not be there when you arrive.

The Pepper Pot is a friendly place where entire families gather to eat, drink, and socialize. The regular customers are residents of Loma and the surrounding communities, but a substantial portion of the business comes from travelers along Highway 87. If you arrive with an appetite, the burgers are quite large and quite good. Homemade soups are also available, and prime rib is featured every Friday and Saturday evening.

At one time, card games were a very popular pastime in the back room. During the early 1950's, two of the card players became involved in a dispute, which eventually led to a fight, which eventually resulted in a dead customer. As the story goes, one of the men was struck, and while falling to the floor, he hit his head on something hard. What it was he hit his head on perplexes modern historians to this day, but whatever it was, it was hard enough to kill the guy. I don't know if the incident played a role in what goes on at the bar today, but you no longer see live poker games at the Pepper Pot Tavern.

SQUARE BUTTE COUNTRY CLUB

OWNER: Charlie Smith

LOCATION: Main St., **Square Butte**

HOURS: 10:00 a.m. to 2:00 a.m. Daily

PHONE: 406-737-4327

HAPPY HOUR: No

BEER: Drafts; Domestics

GAMBLING: Video Poker/Keno

AMUSEMENT: Pool; Horseshoes; Golf Driving Range

LIVE MUSIC: Occasionally

FOOD: Full Menu Cafe

The Square Butte Country Club is on Main Street in Square Butte. A sign on the exterior of the building advertises ice for sale—Cold ice is $1.00 a bag and warm ice is 25 cents a bucket. The moderate-sized barroom has an L-shaped bar, several tables, and an antique back bar that was installed when the saloon first opened in 1914.

Charlie Smith has owned the business since the summer of 1993, and he's been able to maintain the fun and lively atmosphere the Square Butte Country Club has become known for. This is a place where people invent their own forms of entertainment, and entertaining it is. Buffalo Races is the name of one of the local games played at the bar. To compete, the player utilizes small plastic buffaloes, a game board, and a video keno machine. The bar also sponsors an annual gopher hunt in April, and people from all over Central Montana compete for prizes in the event. Contestants spend the first part of the day shooting gophers in nearby fields and the second part of the day comparing their kills with the carcasses brought in by the other contestants. Prizes are awarded for the biggest gopher, flattest gopher, gopher with the most antlers, and various other categories. Saint Patrick's Day is another occasion that always brings a crowd to Square Butte. The parade down Main Street is always followed by festivities at the Country Club. During the 1995 Saint Pat's celebration, someone who may have been celebrating a bit too much rode a green horse through the crowded barroom.

The Square Butte Country Club is a cafe, as well as a bar. The menu features ribeye steaks, and the Rocky Mountain Oysters make great appetizers. When they're not hosting one of their annual events, the bar is often the site of local gatherings such as birthday parties, anniversary parties, or funeral wakes. It's a great place to bring the kids because there's lots of room outside for them to roam around while the adults are inside eating or drinking. There's even a driving range out back, so don't forget to take your driver. If you don't golf, you may want to take your *designated driver* along to make sure you get home safely.

BUM STEER

OWNERS: Gary and Shirley Ruud

HOURS: 8:00 a.m. to 2:00 a.m. Daily

HAPPY HOUR: No

GAMBLING: Video Poker/Keno

LIVE MUSIC: Occasionally

LOCATION: Main Street, **Flaxville**

PHONE: 406-474-2358

BEER: Drafts; Domestics

AMUSEMENT: Darts

FOOD: Full Menu Grill

The Bum Steer is on Main Street in Flaxville. The barroom has a beautifully-restored mahogany bar, back bar, and liquor cabinet along the south wall. The three matching pieces were shipped to Montana from New Orleans in 1920. The bar, back bar, and liquor cabinet were painted in 1959, but the mahogany finish was restored to its original condition during the winters of 1985 and 1986.

The business was established in 1914. Ownership has changed hands fourteen times, but the Bum Steer is still going strong. During prohibition, the bar officially became a root beer stand. Moonshine was also kept on hand, and familiar customers were served from a jug that was kept behind the bar on top of a trap door. If the wrong people entered the building, the trap door could be activated from three different locations in the barroom, allowing the bottle to fall to the basement floor where it would break open and destroy the evidence. Extra bottles of moonshine were stored in hollow wooden ceiling posts in the basement.

Gary and Shirley Ruud have owned the Bum Steer since January, 1983. They run a family-oriented business and serve excellent food at reasonable prices. The meats at the Bum Steer are never frozen, so you always get a fresh cut of beef. Daily lunch specials are available Monday through Friday, and their pizzas are excellent.

The last real excitement to occur at the Bum Steer was in 1963 when two men pulled an armed robbery. The bar owner and two customers were tied up and left in a steel vault in the basement during the ordeal, but they rescued themselves after the robbers left the building. Fortunately, the thieves didn't turn the tumbler on the vault door, because nobody knew the combination. The villains headed to Canada, where they robbed a bank and shot a woman. The Royal Canadian Mounties eventually caught up with the assailants and took them into custody, but everyone figured the stolen loot was gone forever. Several weeks later, the owner of the Bum Steer was astonished to receive a package containing a note and the money that was taken during the robbery. One of the robber's parents was stricken with guilt, so they rounded up the stolen money and mailed it back to the bar.

RY TRAIL

OWNER: Steve Miller

LOCATION: Main Street, Flaxville

HOURS: 8:00 a.m. to 2:00 a.m. Daily

PHONE: 406-474-2201

HAPPY HOUR: No

BEER: Drafts; Domestics

GAMBLING: Video Poker/Keno

AMUSEMENT: Pool; Darts; Video Game

LIVE MUSIC: Occasionally

FOOD: Full Menu Grill

The RY Trail is on the east side of Main Street in Flaxville. The barroom resides in the ground level-floor of a two story wooden structure. An L-shaped bar and several tables occupy the floor space in the south side of the barroom, and a game room and casino area reside in the smaller room in the north side. There's plenty of seating space, and nearly twenty video gambling machines are available if you have some spare change.

The business has been operating out of the same building since it was established in the early 1920s. A fire erupted inside the building in the late 1950s, but damage to the structure wasn't severe enough put the bar out of business. Steve Miller has owned the RY Trail since May, 1988. Besides owning the RY Trail, Steve has a full time job at a local grain elevator, so he normally doesn't work at the bar.

The RY Trail is a family-oriented place where people of all ages gather to relax and socialize with friends. Someone might ride a horse through the barroom every so often just to liven things up, but more often than not, you will find a friendly crowd and a very relaxed environment. Aside from the people who live in and around Flaxville, the RY Trail gets a lot of business from Canadians who cross the border on weekends. The border is less than fifteen miles north of Flaxville, so it's convenient for the Canadians to cross the border to party in the States. The RY Trail also serves as a post-game gathering place for local scholastic sports teams and their spectators. Players and fans alike drop by after the games to play Monday Morning Quarterback and get something to eat.

The RY Trail serves breakfast, lunch, and dinner daily from 8:00 a.m. until 11:00 p.m. Lunch specials are available Monday through Friday, and steak specials are offered every Monday evening. If you have an adventurous appetite, the RY Trail keeps a fresh supply of gizzards and wings on hand. I'm told the gizzards and wings are a favorite among the Canadian customers, but I couldn't work up the nerve to try them when I was there.

WHISKEY BUTTES CLUB 45 BAR

OWNERS: Lawretta and Loren Fladager

LOCATION: Route 248, **Four Buttes**

HOURS: 11:00 a.m. to 2:00 a.m. Daily

PHONE: 406-783-5318

HAPPY HOUR: 5:00 to 7:00 Wednesdays

BEER: Domestics

GAMBLING: Video Poker/Keno; Shake-A-Day

AMUSEMENT: Darts

LIVE MUSIC: Occasionally

FOOD: Full Menu Restaurant

The Whiskey Buttes Club 45 Bar is on the north side of Route 248 in Four Buttes. The building houses a moderate-sized barroom and a spacious dining area. Several ceiling tiles in the barroom have been "adopted" by local residents, businesses, and bar patrons. Customers are allowed, if not encouraged, to advertise their business, leave a message, or just write their signatures on the ceiling tiles. The owners started this practice in 1994 because they didn't want to paint or replace the faded ceiling tiles. So far, it seems to be working.

The business was established as a beer parlor called Terpstra's Place in 1934. The beer parlor operated out of a building across the road from where the bar now stands until 1942. A liquor license was obtained about the same time the bar changed locations. I'm told the bar was a fairly rowdy place in the early days. One man even died as the result of injuries he received during a fight in the barroom. Although the reason for the fight and exact cause of death have been forgotten over the years, the local authorities apparently ruled it a fair fight because no charges were ever filed. Lawretta and Loren Fladager bought the business in June, 1994 and changed the name from the Four Buttes Supper Club to the Whiskey Buttes Club 45 Bar. The name change reflects the original name of the community, Whiskey Buttes, and also incorporates Bar 45 (the brand from Lawretta's father's ranch) into the name of the business.

Today's customers are quiet and friendly. Most of the bar business comes from local residents, but the food attracts people from within a fifty mile radius. Dining room hours are 5:00 p.m. until 9:00 p.m. daily. Prime rib is available every Friday evening, and lunch specials are offered in the bar Monday through Friday from 11:30 a.m. until 2:00 p.m. Besides the regular happy hour on Wednesdays, special drink prices are available on Ladies Night every Thursday from 5:00 until 7:00. The bar also hosts an annual branding party every year in September, complete with a free barbecue and live music. The Whiskey Buttes Club 45 Bar is off the beaten path, but it's worth the drive if you have the time.

DUTCH HENRY'S CLUB

OWNERS: Dutch Henry Gang, LLC

HOURS: 11:00 a.m. to Closing Daily

HAPPY HOUR: No

GAMBLING: Video Poker/Keno; Shake-A-Shift

LIVE MUSIC: Occasionally

LOCATION: Main Street, **Peerless**

PHONE: 406-893-4389

BEER: Domestics

AMUSEMENT: Pool; Darts; Volleyball; Video Games; Horseshoes; Shuffleboard

FOOD: Full Menu Restaurant

Dutch Henry's Club is on Main Street in Peerless. The barroom resides in the north side of the building, and a formal dining room/dance hall is in the south side. The dining room/dance hall is not part of the original structure. It was added during a renovation project that was completed in the late 1980s. If you prefer drinking outdoors, a beer garden is off the south side of the dining room. Among other things, the beer garden serves as a playing field for Rolle Bolle, a Belgian lawn game played with a beveled wooden wheel and metal stakes in the ground.

The business was established as a pool hall, restaurant, and dance hall in 1926. When prohibition ended, the business became a saloon. It's interesting to note that Dutch Henry's Club was named for the legendary leader of a band of outlaws, and the town of Peerless was named after a popular brand of beer in the early 1900s. The Dutch Henry Gang was a colorful group of bandits who roamed the prairies of Northeastern Montana during the late 1800s. The group was notorious for stealing and selling, then re-stealing and re-selling, horses in Montana, Canada, and North Dakota. The town was named during the early 1900s. A group of residents had met to determine what to call their new settlement, and it's said one of the men looked at the label on his beer bottle and said "Peerless". As easy as that, the name of the beer became the name of the town.

Dutch Henry's Club is now owned by the Dutch Henry Gang, LLC, a group of five individuals from Northeastern Montana. The members of the "Gang" work at the bar, so you still get the personal service you would expect at a small town tavern. The barroom enjoys a steady local clientele throughout the year, and the fine dining draws people from all over Northeastern Montana. A lot of tourists also stop by to see the place during the summer. Peerless is a small community in a remote part of Montana, but it's well worth the drive to spend some time at Dutch Henry's Club. You just know there's something special about a bar named after an outlaw in a town named after a beer.

LINDSAY RECREATION BAR AND GRILL

OWNER: Richard Jonas   **LOCATION:** Route 200S, **Lindsay**

HOURS: 11:00 a.m. to Closing Tue-Sat   **PHONE:** 406-584-7478
3:00 p.m. to Closing Sunday; Closed Monday

HAPPY HOUR: No   **BEER:** Domestics

GAMBLING: Video Poker;   **AMUSEMENT:** Darts
Shake-A-Day

LIVE MUSIC: No   **FOOD:** Full Menu Grill

The Lindsay Recreation Bar and Grill is on the north side of Route 200S in Lindsay. The building houses a moderate-sized barroom that is laid out in somewhat of an L-configuration. The bar stands in the south side of the room facing the center wall, and several tables occupy the remainder of the floor space. A kitchen resides in the northwest corner of the building, and a small apartment is attached to the west end. Several painted saw blades are on display throughout the barroom. The saw blades were painted a local artist who can transform just about anything you have laying around the house into a work of art.

Earl Young established the business as the Lindsay Recreation Parlor in 1933. The bar originally resided in a building one block north of its present location, but the business was moved in 1960 because the old building was about to collapse. The existing structure was home to several other businesses prior to the bar moving in. Among other things, the building served as a farm implement dealership and a grocery store. Except for a short period of time during the mid 1940s when the business operated under the name Hagan's Bar, the bar has always been called the Lindsay Recreation. Richard Jonas has owned the business since 1992.

The Lindsay Recreation Bar and Grill is a basic country bar where strangers leave as friends. It's operated to meet the needs of the local community, but people from all over the world have stopped in. There's always a friendly crowd on hand, and the regular customers know they're trusted enough to serve themselves if the bartender is busy in the kitchen. They just settle up when the bartender returns to the bar. There's no formal happy hour at the Lindsay Recreation Bar and Grill, but the drink prices are always kept at a very reasonable level. A Rocky Mountain Oyster feed is held at the bar several times a year, and people commonly gather here to play cards. If you're looking for a bar with a relaxing atmosphere and friendly people, stop in and see the great folks at the Lindsay Recreation Bar and Grill.

STOCKMAN BAR

OWNERS: Gary and Sally Sodt   **LOCATION:** Main Street, **Richey**

HOURS: 10:00 a.m. to 2:00 a.m. Mon-Sat   **PHONE:** 406-773-5752
1:00 p.m. to 2:00 a.m. Sunday

HAPPY HOUR: 7:00 to 8:00 Friday   **BEER:** Domestics
6:00 to 7:00 During Winter Months

GAMBLING: Video Poker/Keno   **AMUSEMENT:** Pool; Foosball

LIVE MUSIC: No   **FOOD:** Grill Items; Pizza

The Stockman Bar is on Main Street in Richey. The wooden struc-ture houses a relatively small barroom in the front portion of the building, and a game room and video rental shop are in the rear. About ten people can be comfortably seated at the bar, and a few small tables are spread throughout the room. If you prefer drinking outdoors, a couple of picnic tables are available on the lawn, and a sheltered patio is just outside the front entrance.

The business was established as John's Place in 1945. It was only one year later when the name was changed to the Stockman Bar. As far as I know, there's nothing in the way of interesting history to report about the Stockman Bar. If anything of great historical signifi-cance has ever taken place at the bar, nobody I spoke with could remember what it was.

Gary and Sally Sodt have owned the Stockman Bar since October, 1991. They run a very friendly establishment, and their customers are typically well-mannered. Most of the bar business comes in the form of local trade. Visiting deer and antelope hunters join the locals in the barroom during the fall, and a lot of out-of-town rodeo fans flock to the bar during the annual Richey Rodeo on the third weekend in July. Like most small town tavern owners in Montana, Gary and Sally are heavily involved in community activities. They host an annual vol-leyball tournament in May, and the bar sponsors a vintage car race every year in June. Winning teams are awarded trophies, and a pig roast is held concurrent with both events. Several of the trophies that were awarded to the winners of recent vintage car races are now on display in the barroom.

During my first visit to the Stockman Bar, I was told by one of the customers to be sure and mention Richey is the horniest town in Montana. I suspect this is a local joke in reference to the numerous sets of deer antlers mounted on the barroom wall; however, I've never spent enough time in Richey to verify whether this is actually the case. I guess you can always find out for yourself the next time you stop by the Stockman Bar.

DUGOUT BAR

OWNERS: Gary and Marian Harris   **LOCATION:** Galen Village, **Galen**

HOURS: 9:00 a.m. to Closing Daily   **PHONE:** 406-693-2140

HAPPY HOUR: 7:00 to 8:00 Mon - Fri   **BEER:** Drafts; Domestics

GAMBLING: Video Poker/Keno   **AMUSEMENT:** Pool; Pinball

LIVE MUSIC: Occasionally   **FOOD:** Frozen Pizza; Pasties

The Dugout Bar is at 1304 Galen Village in Galen. A lot of upgrades have recently been made to the old barroom, but it's obvious the place has been around for a number of years. The low ceiling, plywood bar top, and fixtures inside the building are sure signs this is no modern facility. An L-shaped bar stands in the south side of the barroom, and four small tables surround the pool table in the north side. A concrete patio and a large stone barbecue pit are in the yard off the east side of the building to accommodate outdoor activities.

The bar first opened in the late 1800s in a 12 x 12 foot log structure. The southwest corner of the present-day barroom is all there was to the building in the early days. Over the years, at least two additions have been made to the original building, but the structure had badly deteriorated by the time Gary and Marian Harris bought the business in April, 1996. Gary and Marian somehow managed to keep the bar operating while they made the necessary structural repairs and remodeled the barroom. They now have the place looking pretty good.

The Dugout Bar is usually a quiet place, but gunfire has interrupted the tranquility in the barroom on more than one occasion. One such instance was a simple case of a man accidently shooting a hole in the ceiling with a shotgun. If you look closely above the bar near the wooden ceiling post, you can see a piece of duct tape that was used to patch the hole. The bullet hole in the men's room door was not the result of an accident, however. I'm told it was made by a lady who entered the bar seeking revenge on her unfaithful husband. Apparently, the lady shot her husband through the men's room door while he was standing in front of the toilet taking a leak. A wooden patch covers the hole on the inside of the door, and a beer poster covers the hole from the outside.

Hopefully, the shooting days are over at the Dugout Bar. There's typically a friendly local crowd on hand, and everyone seems to get along. Gary and Marian have done a great job getting the bar back on its feet, and business is going well for them. They even have free pool on Sundays, so you now have an excuse to hold Sunday services at the bar.

PINTLAR INN

OWNERS: Corte, Linda, and Margaret Truax

LOCATION: 13902 Highway 1 W, **Georgetown Lake**

HOURS: 7:30 a.m. to Closing (Summer)
8:00 a.m. to closing Wed-Sun (Winter)

PHONE: 406-563-5072

HAPPY HOUR: No

BEER: Drafts; Domestics; Imports; Microbrews

GAMBLING: Video Poker/Keno; Shake-A-Day

AMUSEMENT: Darts

LIVE MUSIC: Occasionally

FOOD: Full Menu Restaurant

The Pintlar Inn is just east of the junction of Montana Highway 1 and the Denton's Point Road at Georgetown Lake. The entire business consists of the bar, restaurant, banquet facilities, and a seven unit motel. A spacious dining room is housed in the north side of the main building, and a smaller barroom is in the south side facing the highway. A straight bar stands along the east wall of the barroom, and a stone fireplace rises from the floor against the west wall. If you're a nature lover, you're always welcome to take your drink outside and enjoy the view from the wooden deck.

The business was established as the Brown Derby in 1934, but the name was changed to the Pintlar Inn in 1994. The Brown Derby was a relatively peaceful place until the 1960s when the building allegedly became haunted by the ghost of a woman who was killed alongside the road. The lady's name was Mrs. McKuen, and she met her untimely death at the school bus stop. Something apparently distracted the woman as her son got off the bus, because she didn't step aside as the bus pulled away. The mirror on the side of the bus struck Mrs. McKuen on the head, and she died from the impact. Since that time, doors have mysteriously opened and closed, a spoon has "flown" across the kitchen under its own power, and one waitress claims to have been kicked in the rear end when none of her coworkers were nearby. Mrs. McKuen's ghostly figure has even been sighted standing at a video poker machine in the barroom.

Corte, Linda, and Margaret Truax have owned the Pintlar Inn since December, 1995. They promote a friendly atmosphere where people of all ages gather to relax and unwind. A complete breakfast, lunch, and dinner menu is available, and prime rib is featured on weekends. Alabama Slammers are served at the bar throughout the year, and daiquiris and margaritas are available in the summer. Just don't overindulge in the booze, because Mrs. McKuen's ghost might mysteriously appear before your very eyes.

SEVEN GABLES RESORT

OWNERS: Jeff and Carolyn Brock

HOURS: 8:00 a.m. to Closing Daily

HAPPY HOUR: Daily Beer Specials

GAMBLING: Video Poker/Keno

LIVE MUSIC: Karaoke Occasionally

LOCATION: **Georgetown Lake**

PHONE: 406-563-5052

BEER: Drafts; Domestics; Imports; Microbrews

AMUSEMENT: Darts; Horseshoes

FOOD: Full Menu Restaurant

The Seven Gables Resort is at the junction of Route 1 and the Discovery Basin Ski Area road at Georgetown Lake. The barroom, restaurant, and a small convenience store are housed in the main building on the east side of the road. A ten unit motel is also part of the business, and snowmobile rentals are available during the winter. The barroom has a horseshoe-shaped bar surrounded by stools fashioned from small logs. Two buddy bars and a few tables are spread throughout the room, and a couple of very nice pieces of chainsaw artwork are on display.

The Seven Gables was established in the 1950s in a building that stood across the road from its present location. The building that now houses the business was used as a brothel before a fire destroyed the original Seven Gables Resort in 1953. I've heard the original resort had an underground parking garage which was connected to the whorehouse by a tunnel that ran under the road. Men who didn't want to be seen entering the whorehouse would park in the garage and use the tunnel. The configuration of three small rooms in the second story of the existing building provide sound evidence that it was indeed a bordello at one time, but I'm not aware of any physical evidence to support the story about the underground parking garage or the tunnel.

Jeff and Carolyn Brock have owned the Seven Gables since 1989. Although Georgetown Lake is a premier outdoor recreation area, the barroom has a local atmosphere. The Seven Gables is the social center of the area, and the customers are friendly and fun-loving. In conjunction with Anaconda's annual Art in the Park Festival, the Seven Gables Resort hosts the Georgetown Lake Summer Festival, complete with an outdoor barbecue and a street dance. During the 1996 Summer Festival, the winner of Georgetown's unofficial Mayoral election race was announced. It turns out a local boilermaker named Big Ed edged out a local dog named Norton by fourteen votes out of thousands of ballots cast. Norton has protested the decision, claiming Big Ed bribed voters at the ballot box with drinks. I suspect this means there will be another election in the near future.

WARM SPRINGS STORE AND BAR

OWNERS: Arthur and Pauline Cole

LOCATION: Warm Springs

HOURS: 11:00 a.m. to 2:00 a.m. Daily

PHONE: 406-693-9980

HAPPY HOUR: No

BEER: Drafts; Domestics; Imports

GAMBLING: Video Poker/Keno

AMUSEMENT: Pool; Horseshoes; Shuffleboard

LIVE MUSIC: Occasionally

FOOD: Grill Items

The Warm Springs Store and Bar is just south of the Warm Springs Interchange (exit 201) off Interstate 90. The bar and store is the only business in Warm Springs besides the State Mental Hospital, so you shouldn't have a problem finding the place. A convenience store, self-service gas station, and a bus depot operate out of the north side of the building, and the bar is in the south side. The barroom has a straight bar along the west wall, and a couple of tables are available if you can't find an empty barstool. A wood burning stove resides in the north end of the barroom, and a pool table and shuffleboard table are in the south end. It's not an elaborate place, but the barroom is comfortable and inviting.

The history of the bar dates back to the turn of the 20th century when a two story hotel was built across the road from where the Warm Springs Store and Bar now stands. The bar operated out of the hotel building until 1963 when it was moved across the road to its present location. The old hotel was subsequently destroyed, but the bar and store have remained in business.

Arthur and Pauline Cole bought the Warm Springs Store and Bar in 1991. They promote a friendly atmosphere, and their customers are typically quiet and well-behaved. A variety of grilled sandwiches are served in the bar, but the Philly Cheese Steaks are the house specialty. A steady local crowd keeps the store and bar in business throughout the year, and motorists traveling along Interstate 90 frequently stop because of the convenient location. The store is open from 8:00 a.m. to 6:00 p.m. daily, and they stock a good selection of grocery items, gifts, and souvenirs. Avon products are even available if you find yourself running low on cosmetics. When you visit the Warm Springs Store and Bar, be prepared to meet Prinz, a friendly pooch who comes from rottweiler and doberman ancestry. Prinz was only 5-1/2 months old when I last saw him, but he was growing by the day. Don't be alarmed if Prinz approaches you, because he's about as friendly a dog as I've ever met.

SUNDANCE SALOON

OWNER: David Wendler

LOCATION: 4000 LaMarche Creek Road, **Wise River**

HOURS: No Set Barroom Hours

PHONE: 406-689-3611

HAPPY HOUR: No

BEER: Domestics; Imports

GAMBLING: Video Poker/Keno

AMUSEMENT: Pool; Darts; Ping Pong; Foosball; Horseshoes; Volleyball

LIVE MUSIC: Occasionally

FOOD: Full Menu Restaurant

The Sundance Saloon is part of the Sundance Lodge Guest Ranch. The lodge is fourteen miles west of Wise River on Highway 43 and four miles north of the highway on LaMarche Creek Road. The saloon, dining room, and lobby occupy the ground-level floor of the log lodge, and a game room is in the second story. The barroom has several interesting features about it, including hand-crafted log bar stools and memorabilia items that have been donated by former customers. The lobby has a stone fireplace and several big game taxidermy mounts hanging from the wall.

The Sundance Lodge was originally a 250 acre working ranch that was homesteaded in 1917. The existing lodge was built when the LaMarche Creek Ranch became a commercial guest ranch in 1962. The name of the business was changed to the Sundance Lodge in 1970, but the services have basically remained the same. Six lodging rooms and four cabins are available for overnight guests, and the restaurant and saloon provide a comfortable atmosphere for daytime visitors and overnight guests alike.

David Wendler has owned the business since 1989. David's brother and sister-in-law, Crawford and Lou Wendler, manage the lodge for David. Visitors from all over the world spend their vacations here during the summer, big game hunters from around the country descend on the area in the fall, and snowmobilers provide the biggest share of the business during the winter. Twenty-two miles of groomed cross country ski trails are accessible directly from the lodge, and thousands of acres of snowmobile terrain are just out the back door. Horse rentals are available in the summer, and the big game viewing opportunities are endless. Plans are in place to build a 24 x 16 foot addition onto the barroom in the summer of 1997. Legendary hunting guide Billy Stockton will also begin operating his outfitting business from the Sundance Lodge in 1997, so things are only going to get better. The Sundance Saloon at the beautiful Sundance Lodge is a great place to get away from it all.

PLEVNA BAR AND CAFE

OWNERS: Jeff and Sandy Adams

LOCATION: Highway 12, **Plevna**

HOURS: Closed Mondays
11:00 a.m. to Closing (Winter); 4:00 p.m. to Closing (Summer)

PHONE: 406-772-5847

HAPPY HOUR: 5:30 to 7:30 Tue - Sat

BEER: Drafts; Domestics

GAMBLING: Video Poker/Keno;
Shake-A-Day

AMUSEMENT: Pool; Video Games

LIVE MUSIC: Occasionally

FOOD: Full Menu Cafe

The Plevna Bar and Cafe is on Highway 12 in Plevna. The barroom is housed in the north side of the building, and a dance hall and dining room reside in the south side. There's plenty of stools at the long bar facing the west wall, and several tables are available if you want to bring your family along. The interior decor isn't elaborate, but some interesting pieces of locally-crafted artwork hang from the barroom walls.

The business was established as Ed's Place in 1934. The name was changed to the Plevna Bar in 1937. The original bar was housed in a building across from the post office on Main Street, but it was moved along Highway 12 when construction on the metal building was completed in 1974. The dance hall and dining room were added in 1976.

Jeff and Sandy Adams bought the business in February, 1995. The bar basically serves as the community center for Plevna, so it's operated as a family-oriented business. Some of the best chicken in Eastern Montana is served at the Plevna Bar and Cafe. They also serve excellent steaks, and the special on Friday evenings is spaghetti with homemade sauce. Jeff and Sandy are big supporters of scholastic athletics. Home town players and their fans often gather at the bar after sporting events, and visiting teams are given a generous discount on meals.

Customers at the Plevna Bar and Cafe are expected to behave in a reasonable manner, but nobody expects you to walk away thirsty. There's no formal happy hour, but the normal drink prices are pretty much in line with happy hour prices at other taverns in the area. If you're in town on your birthday, Sandy mixes a wicked birthday drink that can knock the horns off a buffalo. If you want to feel real good real fast, tie yourself to a barstool and down a couple Jamaican Mind Blowers (the real name of the drink can't be printed here, but Sandy will know what you mean). The Plevna Bar and Cafe is also the only place I know of where you can get a TWIG TWOUT License for the very reasonable price of $7.50. Ask your bartender for details, and happy fishing.

MICHAEL J's BAR

OWNER: Michael Richards

HOURS: 10:00 a.m. to Closing Daily

HAPPY HOUR: No

GAMBLING: Video Poker/Keno

LIVE MUSIC: Occasionally

LOCATION: 419 Broadway, **Denton**

PHONE: 406-567-2626

BEER: Drafts; Domestics

AMUSEMENT: Pool; Darts; Video Game

FOOD: Full Menu Grill

Michael J's is at 419 Broadway in Denton. You will see the bar on the north side of Highway 81 as you drive through town. The spacious barroom is housed in a modern building that's kept very clean and well-maintained. A long bar and several tables are in the south side of the building, and a large dance floor and a raised bandstand are in the north side. Naturally finished tongue-and-groove woodwork has been used to cover the interior walls, and the suspended cabinets above the bar are made of oak framing with etched glass panels.

The bar was built in 1982. The liquor license was obtained from the old Farmer's Bar in Denton, which closed down a year or two earlier. When the business first opened, it operated under the name D&D Bar. On the night the bar hosted its grand opening party, the floor collapsed under the weight of the people who showed up for the celebration. The bar had to close down for the rest of the evening, so the customers and the band all went down the street to the old Denton Bar and continued the party. In the mean time, work commenced to shore up the floor at the D&D Bar. The Denton Bar ceased operating in the early 1990's, so closing Michael J's today could cause mass panic in Denton.

Michael Richards bought the business in January, 1993. He promotes a very friendly atmosphere, and the customers are generally well-behaved. Local trade keeps the bar going throughout the year, but travelers and hunters provide a boost to the business during the summer and fall. Michael J's has become a popular spot for local celebrations such as birthday parties, anniversary parties, wedding dances, and holiday parties. There's plenty of floor space inside the barroom, and the people always enjoy the hospitality.

Michael J's also offers good food and reasonable drink prices. Daily lunch specials are available at the bar, and the 1/3-pound Boss Burger is an excellent choice for any meal. The last time I checked, twelve ounce draft beers were only a dollar a mug, and pitchers went for $4.00. Free popcorn is provided for the customers during the evening, so you don't have to drink on an empty stomach.

ROY'S BAR

OWNER: Al McKibben

LOCATION: Highway 87,
Grass Range

HOURS: 10:00 a.m. to 2:00 a.m. Daily

PHONE: 406-428-2242

HAPPY HOUR: 5:30 to 6:30 Daily

BEER: Domestics

GAMBLING: Video Poker/Keno;
Shake-A-Day

AMUSEMENT: Pool; Pinball;
Video Game

LIVE MUSIC: Approximately Monthly

FOOD: Full Menu Cafe

Roy's Bar is on the west side of Highway 87 in Grass Range. It's doubtful the name of the business will be Roy's Bar by the time you read this, but it was still called Roy's Bar when the book went to print. The wooden structure houses a cafe in the north side and a spacious barroom in the south side. A curved wooden bar faces the west wall of the barroom, and about a half dozen tables are spread throughout the room. A motel is also part of the business, so you can spend the night in comfort if you need a place to sleep.

The business was established in the early 1960s. All there was to the place at that time was the bar, and the building was much smaller than it is today. Roy Alderink bought the bar in the early 1970s and gradually expanded the business. The barroom was enlarged to over twice its original size, and the cafe was added some years later. Nine motel rooms were built after the cafe was completed. Roy sold the business to Al McKibben in December, 1996. Al indicated he intended on changing the name when the liquor license came up for renewal in the summer of 1997, but he hadn't decided on what to call his new business when I last spoke with him in January, 1997. My impression is Al will be very successful, regardless of what name he chooses.

Roy's Bar has always been a friendly place where people gather to eat, drink, and socialize. Card games are popular during the winter, and livestock shipping parties are commonly held at the bar during the fall. Local residents and travelers provide a steady business throughout the year. Tourists wander in during the summer months, and hunters fill the bar, cafe, and motel during big game season. Al has recently modernized the cafe, and meals are now served on a daily basis from 6:00 a.m. until 10:00 p.m. Prime rib is the special on Friday evenings, steak and shrimp is featured on Saturday evenings, and the Super Ranger Burger (a 3/4 pound beef patty with ham, bacon, and cheese) is available any time. The business may no longer be called Roy's Bar, but it's still a wonderful place to stop for a meal, a drink, or a room for the night.

PIONEER BAR

OWNER: Jerry Ziegler

HOURS: 7:30 a.m. to Closing Daily

HAPPY HOUR: No

GAMBLING: Video Poker/Keno; Shake-A-Day

LIVE MUSIC: Occasionally

LOCATION: Highway 191, **Hilger**

PHONE: 406-538-7572

BEER: Domestics

AMUSEMENT: Pool; Darts; Video Games

FOOD: Full Menu Grill

The Pioneer Bar is on Highway 191 in Hilger. The barroom is fairly large, but it's separated into three different areas. The middle room and back room are basically used as game rooms. The main part of the barroom is housed in the front part of the building. A straight wooden bar and an antique wooden back bar stand along the east wall, the mounted head of a huge elk hangs from the west wall, and numerous old beer cans, beer bottles, and hats are on display near the bar. The hats and most of the beverage containers were donated by various individuals who have visited the Pioneer Bar over the past several years.

The building that houses the Pioneer Bar was a pool hall and gambling parlor during the prohibition years. The old Midway Bar operated out of the building until 1946 when the Pioneer Bar was established. The back bar came from a saloon in the nearby community of Kendall, which is now a mining ghost town. Jerry Ziegler bought the Pioneer Bar in July, 1993, and he continues to operate it today.

The Pioneer Bar is a friendly place where adults, kids, and several local dogs gather to socialize with friends. The bar sponsors dart teams and pool teams for the local leagues, and they host pinochle tournaments every Sunday through the winter. There's usually at least one pooch roaming around the barroom, and one of the local canines even sits at the bar with its owner and drinks rum and coke. Travelers also frequent the bar, as do visiting hunters. Jerry says there's two guys from Wisconsin who have been coming to the bar during hunting season every year for the past thirty-five years, and they don't even bring guns with them any more.

Jerry has developed some very tasty mixed liquors that he serves one shot at a time from a chilled shaker. If you like schnapps, you'll love these mixed drinks. He also serves excellent 1/2 pound broiled burgers and offers specials on meals Monday through Friday. If you're not hungry enough to eat a full meal, free popcorn or peanuts in the shell are always available. The Pioneer Bar is definitely one place worth visiting, so be sure to stop in and say hello to Jerry if you're ever in Hilger.

RAINBOW BAR

OWNER: Bob Landru		**LOCATION:**	Highway 191, **Hilger**
HOURS: 10:00 a.m. to 2:00 a.m. Daily		**PHONE:**	406-538-7313
HAPPY HOUR: No		**BEER:**	Domestics
GAMBLING: Video Poker/Keno		**AMUSEMENT:**	Pool; Darts; Video Game
LIVE MUSIC: No		**FOOD:**	Full Menu Grill

The Rainbow Bar is on Highway 191 in Hilger. The barroom is long and narrow, with a curved bar in the front part of the room and a gaming area in the rear. Wooden squares with brands burned into them line the barroom walls. The markings are authentic brands from nearby ranches that were established in the late 1800's or early 1900's. Each brand has the original ranch owner's signature under it. The barroom decor isn't fancy, but several nice horse figurines line the top of the back bar.

The early history of the Rainbow Bar is somewhat vague. Documents at the Montana Liquor Division indicate the business was operated in the early 1930s by a couple of known bootleggers. The Midway Bar was the name of the business when the first retail beer license was issued in 1934. The name was changed to the Rainbow Bar when the business moved to its present location in 1961. A bank operated out of the building from 1910 until it went out of business in the early 1920's, but the building basically sat vacant until the Rainbow Bar moved in. The old bank vault is still in place, but it's now used only as a storage area.

Bob Landru has owned the Rainbow Bar since 1980. Of the two taverns in Hilger, the Rainbow Bar caters more to the older residents. Travelers occasionally stop by during the summer months, and visiting hunters provide a boost to the business in the fall. The Rainbow Bar has a friendly atmosphere, and it's common for entire families to stop in to eat, drink, and socialize. The 1/2-pound hamburgers are a very popular lunch and dinner item.

According to some of the locals, the Rainbow Bar is haunted by the ghost of a man who died in the second floor apartment several years ago. Some people claim that ever since "Clarence" passed away, they've heard strange sounds coming from the upstairs apartment. Bob says he's never seen or heard the spook, but other people swear they've heard Clarence making noises late at night. Clarence doesn't appear to mean any harm; he just likes to move things around. Perhaps it's just some people's imagination, or perhaps Clarence's spirit still inhabits the second floor apartment and he's trying to rearrange the furniture.

EDDIE'S CORNER BAR

OWNERS: Bauman Family

LOCATION: Junction of Highway 191 and Highway 87, **Moore**

HOURS: 10:00 a.m. to Closing Daily

PHONE: 406-374-2471

HAPPY HOUR: No

BEER: Drafts; Domestics

GAMBLING: Video Poker/Keno; Shake-A-Day

AMUSEMENT: Volleyball

LIVE MUSIC: No

FOOD: Full Menu Cafe

Eddie's Corner Bar is two miles west of Moore at the junction of Highway 191 and Highway 87. Eddie's Corner is actually the name of the entire business, which consists of an automobile and truck refueling station, convenience store, motel, laundry facilities, showers, full RV hookups, picnic area, and the bar. The convenience store and cafe occupy most of the floor space inside the main building, but a small barroom is housed in the east side. The barroom has recently been refurbished with beautiful oak woodwork throughout. The hand-crafted bar has a wooden front and a slate top. About a dozen barstools are available, and a couple of booths line the west wall if you prefer sitting away from the bar. The antique-looking cash register behind the bar is actually a replica, but the two rifles in the oak display cases are collector's series pieces. One gun is a Montana Centennial Series Rifle, and the other is a Wyoming Centennial Series Rifle.

Eddie's Corner was built in the late 1940s, but the bar didn't open until 1950. Duke Bauman bought Eddie's Corner in 1951, and the business has been in the Bauman family ever since. The bar gets a steady business from residents of Moore and the surrounding communities throughout the year. With its location and variety of services, Eddie's Corner is also a popular place for travelers to stop, especially during the summer months. It really doesn't matter who you happen to see in the barroom, because the people at Eddie's Corner Bar are always friendly and courteous.

Home cooked meals are served in the cafe 24 hours a day, 365 days a year. The cafe is never closed, even on major holidays. The portions are very generous, so you won't go away hungry. Daily lunch specials are offered, and a different homemade soup is featured every day of the week. A separate type of special is available in the barroom. Daily drink specials are offered, and you can win five dollars worth of free play on the video gambling machines if your register receipt has a red star on it. Just remember to look closely at the receipt before you throw it away.

OFFICE BAR

OWNER: Jim Bergstrom

LOCATION: Fergus Avenue, **Moore**

HOURS: 8:00 a.m. to 2:00 a.m. Daily

PHONE: 406-374-2441

HAPPY HOUR: No

BEER: Drafts; Domestics Microbrews

GAMBLING: Video Poker/Keno

AMUSEMENT: Pool; Video Games

LIVE MUSIC: No

FOOD: Full Menu Cafe

The Office Bar is on Fergus Avenue in Moore. The bar is only one part of the entire business, which includes a cafe, a small grocery store, and a beauty shop. Two chandeliers made from iron wagon wheel rims hang above the antique wooden bar along the north wall of the barroom. A matching liquor cabinet and a hand-crafted back bar stand against the wall behind the bar. The beautiful back bar has lighted stained glass panels and large mirrors. The bar, back bar, and liquor cabinet were built around the turn of the 20th century. All three pieces were shipped via steamboat up the Missouri River to Fort Benton where they were off-loaded and transported overland by team and wagon to Moore.

The Office Bar was one of six saloons in the town of Moore in 1910. The business started out in a building across Fergus Street, but it was moved to its present location sometime during the 1930s. During the prohibition years, bootlegged booze was stored inside the hollow back bar for customers who wanted something more than soda to drink. A removable stained glass panel at the bottom of either end of the back bar made for easy access to the bottle of hooch. When the bar first moved across Fergus Street, a brothel operated out of the second floor of the building. The Great Depression was in full swing, but it was a great time to be alive in Moore, Montana if you were a young man with a few dollars in your pocket.

Jim Bergstrom has owned the Office Bar since 1973, but the last time I checked, the bar, cafe, grocery store, and beauty shop were all for sale. The sign in the barroom indicates you can buy all or any part of the business. Since I'm not in the market for a bar, I never inquired what the asking price is. The customers at the Office Bar are mostly local residents, but travelers stop by in the summer, and a few hunters wander into the barroom during the fall. With the cafe and grocery store in the building, there's usually a very friendly crowd on hand. The cafe hours vary, but daily lunch specials are always available. If you don't have time to sit down to a prepared meal, you can always buy something in the grocery store to take with you.

LEGION CLUB

MANAGER: Mike Webster

HOURS: 7:00 a.m. to Closing Daily

HAPPY HOUR: No

GAMBLING: Video Poker/Keno; Shake-A-Day

LIVE MUSIC: Occasionally

LOCATION: Main Street, **Roy**

PHONE: 406-464-5588

BEER: Drafts; Domestics

AMUSEMENT: Pool; Pinball; Video Games

FOOD: Grill Items

The Legion Club is on the west side of Main Street in Roy. It's relatively easy to find; just look for the building with the big American flag and the American Legion flag hanging from the pole out front. The spacious barroom has a straight bar that spans almost the entire length of the north wall. A few tables are available in the front portion of the room, and a covered concrete patio is just off the southwest corner of the building. There's plenty of room for large crowds both inside and outside Roy's Legion Club.

The Legion Club has been in Roy since 1952. It is actually part of the National American Legion organization; however, the bar is open to the general public. The town of Roy doesn't have nearly enough people to support the club on private memberships alone, so they allow non-members to take part in everything except official American Legion business. When the club first opened, only the smaller front portion of the building existed. A large addition was made to the west end of the building a few years later, as was the covered concrete patio.

Mike Webster now manages the Legion Club. They can't serve alcohol until 8:00 a.m., but the doors open every day at 7:00 a.m. for morning coffee. It's not uncommon for as many people to be at the bar for morning coffee as there are for evening drinks. The majority of the Legion Club's business comes from local residents, but visiting hunters and fishermen commonly stop by when they're in the area. Roy's Legion Club promotes a family-oriented atmosphere where people of all ages are welcome.

If there is a community center in Roy, the Legion Club is it. The club hosts various parties and social gatherings throughout the year, and they sponsor pool teams for the local leagues. A very popular wild game feed is held at the bar on the day prior to the opening day of hunting season every year, and the Legion Club also hosts livestock shipping parties for the local ranchers. The Legion Club isn't a fancy place by any means, but it's a great place to meet nice people.

ROY BAR

OWNERS: Betty Johnstone & Kelly Wrozesinski

LOCATION: Main Street, **Roy**

HOURS: 8:00 a.m to Closing Daily

PHONE: 406-464-2765

HAPPY HOUR: No

BEER: Domestics

GAMBLING: No

AMUSEMENT: Pool

LIVE MUSIC: Occasionally

FOOD: Grill Items; Frozen Pizza

The Roy Bar is on the east side of Main Street in Roy. You'll recognize the place by the sign out front that reads "FRIENDS MEET AT ROY BAR". The moderate-sized barroom has a straight wooden bar and an antique wooden back bar along the north wall. The back bar was installed when the bar first opened in 1903. I'm told the handcrafted piece was shipped via steam boat up the Missouri River to Montana (probably Fort Benton) where it was off-loaded and transported overland by team and wagon to Roy. The wood burning stove against the south wall provides all the heat for the building during the winter. All-in-all, it's not an elaborate place, but the Roy Bar is a friendly establishment with a comfortable atmosphere.

With a saloon that's been around for nearly 100 years, there's undoubtedly been some interesting times. During prohibition, the Roy Bar officially became a pool hall, gambling parlor, and cigar store. Unofficially, however, the building was a blind pig. The flow of alcohol virtually went uninterrupted during the prohibition years at the Roy Bar.

Betty Johnstone and Kelly Wrozesinski have owned the Roy Bar since 1990. They run a simple business out of the old building, and their customers have come to expect the same. At the Roy Bar, a shot and a beer are considered a mixed drink. It's basically a drinker's bar with few frills attached. Kelly says he's been tending bar fourteen hours a day, seven days a week for the past thirty years, and he's not shy about joining the customers for a drink while he tends bar. He also keeps his chainsaw, sometimes in one piece and sometimes in numerous pieces, on the table near the wood burning stove. When someone asks him why he keeps the chainsaw in the barroom, Kelly simply replies "to cut wood with".

The regular customers at the Roy Bar are residents of Roy and the surrounding communities. A few travelers occasionally wander into the barroom, but it's mostly a local crowd. Although they can't legally serve alcohol before 8:00 a.m., the bar usually opens around 6:00 in the morning to serve coffee. It's a great place to start your day, and an even better place to end it.

TRAILS INN

OWNER: Frank Arthur

HOURS: 10:00 a.m. to 2:00 a.m. Daily

HAPPY HOUR: No

GAMBLING Video Poker/Keno

LIVE MUSIC Occasionally

LOCATION: Main Street, **Winifred**

PHONE: 406-462-5427

BEER: Drafts; Domestics

AMUSEMENT: Pool

FOOD: Deep Fried Foods

The Trails Inn is on Main Street in Winifred. The steel-sided structure has a modern wooden front made from rough cut boards. The barroom is moderate in size, with a straight wooden bar facing the west wall. The wooden elbow rail on the bar is completely covered with carvings of people's names and initials, and brands from local ranches are burned into the pine boards bordering the ceiling. The interior decor isn't elaborate, but several porcelain liquor decanters are on display on top of the wooden beer cooler behind the bar.

The business was established as the Midway Bar in 1935. The building that housed the Midway was destroyed by fire on two separate occasions during the early 1950s, but the bar was rebuilt each time. I'm told the fires also destroyed just about every other building on Winifred's Main Street, including the neighboring Winifred Tavern. The Midway Bar became the Down-B-Lo in 1971. The name was changed to the Trails Inn when Frank Arthur bought the business in 1986. Frank has spent a considerable amount of time over the past several years performing upgrades and renovations to the building, and his efforts show. A new tile flooring has been installed, tongue-and-groove woodwork and new paneling now cover the walls, and a new flakeboard ceiling is in place. The entire facility is modern and well-maintained.

The Trails Inn is a very friendly tavern. I'm told horses, pigs, and motorcycles have been taken into the barroom over the years, but these antics were all done in fun. A steady local clientele keeps the bar going throughout the year, and visiting hunters pack the barroom during big game and bird seasons. With it's close proximity to the Missouri River, the barroom sees its share of boaters and fishermen during the summer. Frank hosts a branding party at the Trails Inn every spring, and he has a Christmas Party and dance every year in December. The Trails Inn basically gets the same customers as the Winifred Tavern next door. The two bars occasionally team up to promote special events such as a Super Bowl Party and Winifred's annual motorcycle rally. Even when they don't have a party going on, the Trails Inn is a great place to visit.

WINIFRED TAVERN

OWNERS: Rex and Lucille Catron

HOURS: 10:00 a.m. to 2:00 a.m. Daily

HAPPY HOUR: No

GAMBLING: Video Poker/Keno

LIVE MUSIC: Occasionally

LOCATION: Main Street, **Winifred**

PHONE: 406-462-5426

BEER: Drafts; Domestics

AMUSEMENT: Pool

FOOD: Frozen Pizza; Appetizers

The Winifred Tavern is on Main Street in Winifred. The moderate-sized barroom has a relatively long bar facing the south wall, and there's plenty of open floor space. It's not what I would call an elaborate place, but there's an interesting collection of beer cans and beer bottles on display on the shelves that line the barroom walls. Most of the containers were donated by out-of-state hunters who visit the area each year. Rex and Lucille have collected so many cans and bottles in recent years that they need to build more shelving to put them on. In the mean time, the cans and bottles continue to accumulate in the back room. About the only other decorations worth mentioning are the several hundred signed Canadian currency bills posted on the wall behind the bar.

The business was established as Fuller's Beer Parlor in 1934. Mr. Fuller took on a partner in 1935, and the name of the bar became the Winifred Tavern. The original structure was destroyed by fire in the early 1950's, but the bar was rebuilt on the same property. Rex and Lucille Catron have owned the business since 1984.

The Winifred Tavern is a place where people of all ages are welcome. Except for hunting season, most of the customers are residents of Winifred and the surrounding communities. The tavern hosts a great Saint Patrick's Day celebration each year, and they also have an annual hunter's stew and dance on the day prior to the start of big game season. Pool tournaments are popular during the winter, and you will commonly find a pitch game going on in the afternoons when the weather is bad.

Although there's usually a quiet crowd on hand, some of the locals like to stir things up occasionally. Over the years, there has been at least one horse, one very large boar, and even a half grown bobcat inside the building. The horse and pig were easy enough to handle, but the bobcat was a bit testy. Apparently, somebody who had trapped the cat let the critter loose in the men's room and left the building. It wasn't long before an unsuspecting customer entered the men's room and came snout to snout with the angry beast. I'm not certain what happened next, but I'm sure the commotion got the attention of the people at the bar.

DEW DROP INN

OWNERS: Rollyn and Judy Okerstrom

HOURS: 11:00 a.m. to 2:00 a.m. Daily

HAPPY HOUR: 4:00 to 6:00 Daily

GAMBLING: Video Poker/Keno; Shake-A-Day

LIVE MUSIC: Weekly

LOCATION: Highway 2, **Coram**

PHONE: 406-387-5455

BEER: Drafts; Domestics; Imports; Microbrews

AMUSEMENT: Pool; Darts; Pinball; Video Games

FOOD: Grill Items

The Dew Drop Inn is approximately one mile east of Coram on Highway 2. The barroom resides in the north side of the building, and a dance hall is in the south side. A wood burning stove stands in the middle of the building. The piece of plywood on the floor in front of the stove covers a hole that was made during a burglary and botched arson attempt several years ago. Apparently, the intruder decided to pull some burning logs out of the stove before leaving the building. Fortunately, the fire burned straight down and didn't spread.

The Dew Drop Inn was established as a logging camp bar in 1929. The place used to be quite a road house, complete with live entertainment and big name celebrities. Earnest Tubbs and Roy Clark are just two of the entertainers who allegedly played at the Dew Drop Inn. Along with the entertainment, there were plenty of wild times in the barroom. I'm told the customers used to get pretty crazy, but things have calmed down considerably in recent years.

Rollyn and Judy Okerstrom bought the Dew Drop Inn in April, 1995. Things were going pretty well for the new owners, but as fate would have it, tragedy struck. A couple of months after Rollyn and Judy bought the bar, a love triangle erupted into a homicide outside the building. As if moving to a new town and starting a business weren't enough to worry about, Rollyn and Judy now had to deal with this random act of violence. They somehow managed to maintain their composure, and things quickly returned to normal at the bar.

Rollyn and Judy run the business in a community-minded manner. A wild game feed and a pool tournament are held every Wednesday through the winter, and the annual banquets for both the men's and women's pool leagues are held at the bar. Wednesday nights during the summer are known as Hump Night at the Dew Drop Inn. College-aged seasonal workers from Glacier Park converge on the bar and party till the proverbial cows come home. It takes them a week to recover, but they always return for more.

PACKER'S ROOST

OWNER: Greg Vorhees

HOURS: 9:00 a.m. to Closing (Summer)
Noon to Closing (Winter)

HAPPY HOUR: 5:00 to 6:00 Mon - Fri

GAMBLING: Video Poker/Keno

LIVE MUSIC: Occasionally

LOCATION: 9640 Highway 2, **Coram**

PHONE: 406-387-4222

BEER: Drafts; Domestics;
Imports; Microbrews

AMUSEMENT: Pool; Horseshoes

FOOD: Full Menu Cafe

Packer's Roost is at 9640 Highway 2 in Coram. The barroom resides in the north side of the building, and a cafe is in the south side. The barroom has a rustic appearance and a comfortable atmosphere. The walls are finished in rough cut wood, tongue-and-groove pine boards cover part of the ceiling, and a river rock fireplace rises from the floor against the north wall. I'm told the wooden ceiling posts in the middle of the barroom mark the dividing point between Coram and Martin City, so you can party in two different towns without ever leaving the building. If you prefer dining or drinking outdoors, there's a large beer garden off the east side of the building and a wooden deck outside the cafe.

The business was established as the Angler's Lodge in the 1930s. A liquor license wasn't issued until 1945, however. Allegedly, over 900 silver dollars were embedded into the original bar top. I have no idea what became of the coins when the old bar top was replaced. The name of the business was changed to Packer's Roost in 1978. Greg Vorhees bought the bar in 1996, and he continues to operate it today.

Packer's Roost is a friendly establishment where people gather to relax and unwind. The specialty drink of the house is called a B-52 (probably because you'll get bombed on it), and some sort of meal special is usually available in the cafe. Montana Nachos, Indian Fried Bread, chili, and 1/2 pound burgers are some of the more popular menu items. On occasion, local residents are invited in to be a guest cook or a guest bartender. This way, the regular employees get to be obnoxious and bark out orders to the people they normally have to serve. It's a great way for the customers to learn what it's like on the other side of the plank.

People from all over the world have been to the Packer's Roost, but perhaps the best known guest is a mannequin named Joe. Joe pretty much keeps to himself, but he gets moved about the barroom on a regular basis just to keep things interesting. If you need someone to listen to your problems, Joe is always available. The only catch is you have to figure out where he is before you can talk to him.

STONER'S INN

OWNERS: In Transition

HOURS: 11:00 a.m. to 2;00 a.m. Daily

HAPPY HOUR: 5:00 to 6:00 Friday

GAMBLING: Video Poker/Keno; Shake-A-Day

LIVE MUSIC No

LOCATION: Highway 2, **Coram**

PHONE: 406-387-5300

BEER: Drafts; Domestics; Imports; Microbrews

AMUSEMENT: Pool; Video Games

FOOD: Frozen Pizza; Snacks

Stoner's Inn is on Highway 2 in Coram. The moderate-sized barroom has a straight bar facing the east wall, and a wooden leaning rail stands beneath the windows on the west wall. A game room is just off one side of the barroom, and a small casino area is toward the rear of the building. Stoner's Inn is not what I would call an elaborate place, but the people are friendly and the atmosphere is very comfortable.

The business was established as Angell's Tavern in 1945. The name was changed to Stoner's Inn when the Stoner Family bought the bar in 1975. There haven't been many changes made to the building or the decor over the years. In fact, the barroom today looks very much like it did when the building was moved to the property and renovated into Angell's Tavern.

Stoner's Inn is friendly establishment where people go to relax and socialize with friends. The bar enjoys a steady local clientele throughout the year, and visiting tourists, motorcyclists, and outdoors enthusiasts stop in during the summer months. Autumn brings a lot of hunters into the barroom, and snowmobilers provide a boost to the business during the winter months. Customers typically drink to the sounds of country and western music played over the CD jukebox or the television set.

Aside from the day-to-day business at the bar, Stoner's Inn commonly hosts social gatherings such as birthday parties, anniversary parties, and wedding receptions. They also hold a pig roast every year on June 22 as a show of appreciation for their customers. The pig roast is funded from money collected throughout the year in the "Cuss Cup". Any customer who says the "F" word or the "C" word at Stoner's Inn is required to donate 25 cents to the Cuss Cup. Apparently, enough people slip up in a years time to fully fund the annual pig roast.

If you're looking for a specialty drink, excellent huckleberry daiquiris are available in the summer. Stoner's Inn also serves a great Bloody Mary, which can either help you get over a vicious hangover or start you on your way to one. Either way, you will enjoy the drink.

FLAGSTOP BAR (IZAAK WALTON INN)

OWNERS: Larry and Linda Vielleux

HOURS: 4:00 p.m. to 2:00 a.m. Daily

HAPPY HOUR: No

GAMBLING: No

LIVE MUSIC No

LOCATION: Izaak Walton Road, **Essex**

PHONE: 406-888-5700

BEER: Domestics; Imports; Microbrews

AMUSEMENT: Pool; Ping Pong; Volleyball; Basketball

FOOD: Full Menu Restaurant

The Flagstop Bar is housed in the basement of the historic Izaak Walton Inn in Essex. If you've never been to the Izaak Walton Inn, it's one you should put on your list of must see places. The thirty-three room hotel building also houses a restaurant, gift shop, lobby, and the Flagstop Bar. Additional lodging facilities are available on the hill across the railroad tracks in the form of train cabooses which have been renovated into lodging quarters. The barroom, as well as the rest of the facility, is primarily decorated with railroad memorabilia. Model trains, antique posters, photographs, and old signs are on display throughout the building. There's even an authentic piece of steel railroad track at the base of the L-shaped bar for customers to use as a foot rail.

The Izaak Walton Inn was built in 1939 to accommodate train crews who serviced the Great Northern Railway. It was also intended to serve as a guest hotel at a proposed new entrance to Glacier National Park; however, interest in the project faded after World War II, and the road was never developed. The Inn was named for Izaak Walton, the patron saint of fishermen, who was born in 1593 at Stafford, England. The name "Izaak Walton" had become synonymous with conservation and restoration of natural resources in the Unites States by the time the Inn was built, so it seems only fitting the name was selected for the new hotel. In early 1985, The Izaak Walton Inn was listed in the National Register of Historic Places.

The Izaak Walton Inn is nestled between the scenic grandeur of Glacier National Park and the Bob Marshall Wilderness. Thirty-five miles of groomed cross country skiing trails are accessible from the lodge, and a million acres of wilderness surround the community. The Inn still preserves its railroad heritage while providing a comfortable and rustic atmosphere for its guests. Whether you choose to gather with friends at the bar or sit alone at the stone fireplace in the lobby, the Izaak Walton Inn offers a unique opportunity to relax and unwind. As the brochure says, this is truly a place where time stands still and lets you catch up.

HALF-WAY MOTEL, CAFE, AND BAR

OWNERS: Ron and Myrna Sullens

LOCATION: Highway 2, **Essex**

HOURS: 9:00 a.m. to Closing (Summer)
Closed Tuesday and Wednesday Afternoons During the Winter

PHONE: 406-888-5650

HAPPY HOUR: No

BEER: Drafts; Domestics; Imports; Microbrews

GAMBLING: Video Poker/Keno

AMUSEMENT: Video Games

LIVE MUSIC: No

FOOD: Full Menu Cafe

The Half-Way Motel, Cafe, and Bar is one mile west of Essex on Highway 2. The entire business consists of four motel units, eight full RV hookups, a general store, and the bar and cafe. The barroom and cafe operate out of an open area in the same building. A small bar faces one wall, and several wooden booths and tables are spread throughout the room. The tops of the two wooden booths along the front wall have checker boards etched into them, and it's not uncommon to see people playing checkers at these booths. The covered concrete deck on the front side of the building is a very popular spot among the customers during the summer months.

The history of the Half-Way Motel, Cafe, and Bar dates back to the 1920s. The business originally consisted of tourist cabins, a grocery store, lunch counter, service station, and a post office. The Park Creek Bar became part of the business when a liquor license was obtained in 1949. The bar originally operated out of the building that now houses the general store. The name of the business was changed to the Half-Way House in 1956 when construction on a new barroom and dance hall was completed. The old barroom was renovated into living quarters after the bar moved out. Ron and Myrna Sullens bought the Half-Way House in May, 1981. Ron and Myrna renovated the living quarters into a cafe in 1985, but they moved the cafe in with the bar in September, 1995. Later that same year, they opened a general store in the adjacent building.

The Half-Way House once had a fairly wild reputation, but the business is managed as a family-oriented establishment today. It's more of a cafe than a bar, and the atmosphere is very calm and relaxed. The cafe is open from 9:00 a.m. until 10:00 p.m. through the summer. Ron and Myrna advertise themselves as an official slow food restaurant, and their slogan has become *Please Keep In Mind Good Food Is Worth The Weight*. The menu features "The Best Food On The Mountain", including chili, burgers, and the Half-Way Cafe's famous Great Northern Chicken. The prices are very reasonable, and the food is delicious.

SNOW SLIP INN

OWNERS: Gary, Darlene, and
Michael Coen

LOCATION: Highway 2, Ten Miles East
of **Essex**

HOURS: 7:00 a.m. to 2:00 a.m. Daily

PHONE: 406-226-9991

HAPPY HOUR: No

BEER: Drafts; Domestics;
Imports; Microbrews

GAMBLING: Video Poker/Keno

AMUSEMENT: Pool; Video Games;
Horseshoes

LIVE MUSIC: Parking Lot Dances Twice Monthly
& Karaoke Weekly (Summer)

FOOD: Full Menu Cafe

The Snow Slip Inn is ten miles east of Essex on Highway 2. The barroom resides in the west side of the building, and a cafe is in the east side. The interior decor isn't elaborate, but the barroom ceiling is covered with hundreds of signed currency bills from all over the world.

The business was established under the name Doc's Place in 1935. I'm told "Doc" was a chiropractor who often performed minor chiropractic services on his bar patrons in the barroom. The name of the business was changed to the Snow Slip Inn in 1955, and a six unit motel was added few years later. During the 1960s, the Snow Slip Inn was a very popular steak house. Tour busses passing through the area commonly stopped at the bar so the passengers could stretch their legs and get something to eat.

The Snow Slip Inn is a peaceful place now, but things weren't always so civilized. Nobody has actually been shot, but there have been several close calls over the years. I'm told the bullet hole in the front of the bar was made by a woman who was angry at her husband, and the hole in the frame of the painting in the cafe was made by a man who took a shot at his ex-wife. There are several bullet holes in the ceiling, but they've been covered by the paper currency bills. There was even one instance several years ago where a man shot the juke box because he got mad at his wife.

Gary, Darlene, and Michael Coen have owned the Snow Slip Inn since 1990. The Coen's run a friendly establishment, and they certainly don't tolerate gunplay. They do serve excellent food, however. Award winning chili, pork fritter sandwiches, and homemade pizza are just a few of the delicious menu items. The Coen's also host several parties at the bar throughout the year. A Rocky Mountain Oyster feed and fish fry is held in March, an outdoor barbecue and dance is the main event on the 4th of July, and a New Year's Eve Party, complete with fireworks and a pig roast, is held to bring in the new year. Even if you don't care for great food and friendly people, you can always walk around and admire the bullet holes.

LOST PRAIRIE LOUNGE

OWNERS: Dave Tousey, Jim Kauffman, and Richard Steinke

HOURS: Noon to Closing (Summer) Winter Hours Vary

HAPPY HOUR: No

GAMBLING: Shake-A-Day

LIVE MUSIC: No

LOCATION: Lost Prairie

PHONE: 406-858-2314

BEER: Drafts; Domestics; Microbrews

AMUSEMENT: Pool; Darts; Horseshoes; Volleyball; Sky Diving

FOOD: Grill Items

The Lost Prairie Lounge is at 3180 Lower Lost Prairie Road in Lost Prairie. To get there from Highway 2, turn north on Lost Prairie Road (Lost Prairie Road is just west of mile post marker 87), and drive 4-1/2 miles until you see a grass airfield and the bar on your right. The main part of the barroom is housed in the north side of a log structure that stands several hundred yards east of the road. The vaulted ceilings, log and wood finish, and covered wooden deck on the front side of the building create rustic appearance and a comfortable atmosphere. A straight wooden bar faces the east wall of the barroom, and a wood burning stove stands in the northwest corner. Thick planks cut from the center of a large log form the shelving on the wall behind the bar. Numerous photographs of sky divers are pasted to the bar top under the polyurethane coating, and several sky diving photographs and posters line the interior walls.

The Lost Prairie Lounge is the only sky diver's bar I know of in Montana. The adjacent Carson Field Airstrip and the Drop Zone Sky Diving School were built in 1980, and the lounge opened for business one year later. Fred Sand owns and operates the sky diving school. Fred can outfit beginners for their first jump, and he can also provide instruction for people to become certified jumpers. The main rule everyone has to abide by is no drinking until after the jump is completed.

The Lost Prairie Lounge is a friendly bar with a casual atmosphere. The bar hosts an annual costume Halloween Party, Christmas Party, and Thanksgiving Day Dinner, but the big attraction here is the sky diving. Every year during the last week of July and the first week of August, a jump boogie takes place at the airfield. Hundreds of sky divers and thousands of spectators from all over the world converge on Lost Prairie for the ten day event. The jump boogie has steadily gained in popularity since the event was first held at Carson Field in 1980. A lot of people camp out on the property for the entire ten days. That way, they can watch the skydivers during the day and drink themselves silly at night.

MACGREGOR LAKE RESORT

OWNER: Bob Hanggi		**LOCATION:**	Hwy. 2 W, Macgregor Lake
HOURS: 7:00 a.m. to Closing Daily		**PHONE:**	406-858-2253
HAPPY HOUR: 4:30 to 6:30 Mon - Fri		**BEER:**	Drafts; Domestics; Imports; Microbrews
GAMBLING: Video poker/Keno		**AMUSEMENT:**	Pool; Video Games; Pinball; Horseshoes;
LIVE MUSIC: Occasionally		**FOOD:**	Full Menu Restaurant

The MacGregor Lake Resort is approximately twelve miles west of Marion on Highway 2. The entire business consists of a bar, restaurant, motel, cabin rentals, RV park, campground, gas station, convenience store, and boat rentals. The bar, restaurant, and convenience store are housed in a large wooden structure that stands on the south side of the highway. The building has a vaulted wooden ceiling and a huge river rock fireplace in the center of the floor. The kitchen and main dining room are in the north side of the building, and a small dining room is adjacent to the barroom in the south side. There's also a wooden deck off the south end of the building overlooking MacGregor Lake.

The resort was built on the north side of the old highway in the early 1950s. The new highway that came through a couple of years later was built on the north side of the resort, which meant the guests no longer had to cross the road to get to the lake. The business was managed almost without incident until 1964 when an elderly couple who owned the resort were brutally murdered during a robbery. The woman was found shot in the head, and the man was viciously beaten to death. The owners were known to keep the till full of money at night, and it's believed the sinister act was performed by someone who knew about the money. Suspects were identified, but the local authorities were never able to gather enough evidence to bring the case to trial.

Bob Hanggi has owned the business since 1992. He caters primarily to travelers and vacationers, but everyone is always welcome. The MacGregor Lake Resort offers some of the best hunting, fishing, and wildlife viewing opportunities in the nation. Deer, elk, and moose are plentiful, and the fishing is great year round. Most of Bob's guests come to the resort for the seclusion and beautiful scenery, and Bob occasionally has special events to draw people to the bar. An ice fishing derby and Fireman's Ball are held at the resort in February, and the Old Time Fiddlers play at the bar once a year.

HILLTOP HITCHIN POST

OWNERS: Dutch and Jane Dutcher

HOURS: 9:30 a.m. to 2:00 a.m. Daily

HAPPY HOUR: No

GAMBLING: Video Poker/Keno; Shake-A-Day

LIVE MUSIC: Karaoke Occasionally

LOCATION: 8225 Hwy. 2 W., **Marion**

PHONE: 406-845-2442

BEER: Drafts; Domestics; Microbrews

AMUSEMENT: Pool; Video Game

FOOD: Grill Items; Broasted Chicken; Pizza

The Hilltop Hitchin Post is at 8225 Highway 2 West in Marion. The bar stands on the north side of the road at mile post marker 100, so you shouldn't have any trouble finding it. The barroom has a Z-shaped bar along the west wall and a brick fireplace in the center of the floor. Several tables are spread throughout the room on both sides of the fireplace. A covered wooden walkway is off both the south and east sides of the building. Self-service gas and a modern motel are also part of the business, so travelers can spend the night and fill their tanks before continuing on with their journey.

The business was established as the Hilltop Tavern in 1946. Hilltop was selected as the name for the bar because the building stands at the top of Idaho Hill. In the early years, a small bar was housed in the west side of the structure, and the rest of the building was used as living quarters. When Dutch and Jane Dutcher bought the bar in July, 1984, they made the entire building a barroom. A seven unit motel was added in 1991, and a twelve foot addition was built onto the east side of the barroom in the spring of 1996. Other modern features include the recent addition of a big-screen TV and new carpeting throughout the facility.

The Hilltop Hitchin Post is a friendly tavern with a relaxed atmosphere. Dutch and Jane don't tolerate rowdy behavior, so you never have to worry about trouble flaring up. You will typically find a local crowd on hand, but visiting hunters, fishermen, and tourists also stop by. The fishing is superb on nearby Bitterroot Lake, so don't be surprised if you hear people talking about the big one that got away. Breakfast, lunch, and dinner are served daily at the bar, and lunch specials are offered throughout the week. Besides the regular grill items, the Hilltop Hitchin Post serves excellent broasted chicken, and their homemade pizza is spectacular. There's nothing like a hot meal and a cold beer after a hard day of fishing, and the Hilltop Hitchin post is just the place to get it. Be sure to say hello to Dutch and Jane while you're there.

DEER LICK SALOON

OWNER: Deb and Skip Kropp

HOURS: 10:00 a.m. to 2:00 a.m. Daily

HAPPY HOUR: 7:00 to 8:00 Daily

GAMBLING: Video Poker/Keno;
Shake-A-Day

LIVE MUSIC: Every Wed/Fri/Sat

LOCATION: 9352 Old Highway 2 East,
Martin City

PHONE: 406-387-5456

BEER: Drafts; Domestics

AMUSEMENT: Pool; Video Games;
Horseshoes

FOOD: Frozen Pizza; Sandwiches

The Deerlick Saloon is at 9352 Old Highway 2 East in Martin City. The exterior walls of the two story structure are covered with cedar shingles, so you shouldn't have any trouble recognizing the place. A spacious barroom, a dance floor, and a sunken game room are housed in one open area in the ground-level floor. The hardwood dance floor has a very unique feature: a one hundred dollar bill has been laminated into the center of the dance floor. A wood burning stove stands in the middle of the room, providing most of the heat for the building in the winter. During the summer season, a lot of the customers take their drinks and head outside to relax in the outdoor beer garden.

The Deerlick Saloon was established in 1945. The name Deerlick was selected because the bar was built on the site of a mineral deposit that attracted deer looking for salt. Somewhere along the line, a couple of unique taxidermy mounts were installed in the barroom to help promote the name of the business. It usually doesn't take long before first time visitors look on the wall above the bar and notice the mounted buck's head licking a mounted doe's rear end. I'm told that during the construction phase of the Hungry Horse Dam, there were fourteen saloons and at least one whorehouse in the area. The Deerlick was the first saloon built in Martin City. The original barroom has been expanded several times over the years, so it now looks nothing like it did when the doors first opened in 1945.

Some interesting moments have occurred at the Deerlick Saloon. Numerous gunshots have been fired inside the barroom over the years, and several bullet holes are still visible. These days, however, the customers are much better behaved. They still kick up their heels on occasion, but gunplay is strictly forbidden. Live bands perform every Wednesday, Friday, and Saturday. The Deerlick Saloon is also an active participant in the local Cabin Fever Days Celebration. An interesting history and friendly people make the Deerlick Saloon a great place to visit. Be sure to say hello to Deb and Skip when you stop by.

SOUTHFORK SALOON

OWNER: Joe Weiland

HOURS: Noon to Closing Daily

HAPPY HOUR: 6:00 to 7:00 Mon - Fri

GAMBLING: Video Poker/Keno; Shake-A-Day

LIVE MUSIC: Occasionally

LOCATION: 225 Central Avenue, **Martin City**

PHONE: 406-387-5971

BEER: Drafts; Domestics

AMUSEMENT: Pool; Horseshoes

FOOD: Frozen Pizza

The Southfork Saloon is at 225 Central Avenue in Martin City. The wooden structure has a covered boardwalk that spans the length of the front side of the building. The barroom has a curved wooden bar facing one wall, two wooden buddy bars and a couple of small tables spread throughout the room, and padded benches along two walls. Some rather interesting taxidermy mounts are on display in the barroom. They've got everything from a full black bear mount on top of the piano to a mounted armadillo on the shelf against the back wall.

The history of the Southfork Saloon dates back to 1946 when Frank Landon opened the Hungry Horse Bar in Martin City. The name was changed to the M&M Bar in 1959 when the bar was moved to another building in town. The M&M Bar became the Southfork Saloon in 1977, and it's been operating under that name ever since. Joe Weiland has owned the business since 1990.

The Southfork Saloon is basically operated as a neighborhood tavern. The customers have been known to get pretty lively at times, but they're always friendly. A different drink special is offered every day of the week, and you get two drinks for the price of one during happy hour. Wild game feeds are commonly held at the Southfork Saloon during the winter, and outdoor barbecues are held in the summer.

The two big events of the year at the Southfork Saloon are the Mountain Man Competition and the ever-popular Barstool Races. The Mountain Man Competition is held during Martin City's Trapper Days Celebration in the summer. Knife throwing, hatchet throwing, and BB gun shooting are just some of the events contestants compete in during the Mountain Man Competition. The Barstool Races are held in conjunction with the local Cabin Fever Days celebration in the winter. Contestants actually ride barstools mounted on skis down a hill to the finish line to compete for prizes. Races are held in three different classes; steerable, non-steerable, and open. Spectators have witnesses some spectacular spills and even a few broken bones over the years, but everyone always has a great time at the barstool races.

STILLWATER BAR

OWNERS: Bill and Bonnie Donsbach

HOURS: 11:00 a.m. to 2:00 a.m. Daily

HAPPY HOUR: No

GAMBLING: Video Poker/Keno

LIVE MUSIC: Occasionally

LOCATION: Highway 93, **Olney**

PHONE: 406-881-2554

BEER: Drafts; Domestics; Imports; Microbrews

AMUSEMENT: Pool; Video Games

FOOD: Grill Items

The Stillwater Bar is three miles south of Olney and fourteen miles northwest of Whitefish on Highway 93. The modern log structure stands on the banks of the Stillwater River at the spillway to Lower Stillwater Lake. The spacious barroom has a rustic appearance and a comfortable atmosphere. The interior walls, rafters, and ceiling beams are made from logs and naturally-stained wood, and the long bar has a thick wooden top. A raised wooden bandstand resides in one corner of the room, a wood burning stove in another, and four very large northern pike mounted on wooden plaques hang from the barroom walls. A partially covered wooden deck overlooks the river and lake.

The business was established in 1946 as a beer parlor called the Stillwater Inn. A full liquor license wasn't obtained until 1951. The original building was destroyed by fire in 1948, so another structure was built and the bar reopened. The bar operated out of the second building until the late 1970s when it too went up in flames. The log structure that now houses the bar was erected soon after the flames from the second fire were doused. Thus far, the building hasn't suffered any fire damage.

Bill and Bonnie Donsbach have owned the Stillwater Bar since 1982. Their regular customers come from Olney, Whitefish, and the surrounding communities. The bar also gets a lot of business from passing motorists. Travelers, especially the Canadians, have discovered the Stillwater Bar is a great place to take a break from driving. Bill and Bonnie operate the bar as a community-minded business. They have live music occassionally, and a pig roast and pot luck dinner is held at least once every summer. A barbecue pit inside the chimney is accessible from the outdoor deck, so the pig cooks while the customers enjoy the fine weather and the beautiful view of the river. The Stillwater Bar also hosts a children's Christmas Party each year, complete with a visit from Santa Claus and gifts for all the kids. If you show up at the right time, you might get to see Saint Nick. Even if you've been naughty over the past year, it's nice to see the kids walk away with something.

DENNY'S

OWNERS: Clint and Nancy Cathcart   **LOCATION:** Highway 2, **Pinnacle**

HOURS: 8:00 a.m. to Closing (Summer)   **PHONE:** 406-888-5720
          11:00 a.m. to Closing (Winter)

HAPPY HOUR: No   **BEER:** Drafts; Domestics;
          Imports; Microbrews

GAMBLING: Video Poker/Keno   **AMUSEMENT:** Pool

LIVE MUSIC: Occasionally   **FOOD:** Full Menu Cafe

Denny's is housed in a log structure on Highway 2 in Pinnacle. If you can't find Pinnacle on your road map, it's six miles west of Essex. The entire business consists of eight motel units, self-service gas, the bar, cafe, and a small gift shop.

The business was established in the early 1930s. Morgan A. "Denny" Densmore bought the bar in 1936 and changed the name to Denny's Underpass Inn. The name was selected because the bar stood near an underpass on the old highway. The road used to be on the south side of the bar, and a railroad bridge created an underpass on the highway. I'm told that before it was legal to sell alcohol to Indians in Montana, Denny's sold more whiskey out the back door to Indians than they legally sold at the bar. Fortunately, they no longer have to sneak the booze to their neighbors.

The original Denny's Underpass Inn was destroyed by a violent explosion and fire in March, 1961. The explosion occurred while a tanker truck was dispensing gasoline into a 500 gallon underground tank in front of the building. Miraculously, nobody was killed during the ordeal. The driver of the truck was severely burned, a man who was working on a concrete entrance to the building was hurled thirty feet through the air but only suffered minor injuries, and a man who was sitting at the bar walked away without a scratch. The present-day structure was erected later that same year, and Denny's reopened the following season.

Clint and Nancy Cathcart have owned Denny's since 1982. Clint claims he was the first person to be served at the new bar, but his drink was a soda because he was only fourteen years old at the time. Clint and Nancy run the business as a family-oriented establishment, so there's never any trouble at the bar. Daily lunch specials are offered featuring excellent homemade soups, sandwiches, and bread. Denny's also has the largest selection of microbrewed and imported beers in the area. If you're at the bar during the summer, you will probably meet Norman, the Cathcart's Cocker Spaniel and official bar mascot. Norman walks around the barroom sporting a T-shirt with an "Eat At Denny's" insignia.

POINT OF ROCKS RESTAURANT AND LOUNGE

OWNERS: Greg and Valerie Johnson

HOURS: 11:00 a.m. to 2:00 a.m. Daily

HAPPY HOUR: No

GAMBLING: Video Poker/Keno; Shake-A-Day

LIVE MUSIC: At Least Monthly

LOCATION: Highway 93, **Stryker**

PHONE: 406-881-2752

BEER: Drafts; Domestics; Imports; Microbrews

AMUSEMENT: Pool; Darts; Horseshoes

FOOD: Full Menu Restaurant

The Point of Rocks Restaurant and Lounge is five miles southeast of Stryker on Highway 93. The barroom resides in the basement, and the restaurant is in the ground-level floor. The barroom is separated into two sections. The larger room has a straight bar facing the north wall, several video gambling machines, and a wood burning stove in one corner. The smaller room has a brick fireplace, a few tables, and a karaoke setup. A covered boardwalk is just outside the barroom beneath the wooden deck off the south side of the dining room. There's also an open wooden deck and a fountain pond in the lawn behind the building.

The business gets its name from nearby rock formations known as the Point of Rocks. Early settlers used the rock formations as landmarks while traveling through the Tobacco Valley. The Point of Rocks Ranger Station previously stood on the property, but the ranger station was no longer in use when the restaurant and lounge first opened in 1953. Greg and Valerie Johnson have owned the business since February, 1995.

The Point of Rocks Restaurant and Lounge is a friendly establishment where residents of Stryker, Olney, and other nearby communities gather to relax and socialize. Grill items are served in the bar throughout the day, and the restaurant opens at 5:00 p.m. daily (2:00 p.m. on Sunday). Steaks and seafood are the featured dinner items, and an excellent prime rib is available seven days a week.

Greg and Valerie treat their customers like guests in their house, and they expect the customers to behave themselves accordingly. Several parties are held at the bar during the year, including a Fourth of July Party, Labor Day Party, and New Years Eve Party. Food and live music are always included with the price for each event. Santa Claus arrives at the bar prior to Christmas Day each year to hand out gifts to children. The gifts are donated to the bar throughout the year by local businesses and individuals. Over 125 kids showed up for the visit from Santa in 1995, and the event gets bigger every year. The way things are going, Santa may have to get a night job to keep up with the demand.

SUMMIT STATION

OWNER: Francine Forrester

HOURS: 4:00 p.m. to Closing Daily
Winter Hours Vary

HAPPY HOUR: No

GAMBLING: Video Poker/Keno

LIVE MUSIC: Weekly During Summer

LOCATION: Highway 2, **Summit**

PHONE: 406-226-4428

BEER: Drafts; Domestics;
Imports; Microbrews

AMUSEMENT: Pool; Foosball

FOOD: Full Menu Restaurant

Summit Station is eleven miles west of East Glacier at the summit of Maria's Pass. The barroom resides in the second floor of the two story structure, and the dining room and kitchen occupy the entire ground-level floor. Windows in the north wall provide the guests with a spectacular view of Summit Peak and the neighboring mountain range on the southern border of Glacier National Park. If you prefer an unrestricted view of the area's natural splendor, there's a large deck off the north side of the building. The wooden wall coverings in the dining room create a rustic appearance and a comfortable atmosphere. The barroom is nicely finished as well, with wood trim covering the bottom part of the plasterboard walls.

The history of Summit Station dates back to 1902 when the Great Northern Railroad used the building as a train depot. I'm told that before Highway 2 was completed, trains served as ferries to get automobiles over Maria's Pass. Summit Station was one of the two points where cars were on-loaded and off-loaded to get over the hill. The depot operated until sometime in the 1960s. In 1982, the building was moved across the railroad tracks and renovated into a restaurant and lounge.

Francine Forrester has owned Summit Station since 1993. The business is now endorsed by the Orvis Company as a destination fishing lodge, but the bar and restaurant will remain open to the general public, at least on a limited basis. The restaurant offers both casual and finer fair dining. Fishing guests receive first priority, however, so be sure to call ahead for reservations if you plan on dining here. If you just want to stop for a drink, the bar stocks an extensive selection of microbrewed and imported beers, including several microbrews on draft which are rotated seasonally.

Anyone who enjoys fishing for trophy-sized trout should check out the guided trips available at Summit Station. The guides have access to lakes and streams on the nearby Blackfoot Indian Reservation, which are not open to the general public. The fish are abundant in these waters, especially since the fishing pressure is so low. Even if you don't like to fish, you should stop by to admire the breathtaking view from the deck.

103

STANTON CREEK LODGE

OWNER: Gregg and Shannon Johnston

HOURS: Winter Hours Vary
7:00 a.m. to Closing Daily (Summer)

HAPPY HOUR: 5:00 to 7:00 Daily

GAMBLING: Video Poker/Keno;
Shake-A-Day

LIVE MUSIC: Twice a Year

LOCATION: Highway 2, **West Glacier**

PHONE: 406-888-5040

BEER: Drafts; Domestics;
Imports; Microbrews

AMUSEMENT: Croquet; Horseshoes;
Volleyball

FOOD: Full Menu Cafe

The Stanton Creek Lodge is sixteen miles east of West Glacier on Highway 2. The bar and cafe are housed in a log-sided structure that stands near mile post marker 170. Two nice chainsaw carvings are on the covered wooden deck off the front side of the main building, and an assortment of professionally-made and hand-fashioned crafts are on display inside the facility. Sunflowers, bears, and crows, in one form or another, have been effectively used as decorations.

The business was established in the early 1930s, and like most bars that have been around that long, some interesting moments have taken place at the bar. Things are peaceful today, but you can still see bullet holes in the floor; remnants of past wilder times. The holes were made by a former owner who sometimes resorted to drastic measures to get people's attention. This same man was known to ride his horse into the barroom, and I've heard he once got kicked out of Montana for two years for causing an accident on the highway in front of the bar. Apparently, he left a big pile of snow on the road while he was plowing out the parking lot, and it wasn't long before a nasty crash occurred. It took the bar a long time to live down its rowdy reputation, but it's no secret that the Stanton Creek Lodge is a very friendly place these days.

Greg and Shannon Johnston bought the business in May, 1993. They've done a wonderful job upgrading the facility, and Gregg's mother gets the credit for the interior decorating. Gregg and Shannon hold a craft show and a free pig roast every Fourth of July weekend, and they host a car show and barbecue on Labor Day weekend. Live bands and prize drawings are part of both events. Great food is always available, whether you make it to one of the barbecues or not. The chicken gobbler sandwich and chicken fried steak are just two of the many items featured on the menu. If you need a place to spend the night, cabins and RV sites are available. After all, the Stanton Creek Lodge is indeed a full service lodge.

FIFTH ACE SALOON

OWNERS: Debbie King & Lou Jasikoff

LOCATION: 77750 Gallatin Road, **Gallatin Gateway**

HOURS: 10:00 a.m. to Closing Daily

PHONE: 406-763-9988

HAPPY HOUR: 5:00 to 7:00 Mon - Fri

BEER: Drafts; Domestics; Imports

GAMBLING: Video Poker/Keno

AMUSEMENT: Pool; Volleyball; Horseshoes

LIVE MUSIC: Occasionally

FOOD: Grill Items

The Fifth Ace Saloon is housed in a log structure on the east side of Gallatin Road (Highway 191), approximately 1-1/4 miles north of the Gallatin Gateway turnoff. The saloon has a rustic appearance and a very inviting atmosphere. A covered boardwalk spans the length of the front side of the building. The spacious barroom has log rafters, a wooden ceiling, a river rock fireplace, and wagon wheel chandeliers. A straight wooden bar faces the east wall, and a few tables are spread throughout the room. A wooden deck and a large barbecue pit are available outside to accommodate outdoor festivities.

Lou Jasikoff built the Fifth Ace Saloon and Motel in 1984. The motel rooms were in the small buildings north of the saloon, but the lodging facilities were eventually renovated into small shops. The shops are currently leased out as separate businesses. Debbie King bought a share of the Fifth Ace Saloon in 1993, and she and Lou now manage the business as a partnership. In an effort to show appreciation to her regular customers, Debbie founded the Fifth Ace Saloon Asshole Club in 1995. Debbie personally determines which customers are qualified for membership into the prestigious organization and posts their names on the membership roster behind the bar. Debbie says she only chooses her best customers for the club, so the name is actually a little misleading.

The Fifth Ace Saloon is basically a local tavern. Guests from a neighboring whitewater rafting guide shop occasionally wander in to drink a few cans of courage, but the bar caters primarily to the locals. A large Blue Tick Hound named Zeke shows up every morning at 11:00 to mooch food, so be careful not to trip over him as you enter the door. The customers are usually friendly, but Debbie says a never-ending line of bullshit flies around the barroom during the evening hours. Pool is a popular activity, and the bar hosts several tournaments throughout the year. The annual pool tournament in June is always held outside on the boardwalk.

STACEY'S OLD FAITHFUL BAR

OWNER: Phyllis Crosby

HOURS: 10:00 a.m. to 2:00 a.m. Mon-Sat
11:00 a.m. to 2:00 a.m. Sunday

HAPPY HOUR: No

GAMBLING: Video Poker/Keno

LIVE MUSIC: Every Weekend

LOCATION: Gallatin Gateway

PHONE: 406-763-4425

BEER: Domestics; Imports

AMUSEMENT: Pool

FOOD: Frozen Pizza

Stacey's Old Faithful Bar is housed in the ground-level floor of a two story brick structure at 300 Mill Street in Gallatin Gateway. Their slogan, "Where The West Is Still The West", provides an accurate description of the atmosphere. The spacious barroom has a long horseshoe-shaped bar in the center of the room, a hardwood dance floor in the west side, and a stone fireplace in the northwest corner. Several initials are carved into the wooden bartop, but you may get a boot up your butt if you try to add to the carvings. Two sets of legs dangle from the drop ceiling in the west side of the room; remnants of past Halloween parties. Hundreds of framed photographs, some dating back to the early 1900s, hang from the rough cut boards covering the barroom walls. Most of the photographs are of local rodeo cowboys, and every picture has a story behind it.

The Old Faithful Bar was established by Mae Ping in 1932. Mae operated the bar in the ground-level floor, and she allegedly ran a brothel in the second floor. Stacey and Phyllis Crosby bought the Old Faithful Bar in 1964, and the business has been in the family ever since. Stacey passed away in 1990, but people who work at the bar believe Stacey's spirit lives on through a ghost named George, who now inhabits the second story. Stacey was a stickler for measuring liquor with a shot glass. I'm told that after his death, the liquor bottles on the shelves would mysteriously start to rattle every time someone poured a shot free-hand. Stacey may be gone, but George is now watching over the hired help.

Except for the photographs on the wall and worn boards on the dance floor, the barroom looks much the same today as it did in 1932. The employees are a very tight-knit bunch, and the customers are very friendly. The barroom has such an old west atmosphere that it's been used as a set for several movies and commercials. Don't think it's all a ploy to attract tourists, because some of the locals still ride their horses to the bar and tie them to the hitching post outside. There's nothing phony about Stacey's Old Faithful Bar. All you have to do is stop in for a visit, and you will understand exactly what I mean.

Stacey's Old Faithful Bar in Gallatin Gateway.

Top Photo: The west side of the barroom.
Numerous rodeo photographs hang from the walls, and a set
of legs dangles from the drop ceiling.

Bottom Photo: Current owner Phyllis Crosby (end barstool).
Founder Mae Ping's photograph hangs from the oval picture
frame behind the bar.

HAPPY HOUR BAR

OWNERS: Bud and Karen Klungervik

HOURS: 11:00 a.m. to Closing Daily
(Open on a Seasonal Basis)

HAPPY HOUR: No

GAMBLING: Video Poker/Keno

LIVE MUSIC: No

LOCATION: 15400 Hebgen Lake Road

PHONE: 406-646-7281

BEER: Drafts; Domestics; Microbrews

AMUSEMENT: None

FOOD: Full Menu Grill

The Happy Hour Bar is just off Hebgen Lake Road (Highway 287) on the north shore of Hebgen Lake. There's a landmark in the form of an old wooden boat with a "Happy Hour Bar" sign on it along the road, so you shouldn't have any trouble finding the place. The moderate-sized barroom is rustic, yet comfortable, consisting of log walls and rafters, a wooden ceiling, and a wooden floor. Three wooden buddy bars and several tables are spread throughout the room, and the stools at the V-shaped bar afford a fantastic view of the lake through large plate glass windows. If you prefer sitting even closer to the lake, there's a wooden deck off the south and west sides of the barroom. Besides the bar, there's a small marina and several cabin rentals available.

The Happy Hour Bar was established in 1972. The building was originally a house, but whoever lived there apparently decided it would make a better tavern than a home. Bud and Karen Klungervik have owned the bar since 1985. Shannon Johnson now manages the business.

The Happy Hour is a fun place with a lively clientele. Visitors commonly leave their hats to be displayed with the hundreds of other hats in the barroom, and some guests even donate a photograph of their butt so it can be put on display on the "Moon Chart" that hangs from the barroom wall. The customers range from local residents to celebrities who visit the area. A lot of snowmobilers also frequent the Happy Hour during the winter months. Complete lunches and dinners are available, and they mix a mean margarita if you care to take on the tequila.

Because of the area's business cycle, the bar operates on a seasonal basis. Summer season typically runs from mid May through October, and the winter season usually goes from the day after Christmas through the end of March. The bar hosts a "Christmas Party" each year on August 25 to raise money for needy local residents. The party comes complete with dinner, a decorated tree, and a visit from Santa Claus. The Happy Hour is also a popular site for both weddings and funeral wakes, so you can never be quite sure whether the people in the barroom are mourning or celebrating.

LAND OF MAGIC DINNER CLUB AND LOUNGE

OWNER: Jim Groenendal

LOCATION: 11060 Front St., **Logan**

HOURS: 2:30 p.m. to Closing Daily

PHONE: 406-284-3794

HAPPY HOUR: Pull Tab Prices Throughout the Afternoon

BEER: Drafts; Domestics; Imports; Microbrews

GAMBLING: Video Poker/Keno

AMUSEMENT: Pool; Pinball

LIVE MUSIC: Occasionally

FOOD: Full Menu Dinner Club

The Land of Magic Dinner Club and Lounge is at 11060 Front Street in Logan. The rustic architecture of the log structure creates a very comfortable atmosphere. Log posts and rafters support the vaulted ceiling in the barroom, and the interior walls in the dining room are partially covered with rough cut boards. A wooden bar faces the east wall of the barroom, and three tall tables stand against the west wall. The bar has a sturdy top that was made by cutting a thick plank from the center of a tree trunk. Brands have been burned into the woodwork throughout the facility to enhance the building's old west appeal.

The history of the business dates back to 1934 when the Logan Cafe became the Logan Beer Parlor. Land of Magic didn't become part of the name until 1971 when the name was changed to the Land of Magic Night Club. Jim Groenendal has owned the business since 1978. Jim survived a fire that destroyed the original building in 1985, and he erected the present-day structure later that same year. To create a rustic appearance in the new building, Jim installed rough lumber on parts of the interior walls and placed old outhouse dormers above the entrance to the dining room and both rest rooms. The lumber was gathered from old building sites around the area, and the dormers came from old outhouses in the region.

Most of the barroom customers at the Land of Magic are residents of Logan and the surrounding communities, but the dining room attracts people from within a seventy mile radius. The menu features steaks and seafood. Special seasonings are cooked into each cut of beef before it's served, and twice baked potatoes accompany every meal. An extensive selection of wines is available, and numerous brands of microbrewed beers are kept on hand, including six microbrews on tap. Whether you're at the bar or in the dining room, you can always expect to find a friendly crowd on hand. The last real trouble at the bar occurred during the 1970s when two brothers got into a fight in the parking lot over who was going to drive home. One thing led to another, and one of the men ended up shooting his brother in the stomach. It wasn't a fatal wound, but I imagine it settled the fight.

WILLOW CREEK CAFE AND SALOON

OWNER: Deane Mitchell/Tim Andrescik

LOCATION: Main St., **Willow Creek**

HOURS: Closed Mondays
7:00 a.m. to Closing (Summer)
Winter Hours Vary

PHONE: 406-285-3698

HAPPY HOUR: Possibly

BEER: Drafts; Domestics; Imports; Microbrews

GAMBLING: Video Poker/Keno

AMUSEMENT: Pool

LIVE MUSIC: Occasionally

FOOD: Full Menu Cafe

The Willow Creek Cafe and Saloon is on Main Street in Willow Creek. The cafe is housed in the ground-level floor of the original two story structure, and the barroom resides in the one story addition on the north side. The building's interior has been beautifully restored and upgraded. The ceiling tile in the cafe is the original decorative tin that was installed in 1912, and a beautiful antique wood stove stands against the south wall. The antique wooden bar facing the west wall of the barroom was built in the 1870s, but it's in immaculate condition. A brass foot rail extends the length of the base of the bar.

The business was established as the Babcock Saloon in 1912. The barroom and a barber shop originally operated out of the first floor of the existing two story building, and a dance hall was in the second story. After the Babcock Saloon closed, the building served as a grocery store, meat market, and a storage facility. David and Bette Roby bought the building in 1983 and transformed it back into a saloon. They added the present-day barroom in 1985 and operated the business under the name Blue Bell Inn. Deane Mitchell and Tim Andrescik bought the business in December, 1996 and renamed it the Willow Creek Cafe and Saloon. The last I heard, plans were to reopen the cafe and saloon in February, 1997.

Deane and Tim were still in the planning stages of operating their new business when this book went to print, but they seemed anxious to get started. Their menu will feature a variety of breakfast items, burgers, hand-cut steaks, and homemade soups. The cafe opens at 7:00 a.m. daily through the summer. Winter hours Tuesday through Friday are 11:00 a.m. until closing, but breakfast is served beginning at 7:00 a.m. every Saturday and Sunday. Although the town of Willow Creek is off the beaten path, the nearby Jefferson River and Willow Creek offer exceptional fishing opportunities, and the golf course in Three Forks is open most of the year. The Willow Creek Cafe and Saloon is a great place to stop either before or after a hard day of catching lunkers or whacking golf balls.

HELL CREEK BAR

OWNERS: Joe and Charlotte Herbold

HOURS: 9:00 a.m. to 2:00 a.m. Daily

HAPPY HOUR: Change of Shift Drink

GAMBLING: Video Poker

LIVE MUSIC: Approximately Monthly

LOCATION: Main Street, **Jordan**

PHONE: 406-557-2302

BEER: Domestics

AMUSEMENT: Pool; Darts; Video Game

FOOD: Broasted Burgers/Chicken

The Hell Creek Bar is on Main Street in Jordan. The barroom is relatively large, with a dance floor, bandstand, and small bar in one side, a gaming area in the center, and the main bar at the other end. The beautiful antique back bar was built in England around the turn of the 20th Century. The back bar allegedly resided in a bar in Hilger during the early 1900s, but it somehow ended up in Jordan's Hell Creek Bar. The large mirrors, embedded stained glass, and solid cherry woodwork have been maintained in excellent condition.

The business was established as a cigar shop in 1905. The cigar shop occupied the part of the building where the main bar now stands. The business became a blind pig during the infamous prohibition years, and after prohibition ended, the cigar shop became a saloon. The open area of the existing barroom where the dance floor and pool table now reside wasn't incorporated as part of the bar until the 1960s. Prior to that time, a wall separated the bar from a gas station and a plumbing shop next door. The bar has gone through several owners over the years. Joe and Charlotte Herbold most recently bought the business in September, 1995.

For the most part, the customers at the Hell Creek Bar are residents of Jordan and the surrounding area. The bar was filled with media maniacs during the Freemen standoff in 1996, but the reporters have all gone home. Travelers and vacationers stop in occasionally, and visiting hunters frequent the bar during the season. Cowboy poet Baxter Black even stopped by the Hell Creek Bar several years ago and wrote a poem about his visit. A copy of the poem is on display in the glass-encased bulletin board near the rest rooms. Speaking of rest rooms, I feel obligated to mention they still put ice in the urinals at the Hell Creek Bar. Male customers who become bored with the conversation at the bar can always look forward to watching ice cubes melt when they pee. And speaking of conversations, the ones at the Hell Creek Bar can range anywhere from hunting and fishing stories to what constitutes good whiskey and how to make moonshine. During my first visit, I got the impression there may be a few folks around Jordan who know their stuff when it comes to making booze.

RANCHERS BAR

OWNERS: Tom Fogle

HOURS: 9:00 a.m. to 2:00 a.m. Daily

HAPPY HOUR: 6:00 to 7:00 Mon - Fri

GAMBLING: Video Poker/Keno; Shake-A-Day

LIVE MUSIC: Occasionally

LOCATION: Main Street, **Jordan**

PHONE: 406-557-2468

BEER: Drafts; Domestics

AMUSEMENT: Pool; Foosball; Video Games

FOOD: Grill Items

The Ranchers Bar is on Main Street in Jordan. The moderate-sized barroom has a straight bar along one wall, and several tables are spread throughout the room. The Ranchers Bar isn't a fancy place, but the facility is relatively modern and well-maintained. And, of course, there's always plenty cold beer on hand.

The business was established in 1946 in a building across Main Street from where the bar now resides. The Blue Ribbon Beer Parlor was the original name of the bar, but it became the Bear Inn in 1950. I'm told the barroom at the Bear Inn had a large painting of two cowboys roping a bear, and I'm sure the painting had something to do with the name. The Bear Inn became the Ranchers Bar in 1959. The business was moved across Main Street to its present location in 1982. Tom Fogle bought the Ranchers Bar in November, 1993, and he continues to operate it today.

The regular crowd at the Rancher's Bar is comprised of local residents of Jordan and the surrounding area. During the Freemen standoff with federal agents at nearby "Justice Township" in the spring of 1996, the Ranchers Bar was a very busy place. The news media drove the locals crazy with requests for interviews, and the Ranchers Bar was one of the places where the media recruited interviewees. Several years before the Freeman standoff occurred, TV talk show host Geraldo Rivera got into a friendly wrestling match with one of the locals at the Ranchers Bar. A hole got kicked through the wall during the scrapple, but nobody got hurt. The man who wrestled Geraldo told me the two departed on friendly terms. The hole in the wall from the wrestling match was repaired, but five bullet holes in the ceiling were still visible when I last visited the Ranchers Bar in 1995. I don't know the entire story, but I'm told two customers were playing cards in the barroom several years ago, and all of a sudden, one of the men pulled out his 22 revolver and shot five times into the ceiling. If you carefully inspect the ceiling between the end of the bar and the entrance to the Men's Room, you might still be able to see the bullet holes. Just don't make any more, please.

BABB BAR

OWNER: Bob Burns

HOURS: 10:00 a.m. to 2:00 a.m. Summer
Noon to Closing Winter

HAPPY HOUR: No

GAMBLING: Video Poker/Keno

LIVE MUSIC: Karaoke on Weekends

LOCATION: Highway 89, **Babb**

PHONE: 406-732-9204

BEER: Domestics

AMUSEMENT: Pool

FOOD: Frozen Pizza

The Babb Bar is on Highway 89 in Babb. The barroom was still housed in a modest wooden building as of January, 1997, but plans were in place to move the bar into the adjacent log structure. Unfortunately, I don't know whether that's occurred yet. As far as the old barroom goes, it is relatively small and simple. A straight wooden bar faces the south wall, a few tables are spread throughout the room, and a lone pool table stands in the middle of the floor. The interior decor primarily consists of signed American and Canadian currency bills on one wall and part of the ceiling. Construction on a new bar, restaurant, and casino began in 1986. When the bar finally does move into the new building, it will be a beautiful facility with hand-crafted woodwork and river rock masonry.

If you're the type of person who doesn't care for confrontations, you may want avoid the Babb Bar. The place has a reputation as a rough and rowdy joint where fighting is as common as drinking. The first shooting occurred shortly after the business opened in 1954. It seems an irate customer charged over the bar in a fit of rage, so the bartender shot the guy in an act of self defense. The bullet went up the man's nostril and lodged in his forehead. The good news is the guy survived the shooting, but the bad news is the bullet could not be removed from his cranium. I'm told the man walks around to this day with a bullet in his forehead.

I'm told things have settled down considerably in recent times, but the Babb Bar has seen more than its share of fights over the years. In the early 1980's, a national publication rated the Babb Bar as one of the ten rowdiest bars in the United States. In those days, a lot of Canadians drove to Babb on the weekends to party, and they often got into battles with the locals from the Blackfoot Indian Reservation. Some outstanding bands used to play at the bar, and that also brought in a lot of people. Although the atmosphere has improved in recent times, you can still find a fight if you're looking for one. Weekends are usually the only busy times during the winter, but the bar stays full throughout the week in the summer when the tourists come to town.

WAGNER'S BAR BJ GUEST RANCH

OWNERS: Bob and Joyce Wagner

HOURS: Barroom Hours Vary

HAPPY HOUR: No

GAMBLING: No

LIVE MUSIC: Occasionally

LOCATION: Duck Lake Road, **Babb**

PHONE: 406-338-5770

BEER: Domestics; Imports; Microbrews

AMUSEMENT: No

FOOD: Full Menu Restaurant

Wagner's Bar BJ Guest Ranch is 3-1/2 miles south of Babb on Duck Lake Road (Route 464). Although I hadn't planned on writing about guest ranches in this book, I decided to include the bar at Wagner's Bar BJ Guest Ranch because it's open to the public year round and local residents commonly stop in for drinks. To get to the ranch, turn east off Highway 89 onto Duck Lake Road (the turn-off is just south of the St. Mary River) and follow the signs. A small bar is housed in the first floor of the 5,000 square foot log structure. A dining room and lounge area are also on the ground-level floor, and nine lodging rooms are in the second story. The building is beautifully finished in natural wood, and the interior decor consists of antiques and mounted big game heads.

Bob and Joyce Wagner opened the Bar BJ Guest Ranch in May, 1993. Bob grew up on the property, so he has grown accustomed to the spectacular view of the eastern border of Glacier National Park. The ranch is also a mere 2-1/2 miles from Duck Lake, which is well known for its monster rainbow trout. It took Bob and Joyce four years to finish the lodge, but their time was well spent. Aside from the beautiful lodge, Wagner's Bar BJ Guest Ranch has RV sites, tepees, and tent sites. You can also enjoy snowmobiling, hiking, and fishing directly from the guest ranch property.

Wagner's Bar BJ Guest Ranch hosts several private parties throughout the year, as well as an annual New Years Party and a Halloween costume party. A lot of their business comes from visiting tourists and fishermen, but they also do a pretty fair local trade. Bar hours vary so the guests upstairs are not disturbed by noise from the bar. Also as a courtesy to the guests, smoking is prohibited inside the lodge, including the barroom. Breakfast is served from 7:00 a.m. until 9:00 a.m., and dinner hours are from 5:30 p.m. until 9:30 p.m. Lunches are not served in the lodge, but pack lunches are available. The dinner menu features steaks, chicken, and seafood. The St. Mary's Lake Whitefish comes highly recommended, as does the delicious Montana Beef. Wagner's Bar BJ Guest Ranch offers a special atmosphere, whether you're lodging, dining, or just drinking.

BLONDIE'S CASINO

OWNER: Brenda Todd

LOCATION: Dawson Ave, **East Glacier**

HOURS: 11:00 a.m. to Closing (Summer)
4:00 p.m. to Closing (Winter)

PHONE: 406-226-9200

HAPPY HOUR: 5:00 to 7:00 Daily

BEER: Drafts; Domestics; Imports; Microbrews

GAMBLING: Video Poker/Keno; Simulcast Horse and Dog Racing

AMUSEMENT: No

LIVE MUSIC: Karaoke Music Weekly

FOOD: Fresh Pizza

Blondie's Casino is housed in a modern log structure at 33 Dawson Avenue in East Glacier. The spacious barroom has a long wooden bar in the north end of the room, a large seating area in the middle of the floor, and a dance hall in the south end. The interior walls and ceiling are covered in natural wood, and a huge stone fireplace rises from the floor against the west wall. A large addition has recently been built onto the northwest corner of the building, so seating is abundant.

The history of the business, as it was first explained to me, is quite bizarre. The entire account includes a hotel that was built with stolen construction materials, an arson fire, insurance fraud, a death threat made during a divorce proceeding, a failed savings and loan institution, bankruptcy, and a ban on gambling on the Blackfoot Indian Reservation. I couldn't possibly describe the details of these events on one page, but a former partner in the business conveyed this information to me. Just suffice it to say that nobody associated with the business today had anything to do with the exploits mentioned above.

The Palomino Supper Club & Lounge operated out of the building from 1978 through 1986. The movie *Heaven Can Wait* was being filmed around East Glacier during that time, and just about everyone associated with the movie went to the Palomino. The Miller Brewing Company even filmed a commercial in the bar during that time. The place was always packed, and it seemed like everyone who came in bought a round of drinks. The barroom stayed open nearly twenty-four hours a day for the movie crew, and the liquor store in Browning could never keep up with the demand for booze.

The movie making days are long gone, but Blondie's Casino is doing very well, especially since gambling was reinstated on the Blackfoot Indian Reservation. Brenda Todd has owned the business since the summer of 1995. Aside from the video gambling machines, Brenda started having simulcast horse and dog races televised in the building. Customers can now place bets directly from the barroom and watch the race as it takes place.

RAMSEY'S FIREBRAND FOOD AND ALE

OWNER: Ramsey Rink

MANAGER: Joseph Jessepe

HOURS: 4:00 p.m. to 11:00 p.m. Daily

HAPPY HOUR: No

GAMBLING: No

LIVE MUSIC: Occasionally

LOCATION: Highway 2, 3 Miles West of **East Glacier**

PHONE: 406-226-9374

BEER: Drafts; Domestics; Imports; Microbrews

AMUSEMENT: No

FOOD: Full Menu Restaurant

Ramsey's Firebrand Food and Ale is three miles west of East Glacier on the north side of Highway 2. The modern wooden structure houses a small bar and a moderate-sized dining area. Although the bar and dining area are in the same room, they are partially separated by a wooden counter and lattice woodwork. A full-service campground, which is open from June through Labor Day weekend, is located directly behind the building. The campground has approximately twenty full RV hookups and coin-operated laundry and shower facilities.

Ramsey Rink established the business in August, 1976. Ramsey named the place after Firebrand Pass, which can be seen in the mountain range to the west of the building. In 1910, fire swept over the pass from the west, igniting several blazes on the east slopes. The resulting "fire brands" on the mountains inspired the name Firebrand Pass. The atmosphere at Ramsey's Firebrand Food and Ale is relaxed and family-oriented. Dinners are served from 4:00 p.m. until 10:00 p.m. daily. The menu features steaks, sandwiches, and a limited number of seafood entrees. Daily dinner specials are offered, and a great steak sandwich is available any time. Private parties for up to thirty people can be held at the restaurant, and take out food orders are available.

During the winter months, the majority of the customers are residents of East Glacier and the surrounding communities. During the summer, however, you will find a lot of tourists in the bar and restaurant. The building is located between Glacier National Park and the Lewis and Clark National Forest, just west of the Blackfoot Indian Reservation and seven miles east of the continental divide. Needless to say, some spectacular scenery surrounds the area. Besides the spectacular view, the ample beer selection and extensive wine list draw people to Ramsey's. They have over fifty brands of beers available, approximately thirty-five of which are either imports or microbrews. With this selection, you're bound to find at least one beer you like.

TRAILHEAD SALOON

OWNER: Marie Robertson

HOURS: 2:00 p.m. to 2:00 a.m. Daily

HAPPY HOUR: 5:00 to 7:00 Mon - Fri

GAMBLING: No

LIVE MUSIC: No

LOCATION: Highway 2, **East Glacier**

PHONE: 406-226-4497

BEER: Drafts; Domestics; Imports

AMUSEMENT: Pool

FOOD: Frozen Pizza; Sandwiches

The Trailhead Saloon is on the south side of Highway 2 in East Glacier. Of all the bars in and around this tourist-oriented community, the Trailhead most resembles what you might think a small town tavern in Montana would be like. The interior walls are covered with wood, in one form or another. A straight bar runs along the east wall, four small tables rest against the west wall, and an empty piano bar stands toward the back of the room. A piano once stood inside the curved piano bar, and customers commonly gathered around the bar making requests and singing along to the music. The piano was removed several years ago, but the curved bar that surrounded it was left behind.

The business was established as the Tepee Bar in 1954. The name was changed to the Park Bar in 1956. The building that presently houses the bar was home to the Palomino Bar from 1955 until 1974. The Park Bar operated out of the building next door during that time. After the Palomino moved out, the wall between the Park Bar and the old Palomino was knocked out. The vacant floor space was used as a dance hall for several years, but the wall was reconstructed in the mid 1980s. I really don't know how it happened, but the barroom ended up on the west side of the wall, which is the opposite side it started out on.

Marie Robertson has owned the business since 1992, and although the saloon stands in the shadow of Glacier National Park, Marie caters more to local residents than tourists. That's not to say tourists aren't welcome at the Trailhead Saloon, because they certainly are. In fact, tourists often comment that the friendly, relaxed environment at the Trailhead Saloon is a welcome change from the high priced, stuffy atmosphere they're accustomed to in barrooms at the resort hotels. As a show of customer appreciation, Marie hosts a barbecue at the Trailhead Saloon every September. The rest of the year she pretty much runs a steady business. Marie doesn't have a lot of rules, but I'm told she charges a 6% bed tax if you fall asleep in the barroom. I highly recommend you visit the Trailhead Saloon, but don't stay too long if you're tired.

KIP'S BEER GARDEN

OWNER: Kip Flammond

HOURS: 4:00 p.m. to Closing Daily
Winter Hours Vary

HAPPY HOUR: No

GAMBLING: No

LIVE MUSIC: DJ Weekly During Summer

LOCATION: Highway 89, **St. Mary**

PHONE: 406-732-9237

BEER: Drafts; Domestics

AMUSEMENT: Pool; Foosball; Video Games

FOOD: Summer Months Only

Kip's Beer Garden is housed in a log building on the west side of Highway 287 in St. Mary. Kip Flammond, who owns the business, spent endless hours cutting the logs and planks used to build the structure and did most of the construction work on his own. Kip initially planned on operating an automobile repair shop out of the building, but his friends convinced him to open a bar instead. Kip's Beer Garden opened in 1972, and the rest, as they say, is history. The moderate-sized barroom has a relatively small wooden bar. The primitive barstools are actually just tree stumps that were placed in front of the bar. Eight wooden picnic tables are spread across the floor, so you don't have to stand if you can't find an unoccupied stump at the bar. The wooden chandeliers suspended from the ceiling are fashioned from authentic wagon wheels that were left behind by settlers who passed through the region during the 1800s. Kip gathered the wagon wheels from the nearby plains in the 1950s, and he made light fixtures out of them when he built the bar.

Kip's is a friendly place where local residents, tourists, and seasonal workers in and around Glacier National Park commonly gather. During the summer, Kip's is a very busy place. A live DJ plays music in the outdoor beer garden once a week, and hot meals are served from the bar on a daily basis. Business is sparse during the winter, however, and the hours of operation vary. Kip may close the bar completely during some winters, depending on whether he can find reliable help to run the place. If you're in need of camping facilities, Kip's just may be what you're looking for. A large campground, complete with twenty full RV hookup spaces and shower facilities, is located just behind the bar.

When you visit Kip's Beer Garden, you may notice some rather large rocks between the parking lot and the building. Aside from their aesthetic value, the rocks have a practical purpose. Kip once had a problem with people driving their vehicles into the front of the building, so he carefully placed the rocks at the end of the parking lot to prevent further damage. Thus far, the rocks have done their job.

COZY CORNER BAR AND CAFE

OWNERS: Miller, Esther, & Terry Boe

LOCATION: Junction of Highway 12 & Route 3, **Lavina**

HOURS: 8:00 a.m. to Closing Daily

PHONE: 406-636-2261

HAPPY HOUR: 6:00 to 7:00 Daily

BEER: Drafts; Domestics

GAMBLING: Video Poker; Shake-A-Day

AMUSEMENT: Pool; Darts; Foosball; Pinball; Video Games

LIVE MUSIC: Occasionally

FOOD: Full Menu Grill

The Cozy Corner Bar and Cafe is at the junction of Highway 12 and Route 3 in Lavina. If you possess a road map and an automobile, you should have no problem whatsoever finding the place. The huge barroom is adjoined by a smaller game room with plenty of video games and such for the kids. The barroom has a long bar facing the south wall, several tables spread throughout the room, and a wooden dance floor with an elevated bandstand in the east side. An immaculate stone fireplace rises from the floor against the north wall of the barroom.

The history of the bar dates back to 1948. A motel was housed in the building at that time, and a small barroom was added to the business. The motel eventually went out of business, so the lodging rooms were renovated into a dance hall. The bar continued operating out of the small room where the kitchen now resides until 1975. The change created a very spacious barroom without substantially reducing the size of the dance hall.

Miller and Esther Boe have owned the Cozy Corner since 1989. They had previously owned the business in the early 1970s, but they took a break for several years before reacquiring the bar. Their son, Terry, now manages the business. There were two bars in Lavina up until 1993. From what I've been told, there were some real characters and some wild times at the other bar, but the Cozy Corner has always been more of a family oriented place. Residents of Lavina and the surrounding farming and ranching communities provide most of the business, but passing motorists also stop by occasionally.

Like many small town taverns in Montana, the Cozy Corner serves as the community center for Lavina. You never know when a crowd might gather, but the weather plays a big role in how busy the place gets because of the agriculture-based economy. If it's too wet in the summer, there will likely be some folks at the bar. The winter weather also dictates business, with snow being the major factor in determining the traveling conditions.

FLECK'S BAR

OWNER: Mildred Fleck

HOURS: 8:00 a.m. to 2:00 a.m. Daily

HAPPY HOUR: 5:30 to 6:30 Daily

GAMBLING: Video Poker/Keno

LIVE MUSIC: Occasionally

LOCATION: 103 1st St. N., **Ryegate**

PHONE: 406-568-2521

BEER: Drafts; Domestics

AMUSEMENT: Pool; Darts; Pinball; Video Games

FOOD: Frozen Pizza; Snacks

Fleck's Bar is on First Street in Ryegate, just one building north of Highway 12. The moderate-sized barroom has a straight bar facing the south wall, and a game room resides in the north side of the building. There's nothing elaborate about the place, but it's kept very clean and well maintained. Fleck's Bar is one place where you never have to worry about encountering unsanitary conditions.

The business was established as Frank's Variety in 1949, but Bill and Mildred Fleck changed the name when they bought the bar in 1950. The couple had owned a bar in Wilsall for fifteen years prior to moving to Ryegate, and they also produced and sold bootlegged booze during prohibition. Millie says she was responsible for brewing the beer, but alcohol has never passed her lips. Smoking is a different story, however, because Millie has been trying to kick the habit for several years. Bill is gone now, but Millie can tell you all about her sixty plus years in the bar business and her stint as a moonshiner. The only catch is you have to arrive at the bar early to talk with Millie, because she has usually already been there and gone by 10:00 a.m.

Mildred was born in 1903. She has lost two of her four children; a son to a heart attack and a daughter to cancer. Peggy Wilson and Billie Zeier are still living. In spite of her age, Millie still takes an active role in the business. She promotes a friendly atmosphere at the bar, and people of all ages are welcome. You will usually find a local crowd on hand, but visiting hunters stop by during the fall, and travelers along Highway 12 occasionally stop in to take a break from driving.

A rather interesting discovery was made under the north side of the building in 1991. During an excavation project that was being performed to replace a broken sewer line, bones in the shape of a human skeleton were unearthed. A forensics team was called to the scene, and they were eventually able to verify the bones were the partial remains from a human body. Nobody knows who the man was or how long he had been buried there, but the bones were removed and the excavation continued.

RYEGATE BAR AND CAFE

OWNERS: Thane and Rhonda Russell & Eddie and Mary Lu Sorensen

LOCATION: 101 1st St. N., **Ryegate**

HOURS: 8:30 a.m. to 2:00 a.m. Daily

PHONE: 406-568-2330

HAPPY HOUR: 6:00 to 7:00 Daily

BEER: Drafts; Domestics

GAMBLING: Video Poker/Keno

AMUSEMENT: Pool; Pinball

LIVE MUSIC: Occasionally

FOOD: Full Menu Grill

The Ryegate Bar and Cafe is on the corner of Highway 12 and First Street in Ryegate. The barroom has an L-shaped wooden bar and an antique wooden back bar facing the east wall, several tables spread throughout the room, and a hardwood dance floor in the northwest corner. Although I'm certain there's some history to the back bar, nobody I spoke with knew where it came from or how long it's been in the building.

The Ryegate Bar and Cafe is housed in one of the oldest structures in town. A mercantile store originally operated out of the building, but the Idle Hour Bar took over occupancy in 1933. The Idle Hour Bar became the Ryegate Bar in 1942. Thane and Rhonda Russell and Eddie and Mary Lu Sorensen were in the process of taking over the business when I last visited Ryegate in December, 1996. The old Ryegate Cafe will be operated out of the building along with the bar, so the name of the business was changed to the Ryegate Bar and Cafe. Meals are served from 6:00 a.m. until 10:00 p.m. daily. Homemade soups and pies are featured, and daily lunch specials are always available.

The Ryegate Bar and Cafe hosts a cribbage tournament each year after calving season ends. It's quite an affair, lasting about six weeks until all but one contestant is eliminated. The big event of the year, however, is the annual Testi-Fest that's held during the second weekend in June. The first Rocky Mountain Oyster Feed was held in 1983, and the event gets bigger each year. In 1995 alone, 350 pounds of bull balls were shipped in, and local ranchers donated a bunch more to feed the 300 or so people who showed up for the event. It's an all-day affair, with the food preparation taking most of the morning and afternoon. Besides the testicles, several gallons of baked beans are prepared, a beef roast is served, side dishes are brought in by local residents, and many other barbecued foods are available. The event has gotten to the point where people from out of state now plan their vacations just so they can be in Ryegate for the festivities. The souvenir T-shirts on sale in the barroom will give you some idea about the popularity of Ryegate's annual Testi-Fest.

CHALET BEARMOUTH

OWNERS: Bob, Linda, & Justin Moser

LOCATION: Exit 138, **Bearmouth**

HOURS: 8:00 a.m. to Closing Daily

PHONE: 406-825-9950

HAPPY HOUR: No

BEER: Drafts; Domestics; Imports; Microbrews

GAMBLING: Video Poker/Keno; Shake-A-Day

AMUSEMENT: Pool; Video Games; Horseshoes; Volleyball

LIVE MUSIC: No

FOOD: Full Menu Restaurant

The Chalet Bearmouth is just east of the Bearmouth Interchange (exit 138) on Interstate 90. The bar and restaurant are housed in the third floor of a four story building. Public laundry and shower facilities, a banquet room, motel, sleeping rooms, and a private residence are also in the building, and a campground with forty-five full RV hookups is part of the business. The barroom has an L-shaped bar, several tables, and a nice stone fireplace on the east wall. If you prefer the great outdoors, there's a covered wooden deck off the south side of the barroom.

The business was established sometime in the early 1970s, but nobody I spoke with knew the exact date. Nothing of great historical significance has ever occurred at the chalet, unless you consider the building being haunted as historically significant. As the story goes, a former owner of the business died in the gift shop several years ago, and since his passing, some people claim the man's spirit now inhabits the building. Strange noises, shutters opening and closing for no apparent reason, and water valves mysteriously opening and closing have all been attributed to George the Ghost. George doesn't appear to mean any harm; he just turns mischievous from time to time to keep people on their toes. Apparently, George's spirit isn't quite ready to go to wherever it is that spirits are supposed to go.

Bob, Linda, and Justin Moser have owned the Chalet Bearmouth since August, 1995. They operate friendly establishment where local residents, travelers, and visiting sportsmen gather to relax and unwind. Breakfast, lunch, and dinner are served seven days a week. All the food is good, and the ribeye steaks are the house specialty. The Chalet Bearmouth is a favorite stop for truckers because they can park their rigs overnight and get a free shower and free coffee. A large campground is also available, and the chalet is only fourteen miles from Garnet, Montana's most intact ghost town. Perhaps Garnet is where George spends his time when he's not getting into mischief at the chalet.

CANYON BAR

OWNER: Bruce King

HOURS: Noon to 2:00 a.m. Daily

HAPPY HOUR: 5:00 to 6:00 Mon - Fri

GAMBLING: Video Poker/Keno; Shake-A-Day

LIVE MUSIC: No

LOCATION: 160 E. Front, **Drummond**

PHONE: 406-288-3306

BEER: Drafts; Domestics

AMUSEMENT: Pool

FOOD: Frozen Pizza; Bar Snacks

The Canyon Bar is at 160 East Front Street in Drummond. The building has a wooden front, and several columns of glass brick on the south and east sides let some daylight pass through the walls. The moderate-sized barroom has a long wooden bar, two small tables, and plenty of open floor space. Several collectors series porcelain figurines, most of which are buffalo figures, line the top of the wooden back bar against the west wall. The mounted buffalo head on the barroom wall has been given the official title of Mortimor Charles Alexander IV, but most people simply refer to the beast as either Buford or Buffy.

The bar first opened in the late 1920s. An old store building was moved to Drummond from the nearby community of Old Chicago and renovated into a tavern. The Turf Bar was the name of the business when the first retail beer license was issued in 1934. The name was changed to the Canyon Bar when the bar moved to its present location in 1949. Some years later, an addition was built onto the north side of the building and the barroom expanded. There haven't been many famous people at the Canyon Bar, but I'm told Spike Popish was once a part time bartender here while he was the Deputy Sheriff of Granite County. You may recall Spike was the last person to arrest a man who was hanged in Montana.

Bruce King has owned the Canyon Bar since November, 1996. Bruce keeps a supply of home-grown and packaged hot peppers on hand, and he provides complimentary samples to his customers. You're welcome to eat as many peppers as you want, but few people can handle more than one. Bruce has also implemented a *Feed The Moose* campaign. Customers donate funds to a rather hideous looking porcelain moose bank behind the bar, and when the moose burps (the bank is full of money), the funds are used for a party. The bar is open 365 days a year. In fact, Christmas is always one of the busiest days of the year at the Canyon Bar. The barroom also gets packed during Drummond's Mule Days Celebration on the first weekend of June, the Drummond Rodeo on the weekend after the Fourth of July, and the annual barbecue that's held at the bar on the first Saturday in August.

PALACE SALOON AND CAFE

OWNERS: Denise and Mark Clark

HOURS: 5:00 p.m. to 2:00 a.m. Daily

HAPPY HOUR: No

GAMBLING: Video Poker/Keno

LIVE MUSIC: No

LOCATION: E. Front St., **Drummond**

PHONE: 406-288-9980

BEER: Drafts; Domestics; Microbrews

AMUSEMENT: Pool; Video Games

FOOD: Full Menu Cafe; Pizza

The Palace Saloon and Cafe is housed in a two story brick structure on East Front Street in Drummond. The barroom resides in the middle of the building, flanked on the west by a cafe and on the east by a game room. A straight wooden bar and a beautiful oak back bar stand along the east wall of the barroom, and plenty of tables are available for additional seating. The hand-crafted back bar has beveled mirrors in the shape of diamonds at each end and a large rectangular mirror in the middle. The back bar was built in the late 1800s. It resided in a hotel in White Sulfur Springs before being moved to the Palace Saloon in 1972.

The Palace Hotel was built in 1911; however, a saloon didn't become part of the business until 1972. The Drummond Bank originally operated out of the west side of the building, a pharmacy and soda fountain were in the middle, and a restaurant, barber shop, and the hotel lobby were housed in the east side. The hotel has been closed since 1956, but the original hotel counter still stands in the old lobby. The twenty-two hotel rooms in the second story are currently being restored. Plans are in place to gradually reopen the hotel as the restoration project continues.

Denise and Mark Clark bought the Palace Saloon and Cafe in 1992. Denise and Mark run a family-owned, family-operated business, and they cater to people of all ages from all parts of the world. Out of town business is always welcomed at the Palace Saloon and Cafe. A lot of people have come in as strangers, but few have left that way. Denise and Mark pride themselves on the friendly service, good food, and family-oriented atmosphere at the Palace Saloon and Cafe. Although the barroom doesn't open until 5:00 p.m., the cafe serves from 3:00 p.m. until 2:00 a.m. Sunday through Thursday and 3:00 p.m. until 3:00 a.m. on Friday and Saturday. Fresh pizza, hot hoagies, breadsticks, and salads can be ordered to eat in or take out, and the food is excellent. Whether you're in the barroom or the cafe, you will always find friendly, courteous people who take a personal interest in you. This type of treatment is the trademark of Drummond's Palace Saloon and Cafe.

SWEDE'S BAR AND CASINO

OWNERS: Craig and Joann Farley

LOCATION: 11 A Street, **Drummond**

HOURS: 8:00 a.m. to Closing Daily

PHONE: 406-288-3652

HAPPY HOUR: 6:00 to 7:00 Mon - Fri

BEER: Drafts; Domestics

GAMBLING: Video Poker/Keno; Live Poker

AMUSEMENT: Pool

LIVE MUSIC: No

FOOD: Grill Items; Broasted Chicken

Swede's Bar and Casino is at 11 A Street in Drummond. The barroom was finished in a 1950s and 1960s-style decor when I last visited Swede's in December, 1996; however, the entire facility was about to receive a major facelift. The pastel formica and worn paint will probably be covered with rustic woodwork by the time you read this. The structure is made almost entirely of brick and mortar, but glass brick windows let some sunlight pass through to the barroom during the daylight hours. Seating is pretty much limited to the fifteen or so stools at the bar, but a padded booth is available if all the barstools are occupied. There's also plenty of open floor space if you don't mind standing.

Swede's Bar was established just after prohibition ended in 1933. A grocery store and clothing store had operated out of the entire building prior to that time. Both stores moved into the north end of the building to make room for the bar after the infamous prohibition amendment was repealed. The stores were vacated after World War II ended, and Swede's Bar expanded into the rest of the building. The two large murals on the south wall of the barroom were painted in 1953. I'm told Swede paid the artist $120.00 when the murals were finished, but the man spent every cent of his earnings drinking in the barroom that very same day. Talk about reinvesting your earnings!

Craig and Joann Farley bought Swede's Bar and Casino on December 17, 1996. They basically operate the business as a neighborhood bar, but tourists and visiting hunters occasionally stop in during the summer and fall. Swede's is a very popular place during the annual Drummond Rodeo in July. Local rodeo cowboys hang out at Swede's throughout the year, and a lot of the circuit riders stop by when they're in town. If you arrive at the bar with an appetite, the grill is open all day long. For people who don't care for fried food, the broasted chicken comes highly recommended. Swede's has a live poker game every Friday night. If you like to gamble but don't care for noisy video gambling machines, you might want to stop in and try your luck at the table.

GEORGETOWN LAKE LODGE

OWNERS: Felix and Tillie Dauenhauer

HOURS: 8:00 a.m. to 2:00 a.m. Daily

HAPPY HOUR: No

GAMBLING: Video Poker/Keno; Live Poker

LIVE MUSIC: Occasionally

LOCATION: Denton's Point Road, Georgetown Lake

PHONE: 406-563-7020

BEER: Drafts; Domestics; Microbrews

AMUSEMENT: Pool; Darts; Video Games

FOOD: Full Menu Restaurant

The Georgetown Lake Lodge is two miles off Route 1 on the Denton's Point Road at Georgetown Lake. The beautiful lodge is a 20,000 square foot peeled log structure with high vaulted ceilings supported by log posts and beams. A spacious barroom and dining room are just inside the main entrance. A huge banquet room resides in the center of the building, and eleven motel rooms are housed in the opposite side. A wooden deck spans the entire length of the front side of the lodge, providing a breathtaking view of Georgetown Lake and the surrounding mountains. Several mounted big game animals are on display throughout the building, including a full mount bighorn ram that gazes over the barroom from his lookout on the huge stone fireplace near the front entrance.

The history of the Georgetown Lake Lodge dates back to the 1940s when Ray Denton built a tackle shop, restaurant, and bar called Denton's Point. Denton's Point enjoyed many successful years of operation, but the building was destroyed by fire in the fall of 1982. Felix and Tillie Dauenhauer owned Denton's Point at that time, and they started planning for a new building soon after the smoke cleared. The new lodge was built completely with natural logs, and the lobby counter from the old Marcus Daly Hotel in Anaconda was obtained and made into the new bar. After a few final touches were added to the building, the new Georgetown Lake Lodge opened on the site of the old Denton's Point business. Felix and Tillie continue to operate the lodge as a family-owned business.

The Georgetown Lake Lodge is open year round. Since the area has such an abundance of recreational opportunities, Felix and Tillie cater to outdoors enthusiasts. A campground, marina, and gasoline are available at the lodge, and a complete breakfast, lunch, and dinner menu is offered. If you're looking for a special meal, try the prime rib. The Georgetown Lake Lodge is also a very popular place for holiday parties, banquets, wedding ceremonies and receptions, and other private parties. The banquet room can seat up to 200 people, so space is rarely a problem.

STOCKMAN'S BAR

OWNER: Sheila Keirnes

HOURS: 1:00 p.m. to Closing Daily

HAPPY HOUR: No

GAMBLING: Video Poker

LIVE MUSIC: Occasionally

LOCATION: Hall

PHONE: 406-288-3842

BEER: Domestics

AMUSEMENT: Pool

FOOD: Frozen Pizza

The Stockman's Bar is housed in a wooden structure just west of Route 1 in Hall. The front portion of the barroom has a straight wooden bar facing the east wall and a couple of small tables spread across the floor. A hardwood dance floor and a brick fireplace with a wood burning insert are in the back of the room. The barstools have been creatively constructed with 2 x 2 wooden slats. The design may be uncommon, but the stools are very sturdy and quite functional. The barroom walls are covered with tongue-and-groove boards, and the wall decorations primarily consist of beer signs, porcelain liquor decanters, a few antiques, antlers, and a mounted cow's head with a cigarette hanging out of its mouth.

I wasn't able to find out exactly when the business was established, but the people I spoke with believe it was sometime during the 1930s—probably soon after prohibition ended. The building has housed several different business over the years. It was a grainery during the early 1900s, and a creamery operated out of the building for a few years prior to the bar moving in. A barber shop was actually part of the barroom for several years, and the local telephone operator's office was in the building alongside the bar when they first got telephones in Hall. The other businesses have all moved out, but the Stockman's Bar is still going strong.

Sheila Keirnes has owned the Stockman Bar since 1978. The building is just off Route 1, a designated scenic route, but Sheila says tourists rarely stop in. Since Sheila relies almost exclusively on local trade to keep the place going, she has to control her overhead costs by maintaining a limited supply of beer and liquor. Along with the local customers, you'll usually find some local critters inside the building. Sheila's cat and dog spend a lot of time in the barroom, and some of the customers are often accompanied by their pets. Everyone, including the customers, are friendly and well-behaved, so you don't have to worry about problems starting. The Stockman's Bar is a very friendly establishment that caters to the needs of the local community, and that's what makes small taverns in Montana so special.

VFW POST 8292

MANAGER: Bob Bowers

HOURS: 11:00 a.m. to Closing Daily

HAPPY HOUR: No

GAMBLING: Video Poker/Keno; Shake-A-Day

LIVE MUSIC: Occasionally

LOCATION: Maxville Road, **Maxville**

PHONE: 406-859-3657

BEER: Drafts; Domestics

AMUSEMENT: Pool

FOOD: Frozen Pizza

The Veterans of Foreign Wars Post 8292 is at 14 Maxville Road in Maxville. This particular VFW is open to the general public, so you don't have to be a member to get served. The building houses a fairly spacious barroom with an L-shaped bar, several tables, and plenty of open floor space. A lone wood burning stove stands near the back of the room, providing heat for the building during the cold weather months. The barroom has recently undergone extensive renovations, so everything is very modern and well-maintained.

The VFW Post 8292 was established in 1992. Prior to that, the community of Maxville had been without a liquor license for nearly 20 years. The Silver Slipper Bar was Maxville's original saloon. I'm told there were some real characters and some very interesting moments at the old Silver Slipper, but the bar was destroyed by fire in the early 1970s. The liquor license was sold to the Chalet Bearmouth, so the residents of Maxville had to leave town to drink until the Boulder Creek Saloon was built in 1990. The Boulder Creek Saloon only had a beer and wine license, but it was better than nothing. In 1992, some local residents got together and decided to establish a VFW Post. A veterans organization liquor license was obtained from the State, and the VFW Post 8292 opened in the Boulder Creek Saloon Building. The good folks of Maxville have been enjoying the benefits of a full liquor license ever since.

At the time this book went to press, Bob Bowers was the manager of the bar. There are approximately twenty-five full time members of Post 8292, but they encourage non-members to come in and join them for a drink. The VFW has become the social center of Maxville. Videos are available for rent, and paperback books are loaned out to people in the community. Frozen pizza, soups, and sandwiches are the only food items served directly from the bar; however, you can order a hot meal from the restaurant next door. They will gladly hand-deliver your meal to the barroom, if you prefer. The food is excellent, and it's a great way to maintain a friendly relationship with the business next door.

D & L BAR

OWNER: Glen Eizoo Terry

HOURS: 3:00 p.m. to 2:00 a.m. Mon-Tues
10:00 a.m. to 2:00 a.m. Wed-Sun

HAPPY HOUR: 6:00 to 7:30 Daily

GAMBLING: Video Poker/Keno

LIVE MUSIC: Every Other Weekend

LOCATION: Highway 87, **Box Elder**

PHONE: 406-352-4440

BEER: Drafts; Domestics

AMUSEMENT: Pool; Rodeo

FOOD: Microwave Sandwiches;
Frozen Pizza

The D & L Bar is housed in a steel-sided structure at the south end of Box Elder on Highway 87. The moderate-sized barroom has a straight bar facing the north wall, and about ten tables are spread throughout the room. An elevated beer garden, which doubles as a bandstand, and a rodeo arena occupy a small parcel of the thirty acres surrounding the building.

The business was established as the Pastime Beer Parlor in 1934. The name was changed to Johnson's Bar in 1958, and over the next eleven years, the place became notorious for fights and underage drinking. It was during this tenure when one of the bartenders fatally shot a man who was a passenger in a vehicle leaving the parking lot. Campbell's Bar was the name of the business when the bar moved to its present location in 1975. The bar's troubled past seemed to follow, because the bar owner's son committed suicide in the new building. The business became the D & L Bar in 1984, and it's operated under that name ever since.

Glen Eizoo Terry bought the D & L Bar in January, 1996. Eizoo is very familiar with the bar's dismal reputation, and he can even show you a couple of bullet holes in the building as evidence of the bar's wild past. Since taking over the business, Eizoo has taken positive steps to cut down on the violent behavior. He doesn't mind if you jump up on a table and start dancing and screaming, but fighting in the bar will get you 86'd in a hurry. Things have settled down considerably, but the D & L Bar still doesn't serve drinks from glass containers because of the potential for someone breaking the glass and using it as a weapon.

Eizoo says about 75% of his business comes from Native Americans from the neighboring Rocky Boy's Reservation. The bar gets very busy on Friday and Saturday nights, especially on dance nights when the happy hour runs from 8:00 to 9:00. As additional entertainment, Eizoo started holding live rodeos at the bar twice a year. Since the arena is already in place, you will be able to bring your horse and go out back for a little calf roping any time you want. If rodeo isn't your thing, the D&L Bar hosts a pool tournament every Sunday. It's $5.00 a stick and 100% payout.

129

LONE TREE BAR

OWNERS: Kevin and Maria Kuhn	**LOCATION:** Route 448, **Box Elder**
HOURS: 8:00 a.m. to 2:00 a.m. Tues-Sun Closed Mondays	**PHONE:** 406-352-3112
HAPPY HOUR: 4:30 to 6:00 Daily	**BEER:** Domestics
GAMBLING: Video Poker/Keno	**AMUSEMENT:** Pool; Video Game
LIVE MUSIC: Approximately Monthly	**FOOD:** Microwave Sandwiches

The Lone Tree Bar is one block west of Highway 87 on Route 448 in Box Elder. Although the exterior of the building could use some work, the interior is very modern. The barroom has a relatively small bar in the southwest corner, and several tables are spread throughout in the middle of the room. A huge tree trunk in the middle of the barroom floor provides support for the ceiling. It's from this tree that the bar got its name, the Lone Tree.

The bar's history dates back to 1911 when the Bear Paw Hotel first opened. Perry's Bear Paw Bar occupied a small portion of the hotel lobby. The hotel closed in the late 1950's, but the bar continued to operate from the first floor of the building. Kevin and Maria Kuhn bought the business in 1990, but they didn't reopen the bar until extensive renovations were completed in October, 1992. Maria tells me the only things in the barroom today that were there prior to the renovations are the wood trim on the walls, the cooler doors, the bar, and the back bar. The barroom now occupies the entire ground-level floor of the structure.

The majority of the customers at the Lone Tree Bar are residents of Box Elder and the neighboring Rocky Boy's Indian Reservation. Among the many interesting people you might meet at the bar is Vernon LaBoy, a very talented local artist. The Lone Tree is a relatively peaceful place now, but things weren't always that way. When Maria and Kevin first opened, some of the customers tested the new owners to see what they could get away with. The numerous bullet holes in the barroom ceiling are examples of the sort of things people did during the first few months to gauge the new proprietors. Things quickly settled down, because Maria and Kevin now have bouncers to respond to unruly behavior. Customers who get out of line these days have to answer to the Friede brothers, also known as the Gentle Giants of the Lone Tree Bar. Things have improved significantly, but Kevin and Maria still don't serve drinks in glass containers. There's an on-going worry that someone might break the glass and use it as a weapon. In due time, that too might change.

BLACKIE'S FRESNO TAVERN

OWNER: Blackie Preeshl

HOURS: 11:00 a.m. to Closing Summer
2:00 p.m. to Closing Winter

HAPPY HOUR: No

GAMBLING: Video Poker

LIVE MUSIC: Occasionally

LOCATION: Highway 2, **Fresno**

PHONE: 406-265-9950

BEER: Domestics

AMUSEMENT: Pool; Darts; Foosball;
Video Games

FOOD: Microwave Sandwiches

Blackie's Fresno Tavern is on the south side of Highway 2 in Fresno. The spacious barroom has a long bar facing the north wall, several tables spread throughout the room, and plenty of open floor space. A fairly extensive hat collection hangs from the ceiling behind the bar. The collection started several years ago when a customer decided to donate his cap to the bar. The idea quickly caught on, and the hats began piling up so fast that Blackie didn't know what to do with them all. She eventually tacked them to the ceiling behind the bar to put them on display.

The Fresno Tavern was established in 1946. The building originally stood approximately 1-1/2 miles west of its present location, but the structure was moved in 1953. The east side of the existing building is actually an addition that was built in the 1960s. Blackie Preeshl has owned the business since 1989. She operates a very friendly establishment, and people of all ages are welcome at the bar. The bar is only two miles from Fresno Reservoir, so boaters and fishermen from all over the world stop by. A lot of Hi-Liners traveling to and from Havre also visit Blackie throughout the year.

If you're in the barroom and all of a sudden see Blackie run for the neon sign at the end of the bar, be prepared to hear a loud train whistle. Blackie has become known among railroad workers from Chicago to Seattle as the person who blinks the neon sign on and off as trains pass by. The train engineers always sound their horns to return the hello gesture. Blackie is also well known among the state's top Walleye fishermen. The Montana Walleyes Unlimited organization holds a fishing tournament at Fresno Lake each year in June, and the bar hosts the rules meeting and a barbecue for the participants. Other parties such as a Super Bowl bash, wedding receptions, and birthday parties are held at the Fresno Tavern throughout the year. If you're looking for a unique gift item for that special person in your life, be sure to pick up a can of Blackie's World Famous Walleye Assholes packed in pure fish gut sauce. They make a great gift for the person who has everything.

GILDFORD BAR

OWNER: Kim Hickman

LOCATION: Main Street, **Gildford**

HOURS: 11:00 a.m. to Closing Daily

PHONE: 406-376-3271

HAPPY HOUR: 5:00 to 6:00 Mon - Fri

BEER: Domestics; Microbrews

GAMBLING: Video Poker

AMUSEMENT: Pool; Darts; Video Game

LIVE MUSIC: Occasionally

FOOD: Grill Items; Deep Fried Foods; Sandwiches

The Gildford Bar is on the corner of Route 449 and Main Street in Gildford. The wooden structure houses a fairly long and narrow barroom. A straight bar runs north and south through the front part of the building, and a game room is in the rear. I'm told the two smaller rooms behind the bar were originally shipping crates that were used to transport heavy equipment. The crates were so sturdy and big that they were attached to the building to make more floor space. The crates have served well over the years, and they now house the kitchen.

The history of the business dates back to 1934 when the Hi-Line Service Station obtained a retail beer license. The business operated under several different names over the years, including Flynn's Tavern, the B&B Tavern, Nordrum's No-No, the Triangle Bar, Hennessy's, the Triple T Bar, and Kelly's Pub. Although you can't see them from the barroom, there are several bullet holes in the wall behind the bar. As the story was told to me, a man who owned the business for a number of years during the 1940's had a large picture of ducks hanging from the wall behind the bar. The picture apparently bothered the guy, because one day without warning, he pulled out a pistol and shot the hell out of the ducks. The bullet holes have been covered with paneling on the bar side of the wall; however, you can still see the holes near the ceiling if you look at the wall from the kitchen side.

Kim Hickman bought what was Kelly's Pub in 1996 and changed the name to the Gildford Bar. I'm not sure what changes will be made, but the last I heard, an addition was scheduled to be built onto the north side of the building in the spring of 1997. It's not likely you will see someone shooting at a picture on the wall when you visit the Gildford Bar, but there's always enough going on that you won't get bored. The customers are a friendly bunch who go out of their way to make strangers feel welcome. If you arrive with an appetite, excellent food is served at reasonable prices. Even if you're not hungry, the Gildford Bar is a great place to visit and meet new friends.

132

HI-WAY BAR

OWNERS: Ross and Terri Alsup

HOURS: 7:00 a.m. to 2:00 a.m. Daily

HAPPY HOUR: 5:00 to 6:00 Mon - Fri

GAMBLING: Video Poker/Keno; Live Poker

LIVE MUSIC: Occasionally

LOCATION: Highway 2, **Hingham**

PHONE: 406-397-3266

BEER: Drafts; Domestics; Imports

AMUSEMENT: Darts; Foosball

FOOD: Full Menu Cafe

The Hi-Way Bar is on the south side of Highway 2 in Hingham. The bar is actually part of a larger business consisting of a grocery store, cafe, gas station, campground with RV hookups, a laundromat, car wash, and the bar. The barroom resides the west side of the building, and the grocery store is in the east side. A long bar faces the south wall of the barroom, and a couple of tables are available for additional seating. The cafe dining area is also in the barroom, just east of the bar.

The Hi-Way Bar was established in 1946. A service station and tourist court known as the White Eagle Cabins had been in operation on the property for several years prior to the bar opening. Numerous changes and improvements have been completed on the property and the building over the years, so the facilities are all very modern.

Ross and Terri Alsup bought the Hi-Way Bar in June, 1993. They run the business as a family-owned, family-operated establishment. The regular customers are local residents of Hingham and the surrounding communities. During the summer months, a lot of tourists stop by to eat, drink, camp, and stock up on supplies. A surprisingly high number of people touring the country on bicycles also visit the bar and grocery store during the warmer months, and custom cutters who come to the area during harvest season provide a boost to the business in the fall. Overall, you can expect to find a fairly quiet, friendly crowd at the Hi-Way Bar.

The Hi-Way Bar sponsors dart teams in the local league, and they occasionally host dart tournaments. The bar also serves as the local coffee house where people gather in the mornings for their daily dose of caffeine. The cafe offers daily lunch specials throughout the week, and great dinner values are available during Monday Night Football broadcasts. When available, the prime rib at the Hi-Way Bar is excellent, and the hamburgers are always good. Aside from the food, the Highway Bar is one of the few places in the area that sells Montana, Tri-West, and Powerball lottery tickets. When you consider all the other products and services available, you truly do have one stop shopping.

INVERNESS HOTEL BAR

OWNER: Dalton Dahlke

LOCATION: Main Street, **Inverness**

HOURS: 9:00 a.m. to Closing Daily

PHONE: 406-292-3801

HAPPY HOUR: 5:30 to 6:30 Mon - Fri

BEER: Drafts; Domestics

GAMBLING: Video Poker/Keno

AMUSEMENT: Darts; Foosball; Video Game

LIVE MUSIC: No

FOOD: Full Menu Supper Club

The Inverness Hotel Bar is housed in a two story structure at the north end of Main Street in Inverness. The barroom resides in the south side of the ground-level floor, and a dining room is in the north side. An L-shaped bar faces the south wall of the barroom, and a couple of tables are spread throughout the room. If things get too crowded in either the barroom or the dining room, overflow seating (or standing) is available in the room immediately to the south of the main barroom.

The Inverness Hotel was built in 1907, but the bar wasn't added until prohibition ended. The room to the south of the main barroom was originally a pharmacy in the adjoining building. Somewhere along the line, the wall was removed, and the old pharmacy became the hotel dance hall. Since they don't have dances anymore, the room has evolved into an overflow seating area. There were sixteen sleeping rooms and three bathrooms on the second floor of the building at one time, but the hotel portion of the business closed in 1975.

There have only been two owners of the Inverness Hotel Bar since it first opened. Dalton Dahlke bought the business from the original owner in 1961, and he continues to operate it today. Dalton and his wife still live in the building, and they use the old hotel rooms as storage areas. Although the hotel is closed, the dining room still brings in plenty of business. Dining room hours are 5:00 p.m. to 11:00 p.m. daily, and they offer a complete dinner menu featuring steaks, seafood, and chicken. If you're a steak lover, the tenderloins at the Inverness Hotel Bar come very highly recommended.

The regular customers at the Inverness Hotel Bar are residents of Inverness and the surrounding communities. The building is not within sight of Highway 2, so they don't get much in the way of tourist business. Because of their large seating capacity and excellent food, the bar hosts a lot of holiday, birthday, and anniversary parties. The building also serves as somewhat of a community center for Inverness, so you will usually find a quiet, friendly crowd on hand.

BANK BAR

OWNERS: Don and Shirley Kline

HOURS: 9:00 a.m. to Closing Daily

HAPPY HOUR: 5:30 to 6:30 Mon - Fri

GAMBLING: Video Poker/Keno

LIVE MUSIC: Occasionally

LOCATION: Reed Street, **Rudyard**

PHONE: 406-355-4143

BEER: Drafts; Domestics

AMUSEMENT: Pool; Darts

FOOD: Frozen Pizza

The Bank Bar is on the southwest corner of Reed Street and Pyper Avenue in Rudyard. The moderate-sized barroom has a wooden bar along the south wall, and a few tables are spread throughout the room. The building today looks very much the same as it did when it was built in the early 1900s. The original decorative tin ceiling is still intact, and the brick on the interior walls has not been covered.

The building originally housed a bank, so it's no mystery how the bar got its name. In fact, the walk-in bank vault is still in the building today. The bank went belly up in 1922. It was during the prohibition years, so some entrepreneurial folks in Rudyard decided to operate a blind pig out of the building. After prohibition ended, a billiard parlor and saloon called the Bank Billiards opened in the building. The pool hall portion of the business was phased out over the years, but the bar is still going strong.

The Bank Bar has been in the same family since prohibition ended in 1933. Don and Shirley Kline currently own the bar, but Don's father obtained the first retail beer and liquor licenses. Don assumed ownership of the Bank Bar from his father in the early 1960's, but he was no newcomer to the business. Don has worked at the Bank Bar since he was seventeen years old, with the only real break from the bar being the time he spent in the service during the Korean War.

Don says the Bank Bar was a hopping place right after World War II. A lot of gambling went on in those days, and the official opening and closing hours didn't have much to do with when the place actually opened and closed. There are at least two bullet holes in the walls and one bullet hole in the ceiling of the barroom. Don said he doesn't know how the two holes in the wall got there, and he doesn't care to discuss the hole in the ceiling. These days, things aren't near as rowdy as they used to be. Virtually all the customers are local residents, and everyone seems to know everyone else. You can always expect to find a friendly crowd at the Bank Bar and maybe even hear a story or two from Don about how things were in the good old days.

SILVER SADDLE BAR AND CAFE

OWNER: Chester and Rose Bullock   **LOCATION:** Basin Street, **Basin**

HOURS: 8:00 a.m. to 2:00 a.m. Daily   **PHONE:** 406-225-9995

HAPPY HOUR: No   **BEER:** Drafts; Domestics

GAMBLING: Video Poker/Keno   **AMUSEMENT:** Pool

LIVE MUSIC: No   **FOOD:** Full Menu Cafe

The Silver Saddle Bar and Cafe is housed in the ground-level floor of a two story brick structure on Basin Street in Basin. The barroom resides in the east side of the building, and the cafe occupies the west side. A straight wooden bar and a wooden back bar stand against the west wall of the barroom. Two chandeliers fashioned from wagon wheels hang from the ceiling, and numerous collectors-series porcelain figurines and liquor decanters decorate the top of the back bar and the shelves in the cafe. Several photographs on the barroom wall depict the old mining town of Basin during its earlier and more profitable years.

The history of the Silver Saddle dates back to 1902 when a hotel called the Skerson Block opened in the building. The Skerson, which was advertised as a modern hotel with steam heat and electric lights, had seventeen hotel rooms, a barber shop, a drug store, and a saloon. The hotel also housed one of eight brothels in Basin during the mining boom days. Somewhere along the line, the name of the hotel was changed to the Wagon Wheel, and in 1944, it became the Silver Saddle. The hotel stayed in business until 1957 when there was no longer enough business to support it. The second floor has been renovated into four apartments, so there are once again residents in the old Skerson Hotel.

Chester and Rose Bullock have owned the Silver Saddle since 1972. They promote a friendly atmosphere, and their customers are typically well-mannered. Most of the bar business comes from residents of Basin and the surrounding communities, but tourists and hunters frequent the bar and cafe in the summer and fall. The Silver Saddle gets very busy during Basin's annual flea market in June, and the place also gets crowded in April when Chester hosts a birthday party for the bar. Several private parties are held at the Silver Saddle throughout the year as well. Daily lunch and dinner specials are offered in the cafe, and a catering service is also available. Mexican food is featured every Friday, and prime rib is the special on Saturdays. The hotel and brothel are no longer in operation, but you can always get plenty to eat and plenty to drink at the Silver Saddle Bar and Cafe in Basin.

VFW CATARACT POST 3648

MANAGER: Bob Mayes

HOURS: 2:00 p.m. to Closing Tue-Sun
Closed Mondays

HAPPY HOUR: 5:00 to 6:00 Tue - Fri

GAMBLING: Video Poker/Keno;
Shake-A-Day

LIVE MUSIC: Occasionally

LOCATION: Frontage Road, **Basin**

PHONE: 406-225-3530

BEER: Drafts; Domestics

AMUSEMENT: Pool; Darts

FOOD: Frozen Pizza, Bar Snacks

The VFW Cataract Post 3648 is on the Frontage Road that parallels Interstate 15 in Basin. A large sign stands along the highway, so you shouldn't have any trouble finding the place. Although the bar is officially a VFW Post, it's open to the general public. Access for non-members is not a problem. The log structure houses a barroom and dance hall on the ground-level floor, and a meeting room and kitchen are in the basement. A straight wooden bar faces the west wall of the main barroom, and two wooden tables and a couple of booths are available if you prefer sitting away from the bar. Most of the vaulted wooden ceiling is covered with beer posters of one form or another, and I suspect the entire ceiling will soon be covered as more posters become available.

The VFW Cataract Post 3648 was established in 1985. I'm told all the logs used to build the structure were donated by the U.S. Forest Service, and VFW members from the local community volunteered their time to erect the building. The dance hall on the west end of the building was added in 1992. The clay plaque on the fireplace was made by a local resident and donated to the post after the dance hall was completed. Bob Mayes currently manages the VFW Post 3648. There were over sixty members the last time I checked.

The VFW Cataract Post 3648 is basically a local tavern where people gather to relax and socialize. The regular customers come from as far away as Butte and Helena, and tourists frequently stop in during the summer months. There's usually an adult crowd at the bar, but everyone is friendly and courteous. A local band comes in during the week for informal jam sessions, and the band appears on a formal basis at the bar about once a month. The VFW Cataract Post 3648 hosts a barbecue each year on the first or second weekend in June in conjunction with a local off-road RV run that takes place in the surrounding Deerlodge National Forest. Regardless of whether you're a member of the VFW, you're always welcome at the Cataract Post 3648 in Basin.

SINGLETREE SALOON A.K.A. CLANCY BAR

OWNERS: Sue Cox and Jack Pyatt   **LOCATION:**   9 E. Clancy St., **Clancy**

HOURS: 1:00 p.m. to Closing Daily   **PHONE:**   406-933-5547

HAPPY HOUR: 4:00 to 6:00 Mon - Fri   **BEER:**   Drafts; Domestics;
                                            Imports; Microbrews

GAMBLING: Video Poker/Keno   **AMUSEMENT:**   Pool; Darts; Horseshoes

LIVE MUSIC: Occasionally   **FOOD:**   Full Menu Steak House

The Singletree Saloon is at 9 East Clancy Street in Clancy. The building houses a moderate-sized barroom in the north side and a dining room in the south side. A long bar with a brass elbow rail is positioned in front of a modern wooden back bar against the west wall. Two buddy bars stand in the middle of the room on the refurbished hardwood floor, and a small bandstand is in the southeast corner. The entire facility has recently undergone extensive renovations. Everything is very modern, and the rest rooms are kept virtually spotless. If you prefer the great outdoors over a barroom, there's a wooden gazebo outside.

As far as anyone I spoke with knew, the saloon was established around the turn of the 20th century. The Sagebrush Bar was the name of the business when the first liquor license was issued in 1937. The name was changed to the Clancy Inn in 1939, and the place is still known to many people around the area as the Clancy Bar. Sometime during the 1980s, the name was changed to the Singletree Saloon. Sue Cox and Jack Pyatt bought the Singletree Saloon in 1993. They didn't completely change the name of the business, but they did add "a.k.a. Clancy Bar" to make the more popular name part of the official name. Sue and Jack have made also made numerous upgrades and renovations to the building. Overall, they've been very successful at bringing new life to the old Clancy Bar.

The Singletree Saloon's slogan has become "One More and We Gotta Go" since most of the regular customers end up repeating those words several times before finally departing for the evening. Food is served throughout the week, but the full dinner menu is only offered Wednesday through Sunday from 5:00 p.m. until 10:00 p.m. It's worth the wait, however, because they serve excellent steaks and broasted chicken. Mondays are "Burger and a Beer 4 a Buck" night, and the Colossal Shrimp Cocktails, which are a small meal in themselves, are available any time. If you're a musician, informal jam sessions are held at the bar every Sunday evening. Sue and Jack have definitely gotten the old Clancy Bar back on the right track, so be sure to stop in the next time you're in the area.

CRIBBAGE BOARD BAR (TINGS)

OWNERS: Bill Meagor & Lewis Perino

LOCATION: 1 S Main, **Jefferson City**

HOURS: 1:00 p.m. to Closing Daily

PHONE: 406-933-8674

HAPPY HOUR: No

BEER: Drafts; Domestics

GAMBLING: Video Poker/Keno; Shake-A-Day

AMUSEMENT: Pool; Darts; Horseshoes

LIVE MUSIC: No

FOOD: Frozen Pizza

The Cribbage Board Bar (formerly Ting's Bar) is housed in a stone and mortar structure at 1 South Main Street in Jefferson City. The barroom resides in the ground-level floor at the south end of the building; the rest of the building now sits vacant. The moderate sized-barroom has an antique back bar with a large silver-backed mirror and a matching bar. Both pieces were hand-crafted from cherry wood around the turn of the 20th Century. The bar and back bar were originally shipped up the Missouri River by steamboat, off-loaded at Fort Benton, and transported overland by team and wagon to a hotel in Townsend. The bar and back bar were moved to Jefferson City and installed in Ting's Bar in 1952.

The history of the business dates back to the 1880s when the building was a stage stop, saloon, and hotel. It's rumored that the Montana Government even operated out of the building for one day while the Capitol was in the process of moving from Virginia City to Helena. A man known as Ting bought the saloon in the early 1950s. Ting was an amusing type who often allowed his customers to serve themselves while he entertained the barroom patrons with his antics, which frequently involved parading around in a clown suit. Ting's was also well known because a neighborhood donkey often wandered into the crowded barroom and drank beer until it got drunk and staggered back home. Bill Meagor and Lewis Perino bought Ting's in 1989. Bill and Lew changed the name to The Cribbage Board Bar because they planned on holding cribbage tournaments with large cash payouts. The State said NO to their cribbage idea, but the name on the liquor license had already been changed to the Cribbage Board Bar.

The Cribbage Board is a friendly place where local residents and travelers stop to relax and socialize. The Cribbage Board doesn't host a lot of special parties, but the Jefferson City Volunteer Fire Department always holds its annual social at the bar on the Saturday prior to Thanksgiving. Between 150 and 300 turkeys are given away at the social, so it's a very popular event. There's no need to wait for the social to visit the Cribbage Board Bar, however, because every day is a fun day.

LAHOOD PARK

OWNER: Steve Wendell

HOURS: Noon to Closing Daily

HAPPY HOUR: No

GAMBLING: Video Poker/Keno

LIVE MUSIC: Occasionally

LOCATION: Route 2, **LaHood**

PHONE: 406-287-3281

BEER: Domestics; Imports; Microbrews

AMUSEMENT: Pool; Volleyball; Horseshoes

FOOD: Full Menu Restaurant

LaHood Park is on Route 2 in LaHood. The barroom and restaurant are housed in a wooden structure that stands just west of an old hotel building on the south side of the road. The barroom has a beautiful mahogany back bar against the east wall. The back bar was built in the late 1800s, but it resided for many years in Butte's Finlen Hotel before being moved to LaHood. A hardwood dance floor and a raised wooden bandstand are in the west side of the barroom, and a wooden deck is just off the south side of the building overlooking the outdoor entertainment arena. Several intriguing paintings hang from the barroom and dining room walls. The paintings were done by Larry Knutson of Bozemen, and they can be purchased at the bar.

The history of the business dates back to the 1920s when Shadan LaHood built the Mountain View Inn Hotel. The hotel was once rated as one of the ten best hotels in the country, and it also served as the headquarters for Morrison Cave, which is now called Lewis and Clark Caverns. The hotel management always demanded the highest of standards, but they also served bootlegged booze during prohibition. The first time alcohol was legally sold at LaHood Park was when a VFW post opened around 1960. A public liquor license was eventually obtained, and the bar became accessible to everyone.

Steve Wendell has owned LaHood Park since 1991. Steve works hard at providing quality entertainment, and he is renovating the old hotel into a bed and breakfast facility. On the weekend prior to Labor Day, Steve holds a bluegrass festival featuring Grammy Award winning musicians. 2,000 people attended the bluegrass festival in 1996, and thousands more come to LaHood to see the excellent musicians that play throughout the year. The old hotel will be restored to its original condition, and most of the rooms will have a view of the Jefferson River. The restaurant is open from 6:00 a.m. until 10:00 p.m. daily, and the dinner menu features seafood, chicken, and some of the best steaks served anywhere in Montana.

EXCHANGE BAR AND SUPPER CLUB

OWNER: Ike Lanning　　　　　　**LOCATION:** **Montana City**

HOURS: 9:30 a.m. to Closing Daily　　**PHONE:** 406-443-9616

HAPPY HOUR: 4:00 to 6:00 Mon - Fri　**BEER:** Drafts; Domestics; Imports; Microbrews

GAMBLING: Video Poker/Keno; Live Keno　　**AMUSEMENT:** Pool; Darts; Pinball; Video Games; Horseshoes

LIVE MUSIC: Approximately Monthly　　**FOOD:** Full Menu Restaurant

The Exchange Bar and Supper Club is on the west side of Interstate 15 at the Montana City Interchange (exit 187). A spacious barroom resides in the west side of the building, a restaurant occupies the east side, and a banquet room is housed in the partial second floor. A long wooden bar with a brass elbow rail extends completely through the east side of the barroom and partially into the west side. Several tables are spread throughout the room, and plenty of video gambling machines are available for people who like to drop a few coins.

Ike Lanning and a partner established the Exchange Bar in December, 1980. The business started out as a small tavern, but the building was expanded eastward, westward, and upward during the mid 1980s to make room for the restaurant, a casino, and the banquet room. Further renovations have been completed since that time, so you probably wouldn't recognize the place if you haven't seen it in a while. Ike bought out his partner's share of the business in 1994, and he now maintains full control over the day-to-day operations.

The Exchange Bar and Supper Club draws most of its customers from Montana City, Helena, and the surrounding communities. They also get a lot of business from tourists in the summer and fall. The customers are always very friendly and well-behaved, so there's never any trouble in the barroom. Daily lunch and dinner specials are offered in the restaurant, and they run a steak, eggs, and Bloody Mary special every day for $5.00. Gamblers who purchase a $10.00 roll of quarters get a free lunch. If you like Rocky Mountain Oysters, the Exchange Bar and Supper Club serves some of the best you'll find anywhere. They also have a large selection of domestic, imported, and microbrewed beers to help you wash down your meal. The Bloody Marys and Caesars served at the Exchange have become quite popular, especially among the customers who come in with a hangover. Of course, these drinks can cause a hangover almost as fast as they can cure one, so be careful about how many you drink.

141

JACKSON CREEK SALOON

OWNERS: David and Darwin Simac

LOCATION: 1 Jackson Creek Road, **Montana City**

HOURS: 11:00 a.m. to Closing Daily

PHONE: 406-443-2866

HAPPY HOUR: No

BEER: Drafts; Domestics; Imports; Microbrews

GAMBLING: Video Poker/Keno; Shake-A-Day

AMUSEMENT: Pool; Darts

LIVE MUSIC: At Least Monthly

FOOD: Full Menu Grill

The Jackson Creek Saloon is at 1 Jackson Creek Road in Montana City. To get there from Interstate 15, take the Montana City Interchange (exit 187) and drive west for approximately 1/4 mile. You will see the saloon on the north side of the road. The wooden structure houses a barroom in the ground-level floor, and a banquet room is in the basement. If you prefer the great outdoors, a covered wooden deck is attached to the west side of the building. The wooden ceiling in the east side of the barroom is vaulted. Several antique signs and big game head mounts hang from the walls in this part of the building, and an L-shaped bar and several tables occupy most of the available floor space. The west side of the barroom is basically used as a game room.

The Jackson Creek Saloon was built in 1986. David and Darwin Simac bought the business in April, 1992, and they have been operating it ever since. The barroom was the only attraction when David and Darwin bought the place, but they've renovated the basement into a banquet room and added the covered wooden deck. The banquet room is a convenient place for people to hold private parties, and the deck has become a popular spot for customers to gather during the summer months.

The Jackson Creek Saloon is primarily operated as a neighborhood tavern. Most of the customers are residents of Montana City, Helena, and the surrounding communities. A few tourists stop in during the summer, and visiting hunters frequent the bar in the fall. A large selection of beers is kept on hand at the bar, and a variety of grill items are available from the lunch and dinner menu. The burgers come highly recommended for lunch, and the broasted chicken has become a very popular dinner item. There's typically a friendly crowd on hand, even on dance nights when the barroom gets very crowded. The Jackson Creek Saloon has live music at least once a month, and the band usually sets up outside during the summer. There's always something interesting going on, which makes the Jackson Creek Saloon a great place to visit.

142

PAPA RAY'S CASINO & HUGO'S PIZZA

OWNERS: Ray and Debbie Thares

LOCATION: Montana City

HOURS: 6:30 a.m. to Closing Daily
(Bar opens at 11:00 a.m.)

PHONE: 406-449-4112

HAPPY HOUR: None

BEER: Drafts; Domestics; Imports; Microbrews

GAMBLING: Video Poker/Keno; Shake-A-Day; Daily Cash Drawing

AMUSEMENT: Darts; Video Games; Horseshoes; Pinball; Volleyball

LIVE MUSIC: Occasionally

FOOD: Fresh Sandwiches; Pizza

Papa Ray's Casino and Hugo's Pizza is on the east side of Interstate 15 at the Montana City Interchange (exit 187). A pizza parlor and sandwich shop reside in the east side of the building, and the barroom is in the west side. The facility is relatively new, and the decor is modern. The barroom has an L-shaped bar, three buddy bars, and a wooden counter along one wall. One big screen TV and two smaller television sets are available to keep the customers entertained during televised sporting events. A large patio is just off the south side of the building, and horseshoe pits and volleyball courts are on the lawn.

Papa Rays Casino and Hugo's Pizza was established in February, 1993. Hugo and Di Hansen and Ray and Debbie Thares were the original partners in the business. Hugo had been operating a small pizza shop in the Exchange Bar and Supper Club under lease agreement, and he had always dreamed of owning his own business. The four partners were able to obtain a liquor license from the old Buckhorn Bar in Wheeler, near Fort Peck, and they joined forces to open Papa Ray's Casino and Hugo's Pizza. Hugo and Di eventually moved on, so Ray and Debbie now operate the entire business.

Papa Ray's Casino and Hugo's Pizza is a family-owned, family- operated business that primarily caters to residents of Montana City and the surrounding communities. The bar doesn't open until 11:00 a.m., but fresh baked pastries and espresso are served beginning at 6:30 a.m. daily. Excellent sandwiches are served, and the pizza is made with homemade sourdough crust and only the freshest ingredients available. A large selection of beers is kept on stock in the bar, including seven different draft beers. The patio is a very popular spot during the summer, and the volleyball court gets plenty of use when the weather cooperates. With all it has to offer, Papa Ray's Casino and Hugo's Pizza is a great place to take the entire family. There's plenty for the kids to do while the adults spend some quality time in the bar.

CABIN CREEK BAR

OWNERS: Ray and Clifford Nottingham

HOURS: 10:00 a.m. to 2:00 a.m. Fri-Wed
3:00 p.m. to 2:00 a.m. Thursday

HAPPY HOUR: 4:00 to 6:00 Daily

GAMBLING: Video Poker/Keno;
Live Poker

LIVE MUSIC: Occasionally

LOCATION: Main Street, **Geyser**

PHONE: 406-735-4334

BEER: Drafts; Domestics

AMUSEMENT: Pool; Darts

FOOD: Full Menu Grill

The Cabin Creek Bar is on Main Street in Geyser. The moderate-sized barroom has an antique wooden bar and a hand-crafted back bar along the south wall, and three tables are lined against the north wall. The bar and back bar were built in Germany in 1898. Although the bar shows some signs of wear, the back bar has been maintained in immaculate condition. The beautiful wooden clock hanging from the wall behind the bar was presented as a gift from a local resident who fashioned the time piece.

The bar first opened around the turn of the 20th century in the original settlement of Geyser. The saloon, along with the rest of the community, was moved approximately 4-1/2 miles to the east when the railroad came through in 1907. I wasn't able to find out what became of the business during the prohibition years, but a suicide, an arson attempt, and a homicide all took place inside the barroom between the late 1930s and early 1940s. Both the suicide and arson attempt can be credited to a dejected individual who was the former partner of the man who owned the business. Allegedly, the guy broke in late one night and set fire to the building before killing himself. Fortunately, the fire was brought under control before any significant structural damage occurred. The homicide took place during a poker game in 1942. I'm told the lights went out in the building for a few moments, and when the lights came back on, one of the card players laid dead on the floor. His throat had been slashed with a broken beer bottle, and nobody seemed to know who did it. Oddly enough, this mysterious case has never been solved.

Ray and Clifford Nottingham bought the Cabin Creek Bar in December, 1993. They run a friendly business where adults, kids, and entire families gather to relax and socialize with friends. Wednesday night poker is a big draw at the Cabin Creek Bar. Some of the best players in the region gather here on a weekly basis, which makes for a very tough table. If poker isn't your thing but eating is, the 1/2 pound burgers are considered the best in the county. And if you just want a beer, they've got plenty of it.

HOBSON BAR AND SUPPER CLUB

OWNER: John Ward

LOCATION: Route 239, **Hobson**

HOURS: 10:00 a.m. to 2:00 a.m. Tue-Sun
Closed Mondays

PHONE: 406-423-5639

HAPPY HOUR: 5:00 to 6:00 Tue-Fri

BEER: Drafts; Domestics

GAMBLING: Video Poker/Keno;
Shake-A-Day

AMUSEMENT: Pool

LIVE MUSIC: Occasionally

FOOD: Full Menu Restaurant

The Hobson Bar and Supper Club is in the ground-level floor of a two story cinder block building on Route 239 in Hobson. A spacious barroom resides in the front part of the building, and a smaller dining room is in the rear. The main part of the barroom is adjoined by a larger area that has a hardwood dance floor, a raised bandstand, and several tables. A long L-shaped bar extends from the barroom into the adjoining room.

Construction on the building was completed in 1910. At that time, a bank and grocery store operated out of the first floor, and a barber shop, pool hall, and the Farmers Union Meeting Hall were in the basement. The Hobson School Gymnasium was housed in the top floor of the building until the bar opened 1939. The bar first operated out of the southwest corner of the ground-level floor, and the rest of the area was used as living quarters. When John Ward bought the business in 1980, he expanded the barroom and added the dance floor. The wood that was used to build the dance floor was taken from the old gymnasium upstairs. In 1985, the dining room was added, and the Hobson Bar became the Hobson Bar and Supper Club. Except for the ground-level floor, most of the building is now unoccupied. The are some mannequins inside the windows of the second floor, and if you look up from the street, you could easily mistake the mannequins for real people. To keep things interesting, the people at the Hobson Bar and Supper Club change the clothes on the mannequins about once a month.

The regular crowd at the Hobson Bar and Supper Club consists of residents of Hobson and the surrounding communities. There's normally an adult crowd on hand in the bar, but they're a friendly bunch. A scene from the movie *Thunderbolt and Lightfoot* was shot inside the barroom, which means the likes of Clint Eastwood, Jeff Bridges, and George Kennedy have all been to the Hobson Bar. You probably won't see any celebrities when you visit, but you can always get a good meal. The supper club starts serving at 5:00 p.m. most days, and they have excellent prime rib on Friday and Saturday evenings.

BLUE NUGGET

OWNER: Mark and Krista Sweckard

HOURS: 10:00 a.m. to Closing Daily

HAPPY HOUR: 6:00 to 7:00 Mon - Fri

GAMBLING: Video Poker/Keno

LIVE MUSIC: Occasionally

LOCATION: Pig Eye Basin

PHONE: 406-423-5541

BEER: Domestics

AMUSEMENT: Pool

FOOD: Grill Items

The Blue Nugget is ten miles southwest of Utica on the Judith River Road. The area is known locally as Pig Eye Basin, but you might find it listed as Sapphire Village on your atlas and gazetteer. The barroom shares the building with a small convenience store and gift shop. Gasoline and propane are also sold at the bar, and RV parking spaces are available outside. An extensive renovation project has recently been completed on the entire building, so the facility is very modern. Log siding covers the exterior walls, new tile flooring has been installed, and tongue-and-groove pine woodwork and pine boards cover the interior walls and ceiling. Several big game head mounts are on display throughout the barroom, and a full mount brown bear with a beer can in its paw stands on its hind legs at the corner of the wooden bar.

The building that houses the Blue Nugget was originally the Pig Eye School House. The Blue Nugget began operating out of the building with a retail beer and wine license in 1969. Blue Nugget was selected as the name of the bar because Yogo (blue) Sapphires are mined in the area. Yogo Sapphires are the highest quality sapphires in the world, and the only known deposit of these rare gems is the Pig Eye Basin. Mark and Krista Sweckard bought the Blue Nugget in May, 1996. They obtained a liquor license from the old Corner Bar in Geyser, and they also moved the bar and back bar out of the Corner Bar into the Blue Nugget. Extensive building renovations were completed before the bar reopened on July 4, 1996.

Mark and Krista are relatively new to the bar business, but they have gotten off to a very good start. They operate the Blue Nugget as a service to local residents and outdoors enthusiasts who come to the area to hunt, fish, and dig for sapphires. The barroom customers are courteous and friendly. This is one place where you can take your entire family without having to worry about barroom brawls or unruly customers. If you're looking for a unique gift or souvenir, some very nice locally-crafted jewelry is available in the convenience store. The ten mile trip from Utica to the beautiful Pig Eye Basin is well worth the time if you plan on stopping at the Blue Nugget.

MINT BAR

OWNER: Nick Obresely

HOURS: 11:00 a.m. to Closing Wed-Mon
Closed Tuesdays

HAPPY HOUR: No

GAMBLING: Video Poker/Keno

LIVE MUSIC: Occasionally

LOCATION: Highway 87, **Raynesford**

PHONE: 406-738-4447

BEER: Drafts; Domestics

AMUSEMENT: Darts

FOOD: Frozen Pizza, Bar Snacks

The Mint Bar is on the north side of Highway 87/200 in Raynesford. A wooden walkway spans the length of the east side of the building, creating somewhat of an old west effect. The barroom has a rustic appearance and a comfortable atmosphere. Rough cut barn wood covers the interior walls, and blue stain pine boards were used to fashion the horseshoe-shaped bar along the east wall. A couple of tables are spread throughout the room, and there's plenty of open floor space.

I'm told the business has been in Raynesford since the early 1900's. Documents from the Montana State Liquor Division show the bar operated under the name Hank's Place until 1945 when the name was changed to the Mint Bar. Allegedly, part of the existing building was an old train station that was moved to the property when the bar first opened. The bar originally operated out of the old train station, which is actually the south side of the barroom as it exists today. At one time, the building allegedly had a second floor that was used as a whorehouse. I wasn't able to find out when or why the whorehouse ceased operations, but it may have had something to do with the second story being torn off the building many years ago. Nick Obresely has owned the Mint Bar since 1993. Nick has done a lot of work on the building, and his efforts show. The barroom has recently been expanded northward, and the interior of the building was completely renovated in 1994.

The majority of the customers at the Mint Bar are residents of Raynesford and the surrounding farming and ranching communities. Visiting hunters and fishermen visit the bar during the summer and fall, and tourists passing through the area occasionally stop in during the summer months. Like most small town taverns, you never know when a crowd might show up at the Mint. You're as likely to find a packed barroom on a weekday afternoon as you are on a weekend evening. About the only thing constant about the customers is they're always friendly and courteous. I guess that's about all a person could ask for when walking into a saloon.

OXEN YOKE INN

OWNERS: Cathy Underwood

LOCATION: Route 239, **Utica**

HOURS: 10:00 a.m. to 2:00 a.m. Daily

PHONE: 406-423-5560

HAPPY HOUR: 5:00 to 6:00 Mon - Fri

BEER: Drafts; Domestics

GAMBLING: Video Poker/Keno

AMUSEMENT: Pool; Darts; Video Games

LIVE MUSIC: Occasionally

FOOD: Grill Items

The Oxen Yoke Inn is housed in a log structure on Main Street in Utica. The spacious barroom has a curved bar and a modern wooden back bar along the north wall, several tables spread throughout the room, and plenty of open floor space. The south wall is covered with passive solar panels. The solar heating system does an excellent job keeping the building warm during the winter months as long as the sun shines, and a wood burning stove provides backup heat on cloudy days. The interior walls and ceiling are covered with rough cut lumber, providing a rustic atmosphere in the barroom. The walls in the men's room are covered with C. M. Russell prints, which have become such an attraction that tour groups from the Russell Museum in Great falls have filed through the barroom and into the men's room just to see them.

The Oxen Yoke Inn was built in 1948. The original building was destroyed by fire in 1982, but a rebuilding effort quickly got underway. The business reopened in a new building later that same year. Although the structure is relatively new, the barroom has already developed a character all its own. Several cowboy hats, along with the name and home town of the person who donated the hat, hang high on the barroom walls amongst the mounted big game heads. People from the local area and all over the United States have left their hats at the bar.

Cathy Underwood has owned the Oxen Yoke Inn since 1991. Cathy runs a friendly establishment, and people of all ages are always welcome. Cathy serves a twelve ounce "Oxen Burger" made from fresh ground beef with a fat content of less that 12%. The burgers have become so popular that foreign visitors occasionally stop in because they've heard about the burgers from friends and relatives. Pitch games are popular at the bar on Sundays, except for the first Sunday in June when they host a branding party. The bar also has a Turkey Fire Dance every year on Thanksgiving weekend in commemoration of a fire that destroyed several houses around Utica on Thanksgiving weekend in 1990. The same musician that was playing at the bar the night the fire went through comes back every year to play at the Turkey Fire Dance.

BAR 87

OWNERS: Joe and Sharon Marshall

HOURS: 4:00 a.m. to 2:00 a.m. Daily

HAPPY HOUR: No

GAMBLING: Video Poker/Keno

LIVE MUSIC: Karaoke Every Weekend

LOCATION: Highway 87, **Windham**

PHONE: 406-566-9936

BEER: Drafts; Domestics

AMUSEMENT: Pool

FOOD: Full Menu Grill

The Bar 87 is housed in a steel-sided structure on the south side of Highway 87/200 in Windham. A long L-shaped bar stands just inside the main entrance in the middle of the building. A spacious seating area, a large dance floor, and a bandstand reside in the west end of the building, and the rest rooms, several tables and a pool table are in the east side. The entire facility was completely renovated in 1995. With the upgrades, the building meets all the requirements of the American's With Disabilities Act, so handicapped access is no problem.

The bar's history dates back to 1949 when a fire destroyed Higg's Beer Tavern in Windham. Small rodeos were commonly held out back of the old tavern, so Mr. Higg needed a plan to keep his business going through the summer rodeo season. As a temporary measure, he moved a small building to the property where the Bar 87 now stands. Later that year, a house from the nearby town of Lehigh was moved onto the property to replace the temporary structure, and the Bar 87 officially opened for business. Joe and Sharon Marshall bought the bar in February, 1995. They spent the next ten months building a large addition onto the west side of the building and completely renovating the rest of the structure. The new and improved Bar 87 reopened on December 20, 1995. Joe and Sharon plan on adding RV parking spaces and an outdoor barbecue pit during the summer of 1997, so there are still some improvements to come.

The big draw at the Bar 87 is karaoke music every Friday and Saturday night. People from all over the surrounding region, many from as far away as Great Falls and Lewistown, come to the bar on the weekends for the live entertainment. Although the barroom gets very crowded, there's usually a friendly bunch of people on hand. Fights and rude behavior are not commonplace in the barroom. Joe and Sharon have invested in an 8 x 10 foot TV screen, so the Bar 87 has become a very popular spot during televised sporting events. Steaks, burgers, and chicken are also served at the bar, so you don't have to drink on an empty stomach. If you haven't been to the Bar 87 in recent years, stop by. I'm sure you will be pleasantly surprised to see what's happened to the old place.

STOCKMAN BAR

OWNER: Fred Gilleard

LOCATION: Highway 93, **Arlee**

HOURS: 10:00 a.m. to Closing Daily

PHONE: 406-726-3870

HAPPY HOUR: No

BEER: Drafts; Domestics

GAMBLING: No

AMUSEMENT: Pool

LIVE MUSIC: No

FOOD: Grill Items

The Stockman Bar is on Highway 93 in Arlee. The barroom has a beautiful antique bar, back bar, and matching liquor cabinet along one wall. The beveled glass mirrors at each end of the back bar are original, but the middle mirror is a replacement that was installed after someone shot out the original fixture. The Great Falls Select Beer sign behind the bar and the Highlander Beer sign on the back wall are valuable collectors items. There are also several collectors item beer cans and beer bottles on display in the glass case at the end of the bar.

Arlee's Stockman Bar was established in 1903. The bar originally operated out of a house that stood near the railroad tracks, but it moved to its present location when the highway came through. The Stockman Bar officially became the Stockman Soda Fountain during prohibition, but it's likely bootlegged liquor was sold along with the soda. The western outdoor scene murals on the walls and the front of the bar were painted in the early 1950s. I'm told the artist completed the project in three days using only a sock and a six inch paint brush. The wall mural originally covered all four walls and the ceiling, but two walls have since been refinished, and a new drop ceiling has been installed. There are at least three other false ceilings above the one that's now visible.

Fred Gilleard has owned the Stockman Bar since 1972. Fred promotes a family oriented atmosphere, and he also hosts benefits throughout the year for local residents in need of assistance. Entire families commonly visit the Stockman, and everyone is friendly and courteous. I've been told that most of the kids in Arlee were raised in the barroom, so you know it's a great place to visit.

One of the more interesting features about the Stockman Bar is the sink in the men's room. The sink is mounted so high on the wall that I nearly needed to stand on a stool to wash my hands. Apparently, the sink was intentionally mounted that high to keep people from peeing in it. I just hope nobody interprets that as a challenge and tries to do it anyhow. If you think the sink is high today, you should have seen it a few years ago. Allegedly, it was even higher on the wall at one time.

SAILING WOLF TAVERN

OWNER: Steve Hauf		**LOCATION:**	Highway 93, **Big Arm**
HOURS: 10:00 a.m. to 2:00 a.m. Daily		**PHONE:**	406-849-5292
HAPPY HOUR: No		**BEER:**	Drafts; Domestics; Imports
GAMBLING: No		**AMUSEMENT:**	Pool; Darts; Horseshoes
LIVE MUSIC: Occasionally		**FOOD:**	Full Menu Grill

The Sailing Wolf Tavern is on the east side of highway 93 in Big Arm. The building stands on a hill overlooking Flathead Lake. The relatively small barroom has an L-shaped bar just inside the front entrance and a few small tables along one wall. It's not what I would describe as a rustic place, but a log front has recently been installed, the floor is made of wood, and log slats cover the interior walls.

The Sailing Wolf Tavern is housed in the old Big Arm Post Office building. A restaurant operated out of the building after the post office moved, and in the late 1960s, a bar called the Pit Stop opened. Steve Hauf bought the bar in November, 1995 and changed the name to the Sailing Wolf Tavern. Steve tells me he selected Wolf as part of the name for his new business because of the recent wolf reintroduction controversy in Montana. The logo for the bar is now a wolf sailing a dingy.

The Sailing Wolf Tavern is a friendly place with a relaxed atmosphere. Pool and darts are popular at the bar, so you may want to sharpen up your game before you visit. Local residents support the business throughout the year, but like most taverns in the area, the Sailing Wolf gets plenty of tourists and outdoors enthusiasts in the summer. You will see boaters, fishermen (and women) vacationers, and just about every other type of recreationist at the bar when the weather is nice. Skiers traveling to and from The Big Mountain Resort in Whitefish occasionally stop by during the winter. It really doesn't matter who happens to be there at any given time, because everyone is friendly. The bartenders are quite pleasant, and they always seem to strike up a conversation with their customers.

When I last visited the Sailing Wolf Tavern in December of 1996, plans were in place to do some major building renovations. Scheduled improvements included expanding the overall size of the barroom and repositioning the bar in front of some new windows in the east wall overlooking the lake. Don't be too surprised if the place looks nothing like what I've described when you arrive.

TERRACE SUPPER CLUB AND LOUNGE

OWNERS: Dave D'Albini, Julia D'Albini, and Steve Swenson

LOCATION: 78571 Highway 83 South, **Big Fork**

HOURS: 4:00 p.m. to Closing Daily
Closed Mon & Tues (Winter)

PHONE: 406-837-5799

HAPPY HOUR: No

BEER: Drafts; Domestics; Imports; Microbrews

GAMBLING: Video Poker/Keno

AMUSEMENT: None

LIVE MUSIC: No

FOOD: Full Menu Supper Club

The Terrace Supper Club and Lounge is on Highway 83 between Big Fork and Swan Lake. The wooden structure houses a moderate-sized barroom in the north side and a dining room in the south side. An L-shaped bar faces the east wall of the barroom, and a few tables are spread throughout the room. The spacious dining room has ample seating for upwards of fifty people. Both the barroom and dining room guests can enjoy a spectacular view of Swan Lake and the surrounding mountains through the plate glass windows in the west wall. Sliding glass doors provide access to an elevated wooden deck overlooking Emerald Bay, and a long wooden stairway leads from the deck to a dock on the shoreline of the lake.

I don't know the complete history of the Terrace Supper Club and Lounge, but I'm told the business originally operated out of a building that stood a few hundred yards to the west on a hill overlooking Emerald Bay. Construction on the present-day dining room was completed in 1965, and the existing barroom was added during a renovation project that was completed a few years after the dining room was built. Over the years, the Terrace Supper Club and Lounge has become a local landmark. It's one of the few commercial buildings along Highway 83 between Swan Lake and Big Fork, so travelers commonly use the structure as a half way marker between the towns.

Dave and Julia D'Albini and Steve Swenson bought the Terrace Supper Club and Lounge in November, 1995. The business had been operating on a limited basis over the three previous years, so the new owners spent a lot of time upgrading the building. The dining room doesn't open until 4:00 p.m., but lunches are served in the bar beginning at 11:00 a.m. from June through August. The dinner menu features hand-cut steaks, pork, pasta, and seafood dishes. Prime rib is the house specialty. If you just want a beer, an extensive selection of domestics, imports, and microbrews is available. I can think of few things in life more relaxing than drinking beer and enjoying the view from the deck at the Terrace Supper Club and Lounge.

BRANDING IRON

OWNER: Loren and Kathy Smith		**LOCATION:**	Main Street, **Charlo**
HOURS: 10:00 a.m. to 2:00 a.m. Daily		**PHONE:**	406-644-9493
HAPPY HOUR: 5:30 to 6:30 Daily		**BEER:**	Drafts; Domestics; Imports
GAMBLING: No		**AMUSEMENT:**	Pool; Pinball; Video Games
LIVE MUSIC: Weekly During Summer Twice Monthly Winter		**FOOD:**	Grill; Broaster

The Branding Iron is on Main Street in Charlo. The barroom is relatively large, with a straight wooden bar along one wall, several tables spread throughout the room, and a bandstand and big-screen TV in one corner. The wooden floor, tongue-and-groove pine woodwork, and brands on the walls enhance the building's rustic charm. The brands are all authentic markings from local ranches, and each year, a few more brands get added to the collection. If you show up at the Branding Iron on a dance night, you will notice they still spread sawdust around so their customers' shoes don't stick to the floor.

The building that houses the bar was originally a grocery store and post office. An upholstery shop also operated out of the building before the Branding Iron opened in 1981. Being that the bar hasn't been around all that long, there's not much in the way of interesting history to report. Horses and goats have been taken into the barroom on more than one occasion, but these antics were all done in fun.

Loren and Kathy Smith have owned the Branding Iron since September, 1996. They promote a family-oriented atmosphere at the bar, and their customers are fun-loving people. Local residents provide a steady business throughout the year. The bar is within eight miles of the National Bison Range, so plenty of tourists stop by during the summer. Big game and water foul hunters also frequent the Branding Iron during the seasons.

The Branding Iron is operated in a very community-minded manner. Loren and Kathy sponsor or co-sponsor several special events each year, none more popular than the annual Mission Mountain Testicle Festival on the first Saturday in June. Several hundred people attend the event, and upwards of 250 pounds of Rocky Mountain Oysters are consumed. Other events worth mentioning include an Eight Ball Shootout on the weekend closest to Valentines Day, a "Fups Basketball Brawl" fund raiser in mid April, the annual Mayor's Day Over-The Hill Race on the third Saturday in June, and the ever popular wild game feed and hunter's ball in November.

IDLE SPUR

OWNER: Calvin Brown

HOURS: 10:00 a.m to Closing Daily

HAPPY HOUR: No

GAMBLING: No

LIVE MUSIC: Every Weekend (Summer)
Occasionally (Winter)

LOCATION: A Street, **Dayton**

PHONE: 406-849-5599

BEER: Drafts; Domestics;
Imports; Microbrews

AMUSEMENT: Pool; Darts; Pinball;
Video Games; Horseshoes

FOOD: Grill Items; Chicken

The Idle Spur is on A Street in Dayton. The barroom is relatively large, and the facility is very modern. The interior walls are covered with tongue-and-groove woodwork, creating a comfortable environment. A curved bar stands along one wall, and several tables are spread throughout the room. If you prefer the great outdoors, the wooden deck provides a fantastic view of Flathead Lake and the surrounding mountains.

The business was established as the Buckboard Saloon in the 1920s. The original barroom was quite small compared to the size it is today, but an expansion project was completed on the building in 1990. Unfortunately, the customers didn't get to enjoy the added floor space for long. Freddie's Bar, as it was called at that time, hosted a celebration just after the building renovations were completed. Sparks from a fire in the barbecue pit set the building on fire, and it was completely destroyed by the blaze. A 30 x 70 foot building was erected later that summer, and the bar was back in business. Since then, a 1,400 square foot addition and a large wooden deck have been added. Up to 140 people can now be seated inside the building, and there's plenty of parking space outside.

Calvin Brown bought the business in January, 1992. One of Calvin's first official acts was to hold a contest to rename the bar. The Idle Spur was selected, and the business has been operating under that name ever since. Calvin says the bar used to have a fairly rowdy reputation, but the customers these days are friendly and well-mannered. A lot of people stop by just for meals. The grill menu features steaks, shrimp, and hot sandwiches. Broasted chicken is the house specialty. If you're a golfer, take note that a closest to the pin golf shootout is held outside the bar every Wednesday evening through the summer. Contestants pay $5.00 apiece for three shots at the flag. The winner gets his money back, but the rest of the money is used to buy drinks for all the participants until the kitty runs dry. The weekly contest has become quite popular, especially since nobody really loses.

154

JUNCTION BAR

OWNER: Janet Sanderson

LOCATION: Junction of Highway 83 & Route 209, **Ferndale**

HOURS: 9:00 a.m. to Closing Daily

PHONE: 406-837-5206

HAPPY HOUR: 5:00 to 6:00 Daily

BEER: Drafts; Domestics

GAMBLING: Video Poker/Keno

AMUSEMENT: Pool; Darts; Pinball

LIVE MUSIC: No

FOOD: Grill Items

The Junction Bar is housed in a wooden A-Frame structure that stands one mile east of Ferndale at the junction of Highway 83 and Route 209. The barroom resides in the ground-level floor, and the second story is used as living quarters. A wooden bar with a steel foot rail faces the south wall of the barroom. The barstools are mounted to the base of the bar, so don't plan on dragging your seat across the room. Stone flooring has been installed in front of the bar, but the rest of the floor is made of wood. The interior decor pretty much consists of various posters attached to the vaulted walls.

The Junction Bar was established in 1973. Some interesting moments have occurred over the years, but probably the most memorable event took place on June 29, 1989. Sparks from the wood stove ignited the cedar shake roof, forcing the customers to evacuate. Everyone went outside until the blaze was brought under control, but they didn't stay outside for long. Once the flames were doused, the bar patrons re-entered the building and resumed their positions at the bar. Fire water was dripping through the ceiling, but a little moisture didn't seem to bother anyone. A lantern was brought in for light, and the drinks started flowing again.

Janet Sanderson has owned the Junction Bar since 1984. She survived the great fire of '89, and she has also been successful at bringing some order to the place. The customers are typically friendly and well-behaved these days, but things weren't always that way. There was a time when people actually sat at the bar with their pistols and used the log ceiling posts for target practice. On one occasion, a man pulled out a 22 caliber pistol and shot his "friend" in the leg. I'm told the two men had been arguing, and I guess one of them decided to let his pistol settle the dispute. It's been a while since the sound of gunfire has echoed through the building, but a lot of cribbage still gets played in the barroom. They also host a great Groundhog's Day Party, complete with food and prizes. If you're interested in visiting the place that was once referred to as the hottest bar in Montana, stop by the Junction Bar near Ferndale.

LAKE MARY RONAN LODGE AND RESORT

OWNERS: Bob and Cheri Shores

LOCATION: Lake Mary Ronan Road, **Proctor**

HOURS: 11:00 a.m. to Closing Daily

PHONE: 406-849-5454

HAPPY HOUR: No

BEER: Drafts; Domestics

GAMBLING: Video Poker/Keno

AMUSEMENT: Darts; Video Games; Horseshoes; Volleyball

LIVE MUSIC: Weekly Through Summer Occasionally in Winter

FOOD: Full Menu Restaurant

The Lake Mary Ronan Lodge and Resort is approximately six miles from Proctor (eight miles off Highway 93) on the Lake Mary Ronan Road. The entire business consists of the bar, restaurant, cabin rentals, a full service campground, and boat rentals. The bar and restaurant are housed in a 4,000 square foot log structure. The informal atmosphere in the lodge is enhanced by the wooden walls and stone fireplace. The barroom and dining room are in separate rooms, and a large wooden deck is attached to the side of the building overlooking the lake. The windows in the barroom provide the guests a spectacular view of beautiful Lake Mary Ronan.

The business was established as a motor inn during the early 1920s. Over the years, the motor inn was transformed into a resort with a very informal atmosphere. Bob and Cheri Shores have owned the Lake Mary Ronan Lodge and Resort since January, 1993. Bob and Cheri spent a considerable amount of time making upgrades and renovations to the grounds and buildings, and their efforts show. Ten cabins were available when I last visited the resort in December, 1996. Bob and Cheri are steadily adding to the lodging facilities, and they now have thirty-eight RV spaces with full hookups on the property.

The Lake Mary Ronan Lodge is a year-round resort. The bar opens at 11:00 a.m. daily, but the restaurant is open for breakfast at 7:00 a.m. through the summer. Dinner specials are available four days a week. The specials include tacos on Monday, pizza on Wednesdays, prime rib on Friday, and baby back pork ribs on Saturday. With its secluded location and great food, the resort is a popular place for private gatherings such as weddings and family reunions. Snowmobilers and cross country skiers provide a lot of business during the winter, but fishing is the biggest attraction throughout the year. Bob's father, Pop, is usually at the boat house, and he can tell you how the fishing is. If you don't have the appropriate bait or lure, Pop will gladly sell it to you. There's nothing like getting a first hand scouting report before casting your line.

MOUNTAIN MEADOWS RESORT & WILDERNESS GOLF COURSE

OWNER: Gene Garrison		**LOCATION:**	Lake Mary Ronan Road, **Proctor**
HOURS: 8:00 a.m. to Closing Daily		**PHONE:**	406-849-5459
HAPPY HOUR: No		**BEER:**	Drafts; Domestics
GAMBLING: No		**AMUSEMENT:**	Pool; Horseshoes; Video Games; Volleyball; Wilderness Golf
LIVE MUSIC: Occasionally		**FOOD:**	Full Menu Restaurant

Mountain Meadows Resort and Wilderness Golf Course is approximately six miles from Proctor on the Lake Mary Ronan Road. The entire business consists of the lodge, cabin rentals, camping facilities, and the infamous Wilderness Golf Course. Drinking and eating facilities are housed in a rustic log structure that's nestled amongst the pines on the shoreline of beautiful Lake Mary Ronan. The building has a wooden floor, log walls, and a cathedral ceiling supported by log posts and beams. Other services available at the lodge include a store, a recreation room, and an arts and crafts gallery featuring Montana wildlife paintings. There's also a large wooden deck off the west side of the building facing the lake.

The campground has been in existence since the 1930s, but the first liquor license wasn't issued to the lodge until 1962. Campbell's Resort was the name of the business at that time, but the lodge has also operated under the names Beartrack Lodge, Lake Mary Ronan Western Sunset, and the Roads End Lodge. The name finally became Mountain Meadows Resort in 1984. Gene Garrison has owned the business since 1992. Gene's philosophy is he doesn't operate a bar; he operates a lodge. Foul language isn't tolerated inside the building. In fact, Gene has a sign posted on the wall which states "THIS IS A LODGE, NOT A BAR...USE FOUL LANGUAGE, AND OUT YOU ARE".

The lake and Wilderness Golf Course are the two big attractions at Gene's lodge. Some of the best Kokanee Salmon fishing in the country can be found on Lake Mary Ronan, and the golf course is something everyone should experience at least once. It's definitely "The World's Worst Golf Course In The Last Best Place". Golfers can bring their own clubs or use one of the implements available in the Not-So-Pro-Shop at the lodge. Be forewarned, however, because even the brochure states "when you're on the greens you're in the rough". The Mountain Meadows Resort and Campground is a wonderful place in a picturesque setting. It's well worth your time to get off the beaten path to see what they have to offer.

157

BUFFALO SALOON

OWNERS: Dell Haugen & Vicki Sherry

LOCATION: Highway 93, **Ravalli**

HOURS: 11:00 a.m. to 2:00 a.m. Summer
2:00 p.m. to Closing Winter

PHONE: 406-745-2666

HAPPY HOUR: No

BEER: Drafts; Domestics; Imports

GAMBLING: No

AMUSEMENT: Pool; Pinball; Horseshoes

LIVE MUSIC: Twice a Month

FOOD: Char-Broiled Items

The Buffalo Saloon is on Highway 93 in Ravalli. The front of the building is covered with log slats, and the interior is finished with logs and wood. The spacious barroom has a straight bar facing the south wall, several tables in the center portion of the room, and a dance floor and a wooden bandstand in the north side. Log posts support the ceiling, and a couple of wooden counter tops have been installed on the log railings that separate the bar area from the dance floor and general seating area.

The business was established as the Buffalo Park Beer Parlor in 1944. The bar was built around the history of Big Medicine, a white buffalo who once lived on the nearby National Bison Range. The fiberglass buffalo on the sign in the parking lot originally stood on the roof of the building. It used to be a tradition for customers to climb onto the roof and ride the buffalo. Of course, most of the riders were in a drunken stupor, and many of them were thrown during their ride. One man who fell from the beast landed on the hood of a car in the parking lot.

Dell Haugen and Vicki Sherry have owned the Buffalo Saloon since July, 1994. They spent a considerable amount of time and money making upgrades and renovations to the building, and their efforts show. Sherry tells me it was a pretty rowdy place when she and Dell first took over, but they've managed to get the customers to settle down. The Buffalo Saloon is still known as the party bar of the area, but fighting and rude behavior are no longer tolerated.

The customers at the Buffalo Saloon come from all age groups and backgrounds. Local residents strongly support the business, and visiting tourists and outdoors enthusiasts stop in throughout the year. The bar is a popular place for people to watch televised University of Montana athletic events, and you will typically see a group of local ranchers and cattle buyers in the barroom on Thursday afternoons. The Buffalo Saloon has become the local meeting place for people to discuss cattle prices after leaving the weekly cattle sale in Missoula.

4 STAR BAR/MORIGEAU'S RESTAURANT

OWNERS: Irene and Calvin Morigeau

LOCATION: Highway 93, **Ravalli**

HOURS: 10:00 a.m. to 2:00 a.m. Summer
Noon to 2:00 a.m. Winter

PHONE: 406-745-3220

HAPPY HOUR: 5:30 to 7:00 Mon - Fri

BEER: Drafts; Domestics;
Imports; Microbrews

GAMBLING: No

AMUSEMENT: Pool; Darts; Pinball;
Video Games

LIVE MUSIC: Every Weekend

FOOD: Full Menu Restaurant

The 4 Star Bar and Morigeau's Restaurant is on the east side of Highway 93 in Ravalli. The barroom resides in the north side of the building, and the restaurant occupies the south side. The bar and pool tables are in the front portion of the barroom, and a spacious dance floor is in the back. A large painting of Big Medicine, a white buffalo who lived on the nearby National Bison Range during the 1950s, hangs from the wall behind the bar. The small mounted deer that stands beside the painting of Big Medicine has come to be known as Little Medicine.

The business was established as the 4 Star Bar and Lunch Counter in 1945. Prior to the bar moving in, the building housed a gas station and grocery store. 4 Star was selected as the name of the bar and lunch counter because the last name of the four people who established the business was Star. The original barroom was only about half the size it is today. The part of the building that now houses the dance floor was built in the late 1960s.

Irene and Calvin Morigeau have owned the business since 1993. Irene manages the restaurant, and Calvin runs the bar. Restaurant hours are 8:00 a.m. to 10:00 p.m. daily. The menu features buffalo steaks and burgers, Indian Tacos, various fry bread dishes, and chicken. Daily lunch and dinner specials are offered during the summer, and the Huckleberry Fry Scream is very good. The restaurant even serves the famous Dixon Burger, which was invented by Joanne Schmauch at the Dixon Bar.

Local residents provide a steady business throughout the year, and plenty of tourist stop by in the summer. The customers are typically friendly, and the atmosphere is relaxed. A pool tournament with a cash payout is held at the bar every Saturday, and you can win a case of beer playing pool during the week. Free drinks and one grand prize are given away during every happy hour, and a different drink special is available seven days a week. The bar's specialty drinks include a 4 Star Slammer, Sex on the Res(ervation), Sex on the Sea, and Sex on the Pool Table.

SWAN BAR & GRILL

OWNERS: David & Dani Carlson and
Jim and Joyce Sedivy

LOCATION: Highway 83, **Swan Lake**

PHONE: 406-886-2170

HOURS: Noon to Closing Daily

HAPPY HOUR: No

BEER: Drafts; Domestics;
Microbrews

GAMBLING: Video Poker/Keno

AMUSEMENT: Pool; Horseshoes;
Shuffleboard

LIVE MUSIC: Once a Year

FOOD: Burgers; Chicken; Snacks

The Swan Bar & Grill, "That Big Little Bar on 83", is on the east side of Highway 83 in Swan Lake. The barroom has an L-shaped bar facing the east wall, and plenty of tables are available for additional seating. A few painted saw blades decorate the interior walls, but most of the barroom decor is sports-oriented. Various team pennants and lots of Minnesota Vikings paraphernalia are on display. Sliding glass doors lead to a partially covered deck off the east side of the building. There's also an enclosed back yard with horseshoe pits and a creek.

The Swan Bar and Grill was established in October, 1990. The building previously housed the Hummingbird Cafe, but by Jim and Joyce Sedivy and Dave and Dani Carlson transformed the old cafe into the Swan Bar and Grill. Jim and Dave built the existing bar from oak flooring. The metal vehicles and airplanes on display behind the bar are actually coin banks. The pieces belong to a collection Dave started several years ago.

The Swan Bar and Grill is a friendly place with a family-oriented atmosphere. The business enjoys a steady local clientele throughout the year, but summers are the busiest season. A lot of summer residents live around Swan Lake, and the picturesque landscape draws tourists and campers to the area. The barroom is typically crowded of Friday evenings when people gather to dine and socialize. It's also a popular spot for people to watch televised sporting events. If you're a sports fan, Dave can usually find some sort of game on the satellite.

The Swan Bar and Grill has live music only once a year. This festive occasion takes place outside on the deck on the first weekend in August. The Swan Bar & Grill also hosts an annual potluck dinner in October to celebrate its anniversary. If you can't make it to one of the scheduled events, you can always order off the menu. The kitchen is open daily from noon to 10:00 p.m. The menu is simple, featuring 1/2 pound burgers, Chester Fried Chicken, and homemade jojo potatoes. The customers never go away hungry at the Swan Bar & Grill.

RAVEN BREW PUB AND GRILL

OWNERS: Chris and Lisa McCreedy

HOURS: 11:00 a.m. to 2:00 a.m. Daily

HAPPY HOUR: 5:00 to 6:00 Mon - Fri

GAMBLING: Video Poker/Keno

LIVE MUSIC: Occasionally

LOCATION: Highway 35, **Woods Bay**

PHONE: 406-83RAVEN

BEER: Drafts; Domestics; Imports; Microbrews

AMUSEMENT: Darts; Pinball

FOOD: Barbecued Foods

The Raven Brew Pub And Grill is on Highway 35 in Woods Bay. For all you microbrew fanatics out there, this is the place where Raven Beer is brewed. The building stands on the east shore of Flathead Lake in the pristine Flathead Valley. The barroom is housed in the first floor, and a game room shares space with a small brewery in the basement. A Z-shaped bar is positioned near the plate glass windows in the west wall of the barroom. On a bright day, the sunlight shining through the windows can be almost blinding. It may take a few minutes for your eyes to adjust, but it's only a temporary inconvenience. The breathtaking view of the water and the surrounding mountains makes you quickly forget about the glare. Two wooden decks overlook Flathead Lake, and a series of steps lead to a dock in the marina. I'm told the fishing is pretty good from the dock, so you don't have to stray far from the bar to cast your line.

The business was established as the Windjammer Bar and Motel in 1974. The motel rooms were in the building across the road, but the rooms are now rented out as apartments. Chris and Lisa McCreedy bought the business in June, 1996. They teamed up with former owners Neil and Patty Brown and started operating a brew pub. Several different kinds of Raven Beer are brewed in the basement. The batch changes on a periodic basis, and seasonal brews are available. Chris and Lisa also serve excellent barbecued foods in the barroom. Ribs, seafood, and cajun entrees are just some of the items featured on the rotating menu.

As you might expect, the Raven gets a lot of business from tourists and recreationists during the summer. Chris tells me the bar has become so popular that it's not uncommon to see boats circling in the marina waiting for a place to dock. Local residents frequent the bar throughout the year, and the Raven is also a popular place among seasonal workers. A lot of college-aged people gather at the bar during the tourist season. Regardless of the time of year, the customers are typically friendly and well-mannered. The only words of caution I would offer is to wear your sunglasses into the barroom if you go there on a sunny day.

SITTING DUCK BAR AND RESTAURANT

OWNERS: Jim and Kathy Barkell   **LOCATION:**   Highway 35, **Woods Bay**

HOURS: 11:00 a.m. to 2:00 a.m. Daily   **PHONE:**   406-837-DUCK

HAPPY HOUR: No   **BEER:**   Drafts; Domestics;
Imports; Microbrews

GAMBLING: Video Poker/Keno   **AMUSEMENT:**   Horseshoes

LIVE MUSIC: Occasionally   **FOOD:**   Full Menu Restaurant

The Sitting Duck Bar and Restaurant is housed in a wooden structure on the west side of Highway 35 in Woods Bay. A huge river rock fireplace rises from the middle of the floor, and log ceiling beams, a vaulted wooden ceiling, and natural wood wall coverings add to the building's rustic charm. A wooden bar with a brass foot rail stands in front of a beautiful oak back bar against the south wall. A silhouette of a barnyard duck is engraved into the middle of the back bar to promote the name of the business. A tiered wooden deck is off the west side of the building, providing the guests with a spectacular view of Flathead Lake and the surrounding mountains.

The business was established as Derry's Marina in the 1940s. Mr. Derry is the man who invented the Derry parachute, which is still used by modern day smoke jumpers. I'm told Mr. Derry also built a small submarine in the basement of the marina building, and he kept his submarine docked along the shore of Flathead Lake. Derry's Marina obtained a liquor license in 1948, and the bar has been going strong ever since. The name of the business was changed from Derry's Marina to the Shoreline in 1981, but it was renamed the Sitting Duck after extensive renovations were completed on the building in 1983. The hand-crafted back bar that's in the building today was installed during the renovation project. Jim and Kathy Barkell have owned the Sitting Duck since September, 1995. They had previously owned the business from 1976 through 1980, but they bought the Moose Bar in Dillon and operated it for fifteen years before returning to Woods Bay.

Although the Sitting Duck has the appearance of a formal dining establishment, Jim and Kathy operate the business in a casual manner. This is one place where you don't have to dress up to get a great meal. Prime rib is the house specialty, but all the food is good. The dining room is open year round, and outdoor barbecues are commonly held during the summer months. If all you want is a drink, the Sitting Duck has an extensive selection of liquors, wines, and beers. Guests are encouraged to sit back, relax, and enjoy the breathtaking view of the beautiful Flathead Valley.

BUCKHORN BAR

OWNERS: Dellwo Family

HOURS: 8:00 a.m. to 2:00 a.m. Daily

HAPPY HOUR: No

GAMBLING: Video Poker/Keno; Live Poker

LIVE MUSIC: Occasionally

LOCATION: 20 Main Street, **Augusta**

PHONE: 406-562-3344

BEER: Drafts; Domestics; Imports; Microbrews

AMUSEMENT: Pool; Darts

FOOD: Broasted Chicken; Sandwiches

The Buckhorn Bar is housed in a log structure on Main Street in Augusta. The spacious barroom has a long wooden bar, several tables, and plenty of open floor space. The brick fireplace and natural wood interior provide a rustic appearance and a comfortable atmosphere. Several unique taxidermy mounts are on display throughout the building, including two full-curl ram's heads, a golden eagle, a bobcat, and a badger.

The Buckhorn Bar has been owned by the Dellwo family since the late 1950s. Gordon, Francis, Frank, and Tammy Dellwo now manage the business. The original bar was destroyed by fire in 1974, so the log structure that now stands on the property was erected and the bar reopened. Things have been relatively calm since the fire, but some interesting moments occurred when the old bar was still standing. One such incident involved two bulls that were herded into the building by an intoxicated rancher who stopped at the bar on his way home from a bull sale. The shit didn't hit the fan, but there was plenty of it on the floor by the time the animals were herded out the door. On another occasion, a man pulled out a pistol and shot several holes in the floor because rainwater was dripping through the roof and forming puddles. Buckets had been placed on the floor under the leaks, but it was raining so hard the buckets were overflowing. I don't know if the holes cleared out the water, but I'm told the gunshots were enough to clear out all the customers.

An occasional fight still breaks out on dance nights, especially when it's a full moon, but there's normally a very friendly crowd on hand. That friendly crowd always swells to capacity level during the annual Augusta Rodeo in June. The bar is open every day of the year except Christmas, and they host a great party on the afternoon of Christmas Eve. The Buckhorn also has a nice Superbowl party, complete with Rocky Mountain Oyster appetizers, and they host several local celebrations throughout the year. They even have a live poker game on Sunday nights if you want to try your luck at the table.

LAZY B BAR AND CAFE

OWNERS: Kathy and Daryll Jensen

HOURS: 10:00 a.m. to 2:00 a.m. Daily

HAPPY HOUR: No

GAMBLING: Video Poker/Keno; Shake-A-Day

LIVE MUSIC: Occasionally

LOCATION: Main Street, **Augusta**

PHONE: 406-562-3550

BEER: Drafts; Domestics

AMUSEMENT: Pool; Darts; Pinball; Video Game

FOOD: Full Menu Cafe

The Lazy B Bar and Cafe is on Main Street in Augusta. The bar and cafe are housed in the ground-level floor of the three story structure, and vacant hotel rooms occupy most of the second and third floors. The front portion of the barroom is relatively narrow, with enough room for a curved bar, a lone wooden buddy bar, and a few video gambling machines. The adjacent game room has a big-screen TV that gets plenty of use during televised sporting events. Hundreds of brands from ranches all over Montana are on display throughout the barroom and cafe. The barroom is also home to the Sidewalk Cowboys Association, a collection of photographs of celebrities who have visited the Lazy B over the years.

The history of the Lazy B dates back to 1883 when a stage stop and hotel called the Augusta House opened. The structure was one of the first buildings in town, and it was one of the very few that survived a massive fire that swept through Augusta in 1901. Some interesting characters have stayed in the hotel over the years, but none have roused people's imagination more than a man who died in his hotel room many years ago. It's rumored that George's spirit still inhabits the building today. Daryll and Kathy Jenson have owned the Lazy B since January, 1995, and they both have met George on more than one occasion. George doesn't appear to be a mean or destructive ghost, but Kathy and Daryll claim they sometimes hear him moving about the facility.

Daryll and Kathy live in the second floor of the building, but they hope to eventually renovate the hotel rooms and rent them out. For the time being, they are trying to keep the bar and cafe operating. Cafe hours in the summer and fall are 6:00 a.m. to 10:00 p.m., but the hours are cut back as business dies off in the winter. Every meal is homemade, and lunch and dinner specials are offered daily. Friday is seafood night, and prime rib is available on Saturdays. The steaks range in size from twelve to twenty-four ounces, so you won't go away hungry. Who knows, you might even get seated next to George the next time you stop in.

WESTERN BAR

OWNERS: Robert and Lottie Berger

LOCATION: 142 Main Street, **Augusta**

HOURS: 10:00 a.m. to 2:00 a.m. Daily

PHONE: 406-562-3262

HAPPY HOUR: No

BEER: Drafts; Domestics; Imports

GAMBLING: Video Poker/Keno; Shake-A-Day

AMUSEMENT: Pool; Darts; Horseshoes

LIVE MUSIC: Twice Monthly

FOOD: Full Menu Grill; Pizza

The Western Bar is at 142 Main Street in Augusta. An L-shaped bar with a wooden awning above it stands in the front portion of the barroom, several tables are spread throughout the room, and a couple of buddy bars are on the middle of the floor. The exterior walls of the rest rooms have been finished to look like his and hers outhouses. There's no need to worry, though, because the facilities are plumbed with running water. A nice outdoor beer garden, complete with a covered wooden bandstand and a barbecue pit, is just outside the building.

The Western Bar resides on the property where Augusta's livery stable stood during the late 1800s and early 1900s. The livery stable was destroyed by a fire that nearly wiped out the entire town in 1901. The rubble from the fire was eventually cleared, and a saloon was built on the lot. The area where the walk-n cooler now resides once housed a barber shop. The barber shop co-existed with the saloon for several years.

Robert and Lottie Berger bought the Western Bar in October, 1995. They maintain a lively atmosphere, and their customers are fun loving types who know how to enjoy themselves. The Western Bar has live music twice a month, and a band plays all three nights during the weekend of the annual Augusta Rodeo. Robert and Lottie host a pig roast for their customers every September, and they sponsor an annual ice fishing derby that pays a handsome sum of prize money to the winner. Maggot races and a time capsule party (messages were written on the old floor before new flooring was installed) are just a few of the other interesting events that have been held at the Western Bar. There was even one occasion when grown men and women wagered on where a parrot would poop on the floor.

Besides the lively atmosphere and friendly customers, the Western Bar serves some very good food. Their homemade pizzas are delicious, and the hamburgers range in size up to a full pound of fresh ground beef. Daily lunch specials featuring homemade soups and sandwiches are available, and the steaks come highly recommended for dinner. They even serve hard cider if you're looking for a sweet drink that packs a punch.

BOWMAN'S CORNER

OWNERS: Mel Winkels

HOURS: 10:00 a.m. to Closing Daily

HAPPY HOUR: Friday, 6:00 to 8:00

GAMBLING: Video Poker/Keno; Shake-A-Day

LIVE MUSIC: Occasionally

LOCATION: Bowman's Corners

PHONE: 406-562-9231

BEER: Drafts; Domestics; Imports; Microbrews

AMUSEMENT: Pool

FOOD: Full Menu Restaurant

Bowman's Corner is at the junction of Highways 200 and 287 north of Wolf Creek. The junction is known locally, but unofficially, as Bowman's Corners. The structure is made of cinder blocks, but a rustic wooden front has been added which greatly improves the aesthetic qualities of the building's exterior. The barroom and dining area share one open room inside the building. A straight wooden bar with a log foot rail faces the east wall, and several tables are spread throughout the northwest corner of the room.

Howard Bowman established Bowman's Corner in 1947. Howard converted a house that stood on the property into a bar and cafe, and he moved an old schoolhouse onto the lot and renovated it into a motel. The original buildings were destroyed by fire in January, 1964. The structure that now houses the bar and restaurant was erected in the spring of that same year, and the business has been operating out of the building ever since.

Mel Winkels has owned Bowman's Corner since November, 1994. Mel promotes a family-oriented atmosphere at the bar, and his customers are typically friendly and well-behaved. Restaurant hours are 11:00 a.m. to 10:00 p.m. daily. Excellent prime rib, burgers, and cajun barbecued shrimp are just a few of the menu items available. Bowman's Corner also offers drink specials seven nights a week. The Ladies Night specials on Thursday from 6:00 p.m. to 10:00 p.m. and the happy hour on Fridays from 6:00 p.m. to 8:00 p.m. are just two of the specials offered.

Plenty of activity occurs inside the barroom, but Mel also utilizes the surrounding property. Several full RV hookups have been installed, and a large corral occupies a sizeable chunk of land to the west of the building. Team steer roping competitions are held in the corral throughout the summer, and motorcycle rodeos have been held here on occasion just to keep things interesting. Plans are in place to add six rustic cabins in 1997, so lodging will also be available. There's always something going on at the bar, so you don't have to worry about getting bored. Good food, cold beer, and friendly people make Bowman's Corner a great place to stop.

GLASS SLIPPER LOUNGE AND GROCERY

OWNERS: Bob and Donna Glass

LOCATION: 5720 Canyon Ferry Road, **Canyon Ferry**

HOURS: 11:00 a.m. to Closing Daily

PHONE: 406-475-3230

HAPPY HOUR: No

BEER: Drafts; Domestics

GAMBLING: Video Poker/Keno

AMUSEMENT: Pool; Darts; Pinball; Video Games; Horseshoes

LIVE MUSIC: No

FOOD: Frozen Pizza; Snacks

The Glass Slipper Lounge and Grocery is at 5720 Canyon Ferry Road between Helena and Canyon Ferry Reservoir. The building stands on the southwest corner at the intersection of Canyon Ferry Road and Spokane Creek Road (Route 284). The steel-sided structure houses a barroom and a small grocery store with video rentals. The barroom has a long Z-shaped bar with a brass foot rail, and a few tables are spread throughout the room if you prefer some privacy.

The Glass Slipper first opened on Thanksgiving Day in 1981. Bob and Donna Glass established the business, and they continue to operate it today. The Glass Slipper is really more of a community center than a bar and store. People of all ages stop in to rent videos, buy groceries, and socialize with their neighbors. Bob and Donna operate the Glass Slipper as a service to the local residents. They host several benefits and fund raising events throughout the year, and they also sponsor dart and horseshoe teams for the local leagues. Private parties such as wedding receptions, anniversary parties, and birthday parties are commonly held at the Glass Slipper, and a Bob and Donna host a great Christmas Party every year on Christmas Eve.

Because of the bar's close proximity to Canyon Ferry Reservoir and the surrounding national forests, a lot of outdoors enthusiasts stop at the Glass Slipper. Boaters, hunters, fishermen, hikers, and tourists from all over the world have stopped by over the years. Exceptional wildlife viewing, big game and bird hunting, and fishing are all within ten miles of the Glass Slipper. A popular eagle viewing spot at the base of Canyon Ferry Dam is within a few miles of the bar, and the region also boasts some of the best sapphire digging in the United States. The recreational opportunities around the area are abundant, and the Glass Slipper is an excellent place to stop after a long day in the great outdoors. If that's not enough incentive for you to stop, Bob says he will buy a free drink for anyone who brings a copy of this book into the bar.

167

O'MALLEY'S

OWNER: Matt Gould & Claire O'Malley

LOCATION: 8030 Canyon Ferry Road, **Canyon Ferry**

HOURS: 8:00 a.m. to Closing Daily

PHONE: 406-475-3899

HAPPY HOUR: No

BEER: Drafts; Domestics; Imports; Microbrews

GAMBLING: Video Poker/Keno; Shake-A-Day

AMUSEMENT: Pool; Darts; Pinball; Video Games; Foosball; Horseshoes

LIVE MUSIC: Occasionally

FOOD: Full Menu Restaurant

O'Malley's is approximately two miles east of the Canyon Ferry Dam on Canyon Ferry Road (Route 284). The main barroom in the center of the building is flanked on one side by a game room and on the other by a dining room. Ample seating is available at the long bar, and plenty of tables are spread throughout the room if you don't want to risk falling off a barstool. When the barroom gets crowded, you can head for the deck outside the dining room and enjoy the view of Canyon Ferry Reservoir.

The business was established as the Golden Pine Club in 1948. The Montana Liquor Division repeatedly denied early applications for a liquor license, mainly because the Bureau of Land Management didn't want any liquor sold within five miles of the Canyon Ferry Dam construction site. A suit was filed against the Liquor Division, and a license was eventually issued. I normally don't write about lettuce, but I'm told the first salad bar in Montana operated out of the building. What historical significance this has, I don't know, but I thought it was worth mentioning.

Matt Gould and Claire O'Malley, both natives of Ireland, bought what was Riley's Bar in April, 1996 and changed the name to O'Malley's. Matt and Claire take a personal interest in their customers, and they display a wonderful sense of humor. They also serve excellent food at the bar. The dinner menu features steaks and seafood, and Irish Beef Stew is sometimes available. My personal favorite at O'Malley's, besides the Olympia Beer, is the 1/2 pound cheeseburger and hand-cut fries.

Several special events are held at O'Malley's throughout the year; none more popular than the annual Saint Patrick's Day celebration. The number of days remaining until the big party is updated daily on a plastic clover leaf in the bar. Claire plans on hosting a St. Patrick's Day party that rivals the one in Butte. That would be quite an accomplishment, but if anyone can do it, I'm sure it will be Matt and Claire at O'Malley's.

YACHT BASIN

OWNER: Orville Johnson

LOCATION: 7035 Canyon Ferry Road, **Canyon Ferry**

HOURS: 8:00 a.m. to Closing Daily

PHONE: 406-475-3125

HAPPY HOUR: No

BEER: Drafts; Domestics; Imports; Microbrews

GAMBLING: Video Poker/Keno

AMUSEMENT: Pool

LIVE MUSIC: No

FOOD: Full Menu Restaurant

Yacht Basin is at 7035 Canyon Ferry Road near the Canyon Ferry Dam. The building stands on a hill overlooking the reservoir, providing the guests with a spectacular view of the lake and surrounding mountains. The barroom resides in the west side of the building, and the dining room is in the east side. Customers in either room can peer out across the water through large plate glass windows. The barroom decor is relatively simple, but the dining room is finished in a more formal manner. Among the many interesting features in the dining room is a huge antique mirror that was shipped to Montana via team and wagon from Chicago. The mirror originally resided in a furniture store in Helena. The store was destroyed by fire in the 1970s, and the mirror was moved to Yacht Basin in 1984.

The business was established as Sherriff's Place in 1947. The initial request for a liquor license was denied because of a Bureau of Land Management request that liquor not be sold within five miles of the Canyon Ferry Dam construction site, so the bar operated with only a retail beer license for the first several years. The name was changed to the Canyon Ferry Club in 1948 when the original owner took on two partners. A full liquor license was issued in 1953, just one year prior to the bar moving to its present location. The business became Yacht Basin in 1964. Fire destroyed the building in 1977, so a modular building was moved in and renovated into a barroom. The existing dining room is an addition that was built onto the west side of the modular building in 1982.

Orville Johnson has owned Yacht Basin since 1978. Orville's busiest season is the summer when tourists and outdoors enthusiasts join the steady crowd of locals at the bar and restaurant. The restaurant opens at 5:00 p.m. daily during the summer, but dinners are served only on weekends through the winter. The menu features a variety of steak and seafood entrees, all of which are delicious. If all you want is a drink, the bar opens at 8:00 a.m. daily. You're bound to meet some interesting characters at the bar, especially if you talk to the regular day shift bartender.

CRAIG BAR

OWNERS: Joe and Juanita Duvall

LOCATION: Craig

HOURS: 8:00 a.m. to 2:00 a.m. Daily

PHONE: 406-235-9994

HAPPY HOUR: No

BEER: Drafts; Domestics; Imports; Microbrews

GAMBLING: Video Poker/Keno; Shake-A-Day

AMUSEMENT: Pool

LIVE MUSIC: Occasionally

FOOD: Sandwiches; Bar Snacks

The Craig Bar is in downtown Craig, and believe me, that's all the directions you need to find the place. The moderate-sized barroom is laid out in somewhat of an L-configuration. A large horseshoe-shaped bar occupies most of the floor space in the south side of the building, and a pool table fills the smaller room on the north side. A couple of small tables stand near the stone fireplace toward the center of the barroom if you prefer sitting away from the bar.

The business was established as Lee's Place in 1950. The building was a lot smaller when the bar first opened, but several additions have been made over the years. The bar was called Kay's Tavern between 1952 and 1964, and it operated under the name Coachman Bar and Cafe from 1964 until it became the Craig Bar in 1974. Joe and Juanita Duvall bought the business in 1986, and they continue to operate it today.

The Craig Bar is seven miles from Holter Lake and about 200 yards from a popular fishing access site on the Missouri River, so it's no surprise that a lot of fishermen frequent the bar. Fly fishermen (and women) from all over the world stop at the Craig Bar during the spring, summer, and fall, and ice fishermen commonly stop in during the winter. If you plan on floating the river during the off-season, you can usually get someone in the bar to shuttle your vehicle to the next boat access point for a minimal fee. The bar also sells live bait and a limited selection of fishing accessories if you run short.

One of the featured attractions at the Craig Bar occurs on January 1 each year when members of the Craig Bar Polar Bear Club convene for their annual dip in the Missouri River. People from all over the region come to participate in the plunge, and they have a great party in the bar afterwards. Members who can't make it to Craig on New Year's Day must perform a make-up swim sometime during the winter to remain a member in good standing. Several certificates of participation are posted on the barroom wall showing the date a particular person swam and the outdoor temperature on that day. Some minus 20 degree swims are on record.

LAKESIDE RESORT

OWNER: Clete Daily

HOURS: 9:00 a.m. to 2:00 a.m. Daily

HAPPY HOUR: No

GAMBLING: Video Poker/Keno

LIVE MUSIC: Occasionally

LOCATION: 5295 York Road, **Lakeside**

PHONE: 406-227-6076

BEER: Drafts; Domestics

AMUSEMENT: Pool; Darts; Volleyball; Pinball; Horseshoes; Video Games

FOOD: Grill Items

Lakeside Resort is on York Road in Lakeside, a small community on the west shore of Hauser Lake. The bar is part of a larger business, which includes a marina, paddle boat rentals, an RV campground, and a tackle shop. Nine acres of lakefront property surround the bar. Plate glass windows on the east side of the building afford a fantastic view of the lake for customers inside the barroom, and outdoor seating is available on the covered deck that also faces the water.

The Lakeside Resort was established in the 1940s. A retail beer license was obtained in 1947, and a liquor license was subsequently obtained in 1949. The business has expanded significantly since the bar first opened, but with only one exception, the barroom has always been a peaceful place. That one exception occurred many years ago when an armed man entered the bar to rob the place. Unbeknownst to the would-be robber, the bartender kept a loaded shotgun hidden behind the bar. To make a long story short, the unwelcomed intruder ended up dying in the parking lot with a gut full of shotgun pellets. It wasn't long until the peaceful atmosphere returned at the Lakeside Bar, and to the best of my knowledge, nobody has since attempted to rob the place.

Clete Daily has owned the Lakeside Resort since 1978. Clete is a community-minded individual who often hosts fund raising events at the bar for local organizations such as the volunteer fire department. The resort is also a popular place for class reunions, weddings, and company picnics. The busiest times of the year are during the summer and fall when boaters, fishermen, and sightseers swarm to the area for the outstanding wildlife viewing and recreational opportunities. Possibly the best kokanee salmon fishing in Montana is on Hauser Lake, and hundreds of bald eagles flock to the lake every fall to feast on spawning salmon. Marina reservations can be obtained by calling 227-6413. Up to 100 boats can be docked at any one time, and 68 RV spaces are available on the property.

MARYSVILLE HOUSE

OWNERS: Steve and Vanessa Sobonya

LOCATION: Main Street, **Marysville**

HOURS: 5:00 p.m. to Closing Tue-Sat
1:00 p.m. to Closing Sat/Sun
Closed Monday (Summer) and Monday and Tuesday (Winter)

PHONE: No Phone

HAPPY HOUR: No

BEER: Drafts; Domestics; Imports

GAMBLING: No

AMUSEMENT: Horseshoes

LIVE MUSIC: No

FOOD: Restaurant

The Marysville House is on Main Street in historic Marysville. If ever a place should be described as rustic, the Marysville House is that place. The floors, walls, ceiling, and fixtures are mostly fashioned from wood, in one form or another. Illumination is provided by kerosine lamps, and the primary heat sources are a wood burning stove and a stone fireplace. The barroom has a wooden bar with a thick top made from planks cut from a single tree trunk. The foot rail at the base of the bar is an old mine car track taken from a local mine. Photographs of old Marysville hang from the barroom walls, and the dining room decor consists of antique skis and snowshoes. Don't let the building's appearance fool you, however, because the Marysville House serves some of the best food in Montana.

The building that houses the Marysville House is well over 100 years old, but it hasn't always stood in Marysville. The wooden structure was originally the train depot in the nearby community of Silver City. It was moved to Marysville in the early 1970s when the Marysville House first opened. A few minor renovations were made, but the building today looks much like it did when it served as a train station. Steve and Vanessa Sobonya have owned the business since 1982. They started serving meals three years later, and the menu has never changed. The few steak, seafood, and chicken entrees listed on the chalk boards attached to the walls are all that's available. Steve and Vanessa never get complaints about an inadequate selection of food because what they do serve is outstanding.

The one thing that sets the Marysville House apart is the unique combination of fine dining and informal atmosphere. The place is the epitome of exquisite meals served in a casual environment. You can't call ahead for reservations, so it's a first-come, first-served seating policy. The meals are prepared outside on propane grills, and dining room guests are seated at wooden picnic tables and served from paper plates. Of course, you don't have to have dinner when you visit the Marysville House. The full service bar has the same great atmosphere as the dining room.

MONTANA AL'S SILVER CITY BAR AND GRILL

OWNER: Al and Cheryl Potter

LOCATION: Lincoln Hwy. & Birdseye Road, **Silver City**

HOURS: 8:00 a.m. to 2:00 a.m. Fri/Sat/Sun 11:00 a.m. to Closing Tue-Thur

PHONE: 406-443-9702

HAPPY HOUR: No

BEER: Drafts; Domestics; Microbrews

GAMBLING: Video Poker/Keno; Shake-A-Day

AMUSEMENT: Pool

LIVE MUSIC: Original Live Music Every Friday and Saturday

FOOD: Full Menu Grill

Montana Al's Silver City Bar and Grill, home of the world's largest and most complete collection of Fender instruments, is at the junction of Lincoln Highway and Birdseye Road in Silver City. The main barroom resides in the west side of the building, an elevated stage overlooks a spacious dance floor in the east side, and Fender instruments of all shapes and sizes are on display in show cases high on the barroom walls. Aside from the instruments, the interior decor is primarily western. The main bar has a log foot rail and a thick top made from planks cut from the middle of a tree trunk. Painted animal skulls and weathered cowboy hats hang from the walls, old corral gates stand along the wall near the dance floor, and the woodwork throughout the building has been scarred with hot branding irons.

The business was established as the Silver City Supper Club in 1981. Al and Cheryl Potter bought the place in 1990 and started transforming it into a country and western bar and a museum for Al's instruments. With over 400 pieces in his possession, Al Potter has the worlds largest, most complete collection of Fender electric and acoustic guitars, lap steels, fiddles, banjos, basses, pedal steels, and mandolins. Approximately eighty string instruments were on display in the barroom as of January, 1997; however, Al plans on adding at least 300 more by the time he's done. Al and Cheryl also built a thirty foot addition onto the original building, and they've completely renovated the interior.

Montana Al's attracts a steady flow of local residents throughout the year, and they also see plenty of tourists, sportsmen, and outdoors enthusiasts who visit the area. The bar becomes quite busy during the annual ultralight plane convention that's held in Silver City, especially since the landing field is just across the road. And, of course, I can't forget to mention the weekend crowd. The barroom is usually packed with people who come to listen and dance to the original music of Montana Al's World Famous Band on Friday and Saturday nights.

173

THE FRENCHMAN AND ME

OWNERS: Tom and Jerrelyn Powell   **LOCATION:** Main Street, **Wolf Creek**

HOURS: 7:00 a.m. to 2:00 a.m. Daily   **PHONE:** 406-235-9991

HAPPY HOUR: No   **BEER:** Drafts; Domestics; Imports; Microbrews

GAMBLING: Video Poker/Keno   **AMUSEMENT:** No

LIVE MUSIC: Occasionally   **FOOD:** Full Menu Cafe

The Frenchman and Me is housed in a brick structure on Main Street in Wolf Creek. The moderate-sized barroom has an L-shaped bar along the north wall, and additional seating is available at the tables in the south side of the room. The interior decor isn't fancy, but there are some interesting antique lamps, farm and ranch implements, and porcelain figurines on display. If you're interested in buying souvenirs, the gift shop next door sells Montana-made crafts and gifts.

The bar was built in 1895. The walls of the building are twenty-one inches thick, so it comes as no surprise that the structure is still standing over 100 years later. In fact, the building has withstood at least one major earthquake, an intense fire, and several gunshots without suffering any structural damage. I believe it's safe to say the place will be around for at least another 100 years.

Tom and Jerrelyn Powell have owned the Frenchman and Me since 1991. They promote a family-oriented atmosphere, and people of all ages are welcome at the bar. There's a school bus stop in front of the building, so it's not uncommon to see small children inside the barroom waiting for the bus on mornings when the weather is bad. The bar is also a popular morning gathering spot for adults who stop in for breakfast and to catch up on the latest news around town.

The Frenchman and Me is a great place to relax and unwind. You can even enjoy wildlife viewing at the bar because several bighorn sheep usually wander down the mountain into the back yard in the evenings. The bar does a steady business throughout the year, but the place is always packed during the annual Hunters Ball in mid November. Tom and Jerrelyn also host several outdoor barbecues for their customers each year. Homemade meals are served from 7:00 a.m. until 9:00 p.m. daily. Lunch and dinner specials are available, and the steaks and broasted chicken are always good. If you're a fisherman, take a look at the special "Lady Killer" flies they sell at the Frenchman and Me. These interesting pieces of tackle are certain to lure in a trophy.

OASIS BAR AND CAFE

OWNERS: Paul and Cathy Schulte

HOURS: 10:00 a.m. to Closing Daily

HAPPY HOUR: No

GAMBLING: Video Poker/Keno

LIVE MUSIC: Occasionally

LOCATION: Old Hwy. 91, **Wolf Creek**

PHONE: 406-235-9992

BEER: Drafts; Domestics

AMUSEMENT: Pool; Video Game

FOOD: Full Menu Cafe

The Oasis Bar and Cafe is on Old Highway 91 in Wolf Creek. The barroom resides in the south side of the building, and a cafe occupies the addition on the north side. The barroom has a vaulted wooden ceiling supported by log beams. A horseshoe-shaped bar stands just inside the main entrance, and a couple of tables are available along the east wall. Several hundred currency bills are tacked to the barroom walls and ceiling beams. A lot of foreign currency is mixed among the American money, and most of the bills have a signature and short message written on them by the individuals who left them at the bar.

The Oasis Bar and Cafe was established in 1945. The original bar, dining room, and kitchen were all housed in the south portion of the building where only barroom resides today. Things were a bit cramped, to say the least, so a large addition was built onto the north side of the structure in 1980. The dining room and kitchen were moved into the new addition, and the barroom was enlarged to its current size.

Paul and Cathy Schulte bought the Oasis Bar and Cafe in 1981. Local residents provide a steady business throughout the year, but a lot of outdoors enthusiasts and travelers also stop by for meals and drinks. The surrounding Big Belt Mountains provide abundant opportunities for big game hunting, and the nearby Missouri River and Holter Lake are popular fishing and boating attractions. Most of the travelers who stop at the Oasis do so by choice, but Cathy says a lot of them turn out to be stranded motorists who need to make a phone call for roadside assistance. Wolf Creek just seems to be one of those places where vehicles decide to quit running.

The Oasis hosts several community support and customer appreciation events each year. Proceeds from the annual Saint Patrick's Day celebration and wild game feed are donated to the local volunteer fire department, and the annual Survivor's Day party is a customer appreciation bash that's held to celebrate the bar's anniversary. The Oasis also hosts a terrific Halloween party, complete with live music and costume prizes. If you can't make it to any of their parties, it's always fun just to stop in and say hello. Hopefully, you won't be there because of car trouble.

YORK BAR

OWNERS: John and Carol Skufca

HOURS: 11:00 a.m. to Closing Daily

HAPPY HOUR: No

GAMBLING: Video Poker/Keno; Shake-A-Day

LIVE MUSIC: No

LOCATION: 7500 York Road, **York**

PHONE: 406-475-9949

BEER: Drafts; Domestics; Imports

AMUSEMENT: Pool; Pinball; Darts; Horseshoes

FOOD: Grill Items

The York Bar is at the intersection of York and Nelson Roads in the historic mining community of York. The main part of the barroom is housed in the south side of the building, and a game room resides in the north side. A wooden bar with a steel foot rail and a padded elbow rail stands along the east wall of the barroom. The sturdy bar top is made from thick planks that were cut from the center of a large tree trunk. A stone fireplace rises from the floor against the west wall, creating a comfortable setting. Black and white photographs taken of the surrounding area, including both Hauser and Canyon Ferry Dams, hang from the walls. A covered wooden walkway is off the south side of the building, and a tiered wooden deck is off the north side.

The business was established as a store, gas station, and post office in the late 1930s. After the mining died down, the store owners bought the old schoolhouse next door and renovated the building into a tavern. The original name of the bar was the Friendly Tavern, and the York Bar is still widely known as the Friendly York Bar. The existing game room was added to the original building sometime during the 1950s. Although the store, gas station, and post office have all gone out of business, the bar is still going strong.

John and Carol Skufca bought the York Bar in March, 1995, and they've kept the friendly atmosphere very much alive. Friendly sometimes turns feisty, but rarely does trouble start. John says people have ridden horses through the building, but he was somewhat surprised when someone recently drove a Harley into the barroom. Everyone got a good laugh over the antic, so no harm was done. The York Bar is always busy on the third Friday in May (the day before fishing season opens) for the annual Rocky Mountain Oyster feed. Fried bull testicles are the food of choice for one day, but the grilled burgers keep people returning the rest of the year. People from all over the United States and several foreign countries have stopped in just to try the famous burgers at the Friendly York Bar.

JOPLIN BAR

OWNER: Ken Snyder, Jr.

HOURS: 11:00 a.m. to Closing Daily

HAPPY HOUR: 5:00 to 6:00 Mon - Fri

GAMBLING: Video Poker/Keno; Shake-A-Day

LIVE MUSIC: Occasionally

LOCATION: Route 224, **Joplin**

PHONE: 406-292-3245

BEER: Drafts; Domestics

AMUSEMENT: Pool; Darts; Horseshoes

FOOD: Microwave Foods; Frozen Pizza

The Joplin Bar is on the corner of 2nd Street and Route 224 in Joplin. The moderate sized barroom has a straight bar along the east wall, and a few tables are available if you can't find an empty barstool. There's nothing elaborate about the place, but the people are friendly and the beer is always cold. What more could a person ask for?

At one time, Joplin was a thriving community with three saloons. Things have certainly changed, because the Joplin Bar is the only watering hole in town today. The business was established as the Palace Bar in 1945. The bar operated out of an old church building for a while, but it was destroyed by fire in 1949. Another structure was moved onto the lot, and the Palace Bar operated out of that building until the present-day structure was built in 1975. The bar operated under the name Schmuckers from 1980 until 1991 when it became the Joplin Bar.

Ken Snyder bought the Joplin bar in August, 1994. Most of Ken's customers live in Joplin and the surrounding communities, but a few travelers stop in from time to time. Ken's busiest days of the year occur on Super Bowl Sunday and during an annual pig roast he holds in early October. Roasted pig keeps them coming back year after year in October, but rattlesnake is the food of choice on Super Bowl Sunday. Ken is quite the snake hunter, and he serves rattlesnake meat to his customers during the Super Bowl. Ken also makes belts and hat bands out of the snake skins and sells them at the bar. The snake stuff has become so popular that the Joplin Bar's official logo is now a rattlesnake caught in a trap.

Things are usually pretty calm at the Joplin Bar, but occasionally something exciting happens. Several years ago, an alcohol-impaired bar owner inadvertently discharged his pistol while showing the piece to a couple of customers. The bullet went between two people sitting at the bar and ricocheted off the bar top into the ceiling. Nobody was hurt, but there's speculation that a couple of customers may have soiled their undergarments. The scar in the bar top and mark in the ceiling are still there if you're interested in tracing the path of the stray bullet.

177

HALF WAY HOUSE

OWNER: Billy Joe Davis

LOCATION: 14799 Bull Lake Road, **Bull Lake**

HOURS: 10:00 a.m. to 2:00 a.m. (Summer) Noon to Closing (Winter)

PHONE: 406-295-4358

HAPPY HOUR: 4:00 to 6:00 Mon - Fri

BEER: Drafts; Domestics

GAMBLING: Video Poker/Keno; Shake-A-Day

AMUSEMENT: Pool; Darts; Horseshoes

LIVE MUSIC: Frequently Through The Summer

FOOD: Sandwiches; Fresh Pizza; Chicken

The Half Way House is at 14799 Bull Lake Road (Highway 56). The spacious barroom has an open floor plan, with the bar in the front portion of the room and a dance floor and bandstand in the rear. A beautiful antique bar and back bar stand just inside the main entrance along the north wall. Both pieces were fashioned from oak during the late 1800s, and they have been maintained in excellent condition. The hand-carved back bar has a large mirror in the center and a smaller mirror on each end. Allegedly, the bar and back bar resided in a hotel in Noxon before being moved to the Half Way House. The lawn off the east side of the building serves as a beer garden and outdoor dance hall. The beer garden, bar, and outdoor bandstand get plenty of use during the summer months.

Tallmadge Service was the name of the business in 1947 when the first off-premises beer license was issued. A liquor license was obtained in 1950, and the business became known as the Half Way House. The new name was selected because the bar is half way between Noxon and Troy. The Bull Lake Road was gravel at that time, and travelers often stopped at the bar to stretch their legs before continuing on with their journey. The original barroom was less than half the size it is today. Several additions have been made since the bar first opened.

Billy Joe Davis has owned the Half Way House since 1986. Although business is somewhat slow during the winter, big crowds show up in the summer to attend the various gatherings Billy Joe Hosts. Some of the more popular events include the Lost Brothers Poker Run on the third weekend in June, the Country Music Campout on the fourth weekend in July, and the Big Sky Rendezvous on the third weekend in August. Billy Joe leases a piece of property across the road from the bar on the east shore of Bull Lake, so his customers can camp overnight and have access to the water. Be sure to arrive early if you plan on staying the weekend of the Big Sky Rendezvous, because over 1,000 people a year attend the three day event, and camping space is limited.

JERRY'S SALOON

OWNER: Noreen Syth

HOURS: Noon to 2:00 a.m. Daily

HAPPY HOUR: No

GAMBLING: Video Poker/Keno

LIVE MUSIC: Karaoke on Occasion

LOCATION: 1st Ave. S., **Fortine**

PHONE: 406-882-4474

BEER: Drafts; Domestics; Imports; Microbrews

AMUSEMENT: Pool; Horseshoes; Golf

FOOD: Full Menu Grill

Jerry's Saloon is on 1st Avenue South in Fortine. The barroom, dining room, and a small pro shop are housed in the east side of the building, and a multiple-use room is in the steel sided addition on the west side. The obvious question that comes to mind is "why is there a pro shop in a saloon?". Unless you've been to Fortine, the not-so-obvious answer is "because Jerry's Saloon has its own golf course". I realize most golf courses have a bar in the clubhouse for the convenience of the golfers, but Jerry's Saloon is the only place I know of that has a golf course as an added attraction for the bar. There are also twenty RV spaces on the property, so the saloon has its own campground as well.

Jerry and Noreen Syth established Jerry's Saloon in 1966. Jerry and Noreen started out with a retail beer license, but they obtained a full liquor license in 1971. The Meadow Creek Golf Course, a nine hole, par 3 course, was added in 1990. Things went well for Jerry and Noreen until January, 1996, when Jerry was tragically killed by a Lincoln County Sheriff's Deputy. Jerry had gone to the bar in the early morning hours to investigate an intruder Noreen saw from her bedroom window, and in the mean time, Noreen dialed 911 to report the incident. Soon after the deputy arrived on the scene, shots were fired. Controversy exists over who fired the first shot, but Jerry was struck with several bullets, and the deputy was struck with the only shot Jerry fired. The deputy was eventually cleared of any wrongdoing, but the town of Fortine lost a great man.

Noreen continues to operate the business. She gets a lot of support from local residents, and snowmobilers, hunters, and tourists also stop in to eat, drink, or spend the night. Packaged liquor is sold at the bar, and meals are served in the spacious dining room overlooking the golf course. The Pro Special Sirloin and the Par 3 Steak and Shrimp are popular dinner selections, and a wide variety of beers and liquors are available. Whether you're a golfer who wants to relax in the bar after a hot day on the course or a drinker who wants to relax on the golf course after a hard day in the bar, Jerry's Saloon can accommodate your interests.

HAPPY'S INN

OWNERS: Happy's Inn, Inc.

HOURS: 8:00 a.m. to Closing Daily

HAPPY HOUR: 5:30 to 6:30 Mon - Fri

GAMBLING: Video Poker/Keno

LIVE MUSIC: Occasionally

LOCATION: Highway 2, **Happy's Inn**

PHONE: 406-293-7810

BEER: Domestics; Microbrews

AMUSEMENT: Pool; Horseshoes

FOOD: Full Menu Restaurant

Happy's Inn is at 39704 Highway 2 South (40 miles south of Libby) in the community of Happy's Inn. The bar is only part of the entire business, which includes a convenience store, gas station, restaurant, campground, cabin rentals, and public laundry and shower facilities. The barroom, convenience store, and a coffee counter occupy one open area in the north side of the building, and a spacious dining room is in the south side.

Happy's Inn was established as a saloon and tourist cabin rental business by Happy Townsend in 1924. Chicken dinners were served at the bar, but only on weekends. The road was still gravel at the time, but the chicken was so good that people commonly made the eighty mile round trip drive from Kallispell and Libby just for the food. Another attraction was a local deer that would walk into the saloon and drink at the bar. It's hard to imagine a wild animal wandering into a barroom, but photographs showing the deer and the original saloon now hang from the west wall of the dining room. Gas pumps were installed and a restaurant was built when the new highway came through in 1952. The bar moved into the restaurant building, and the original saloon was eventually destroyed.

Happy's Inn was purchased in 1973 by a group of local property owners who call themselves Happy's Inn, Inc. The property owners were concerned that someone unfamiliar with the area might buy the Inn and change the way it was operated, so they joined forces and bought the business. The Inn still caters to the needs of local residents, but it also serves as a convenient stop for motorists traveling along Highway 2.

The barroom customers thrive on innovative forms of entertainment. One of the big events of the year occurs during ice fishing season when Happy's Inn hosts the ever-popular maggot races. Contestants place their maggots into the center of a circle on the floor, and the owner of the first maggot out of the circle is declared the winner. Another popular event is the annual St. Patrick's Day Ugly Auction. People make blind bids on items wrapped in brown paper bags, and although there's never anything of value in the bags, everyone has a great time. The proceeds raised from the Ugly Auction are donated to the local volunteer fire department.

180

KICKIN HORSE SALOON

OWNERS: Pattye and Doc Judd

HOURS: Noon to Closing Daily

HAPPY HOUR: 5:30 to 6:30 Mon - Fri

GAMBLING: Video Poker/Keno

LIVE MUSIC: Occasionally

LOCATION: Highway 2, **Happy's Inn**

PHONE: 406-293-8532

BEER: Drafts; Domestics; Imports; Microbrews

AMUSEMENT: Pool; Shuffleboard; Video Game; Pinball; Horseshoes

FOOD: Pizza; Chicken

The Kickin Horse Saloon is housed in a wooden structure at 39943 Highway 2 South (40 miles south of Libby) in the community of Happy's Inn. The owners of the saloon refer to the area as Nowhere, Montana, but most road maps list it as Happy's Inn. A straight wooden bar and a modern wooden back bar stand along the west wall of the barroom, and a dance floor and raised bandstand are in the east side. The floor is carpeted, except for the dance floor, and the walls are finished with tongue-and-groove pine boards. Bent and twisted logs were installed as railing around the bandstand and the wooden decks off the south and east sides of the building. An old chainsaw is embedded in the thick log post that supports the ceiling above the dance floor.

The business was established as the Whistle Stop in 1971. I'm told the man who built the bar did so in response to a challenge issued by the owner of Happy's Inn across the road. Allegedly, the man complained because he couldn't get a discount on a large quantity of beer he bought from Happy's Inn for a party. The owner of Happy's Inn basically said if he didn't like the price, he could build his own bar. Shortly thereafter, the Whistle Stop opened for business across the road from Happy's Inn. Pattye and Doc Judd bought the bar in 1992 and changed the name to the Kickin Horse Saloon. They doubled the size of the original barroom in 1995 when they added the dance hall.

The Kickin Horse Saloon is a friendly place with fun-loving people. Pattye and Doc go out of their way to make sure their customers enjoy themselves. A wild game cookoff is held every March, and Pattye and Doc sponsor an annual Uglymobile Run on the Fourth of July. The Uglymobile Run contestants drive all sorts of old beater cars over a designated gravel road course, and any vehicle that doesn't make it back to the bar is pulled in with a tow truck. A pig roast and live music take place after the Uglymobile Run, so everybody goes home with a full stomach.

LITTLE JOE'S MONTANA

OWNER: Peggy Trout	**LOCATION:** Highway 56, **Little Joe**
HOURS: 9:00 a.m. to Closing Daily	**PHONE:** 406-295-9701
HAPPY HOUR: 4:00 to 6:00 Mon - Fri	**BEER:** Drafts; Domestics
GAMBLING: Video Poker/Keno; Shake-A-Day	**AMUSEMENT:** Pool; Darts; Horseshoes; Volleyball
LIVE MUSIC: Several Times A Year	**FOOD:** Full Menu Cafe

Believe it or not, Little Joe's Montana is in a place called Little Joe, Montana. The post office pulled out several years ago, however, so you won't find Little Joe on your road map. The community of three permanent residents is approximately fourteen miles south of Troy on Highway 56, and the only commercial building in town is the bar. The bar's logo reads "Famous For Absolutely Nothing So Far", but it's a great place to stop nonetheless. A barroom, cafe, and dance hall share the floor space inside the building, and a partially covered deck and an outdoor bandstand are on the three acres of property that surround the bar. The barroom has an L-shaped bar and a few small tables in the back portion of the room, a wood burning stove in the middle of the floor, and several wooden picnic tables and two bird cages near the front entrance. The dance hall is housed in an adjacent room off the north side of the barroom.

The bar gets its name from the man who established the business. Little Joe, as he was called, opened the Broken Wheel Bar in 1968. Little Joe was in the process of changing the name of the business to Little Joe's Bar when he met an untimely death. It was July, 1976, and Joe was shot to death in his own bar by his own friend. I don't know all the details of the shooting, but I'm told the two men were in the barroom late one night playing pool when the shooting took place. Nobody I spoke with could say for sure why Joe's friend shot him, but the rumors allege everything from a love triangle to a dispute over the pool game.

Peggy Trout has owned Little Joe's Montana since 1993. Peggy caters primarily to local residents, but visiting hunters, fishermen, and snowmobilers also stop by. There's usually a friendly crowd on hand, if you don't count the two talking birds in the cages. Peggy keeps a macaw and a yellow naped amazon at the bar, and the birds have developed a rather interesting vocabulary from the customers. If you care to hear some vulgar language from a couple of parrots, all you have to do is stand near the bird cages and wait until they speak. You will either be offended or amused, and you may even learn a few new words.

FIRST AND LAST CHANCE BAR

OWNER: Dave Clark

LOCATION: Highway 93, **Roosville**

HOURS: 8:00 a.m. to 2:00 a.m. Daily

PHONE: 406-889-3443

HAPPY HOUR: No

BEER: Drafts; Domestics; Imports; Microbrews

GAMBLING: Video Poker/Keno

AMUSEMENT: Pool; Video Games

LIVE MUSIC: Occasionally

FOOD: Grill Items

The First and Last Chance Bar is at the Roosville Point of Entry at the Canadian Border on Highway 93. A spacious barroom resides in the center portion of the building, a liquor store and gift shop are in the north end, and the 3 CCC's Restaurant operates out of the south side. The barroom has a straight wooden bar facing the east wall, a few tables spread throughout the room, approximately twenty video gambling machines, and a big-screen TV against the south wall.

The First and Last Chance Bar was established in 1972. The business initially consisted of only the barroom, but five additions have been made to the building over the years. The latest addition occurred in 1990 when the 3 CCC's Restaurant was built. The restaurant is presently leased out as a separate business, and they were operating on limited hours when I last visited the bar in October, 1996. The First and Last Chance Bar has been in the Clark family since it first opened. Dave Clark currently owns and operates the business.

The regular customers at the First and Last Chance Bar consist of American and Canadian residents. Eureka, Montana and Grasmere, Brittish Columbia, Canada are the closest communities to the Roosville Point of Entry, and people from both towns like to party at the First and Last Chance Bar. Tourists stop in during the summer, and skiers who drive between Canada and the Big Mountain Ski Area in Whitefish, Montana frequent the bar during the winter. Dave says he used to get a lot more Canadian trade, but due to a combination of factors, the Canadians don't drive to the States and party like they used to.

The duty free liquor, cigarettes, and souvenirs still attract some Canadian travelers, and Dave has live music a couple of times a year to help promote the business. An annual Patio Party is held in the parking lot on the first Saturday in July. The Patio Party used to be held on the patio off the south side of the barroom, but the patio was enclosed and renovated into the restaurant in 1990. The party was so popular that Dave decided to keep having it, whether he had an actual patio or not.

STATE LINE HOUSE

OWNERS: Meg and Ed Boggers

HOURS: Noon to Closing Tue-Sun
Closed Monday

HAPPY HOUR: No

GAMBLING: Video Poker/Keno;
Live Poker; Bingo

LIVE MUSIC: Occasionally

LOCATION: Highway 2, State Line
at **Montana/Idaho Border**

PHONE: 406-295-4589

BEER: Drafts; Domestics;
Microbrews

AMUSEMENT: Pool; Horseshoes

FOOD: Frozen Pizza; Bar Snacks

The State Line House is on the south side of Highway 2 at the Montana/Idaho border. The barroom resides in the east side of the building, a poker room is in the middle, and a dance hall/bingo parlor is in the west side. An L-shaped bar stands in the southwest corner of the barroom, and several tables are spread across the floor. The barroom ceiling is completely covered with hats that have been donated to the bar by people from all over the world. The hat collection was started in 1966, and everything from sombreros to motorcycle helmets now hang from the ceiling. The dance hall walls are uniquely adorned as well. The decorations include old paper currency and mounted heads from exotic big game animals.

The State Line House was established in 1952 when the new highway was built. The business started out as a relatively small bar, but several additions were made to the building after Ellis Schanck bought the business in 1966. Ellis hung the first hat on the barroom ceiling, and the wall decorations in the dance hall came from a collection of items Ellis had gathered over the years. When the stone fireplace was built in the dance hall, Ellis had three unusual stones placed among the rocks so his fireplace would have a characteristic all its own. If you look closely at the face of the fireplace, you can see one stone shaped like Montana, one stone shaped like Idaho, and one stone shaped like Nevada. Ellis passed away in 1995. His daughter, Meg Boggers, now runs the business along with her husband, Ed.

The State Line Club is a friendly bar that attracts customers from the surrounding communities of Montana and Idaho. The bar has live bingo every Sunday, a pool tournament every Saturday, and live poker two nights a week. Fireworks are sold throughout the summer, and a huge swap meet is held in the parking lot every Memorial Day Weekend. Everything from hand-made crafts to household appliances are sold at the swap meet, and it's convenient for the husbands to drink at the bar while their wives shop.

GOLDEN NUGGET SALOON AND GRILL

OWNERS: John and Vi Holt

LOCATION: 12824 Yaak River Road, **Sylvanite**

HOURS: Noon to Closing Daily

PHONE: 406-295-4561

HAPPY HOUR: 5:00 to 7:00 Mon - Fri

BEER: Drafts; Domestics; Imports; Microbrews

GAMBLING: Video Poker/Keno; Shake-A-Day; Live Poker

AMUSEMENT: Pool; Darts; Horseshoes

LIVE MUSIC: Every Saturday Night

FOOD: Full Menu Grill

The Golden Nugget Saloon and Grill is at 12824 Yaak River Road in Sylvanite, an old mining community located twenty-three miles north of Troy. The barroom is in the west side of the building, and a dining room, a dance floor, and an elevated bandstand are in the east side. The barroom is quite rustic in appearance. The V-shaped bar along the south wall has a log foot rail, and every barstool was hand-carved from a tree stump. Various pieces of locally-crafted artwork are on display throughout the building, including painted saw blades, portraits, and wood carvings.

Clyde Thornton established the business as the Golden Nugget Lounge in 1958. Clyde built a small bar on the tailings pile from the old Golden Nugget Mine which started operations in 1896. A man named Ellis Skinner ran the bar for several years, and the Golden Nugget was such an integral part of his life that some folks in Sylvanite believe Ellis' ghost still inhabits the building. Ever since Ellis died, people have witnessed the lights in the barroom blinking on and off, unexplained noises, and the crank on the old cash register turning under its own power. People no longer panic when these strange events occur in the barroom, but they immediately start mentioning Ellis' name.

John and Vi Holt have owned the Golden Nugget Saloon and Grill since June, 1993, and it doesn't bother them a bit that they share the building with Ellis' ghost. The business is operated in a family-oriented manner, so the customers are always friendly and well-behaved. The Golden Nugget is open 365 days a year. John and Vi host a party at the bar on every major holiday, and they also play live music every Saturday night. John and Vi like to tell people they play both kinds of music at the Golden Nugget; Country, and Western, so everyone gets to hear what they want. If you've overindulged and don't want to risk driving, cabin rentals, RV parking, and sleeping rooms are available. That way, you know you will be alive the next morning to scream out "I survived the Yaak Attack!", which is the slogan of every saloon in the valley.

WILLY AND RICK'S DIRTY SHAME SALOON

OWNERS: Willy and Rick Carsello

HOURS: 10:00 a.m. to 2:00 a.m. (Summer)
Noon to Closing (Winter)

HAPPY HOUR: No

GAMBLING: Video Poker/Keno;
Shake-A-Day

LIVE MUSIC: Occasionally

LOCATION: 29453 Yaak River Road,
Yaak

PHONE: 406-295-5439

BEER: Drafts; Domestics;
Imports; Microbrews

AMUSEMENT: Pool; Darts; Horseshoes

FOOD: Burgers; Appetizers

Willy and Rick's Dirty Shame Saloon is on Yaak River Road in Yaak. The barroom is mostly finished in wood, creating a casual and inviting atmosphere. The front of the bar in the east side of the room is covered with log slats, a wooden plank supported by two peeled logs stands along the opposite wall, and several chainsaw carvings are on display. The deck on the west end of the building is a popular spot during the summer, and the bandstand on the lawn gets plenty of use during outdoor festivities.

The business was named the Yaak Lodge when the bar opened in 1950. An air force radar base was just built in town, and a local man opened the bar to make a few bucks off the airmen. There's some dispute over whether the "lodge" was actually an old goat pen or a chicken coop, but it was a filthy shack, nonetheless. It was the only bar within forty miles, however, so people put up with the conditions. I've heard two versions of how the name Dirty Shame came about. The version I heard the first time I visited the bar has two beer-craving airmen entering the barroom only to discover the place was out of beer. One man said "That's a shame", and the other replied "No, that's a dirty shame". Dirty Shame became the popular name, but the official name of the bar remained the Yaak Lodge until 1971.

Willy and Rick Carsello bought the Dirty Shame Saloon in 1993. The name of the bar is enough to draw customers, but it's the people that make the place so special. Willy and Rick host numerous parties throughout the year, the most popular being the Cajun Crawfish Festival and Craft Fair on the 3rd weekend in April. Rick makes what he calls a "Twelve O'Clock Margarita" by measuring the amount of tequila poured into a pitcher by the count one o'clock...two o'clock...etc., and Willy counters with her own version of a huckleberry daiquiri. The customers at the Dirty Shame are also wonderful people. A couple named Gail and Carol Bennett used to call the Dirty Shame from Alaska, where they both worked for several years, and buy rounds of drinks for everyone at the bar. Gail and Carol have since moved back to Yaak, but they haven't stopped buying rounds.

The world renowned Dirty Shame Saloon in Yaak.

ALDER STEAK HOUSE AND BAR

OWNERS: Alice and Ralph Northway

LOCATION: Route 287, **Alder**

HOURS: Noon to Closing (Summer)
4:00 p.m. to Closing Fri-Sun (Winter)

PHONE: 406-842-5159

HAPPY HOUR: No

BEER: Drafts; Domestics;
Imports; Microbrews

GAMBLING: Video Poker/Keno

AMUSEMENT: Pool; Darts; Video Game

LIVE MUSIC: Weekends Through Summer

FOOD: Full Menu Steak House

The Alder Steak House and Bar is on the west side of Route 287 (the "Rong" Side of the Tracks) in Alder. Their slogan reads "Stale Beer, Cheap Whiskey, Lousy Service, and the Best Damn Steaks in the West", but only the part about the steaks is accurate. The barroom is housed in the north side of the building, and the dining room is in the south side. The barroom has an L-shaped bar with a thick wooden top, and a few tables are available for additional seating. Several old photographs of gold dredges that were used in local mining operations during the early 1900s hang from the dining room walls along with a few newspaper stories about the region.

The history of the Alder Steak House and Bar dates back to 1902 when the Alder Hotel was built. The two story building is still intact, but additions have been made to the north and south sides of the first floor. The hotel has been closed for some time, but I'm told the second story is still inhabited by a few ghosts from years gone by. One of the ghosts is believed to be the spirit of a sheepherder who died in his hotel room. The spirits of the other ghosts have not yet been identified, but the spooks seem to enjoy moving about the building making noise and frightening unsuspecting people in the first floor.

Alice and Ralph Northway have owned the Alder Steak House and Bar since 1989. The barroom holds its own, but the steak house portion of the business is the big draw. Steaks and seafood are featured on the dinner menu, and grill items are available for lunch. The food is so good that the dining room is typically booked with reservations for weekend diners several days in advance. People from all over the world have been to the Alder Steak House and Bar. Rubys and garnets are plentiful in the area, so a lot of people who come to Alder in search of gems stop in for meals and drinks. Hunters and fishermen also flock to the region for trophy big game animals and lunker trout. Live entertainment is provided every weekend through the summer by a local man known as Bert the Singing Cowboy. Bert plays and serenades, customers dance and sing along, and the ghosts in the second floor wait until things get quiet to make their presence felt.

CHICK'S BAR

OWNER: Diane Sabo

HOURS: 8:00 a.m. to 2:00 a.m. Mon-Fri
10:00 a.m. to 2:00 a.m. Sat/Sun

HAPPY HOUR: No

GAMBLING: Video Poker/Keno; Live
Poker; Shake-A-Day

LIVE MUSIC: Occasionally

LOCATION: Route 287, **Alder**

PHONE: 406-842-5366

BEER: Drafts; Domestics

AMUSEMENT: Pool; Shuffle Board;
Video Game

FOOD: Frozen Pizza; Snacks

Chick's Bar is on Route 287 in Alder. The spacious barroom has a horseshoe-shaped wooden bar toward the back of the room, and a couple of tables are spread across the floor for additional seating. Tongue-and-groove pine boards cover the interior walls. Glass brick has been utilized to allow natural light to pass into the barroom though the building's diamond-shaped windows and the vestibule at the front entryway. The mounted six point elk head hanging behind the bar is from an animal that was shot in 1918. The full-mount bobcat standing in the glass case above the entrance to the ladies's room was trapped in the local area in 1991.

Chick's Bar was established in 1949 by Chick McClain. Instead of building the bar from the ground up, Chick moved an old dance hall from the nearby community of Rubytown onto the property and renovated it into a tavern. Soon after the bar opened, Chick had nearly 300 brands from local ranches painted on the barroom walls. The brands and the names of the corresponding ranch owners are still very visible today. The barroom hasn't changed much since the place first opened. Some of the original hardwood flooring has been covered with carpeting and linoleum, but the old floor is still exposed in the northwest corner of the barroom. There have only been three owners of Chick's since it first opened, the latest being Diane Sabo who bought the bar in January, 1986.

Diane promotes a friendly atmosphere at Chick's, and her customers are courteous and well-mannered. A lot of the locals refer to Chick's as "The Office" because it seems like they get more phone calls at the bar than they do at home. Local trade keeps the place going throughout the year, but Chick's also gets plenty of business from visiting hunters, fishermen, and tourists. Hunting season is always the busiest time of year, and the locals get along just fine with their out-of-state guests. Chick's Bar is open every day of the year, and they host a pot luck dinner on Thanksgiving and Christmas days. If you happen to be traveling through Alder on a holiday, you can always find some company at Chick's Bar.

BLUE MOON SALOON

OWNER: Joann Clark

HOURS: 10:00 a.m. to Closing Mon-Sat
11:00 a.m. to Closing Sunday

HAPPY HOUR: 6:00 to 7:00 (Winter Only)

GAMBLING: Video Poker/Keno;
Shake-A-Day

LIVE MUSIC: Occasionally

LOCATION: Highway 287, **Cameron**

PHONE: 406-682-4612

BEER: Drafts; Domestics;
Imports; Microbrews

AMUSEMENT: Pool; Pinball;
Video Games

FOOD: Grill Items; Bar Snacks

The Blue Moon Saloon is on Highway 287 in Cameron, the town that's always for sale. The saloon occupies the south side of a wooden structure that's adjoined by a restaurant and general store. Self service gas, cabin rentals, and an RV park are also available. The front part of the barroom is relatively small, with a straight bar facing the west wall and a few tables spread throughout the room. A corridor leads to a larger game room in the back of the building. Cameron has become known as the town that's always for sale because everything except the post office is usually on the real estate market. All the businesses are part of one piece of property, and it seems like everyone who buys the place immediately wants to sell it.

The Blue Moon Saloon was built by Ed and Dorothy McAtee in 1938. The bar was named for a blue paper moon cutout that was placed over a light bulb in the barroom. The back room was originally used to lodge travelers on their way to or from the Cliff Lake area, but it became a dance hall after Ed and Dorothy's son and daughter-in-law, Leonard and Janet McAtee, bought the business in 1948. The bar portion of the building was remodeled to the existing configuration in 1966. The business remained in the McAtee Family until 1981, but there have been five owners since. Joann Clark, who previously managed the bar, bought the liquor license in August, 1996. She now has a ten year lease on the saloon building.

The people at the Blue Moon Saloon are friendly and quick to offer a helping hand. If you don't count the time a jealous husband fired a warning shot into a light shade that hung above the bar where his wife and another man were sitting, the customers have always gotten along. Locals frequent the bar throughout the year, and a lot of repeat business comes in the form of visiting hunters, fishermen, and tourists. Joanne serves the coldest beer in the Madison Valley, and quite likely the coldest beer that's still in liquid form anywhere. The compressor that was installed in the cooler is actually designed for a freezer, so Joanne sometimes has to turn the compressor off at night to keep the beer from freezing.

TOBACCO ROOT TAVERN & SUPPER CLUB

OWNER: Suzette Rush

LOCATION: Highway 287, **Harrison**

HOURS: 11:00 a.m. to 2:00 a.m. Daily

PHONE: 406-685-3211

HAPPY HOUR: No

BEER: Drafts; Domestics; Imports; Microbrews

GAMBLING: Video Poker/Keno; Live Poker; Shake-A-Day

AMUSEMENT: Pool

LIVE MUSIC: Twice a Year

FOOD: Full Menu Supper Club

The Tobacco Root Tavern and Supper Club is on Highway 287 in Harrison. A covered boardwalk spans the length of the front side of the building, providing a rustic, old west appearance. The barroom resides in the front portion of the building, and a separate dining room is in the rear. The antique wooden bar and back bar along the west wall originally resided in a Saloon in Logan. A modern bar and back bar were added alongside the antique pieces when the barroom was expanded. The Total Fusion Pool Table is a recent addition. This double right angle billiard table is the only one of its kind in the Northwestern United States.

The Tobacco Root Tavern and Supper Club was established as Ely and Al's Bar in 1945. The name of the business was changed to Duffy's Tavern in 1947. Duffy's was destroyed by fire in 1972, but the owner was quick to rebuild. The fire insurance settlement didn't provide enough money to build to the original standards, so a relatively small structure was built to get the business back on its feet. Duffy's reopened in a building that occupied only the southwest corner of the existing barroom, but additions were made in subsequent years as building funds became available.

Suzette Rush changed the name of the bar to the Tobacco Root Tavern and Supper Club when she bought Duffy's Tavern in 1991. Suzette operates a community-minded business, and she caters to the needs of the local residents. The Tobacco Root Tavern and Supper Club is a place where entire families gather. Customers can choose between the small town tavern atmosphere in the barroom and the formal banquet setting in the dining room, or they can get the best of both worlds during one visit. The dinner menu features steaks, chicken, and seafood, and twice baked potatoes are served with every dinner entree. Homemade finger steaks and burgers are even available for the kids. The dining room has been awarded a four star rating, and a great selection of wines and beers is available from the bar. The Tobacco Root Tavern and Supper Club offers a unique combination of neighborhood tavern atmosphere and fine dining experience. You won't find that in very many places these days.

VIGILANTE STEAK HOUSE

OWNERS: Harold & Doris Schandelmeier   **LOCATION:** **Laurin**

HOURS: 4:00 p.m. to Closing Wed-Sun   **PHONE:** 406-842-5982
Typically Closed December - April

HAPPY HOUR: No   **BEER:** Domestics

GAMBLING: No   **AMUSEMENT:** No

LIVE MUSIC: No   **FOOD:** Full Menu Steak House

The Vigilante Steak House is just off Montana Highway 287 in Laurin. It's primarily an eating establishment, but there is a bar in the west end of the building if you just want to stop for a drink. The building's exterior basically consists of four-sided logs and wood siding covered with white paint. You can tell the structure has been around a while by looking at it from the street. The interior, on the other hand, is very modern. A round brick fireplace with a metal hood overhead stands just inside the main entrance. Beautiful tongue-and-groove pine woodwork covers the interior walls, and modern tile flooring has recently been installed. An assortment of mounted big game heads hang from the wall in the center portion of the building.

The history of the Vigilante dates back to 1934 when the business was still Richard's Store and Service Station. A retail beer license was issued to the store that year, and the store and service station slowly transformed into a tavern. The name was changed to the Vigilante Inn in 1937, probably in reference to the vigilante groups that roamed the area during the gold boom days of the 1800s. I'm told the original hanging tree used by the local vigilantes is still standing in the yard behind the Vigilante Steak House. The building has been expanded at least twice over the years. Additions have been built onto the east and west sides of the original log structure.

Harold and Doris Schandelmeier have owned the Vigilante Steak House since October, 1993. The building isn't visible from the main highway, so they don't get a lot of tourist traffic. People from Laurin and the surrounding communities provide a steady business throughout the year, but hunting season is by far the busiest time at the Vigilante. The region's trophy deer and elk draw big game hunters from all over the world. The dinner menu features steaks, seafood, and chicken entrees. Prime rib, the house specialty, is available on Friday, Saturday, and Sunday. Besides the day-to-day business, Harold and Doris host a lot of banquets and private parties. The atmosphere is relaxed, and the food is exceptional.

GRIZZLY BAR AND GRILL

OWNER: Eric Smith

LOCATION: Hwy. 287, **Madison Valley**

HOURS: 11:00 a.m. to Closing (Summer) Winter Hours Vary

PHONE: 406-682-7118

HAPPY HOUR: No

BEER: Domestics; Imports; Microbrews

GAMBLING: Video Poker

AMUSEMENT: No

LIVE MUSIC: Occasionally During Summer

FOOD: Full Menu Restaurant

The Grizzly Bar and Grill is approximately twenty-four miles south of Cameron on Highway 287. The building's interior is finished entirely with natural wood, and every table, chair, and barstool in the building was hand-crafted from logs and wood. A small wooden bar with a thick log bar top stands in the northwest corner of the bar-room, and an open pit grill constructed of stone and mortar is in the southwest corner. Wooden dining room tables cover the majority of the floor, and several wooden picnic tables are available on the out-door deck.

The bar's history dates back to 1974 when Sturdy's Bar first opened in a 600 square foot building. Sturdy was known to keep live bait in the refrigerator alongside the food he served to customers, but he ran an honest business nonetheless. Eric Smith bought Sturdy's in 1978 and changed the name to the Grizzly Bar and Grill. Eric completed the first of several additions to the original structure in 1984, and he also hand-fashioned every piece of furniture you see inside the build-ing. Today's Grizzly Bar and Grill bears no resemblance whatsoever to the old Sturdy's Bar. The photograph of Sturdy's Bar on the bulletin board near the front entrance will give you some idea of how much work Eric has done since taking over.

Eric got rid of the live bait left behind by Sturdy, and he's worked very hard to establish a reputation for serving excellent meals in a relaxing environment. His efforts have certainly paid off, because people from all over the world have been to the Grizzly Bar and Grill to enjoy the dining experience. All the steaks, seafood, and burgers are cooked over flaming quaking aspen coals in the open pit grill, which gives them a flavor second to none. Entire families from as far away as West Yellowstone and Ennis regularly visit the Grizzly Bar and Grill, and fly fishermen stop in for drinks and meals throughout the summer and fall. Eric keeps the kitchen open until well after dark to accommodate people getting off the river, so don't be shy about sloshing in with your waders at 10:00 p.m. and ordering dinner.

SAGEBRUSH SALOON AND GRILL

OWNERS: Dan and Darcie Stroud   **LOCATION:** Hwy. 287, **Madison Valley**

HOURS: 9:00 a.m. to 10:00 p.m. Mon-Sat   **PHONE:** 406-682-7935
10:00 a.m. to 10:00 p.m. Sunday

HAPPY HOUR: No   **BEER:** Domestics; Microbrews

GAMBLING: Video Poker/Keno   **AMUSEMENT:** None

LIVE MUSIC: No   **FOOD:** Full Menu Grill

The Sagebrush Saloon and Grill is at mile post marker 11 on Highway 287 North. The building stands on the west side of the road approximately 2-1/2 miles north of the junction of Highways 287 and 87. A covered wooden deck with log railings spans the front side of the wooden building. The barroom ceiling is covered with tongue-and-groove pine boards, and new paint and carpeting cover the walls and floor. A Z-shaped wooden bar is in the south end of the building, and several tables are spread throughout the north side of the room. The bar and dining area are have no physical separation between them, but the clientele is such that the dining room customers are not interrupted by loud noises from the bar patrons. The building is basically brand new, so everything is very modern.

The Sagebrush Saloon and Grill was established on May 1, 1996. It is the newest bar I've written about, so there's obviously not much in the way of history to report. Dan and Darcie Stroud opted to go into the bar and restaurant business, so they obtained a liquor license from the old Star Bar in Silver Star, built the saloon on some land they owned, and opened the doors for business. Dan and Darcie were just getting their feet wet when I last visited the Sagebrush Saloon in July, 1996, but Darcie said business had been good to that point.

The Sagebrush Saloon and Grill is more of an eating establishment than a tavern. Closing time is 10:00 p.m. daily, so it's not the type of place where you will run into a bunch of drunks falling off their barstools. Homemade pies, cheesecakes, milkshakes, and malts are available, and items off the breakfast menu are served throughout the day. Business hours will probably change somewhat during the winter, but they will be open throughout the year to accommodate snow-mobilers and anyone else who braves the snowy roads to get to the saloon. Local residents from as far away as Bozeman and West Yellowstone have supported the business so far, and a lot of fishermen off the Madison River stop in during the summer. The food is good, the people are friendly, and the place is brand new, so why not stop in the next time you're in the area.

BEAR CLAW BAR AND GRILL

OWNER: Bob Miller

HOURS: 11:00 a.m. to Closing Daily

HAPPY HOUR: No

GAMBLING: Video Poker/Keno

LIVE MUSIC: Occasionally

LOCATION: Highway 287, **McAllister**

PHONE: 406-682-4619

BEER: Domestics; Imports; Microbrews

AMUSEMENT: Pool; Horseshoes

FOOD: Full Menu Restaurant

The Bear Claw Bar and Grill is housed in a log structure on the east side of Highway 287 in McAllister. A moderate-sized barroom resides in the front portion of the building, and a spacious dining room is in the rear. The barroom walls are covered in rough cut lumber, creating a rustic appearance, and the stone fireplace against the east wall in the dining room provides a cozy atmosphere for the dinner guests. The straight wooden bar along the south wall has a sturdy wooden top that was made by cutting a thick plank from the middle of a tree trunk.

The bar's history dates back to the late 1920s when a house from a nearby ranch was moved to the property and renovated into a tavern. The dining room was added several years later when another house was moved in and attached to the existing structure. Bob Miller, who just goes by Miller, bought what was the McAllister Inn in 1993. He changed the name to the Bear Claw Bar and Grill in reference to the name of a bar he had worked at in Jackson Hole, Wyoming for several years. Miller and Deborah Gregg currently manage the business.

The Bear Claw Bar and Grill offers a complete dinner menu, and they also have an extensive wine selection. Dining room hours are 5:30 p.m. until 10:00 p.m. daily, and items on the lunch menu are served from 11:00 a.m. until 10:00 p.m. in the bar. The dinner menu features steaks and seafood, and an excellent 1/2 pound burger is on the lunch menu. The dining room gets very crowded during the summer, so be sure to get reservations if you plan on having dinner.

The regular customers at the Bear Claw Bar and Grill come from all over southwestern Montana. A lot of tourists and fishermen frequent the establishment during the summer, and visiting hunters flock to the bar and restaurant in the fall. Actor Steven Segal, who owns a ranch in the area, has even been to the Bear Claw Bar and Grill. It doesn't really matter who's there at any given time because there's always a very friendly crowd on hand. This is definitely not the kind of place where you have to worry about your safety.

NORRIS BAR

OWNER: Pegge Seriva

HOURS: 10:00 a.m. to 2:00 a.m. Daily

HAPPY HOUR: 5:00 to 6:30 Mon - Fri

GAMBLING: Video Poker/Keno; Shake-A-Day

LIVE MUSIC: Occasionally

LOCATION: Highway 287, **Norris**

PHONE: 406-685-3304

BEER: Drafts; Domestics; Imports

AMUSEMENT: Pool; Pinball

FOOD: Grill Items

The Norris Bar is at the Junction of Highway 287 and Route 84 in Norris. The main barroom, which resides in the west side of the building, has an L-shaped wooden bar, an antique back bar, and a matching liquor cabinet. A spacious dance hall with a sunken floor is housed in the wood-framed addition on the east side of the structure. A log railing surrounds the dance floor on all four sides, and several tables are lined against the walls on the elevated portion of the floor.

The part of the building where the main barroom now resides was originally a schoolhouse. In 1949, the old schoolhouse was renovated into the Norris Bar. The bar, back bar, and liquor cabinet were obtained from another bar in town that had closed down years earlier. When the dance hall was added in 1972, the original bar was lengthened. The straight wooden bar that was placed in the building in 1949 is now a long L-shaped bar that extends into the dance hall.

Pegge Seriva has owned the Norris Bar since 1982. She manages the business as a friendly establishment, and her customers like to have a good time. The only known shooting to occur at the bar took place during the early 1970's, and that didn't result in anything more than a wounded boot. Apparently, the lady who ran the bar was having problems getting an unruly customer to leave, so she pulled out a gun and shot the heel off the man's boot. The warning shot was apparently enough to convince the customer he was no longer welcome, because he left in quite a hurry.

Problem customers are a rarity at the Norris Bar today. The regulars all know each other, and they're very courteous when they see unfamiliar faces. Pegge says she gets a lot of repeat business from tourists and fishermen who come to the area every year, which can be attributed to the fun and friendly atmosphere in the barroom. A group of Vietnam Veterans also gathers at the Norris Bar on an annual basis, and the bar hosts an Old Time Fiddlers Jamboree every May. The Norris Bar also has free pool on Sundays and the best dance floor in Madison County, so you really have no excuse for not stopping in the next time you're in town.

PONY BAR

OWNERS: Dave and Jan Chapman

HOURS: Noon to Closing Daily

HAPPY HOUR: No

GAMBLING: Video Poker/Keno

LIVE MUSIC: Occasionally

LOCATION: 108 Broadway, **Pony**

PHONE: 406-685-3386

BEER: Drafts; Domestics; Imports; Microbrews

AMUSEMENT: Pool; Bumper Pool; Video Games

FOOD: Frozen Pizza; Snacks

The Pony Bar is on Broadway Street in Pony. Broadway is an extension of the road between Harrison and Pony, so you shouldn't get lost on your way to the bar. The barroom is actually housed in two separate buildings. The east and west sides of the room are partially separated by a wall that now has archways cut through it in the north and south sides. A straight wooden bar faces the center wall from the west side of the room, and a smaller U-shaped bar faces the center wall from the east side. An opening has been cut through the middle of the wall to enable one bartender to serve people on both sides of the room.

The history of the Pony Bar dates back to the late 1800s when Pony was a booming mining town. The bar originally operated out of the single story building that now houses the east side of the barroom. The two story building that now houses the main part (west side) of the barroom was originally a hotel. The building was later used as a boarding house, and at one time, it was the town's whorehouse. The bar eventually moved into the old hotel building next door. During the late 1980's, openings were cut between the two buildings at both ends of the bar to allow for an expansion of the barroom.

Dave and Jan Chapman bought the Pony Bar in 1993. They operate the business as a neighborhood tavern, and as far as Dave is concerned, it's going to stay that way. Pony is far enough off the beaten path that tourists don't stop in too often. About the only time of year they get a big influx of outsiders is during hunting season. Believe it or not, the population of Pony approached 10,000 during the late 1800's. Numerous photographs on the barroom walls depict the town and people of Pony from years past. You can usually find someone in the barroom to tell you about the people and places in the pictures. The folks of Pony are very friendly and proud of their community, so it's easy to make new friends at the Pony Bar. In most ways, this is good, but be prepared to keep up a frenzied drinking pace. The free drink wooden nickels tend to accumulate rapidly.

BLUE ANCHOR BAR AND CAFE

OWNERS: Russell Anderson/Bob Graham

LOCATION: 102 N Main, **Twin Bridges**

HOURS: Noon to Closing Daily

PHONE: 406-684-5655

HAPPY HOUR: 5:00 to 6:00 Mon - Fri

BEER: Drafts; Domestics; Imports

GAMBLING: Shake-A-Day

AMUSEMENT: Pool

LIVE MUSIC: Occasionally

FOOD: Full Menu Cafe

The Blue Anchor Bar and Cafe is housed in the ground-level floor of a two story brick structure on Main Street in Twin Bridges. A spacious barroom is in the south side of the building, and the cafe is in the north side. A beautiful antique back bar with a large rectangular mirror in the middle and arched mirrors on each end stands against the north wall of the barroom. The back bar and the section of the bar that stands directly in front of the back bar were built in the late 1800s. Both pieces originally resided in a saloon in Rochester, a nearby abandoned mining community. The open room off the east side of the barroom serves as a dance hall. The hardwood flooring was taken out of an old dance hall that was in the second story of the building.

Phil and Jamian Cook established the Blue Anchor Bar and Cafe in 1949. Phil and Jamian managed the business together for many years, but they allegedly fought like cats and dogs when they were drinking. In fact, the only mark in the mirror on the back bar is said to have come from an object Jamian threw at Phil while they were having an argument. Phil passed away several years ago, but it's rumored his spirit still inhabits the basement. People claim that after Phil died, they've heard strange noises and felt mysterious air currents moving through the basement of the building. Phil's ghost has become such a nuisance that people have become very hesitant about going downstairs to stock beer.

Russell Anderson and Bob Graham have owned the Blue Anchor Bar and Cafe since 1980. Russell and Bob operate a friendly business, and people of all ages are welcome. The cafe hours are 7:00 a.m. until 9:00 p.m. daily. They offer an extensive breakfast, lunch, and dinner menu, and daily lunch specials are available. The barroom customers are typically friendly and courteous. Residents of Twin Bridges and he surrounding communities provide a steady business throughout \e year, and visiting hunters, fishermen, and tourists stop in during e summer and fall. Phil's ghost stays in the basement, so you don't \ve to worry about being spooked if you're only stopping in for a \rink or a meal.

LOST CABIN BAR

OWNERS: Ted and Mary Ann Nelson **LOCATION:** 109 S Main, **Twin Bridges**

HOURS: 1:00 p.m. to 2:00 a.m. Mon-Fri **PHONE:** 406-684-5482
11:00 a.m. to 2:00 a.m. Sat/Sun

HAPPY HOUR: 5:00 to 6:00 Mon - Fri **BEER:** Domestics

GAMBLING: Video Poker **AMUSEMENT:** Pool

LIVE MUSIC: No **FOOD:** Frozen Pizza

The Lost Cabin Bar is at 109 South Main Street in Twin Bridges. The plate glass window in the front of the building has a painting of a log cabin standing alone in the wilderness, so you shouldn't have any trouble recognizing the place. The barroom is relatively long and narrow, but there's plenty of seating and plenty of open floor space. A long L-shaped bar with a solid oak top stands along the north wall, and three padded booths are in the front part of the room against the south wall.

The Lost Cabin Bar is the oldest tavern in Twin Bridges. Nobody I spoke with knew exactly when the business was established, but the beautiful oak bar top was installed in 1938. Ted and Mary Ann Nelson bought the bar in 1985. The painting on the front window was done later that same year by a man who needed money to support his drinking habit. Ted and Mary Ann didn't plan on leaving the painting on the window for very long, but they soon began to notice the painted scenery seemed to fluxuate according to the season. The trees and ground appear to be covered with a thick layer of snow during the winter, but the snow fades away as summer approaches. Nobody can explain this phenomenon, but the customers at the bar all agree the snow in the painting comes and goes to correspond with the actual seasons of the year.

The Lost Cabin Bar is a neighborhood tavern, period. The business is operated as a service to the community, and bar patrons appreciate the treatment they receive. The Lost Cabin Bar does not provide entertainment to entice new business. Ted and Mary Ann are more interested in providing quality service in a consistent manner. This way, the customers always know what to expect. You won't find any gimmicks at the bar, but you can get a drink for a very reasonable price and still shoot a game of pool for a quarter. The business was for sale when I last visited Twin Bridges, but the current owners are so conscious about the community that they are being very selective about who they sell it too. It may be a long time before Ted and Mary Ann find a buyer who can live up to their standards of service, but they're willing to wait until the right person comes along.

BROCKWAY BAR

OWNERS: Wayne French & Perry Kuntz

HOURS: 10:00 a.m. to 2:00 a.m. Daily

HAPPY HOUR: No

GAMBLING: Video Poker/Keno; Shake-A-Day

LIVE MUSIC: Occasionally

LOCATION: Highway 200, **Brockway**

PHONE: 406-485-2036

BEER: Drafts; Domestics

AMUSEMENT: Pool; Darts; Foosball

FOOD: Full Menu Grill

The Brockway Bar is housed in a metal-sided structure on the north side of Highway 200 in Brockway. The main barroom is in the east side of the building, and a dance hall/dining room is in the west side. A very sturdy bar faces the north wall of the barroom. The bar top was made by splitting a very thick log down the middle and placing it on top of the bar with the flat side facing up. A log foot rail is attached to the base of the bar, and a wood-shingle awning hangs from the ceiling above it. The dance hall/dining room has a sunken floor in the center of the room. Several wooden tables and booths line the walls surrounding the dance floor, and wagon wheel chandeliers hang from the ceiling.

The Brockway Bar was still on Main Street in Brockway as of September, 1996, but it was scheduled to move to the metal building along Highway 200 in the spring of 1997. The original bar building was a bank during the early 1900s. A pool hall began operating out of the building after the bank closed in 1928. The antique till that's in the bar today is the same till that was purchased by the Allen brothers when they opened the pool hall. After prohibition ended, J. R. George and Sam Borgen established the Brockway Bar. At one time, it was relatively common for people to ride horses into the old barroom, but the building eventually deteriorated to the point where the weight of a horse might be enough to cause the floor to collapse. Things finally got so bad that the weight of a person might be enough to cause the floor to collapse, so the owners decided to move the business into the old Cowboy Bar building along Highway 200.

Wayne French and Perry Kuntz have owned the Brockway Bar since 1985. Most of their customers are local residents, but motorists traveling along Highway 200 occasionally stop by, especially those who have stopped before. There's typically a very friendly crowd on hand, even on dance nights. The busiest time of year is during the third weekend of July when Brockway hosts its Dairy Day Celebration. Dairy Day is always on Saturday, but the bar stays packed throughout the entire weekend.

COUNTRY CLUB OF VIDA

OWNERS: Tim and Diane London

LOCATION: Route 13, **Vida**

HOURS: 11:00 a.m. to 2:00 a.m. Mon-Sat
Closed Sundays

PHONE: 406-525-3724

HAPPY HOUR: No

BEER: Drafts; Domestics

GAMBLING: Video Poker/Keno

AMUSEMENT: Pool; Video Game

LIVE MUSIC: Occasionally

FOOD: Full Menu Grill

The Country Club of Vida is on the west side of Route 13 in Vida. The name of the business is somewhat misleading since there's no golf course, clubhouse, or swimming pool. There is a bar, however, and that's the important thing. A straight bar faces the south wall of the barroom, and several tables are available for additional seating. A spacious dance hall is housed in the adjacent room on the north side of the building.

The bar has been in Vida longer than anyone I spoke with could remember. The original tavern was across the road, but the bar was moved after a fire destroyed the building in the mid 1940's. Tim and Diane London bought the bar in 1972 and changed the name from Howard's Club to the Country Club of Vida. They often get solicitations from people trying to sell them items for the golf course or clubhouse, but this has not yet convinced them to rename the business. I don't know if the old till behind the bar is from the original tavern, but it is approximately 100 years old and still fully functional.

The regular customers at the Country Club of Vida are residents of Vida and the surrounding farming and ranching communities. Travelers passing through the area stop in occasionally, and visiting hunters frequent the bar during deer, antelope, and pheasant seasons. The bar commonly hosts local celebrations such as wedding dances, birthday parties, and anniversary parties. Business is good most of the year, but Diane indicated things slow down tremendously during the winter months.

Every ceiling tile in the building is covered with writing. Diane explained that shortly after she and Tim bought the bar, it became popular for people to pay $3.00 apiece to write their name or leave a message on the ceiling. The practice became so popular that the ceiling soon became completely covered with writing. Diane indicated they once considered painting over the writing and starting all over again, but several of the message writers have passed away. Sentimental reasons prevent them from covering the words that were left by past friends, so it's not likely you will be able to add to the graffiti when you stop in.

CHECKERBOARD INN

OWNERS: Rick and Judy Geordge

HOURS: 8:30 a.m. to Closing (Summer)
9:30 a.m. to Closing (Winter)

HAPPY HOUR: No

GAMBLING: Video Poker/Keno;

LIVE MUSIC: Occasionally

LOCATION: Checkerboard

PHONE: 406-572-3373

BEER: Domestics

AMUSEMENT: Pool; Video games

FOOD: Microwave Foods;
Grill Items

The Checkerboard Inn stands just north of Highway 12 in the community of Checkerboard. You can't see the building very well from the highway, but there's a neon sign along the road to guide you to the bar. Besides the bar, a few sleeping cabins, RV parking spaces with electrical hookups, a small grocery store, and a gas station are part of the business. The main barroom is relatively small, but additional space is available in the adjacent game room. The antique cash register behind the bar came from a saloon in Marysville.

The history of the Checkerboard Inn dates back to 1923 when Fred Sumpter built a dance hall, poker parlor, and cafe called the Sumpter Inn. The Sumpter Inn, known locally as Fort Sumpter, also served bootlegged booze that was distilled in the basement. Rick Geordge's grandparents bought the business in 1945 and changed the name to the Checkerboard Inn. Rick and his wife, Judy, took over the business in June, 1990, and they continue to operate it today.

Visiting hunters and fishermen provide the majority of the business at the Checkerboard Inn from Memorial Day through November. The rest of the year is relatively slow, since the seventeen or so residents of Checkerboard can only supply so much business. With the gas pumps, bar, small grocery store, and limited lodging facilities, the Checkerboard Inn offers everything you need to survive a hunting or fishing trip to the area. They probably don't have everything you want, but they have everything you need. Being that the Checkerboard Inn is the only member of the Checkerboard Chamber of Commerce, you don't have a lot of choice on where you purchase your goods.

If you're into minerals (and who isn't these days?), Rick has several samples of "stuff" he has dug up while mining in the area. Rick is a miner by trade, and he works the only operating hard rock mine left in the area when he's not at the bar. Rock hounds are always welcome at the Checkerboard Inn to look at Rick's rock specimens and talk mining lingo. Of course, non-rock hounds are always welcome as well.

FOREST GREEN RESORT

OWNER: Chilly Park   **LOCATION:** Hwy. 89, **Kings Hill**

HOURS: 10:00 a.m. to Closing Sat/Sun   **PHONE:** 406-547-3496
Noon to Closing Tue-Fri.; Closed Mondays

HAPPY HOUR: No   **BEER:** Domestics

GAMBLING: Video Poker   **AMUSEMENT:** None

LIVE MUSIC: Occasionally   **FOOD:** Full Menu Restaurant

The Forest Green Resort is on the west side of Highway 89, seven miles south of the summit of Kings Hill and approximately twenty-five miles north of White Sulfur Springs. The barroom resides in the northeast corner of the main log building on the property. There's also two separate dining rooms in the building to handle large groups of hungry people.

The Forest Green Resort was built on an old sheep ranch. The older green cabins that stand to the north of the main building were built during the 1930's to house local loggers, pulp mill workers, and visiting fishermen. The resort didn't begin operating until the mid 1940's when the log building was erected. An eight unit motel was added in the early 1960's, and a second dining room was built some time later. Chilly and Jay Park bought the resort in 1970. Jay has passed away, but Chili still manages the resort as a family-owned, family-operated business.

Customers at the Forest Green Resort range anywhere from local residents to foreign visitors. Surrounded by the Little Belt Mountains and the Lewis and Clark National Forest, the resort is in the middle of one of Montana's finest outdoor recreation areas. Skiers come here to enjoy the numerous cross country trails throughout the region and the slopes of Showdown Ski Area, which is only seven miles north. Snowmobilers can access over 250 miles of trails directly from the resort. It's also a convenient stop for visiting hunters and fishermen.

The Forest Green Resort is a friendly place with a family-oriented atmosphere. The lodge stays busy throughout the summer, but weekdays are normally slow during the winter. The bar and restaurant are usually closed on Mondays; however, they stay open every day of the week during hunting season. Excellent meals are served, so the resort has become a popular place for private banquets and holiday parties. With its scenic location, reasonable prices, and friendly atmosphere, the Forest Green Resort is a great place to stop. Whether you spend an afternoon or an entire week, you'll enjoy your stay.

MINT BAR

OWNERS: Dan and Susan McLaughlin   **LOCATION:** 107 Main, **Martinsdale**

HOURS: 11:00 a.m. to 2:00 a.m. Daily   **PHONE:** 406-572-9998

HAPPY HOUR: No   **BEER:** Domestics

GAMBLING: Video Poker   **AMUSEMENT:** Pool

LIVE MUSIC: Occasionally   **FOOD:** Grill Items

The Mint Bar is at 107 Main Street in Martinsdale. Rough cut log slabs cover the front of the building, and a wooden awning hangs above the sidewalk between the street and the main entrance. An antique wooden bar and a hand-crafted back bar stand against the north wall in the front part of the room. Although both pieces are over 100 years old, they have been maintained in excellent condition. The dozen or so mounted deer heads on the wall were shot in the local area during the 1940's. I'm told you won't find as many trophy deer in the area these days because of increasing pressure from hunters. There's also a wild boar's head and a mounted deer's butt hanging from the wall, but I don't know what the story is behind these two trophies. The wood burning stove in the back corner serves as the only heat source for the building during the winter months.

I'm told Martinsdale had seven saloons at one time, but the Mint Bar is the town's only watering hole today. A framed photograph of Martinsdale as it looked in 1916 hangs from the back wall of the barroom, and you can see it was a much livelier place in those days. The Mint first opened in the early 1930s in a building next door to where it now stands. The business was moved to its present location in 1938. The antique wooden bar and back bar came from a tavern in Castletown, which is now a ghost town approximately twenty-five miles west of Martinsdale.

The Mint Bar has had several owners since it first opened. Dan and Susan McLaughlin most recently bought the business in November, 1995. Most of the customers are residents of Martinsdale and the surrounding communities, but visiting hunters and fishermen also frequent the bar. The Mint is a friendly place where people of all ages gather to socialize with friends. The only gripe Susan has about the customers is cleaning up after certain slobs who use the men's room. It eventually got to the point where Susan posted a rather threatening sign on the men's room wall to inform people the penalty for peeing on the wall or throwing chewing tobacco into the urinal is the loss of a certain reproductive organ. The sign had been removed when I last visited the Mint Bar in December, 1997, but I was still very careful with my aim when I went to relieve myself.

JT'S BAR AND SUPPER CLUB

OWNERS: Darin and Sandy Bushnell

HOURS: 11:00 a.m. to Closing Tue-Sun
Closed Mondays

HAPPY HOUR: No

GAMBLING: Video Poker/Keno;
Shake-A-Day

LIVE MUSIC: Occasionally

LOCATION: 101 Main St., **Ringling**

PHONE: 406-547-3406

BEER: Drafts; Domestics;
Imports

AMUSEMENT: Pool; Darts; Pinball;
Video Games; Horseshoes

FOOD: Full Menu Restaurant

JT's Bar and Supper Club is on Main Street in Ringling. The front of the building is covered with rough cut log slabs, but it's basically a brick structure. A moderate-sized barroom is housed in the north side of the building, and a dining room resides in the smaller room on the south end. A horseshoe-shaped bar stands along the west wall, and a couple of tables are spread throughout the room.

The business was established during the early 1900's. The original building was destroyed by fire, so the bar was moved to the south bay of the adjacent building. The barroom co-existed for several years with a blacksmith shop, a grocery store, and a post office, but the other businesses have all closed down or moved out. Fortunately, the bar has managed to survive. During the early 1970's, the barroom moved out of the south bay and took over the larger room in the north side of the building.

When Darin and Sandy Bushnell bought JT's Bar in September, 1993, they renovated the south room into a dining area and opened a supper club. Dining room hours are 5:00 p.m. until 9:30 p.m. Thursday through Saturday. Every piece of meat served at JT's is cut fresh off the hock as it's ordered and char-broiled. Side dishes are made from scratch, so everything on the menu is guaranteed to be fresh. The prime rib specials on Friday and Saturday evenings have become so popular that you need reservations to get in the door, so be sure to call ahead.

Darin and Sandy always have something going on at the bar to keep their customers entertained. Annually, JT's hosts such prestigious events as a PGA (Pasture Golf Association) golf tournament in the pasture next to the bar, a gopher shoot, and the always popular, but sometimes controversial, coyote derby. The coyote derby received national media attention in 1994 after Darin got several threatening letters and even a death threat from animal rights activists. None of the cowards who made the anonymous threats dared show up at the coyote derby to protest in person, however, and the event went on as scheduled.

CHET'S BAR

OWNERS: Butch and Vendy Miner

HOURS: Noon to Closing Daily

HAPPY HOUR: 6:00 to 7:00 Daily

GAMBLING: Video Poker/Keno

LIVE MUSIC: Informal Jam Sessions

LOCATION: Railroad Ave., **Alberton**

PHONE: 406-722-4516

BEER: Drafts; Domestics

AMUSEMENT: Pool; Horseshoes

FOOD: Frozen Pizza; Sandwiches

Chet's Bar is at 516 Railroad Avenue in Alberton. Their motto, "A Bar That Loves The 1800s", is a pretty accurate description of what you will find when you enter the front door. A beautiful antique bar, back bar, and liquor cabinet stand along the west wall in the front part of the room. The three matching pieces were hand-crafted from cherry wood around the turn of the 20th century. The back bar has a large rectangular mirror, and stained glass is embedded in the woodwork. Framed photographs of some of the earlier residents of the community hang from the barroom walls. Most of those pictured have passed away, but you can bet there's at least one very interesting story behind every photograph in the bar.

Nobody I spoke with knew exactly when the business was established, but the bar, back bar, and liquor cabinet were installed in 1912. The original barroom was quite small, but the building has been expanded at least twice since the bar first opened. The crack in the mirror on the back bar is actually a stress fracture that occurred in 1951. A heavy cooler that was placed beside the back bar caused the floor to sink, resulting in the fracture. The floor was reinforced to prevent further damage, and the cooler has since been moved.

Butch and Vendy Miner have owned Chet's Bar since March, 1994. Chet's has always been a friendly tavern with a comfortable environment, and Butch and Vendy have maintained the home town atmosphere. There's usually a local crowd on hand, but white water rafters and hunters wander in from time to time. Chet's is also a popular stop for motorcyclists traveling to and from the annual biker's rally in Sturgis, South Dakota. Butch and Vendy occasionally host an 1800s Night at the bar. Guests dress in traditional 1800s clothing, and kerosene lanterns are used in lieu of incandescent bulbs for lighting. Chet's Bar also has dinners on holidays throughout the year, and they host an anniversary party in June. Live music isn't a scheduled event, but it's not uncommon for local musicians to stop by and break out their instruments for a good old jam session. You never know what's going to happen, but you can be assured of having a great time with the folks at Chet's Bar in Alberton.

SPORTSMAN'S TAVERN

OWNERS: Al Benson

LOCATION: Railroad Ave., **Alberton**

HOURS: Noon to 2:00 a.m. Daily

PHONE: No Phone

HAPPY HOUR: No

BEER: Drafts; Domestics

GAMBLING: No

AMUSEMENT: Pool; Electronic Bowling

LIVE MUSIC: Informal Jam Sessions

FOOD: Frozen Pizza; Sandwiches

The Sportsman's Tavern is at 618 Railroad Avenue in Alberton. The barroom has a straight wooden bar that spans almost the entire length of the east wall, and a few small tables are available if all the barstools are occupied. Numerous black and white photographs depicting Alberton and residents of the town during its early years are encased under the polyurethane finish on top of the bar. An old cow bell hangs above the bar, ready to ring out a chime when someone buys a round for the house. Rough cut boards cover the interior walls, and the original hardwood floor is still intact. The Sportsman's Tavern definitely isn't an elaborate place, but it's quite comfortable and very inviting.

The building that houses the bar was originally a grocery store in a nearby community called Lothrup. In 1908, the entire structure was ferried across the Clark Fork River to Alberton and renovated into the Lacasse Saloon. A black and white photograph of the old Lacasse Saloon used to hang from the east wall of the barroom, but it had been taken down the last time I visited the bar in October, 1996. Hopefully, the picture has been placed back on the wall, because it's interesting to see how the original building looked.

Al Benson has owned the Sportsman's Tavern since 1983. Al tells me the Sportsman's has a history of attracting customers that are friendly, fun-loving, and sometimes slightly crazy. Many years ago, a customer shot the cow bell from across the crowded barroom with a 22 caliber pistol to announce he was buying a round of drinks. The bullet ricocheted harmlessly into the ceiling, but a few people politely declined the free drink and ran for safety. The bullet hole is still in the ceiling today. People have also ridden horses and motorcycles through the barroom, but like most of the other crazy stunts, it was all done in the name of fun. It's not always the customers who make life interesting at the Sportsman's Tavern. The man who owned the business in the early 1970s inadvertently drove his brand new Lincoln Continental through the front of the building and smashed into the bar. He apparently mistook the gas pedal for the brake pedal and accelerated into the barroom before he knew what happened.

PINECREST LODGE

OWNERS: Laddie and Jane Stanton   **LOCATION:** DeBorgia

HOURS: Noon to Closing Daily   **PHONE:** 406-678-4360

HAPPY HOUR: 5:30 to 6:30 Mon and Thurs   **BEER:** Drafts; Domestics; Imports; Microbrews

GAMBLING: Video Poker/Keno; Shake-A-Day   **AMUSEMENT:** Pool; Darts; Horseshoes; Volleyball; Video Games

LIVE MUSIC: Occasionally   **FOOD:** Full Menu Grill

The Pinecrest Lodge is on the Frontage Road just north of Interstate 90 at the DeBorgia Interchange (exit 18). The wooden structure houses a spacious barroom with a long bar, several tables, and video gambling machines in the east side and a dance floor and game room in the west side. The barroom has a rustic appearance and a comfortable atmosphere. Rough cut boards cover the walls, three wagon wheel chandeliers hang above the bar, and a wood burning stove stands in one corner. Several mounted big game heads hang from the walls in the west side of the building beneath the wooden beams that support the vaulted ceiling.

The bar was established during the 1920s in a small building that stood just west of the present-day lodge. Along with the bar, several tourist cabin rentals were part of the original business. The structure that now houses the barroom was built in 1973. Three of the old cabins are still rented out, but they are available only on a seasonal basis from Memorial Day weekend through the end of hunting season. Present owners Laddie and Jane Stanton bought the business in March, 1990. Laddie tells me the bar had gained a reputation as a rough and rowdy place during the highway construction days, but things have settled down considerably in recent years. These days, you will typically find a friendly, well-mannered crowd on hand.

The Pinecrest Lodge serves excellent food. In fact, the broasted chicken and grilled burgers have obtained world famous status. People from all over the world have stopped to eat based on recommendations from friends and relatives, and nobody has ever gone away disappointed. Aside from serving great food, Laddie and Jane host a hunter's ball every year during big game season, and they hold a party every winter during a local snowmobile poker run. Hundreds of people turn out for these events, and everybody has a great time. It really doesn't matter whether you make it to one of the scheduled parties, because you can always count on enjoying your visit to the Pinecrest Lodge.

RIVERSIDE INN

OWNER: Tony and Irene Drazan

LOCATION: Frontage Road, **DeBorgia**

HOURS: 2:00 p.m. to 2:00 a.m. Daily

PHONE: 406-678-4226

HAPPY HOUR: 4:30 to 5:30 Mon - Fri

BEER: Drafts; Domestics; Imports

GAMBLING: Video Poker/Keno; Shake-A-Day

AMUSEMENT: Pool; Pinball; Horseshoes

LIVE MUSIC: Occasionally

FOOD: Frozen Pizza, Bar Snacks

The Riverside Inn is housed in a log structure one mile west of DeBorgia on the Frontage Road that parallels Interstate 90. You can either take exit 16 and drive one mile east or take exit 18 and drive one mile west to get to the Inn. A large L-shaped bar and a few tables reside in the east side of the barroom. The west side of the room basically serves as a game room, dance hall, and seating area. An elevated bandstand against the south wall overlooks the dance floor in the center of the room, and several booths and a picnic table are spread across the sunken floor in the north side. The old piano standing against the west wall is still in tune, but it doesn't get much use anymore.

The business was established as the Riverside Beer Parlor in 1934. It became the Riverside Inn when a full liquor license was issued in 1937. The bar originally resided in the west side of the building, and a cafe was in the east side. The bar has since been moved to the opposite side of the room, and the cafe is gone altogether. The large wooden sign that now hangs from the north wall was created as a memorial to a former owner of the bar. Hundreds of coins embedded in the wood spell out the words "Riverside Inn", and the people who contributed to the sign have their names carved into the wood. A lot of people donated both their time and their coins to complete the project.

Tony and Irene Drazan bought the Riverside Inn in 1989. They run a friendly establishment, and their customers are fun-loving people. Tony and Irene host a hunters ball every year during big game season, and they have great pot luck dinners on just about every major holiday. The outdoor barbecue pit gets plenty of use during the summer months for pig roasts and wild game feeds. Another great thing about the Riverside Inn is the drink prices. The last time I checked, four different brands of beer were available for $1.00 a can. As if that isn't reasonable enough, the price is reduced to 75 cents during happy hour. If you can't afford these prices, you might as well give up drinking.

LINCOLN'S 10,000 SILVER $ BAR

OWNER: Rex Lincoln

HOURS: 8:00 a.m. to 11:00 p.m. Daily

HAPPY HOUR: No

GAMBLING: Video Poker/Keno

LIVE MUSIC: No

LOCATION: Haugan

PHONE: 406-678-4242

BEER: Domestics; Imports; Microbrews

AMUSEMENT: No

FOOD: Full Menu Cafe

Lincoln's 10,000 Silver $ Bar is on the north side of Interstate 90 at the Haugan Interchange (exit 16). The enormous wooden structure houses a large barroom, a huge gift shop, and a cafe. Over 30,000 silver dollars are embedded in the two wooden bar tops and the wooden plaques hanging from the walls. Over 10,000 pieces are authentic silver dollars, and the rest are Eisenhower dollars. The coin collection grows by an estimated 1,500 a year, and a tally of the current number of silver dollars in the barroom is maintained on a sign behind the bar. The place is obviously a tourist trap, but the bar attracts a local crowd as well as travelers.

The history of Lincoln's 10,000 Silver $ Bar dates back to 1951 when Gerry and Marie Lincoln opened the Cherry Springs Bar two miles west of Alberton along Highway 10. Gerry hammered the first silver dollar into the bar top and inscribed he and Marie's names beneath it on October 1, 1953 as an attraction to draw customers. Over 2,000 people had added their coins and names to the top of the bar by the end of 1953, so the name of the business was changed to Lincoln's 2,000 Silver $ Bar. The bar, along with over 6,000 silver dollars, moved to Haugan when the highway construction began in 1956. A gift shop was added at that time, and the coin collection continued to grow. The bar and gift shop moved into the existing building in 1975. A cafe, gas station, campground, and motel have since been added. People from all fifty states and over forty foreign countries have left their silver dollars at the bar. The top of the bar in the south side of the existing barroom is the original bar top from the Cherry Springs Bar, and believe it or not, the original coins are still intact.

Gerry and Marie's son, Rex, now owns the business. The majority of the information you've just read was taken from a pamphlet that was written by Gerry and Marie's granddaughter, Brooke Lincoln. The pamphlet contains a much more detailed history of the business, so I recommend you stop at the bar or gift shop and pick up a copy. Better yet, why not bring in your own silver dollar and become a part of the colorful history of Lincoln's 10,000 Silver $ Bar.

Lincoln's 10,000 Silver $ Bar in Haugan.

Top Photo: A view from the parking lot.

Bottom Photo: Over 30,000 silver dollars are on display
in the barroom.

LOZEAU RETREAT TAVERN

OWNER: Bill Manlove

LOCATION: Crossover Road, **Lozeau**

HOURS: 11:00 a.m. to Closing Daily

PHONE: 406-822-4846

HAPPY HOUR: No

BEER: Drafts; Domestics

GAMBLING: Video Poker/Keno

AMUSEMENT: Pool; Horseshoes

LIVE MUSIC: No

FOOD: Grill Items; Chicken

The Lozeau Retreat Tavern is on the north side of Interstate 90 at the Lozeau Interchange (exit 55). The log structure houses a moderate-sized barroom, and a covered wooden deck is just off the north side of the building. The barroom has log walls and roof supports, and natural wood covers the floor and ceiling. The straight bar along the west wall has a thick wooden top that was made by cutting a single plank from the middle of a tree trunk. Brands from local ranches were burned into the bar top prior to the polyurethane coating being applied. The interior decor isn't fancy, but some interesting antiques hang from the ceiling beams.

The business was established in the late 1940s as the Taft Bar. The Taft Bar was forced to relocate in 1969 when Interstate 90 was built, so it reopened in a trailer in Tarkio. It was during this time when a man was fatally shot in the barroom. Not long after the shooting, the trailer was moved to Lozeau. The bar continued operating out of the trailer until 1983 when construction on the log building was completed. Unfortunately, I failed to inquire whether there was any connection between the shooting and the bar moving to Lozeau. I planned on asking about this when I was at the bar, but I became distracted when two officers from the Mineral County Sheriff's Department escorted me from the barroom and searched my vehicle. It turns out I was a suspect in a string of casino burglaries in Central Montana, but the kind officers let me go after a thorough search of my truck failed to turn up any incriminating evidence.

Bill Manlove bought the Lozeau Retreat Tavern in July, 1993. Bill serves excellent burgers and broasted chicken at the bar, and he even offers a Platter Feast featuring a variety of menu items. The Lozeau Retreat Tavern is a friendly place where people gather to relax and unwind. There's never any trouble at the bar, but customers have been known to get stuck while attempting to crawl through a hole in one of the log ceiling posts. The log splits into two branches, but the branches rejoin to form a hole that's just big enough for a small person to crawl through. More than one person who tried to crawl through the hole has become wedged between the branches and required assistance getting out.

212

SHEEP RANCH INN

OWNERS: Alan and Rosie Howes

LOCATION: 23580 Hwy. 93 N., **Arlee**

HOURS: 2:00 p.m. to Closing Weekdays
Noon to Closing Weekends

PHONE: 406-726-3332

HAPPY HOUR: No

BEER: Drafts; Domestics;
Imports; Microbrews

GAMBLING: No

AMUSEMENT: Pool; Horseshoes

LIVE MUSIC: Live Band Saturday & Sunday
Karaoke Wednesday & Friday

FOOD: Full Menu Restaurant

The Sheep Ranch Inn is approximately five miles south of Arlee on Highway 93 North. The barroom resides in the north side of the building, and a separate dining room is in the south side. The atmosphere at the Sheep Ranch Inn is very inviting. The dining room has a stone fireplace on the south wall, and windows in the east wall provide a spectacular view of the surrounding mountains. The barroom is finished in a more casual manner. Rough cut lumber covers the walls, tongue-and-groove pine boards cover the ceiling, and a wood burning stove stands in the northeast corner. Several tables surround the wooden dance floor in the center of the room, and an L-shaped bar stands in the southwest corner.

The business was established in 1975. The building stands on the site of a former sheep ranch, so it's no mystery how the place got its name. I'm told all the ram's skulls hanging near the ceiling surrounding the dance floor came from animals that lived on the original ranch. The Sheep Ranch Inn has changed hands four times since it first opened. Alan and Rosie Howes most recently acquired the business in October, 1996. They were really just getting acquainted with the business when I last visited in December of that same year, but plans were already in place to add a bed-n-breakfast and an RV park during the summer of 1997.

The Sheep Ranch Inn has gained an excellent reputation for its fine dining and pleasant atmosphere. The business has always been operated in a friendly, family-oriented manner, and things are only improving as time goes by. The view from the outdoor deck is nothing less than spectacular, and the food is superb. The dinner menu features steaks and seafood, and the Sheep Ranch Inn serves only certified Black Angus Beef. They also serve an assortment of mixed and blended drinks and stock an extensive selection of beers. Twenty-four acres of ground surround the building, so it's common to see wildlife wandering through the property. Occasionally, a bear will even come by to feast on trout in the pond. It's not often you can witness such a sight, especially from the comfort of your barstool.

CLEARWATER BAR AND CAFE

OWNER: Jim "Looney" Loran

LOCATION: Clearwater Junction

HOURS: 8:00 a.m. to 2:00 a.m. Daily
Winter Hours Vary

PHONE: 406-244-9535

HAPPY HOUR: No

BEER: Drafts; Domestics;
Imports; Microbrews

GAMBLING: Video Poker/Keno

AMUSEMENT: Pool; Pinball

LIVE MUSIC: Occasionally

FOOD: Full Menu Cafe

The Clearwater Bar and Cafe is at Clearwater Junction, which is the local name for the area where Highways 200 and 83 intersect. The bar and cafe are housed in the second floor the building, and four motel rooms occupy the bottom floor. The barroom has an L-shaped bar, several tables, and an open pit stone fireplace surrounding a wood burning stove in the middle of the room. The dining room can seat up to 100 people. Both the barroom and dining room have sliding glass doors leading to a small concrete patio on the east side of the building.

The Clearwater Bar and Cafe was established in 1969. Missoula native Jim Loran has owned the business since 1985. Jim spent several years working the oil fields in Texas prior to buying the bar. He had married a Texas city girl, and when Jim's in-laws heard their daughter was moving to Montana, they told Jim he was looney if he thought the girl would be able to adapt to life in Big Sky Country. Jim's wife only lasted three years, but the nickname Looney has become permanent. That's fine with Jim, because his Looney Burgers have become a very popular menu item. Jim also serves a great chicken fried steak and offers a daily soup and sandwich lunch special in the cafe.

There's not much of a local population around Clearwater Junction, so Looney primarily depends on motorists traveling through the area for his business. The place is typically very busy from April through November, but it slows down substantially the rest of the year. Perhaps the most famous guest Looney has ever entertained is Prince William, the son of England's Prince Charles and Lady Diana. The prince, along with several other guests at a nearby dude ranch, attended a dance at the Clearwater Bar and Cafe during the summer of 1992. Reporters from the British tabloids didn't find out the prince was in Montana until he had already gone back to England, but when they did find out, Looney was overwhelmed with requests for information. I'm told Prince William was very well-behaved during his visit, but the Brittish reporters were a royal pain in the butt.

POOR HENRY'S BAR

OWNERS: Dan and Dave Russell

HOURS: 10:00 a.m. to 2:00 p.m. Daily

HAPPY HOUR: 6:00 to 7:00 Daily

GAMBLING: Video Poker/Keno; Shake-A-Day

LIVE MUSIC: Approximately Monthly

LOCATION: 19150 Hwy 10 E., **Clinton**

PHONE: 406-825-9930

BEER: Drafts; Domestics; Microbrews

AMUSEMENT: Pool; Darts; Pinball

FOOD: Grill Items; Broasted Chicken

Poor Henry's Bar is housed in a wood and log structure on Old Highway 10, approximately one mile west of the Clinton Interchange (exit 121) off Interstate 90. The barroom resides in the south side of the building, and a large dance hall is in the north side. The barroom has a long Z-shaped bar with a brass foot rail, several tables in the middle of the floor, and a game room in the east side. The interior walls and ceiling are made from logs and natural wood, and the floor is bare concrete. Construction on an adjoining dance hall was still in progress when I last visited the bar, but plans were in place to install a raised bandstand, a spacious dance floor, and plenty of seating.

Frank Miller established the business as the Clinton Bar in 1947. The name was changed to Poor Henry's in 1951 when Frank took on Henry Bertholf as a partner. The bar originally operated out of another building in Clinton, but it was moved to its present location in 1954 to be more accessible to people traveling along Highway 10. The log addition on the east side of the barroom was built in the mid 1980s. Dan and Dave Russell bought the business in January, 1996. They made some minor renovations to the barroom and added the dance hall on the north side of the building later that same year.

Poor Henry's Bar is a popular gathering spot for the local working class people. The business has always been operated as a neighborhood bar, and there's little chance that will change. Visiting hunters and fishermen stop in from time to time, but most of the business comes people who live in the immediate area. Great bands play at the bar on dance nights, and Poor Henry's sponsors pool, dart, and softball teams for local leagues. The number and size of the trophies in the barroom indicate some very successful softball teams have worn Poor Henry's jerseys. Excellent broasted chicken is available if you're in need of a good meal, so there's no sense drinking on an empty stomach. Judging from all I've seen and heard, Poor Henry's does an outstanding job of customer satisfaction.

215

LIQUID LOUIE'S

OWNER: Rollie Bigley

HOURS: Noon to Closing Daily

HAPPY HOUR: No

GAMBLING: Video Poker/Keno

LIVE MUSIC: Occasionally

LOCATION: Highway 83, **Condon**

PHONE: 406-754-2391

BEER: Drafts; Domestics; Microbrews

AMUSEMENT: Pool; Darts; Horseshoes; Bumper Pool; VideoGames

FOOD: Frozen Pizza

Liquid Louie's is 3-1/2 miles south of Condon on Highway 83. The barroom has a horseshoe-shaped bar facing the south wall, a lone wooden buddy bar in the middle of the room, and a couple of small tables against the north wall. If you don't care for the confined quarters of a barroom, you and whatever you're drinking are welcome to wander off to the fenced-in party yard behind the building. Several picnic tables are available if you want to sit down, and there's plenty of walking around space. There's also an outdoor bar, a covered lunch counter, and a bandstand in the back yard, but they only get used on special occasions.

The business was established in 1948 by a man named Louie Krause, who was said to have been his own best customer. Louie opened the bar and a small restaurant in a log structure that stood on the west side of the highway. Louie eventually ditched the restaurant and moved the bar across the road. If you don't count the time a lady drove the front end of a pickup truck into the barroom (there's a picture on the barroom wall to prove this really happened), the building has held up well over the years.

Rollie Bigley bought Liquid Louie's in July, 1987. Rollie promotes a friendly atmosphere, and his customers are fun-loving people. If you're short on cash but have a wooden nickel from another bar, you can get a drink with it at Liquid Louie's. Rollie accepts wooden nickels from other bars with hopes the other business owners do the same. Several years ago, Rollie founded Liquid Louie's Horse Racing Association Thoroughbred Club, an organization whose members occasionally gather at the bar to race around the back yard on wooden ponies. I don't know all the rules, but a rider's progress toward the finish line is dependant on a roll of the dice. If the weather is uncooperative on the day of the big race, small plastic pigs and a game board are used in lieu of the wooden ponies and the back yard. The horse races are for members only, but Liquid Louie's anniversary party is open to anyone. The party is always held on the last Saturday of July, and there's free food, $1.00 beers, and live music.

BUCK SNORT RESTAURANT, BAR, & CASINO

OWNERS: Gary and Kathi Stone

HOURS: 10:00 a.m. to Closing Tue-Sun
Closed Mondays

HAPPY HOUR: No

GAMBLING: Video Poker/Keno

LIVE MUSIC: No

LOCATION: 16995 Highway 93, **Evaro**

PHONE: 406-726-4190

BEER: Drafts; Domestics;
Imports; Microbrews

AMUSEMENT: Volleyball

FOOD: Full Menu Restaurant

The Buck Snort Restaurant, Bar, and Casino is housed in a modern log structure on the west side of Highway 93 in Evaro. A casino, bar, and lounge area occupy the south side of the building, and the dining room, banquet room, and kitchen reside in the north side. The entire facility is modern and well-maintained. Custom-designed features include an L-shaped wooden bar with a log front, a sunken lounge area, a gas fireplace, and several elk horn chandeliers hanging from the log beams supporting the vaulted ceilings. The atmosphere at the Buck Snort is somewhat formal, but at the same time, very relaxed.

The business started out as a small cafe in 1981. A liquor license was obtained shortly thereafter, and a bar was born. Gary and Kathi Stone bought the Buck Snort in 1987, and they have been making various upgrades, additions, and renovations since they took over. It looks like Gary and Kathi are finally getting to the point where things are just about the way they want them. The size of the building has more than doubled since they bought the business, and the Buck Snort has become one of the most popular dining establishment in Western Montana.

Although the Buck Snort is known primarily as an outstanding restaurant, they stock a large selection of beers, including several imports and microbrews. There's also plenty of video gambling machines in the casino if you'd like to try your luck dropping coins. The restaurant opens at 5:00 p.m. daily, and breakfast is served beginning at 9:00 a.m. on Saturday and Sunday. The extensive dinner menu features steaks, seafood, chicken, and pasta dishes. The Buck Snort serves one of the best prime ribs you will ever sink your teeth into, and daily dinner specials are also available. Don't worry about going home hungry, because the gourmet chefs at the Buck Snort serve very generous portions of food. In fact, most people end up leaving food on their plates or taking some home in a doggy bag. The only word of caution I have about eating at the Buck Snort is to call ahead for reservations, especially if you plan on being there on a Friday or Saturday evening.

EVARO BAR & CASINO

OWNERS: Corky and Jo Farwell

HOURS: 11:00 a.m. to 2:00 a.m. Daily

HAPPY HOUR: 4:30 to 6:00 Mon - Fri

GAMBLING: Video Poker/Keno; Shake-A-Day

LIVE MUSIC: Every Other Weekend

LOCATION: 17025 Highway 93, **Evaro**

PHONE: 406-726-3040

BEER: Drafts; Domestics

AMUSEMENT: Pool

FOOD: Grill Items

The Evaro Bar and Casino is housed in a log structure on the west side of Highway 93 in Evaro. The spacious barroom has a large dance floor and a wooden bandstand in the north end, several tables in the middle of the room, and a bar in the south end. The interior decor consists mostly of locally-crafted Indian artwork hanging from the logs and rough cut boards that make up the barroom walls.

The business was established as Yoakum's Beer Parlor in 1945. I don't believe anyone has ever been shot in the barroom, but one of the former owners was a pistol-toting man who used lay on top of the bar and shoot flies off the ceiling. I'm told a customer once approached the bar to complain about his beer being frozen, so the owner calmly drew his pistol and shot the beer can out of the guy's hand. He was apparently bored with shooting flies, and the frozen beer was just the excuse he needed to change targets.

The building was damaged by a chimney fire that broke out during a New Years Eve Party in 1990. The local volunteer fire department arrived on the scene to douse the flames, but the structure suffered extensive water and smoke damage. That didn't seem to bother the people at the New Years Eve Party, because they continued to drink at the bar until closing time. The building was completely reconstructed later that year, so people didn't have to worry about water dripping on their heads when it rained.

Corky and Jo Farwell bought the Evaro Bar in 1992. Corky says it was a pretty rowdy place when he and Jo first took over, but they've settled things down a lot. An occasional fight still breaks out, but it's nothing like it used to be. Corky and Jo treat their customers well, as long as they behave themselves, and the customers appreciate that. Some excellent country and western bands play at the Evaro Bar, and Corky and Jo host a party on just about every holiday. The bar also hosts several benefit auctions and private parties throughout the year, and a pool tournament is held every Sunday during the winter. No matter what time of year it is, there's always something going on at the Evaro Bar & Casino

218

JOE'S SMOKE RING

OWNER: Dorothy Clinkenbeard	**LOCATION:** Highway 93, **Evaro**
HOURS: 4:00 p.m. to 10:00 p.m. Daily	**PHONE:** 406-726-3778
HAPPY HOUR: No	**BEER:** Drafts; Domestics; Imports; Microbrews
GAMBLING: No	**AMUSEMENT:** Pool
LIVE MUSIC: No	**FOOD:** Fresh Pizza; Deli Foods

Joe's Smoke Ring is north of Evaro on Highway 93. The barroom resides in a small paneled-off area in a building that also houses a general store, a self-service gas station, and a delicatessen. The makeshift barroom has just enough space to accommodate an L-shaped wooden bar, a few tables, and a pool table. There's nothing elaborate about the place, but the people are very friendly.

Dorothy Clinkenbeard and her brother, Joe, established Joe's Smoke Ring in 1972. The business was initially a tax free cigarette stand along Highway 93 on the south end of the Flathead Indian Reservation. Joe and Dorothy built an A-frame structure that same year and opened a bar in the building. Unfortunately, Joe passed away in 1973. Dorothy continued on with the business, eventually building it into a successful entertainment emporium. Dorothy built the new store and bar in 1985, and she added the Mule Palace, a 7,500 seat outdoor arena, in 1987. The likes of Dan Seals, Lori Morgan, Merle Haggard, Tanya Tucker, and the Bellamy Brothers have entertained thousands of people at the Mule Palace. The Mule Palace was also home to the National Mule Race (a marathon where contestants ride mules over a twenty-six mile course) at one time, and rodeos were commonly held in the arena.

The business was thriving until April, 1993 when the State imposed a ban on gambling on the Flathead Reservation because of a dispute over tax revenues. Since that time, business has suffered substantially. The Mule Palace sits idle, the live entertainment has ceased, and the barroom now operates on limited hours in a stand-by mode. When the State and Tribal Leaders finally come to terms over gambling revenues, the hours of operation and size of the barroom will be expanded to accommodate the increase in business (that agreement had not been reached as of the date this book went to press, and nobody seemed to know when it might happen). In the mean time, you can still stop in for a cold beer and enjoy the company of the friendly people who frequent Joe's Smoke Ring. They may not have gambling, but it's still a great place to stop.

ALCAN BAR AND CAFE

OWNERS: Tom and Chris Porter

HOURS: 10:00 a.m. to 2:00 a.m. Mon-Sat
11:00 a.m. to Midnight Sunday

HAPPY HOUR: No

GAMBLING: Video Poker/Keno

LIVE MUSIC: Occasionally

LOCATION: Beckwith Street, **Frenchtown**

PHONE: 406-626-9930

BEER: Drafts; Domestics

AMUSEMENT: Pool; Darts; Video Game

FOOD: Full Menu Grill

The Alcan Bar and Cafe is housed in a wooden structure on the north side of Beckwith Street in Frenchtown. A straight wooden bar with an upholstered front faces the east wall of the barroom, several wooden buddy bars and small tables are spread throughout the room, and a dance floor/game room is in the west side. There's nothing fancy about the Alcan, but the beer is cold and the people are friendly. Brands from local ranches have been burned into the wooden bar top, adding a touch of local flavor. There are also several brands burned into the ceiling posts and the boards hanging above the archway in the middle of the room.

The business was established as the Frenchtown Beer Parlor in 1934. The name was changed to the Log Cabin Bar in 1940 when the beer parlor got its first liquor license. The business became known as the Alcan Bar in 1950, and it's operated under that name ever since. The original barroom was much smaller than it is today. At least one addition has been built to make room for the dance floor. I can't say for sure that nothing of great significance has ever occurred at the Alcan Bar, but a sign posted on the wall behind the bar is a pretty good indicator that the Alcan has lived a relatively peaceful life. The sign reads: ON MAY 15th, 1867, DURING THE WAR BETWEEN THE STATES, ON THIS SITE, THE ALCAN BAR, NOT A GODDAMN THING HAPPENED.

Tom and Chris Porter bought the Alcan Bar in August, 1996. Although they're relatively new to the bar business, Tom and Chris continue to promote the same friendly atmosphere the Alcan Bar has become known for. The Alcan has always been a family-oriented place where people of all ages are welcome. It's definitely not the type of place where you have to worry about obnoxious customers or fights breaking out every five minutes. There's usually a local crowd on hand, but the bar gets some highway traffic off Interstate 90. If you arrive hungry, the Alcan Bar serves excellent burgers. In fact, lot of people who live in Missoula frequently drive to Frenchtown just to get a Wimpy Burger at the Alcan Bar.

FRENCH CONNECTION

OWNER: Greg Tabish

HOURS: 10:00 a.m. to Closing Mon-Sat
11:30 a.m. to Closing Sunday

HAPPY HOUR: No

GAMBLING: Video Poker/Keno

LIVE MUSIC: No

LOCATION: 16875 Beckwith Road,
Frenchtown

PHONE: 626-4006

BEER: Drafts; Domestics;
Microbrews

AMUSEMENT: No

FOOD: Grill Items; Fresh
Pizza; Sandwiches

The French Connection is a sports bar and casino located at 16875 Beckwith Road in Frenchtown. The bar and casino are housed in the east side of the building, and a self-service gas station and a convenience store reside in the west side. The barroom has a relatively small bar with a brass elbow rail and a brass foot rail. Several tables with cushioned seats are spread throughout the room, and three television sets are positioned at various locations. Large mirrors surround the video gambling machines in the east side of the barroom.

The French Connection was established in October, 1993. The barroom and casino were added onto the east side of the existing gas station and convenience store when an expansion liquor license became available. Greg Tabish owns the French Connection, and he typically broadcasts some type of televised sporting event in the barroom. There's plenty of University of Montana (UM) Grizzlies fans in this part of the state, and just about every UM sporting event that gets televised will be on at least one of the TVs at the French Connection. You can also stop in to see a wide variety of other major college and professional sporting events such as baseball, basketball, football, and boxing.

If you don't necessarily care for sports, you might want to try your luck at one or more of the twenty video gambling machines in the casino. If you don't care for sports or gambling, you can always stop in for a meal. The French Connection serves excellent burgers, fresh submarine sandwiches, and homemade pizza. Daily lunch specials are available at the bar, and you can get take out orders from the regular menu. A good selection of beers is available, and they even keep cold root beer on tap if you've drawn designated driver duties. With the convenience store and gas station right next door, the French Connection offers one stop shopping. It's a great place to stop, whether you need to fill your gas tank or fill your stomach.

FRENCHTOWN CLUB

OWNERS: John and Carol Greenwood

HOURS: 9:00 a.m. to 2:00 a.m. Daily

HAPPY HOUR: 5:00 to 6:00 Daily

GAMBLING: Video Poker/Keno

LIVE MUSIC: Twice Monthly

LOCATION: 15155 Beckwith Street, **Frenchtown**

PHONE: 406-626-5720

BEER: Drafts; Domestics

AMUSEMENT: Pool; Video Games; Horseshoes

FOOD: Frozen Pizza

The Frenchtown Club is on the corner of Beckwith and Demers Streets in Frenchtown. The barroom is relatively large, and there's plenty of seating available. A horseshoe-shaped bar faces the east wall of the barroom, five wooden buddy bars stand in the middle of the floor, and an open area with several tables and plenty of unoccupied floor space resides in the west side. A liquor store is also part of the business, so you can always pick up a bottle to take home with you.

The history of the Frenchtown Club dates back to 1940 when the Hi Ho Club first opened on Main Street in Frenchtown. The Hi Ho Club operated out of the building on Main Street until 1973 when the Frenchtown Community Church Council purchased the property. The bar and the church were next door to each other, and everyone agreed it would be in the best interests of all parties involved if the church bought the property and the bar moved. The liquor license was transferred to the new bar that was built on the corner of Beckwith and Demers Streets, and the business reopened as the Frenchtown Club.

John and Carol Greenwood bought the Frenchtown Club in April, 1996. Although they're relatively new owners, John and Carol plan on continuing the community-minded spirit the Frenchtown Club has become known for. The bar is the headquarters of the Six Pack Club, an organization devoted to raising money for local residents in need. Various fund raising events are held at the bar throughout the year, and a children's Christmas party, complete with free gifts and a visit from Santa Claus, is the main event in December. John and Carol also have karaoke music at least once a month, and they host a summer picnic, pig roasts, and several customer appreciation days throughout the year. The Frenchtown Club even sponsors a commercial bus that makes frequent stops at various bars in Missoula on Saint Patrick's Day. The regular customers are a mix of local loggers, ranchers, and businessmen. The customers get along great with each other, and there's always room for one more at the bar.

LARRY'S SIX MILE TAVERN

OWNERS: Larry and Phyllis Bardwell

HOURS: 8:00 a.m. to Closing Daily

HAPPY HOUR: No

GAMBLING: Video Poker/Keno

LIVE MUSIC: No

LOCATION: Huson

PHONE: 406-626-5573

BEER: Drafts; Domestics; Microbrews

AMUSEMENT: Pool

FOOD: Full Menu Cafe

Larry's Six Mile Tavern is just south of Interstate 90 at the Huson Interchange (exit 85). The moderate-sized barroom is sparsely decorated, but the facility is very clean and well-maintained. A straight bar faces the north wall, and a few tables are lined neatly against the south wall. The owners haven't spend a lot of time or money on fancy decorations, but new paneling, linoleum, and carpeting have recently been installed. There's also a small wooden deck and a few picnic tables off the west side of the building if you would rather drink outside.

The Six Mile Tavern was established by McCoy and Imogene Rice in 1952. The name Six Mile was selected because the original bar stood six miles west of Frenchtown, which was once an important transportation hub in Western Montana. The present-day structure was built in 1961. It stands approximately two miles east of the original Six Mile Tavern, but the name was never changed.

Larry and Phyllis Bardwell have owned the Six Mile Tavern since June, 1979. They operate the business as a neighborhood bar where people gather to relax and socialize with friends. A lot of people have moved into the area since about 1990, and the local trade is what keeps the place going. Bikers, snowmobilers, log truck drivers, and tourists also stop in, but even with this mix of people, there's rarely any trouble at the bar. A lot of the tourists who stop by say they pulled off the highway at Huson because they're tired of fast food restaurants. They never leave the Six Mile Tavern disappointed, because Larry and Phyllis serve great food. Breakfast, lunch, and dinner are served daily, and lunch specials are offered throughout the week. Broasted chicken is the house specialty, and it's some of the best you will find in Montana.

Aside from the day-to-day operation of the tavern, Larry and Phyllis host several benefits each year to raise money for local organizations and people who have recently experienced tragic events. They take a personal interest in their customers and their community, and that's just one of the things that makes Larry's Six Mile Tavern such a special place.

KOZY KORNER STEAK HOUSE AND BAR

OWNERS: Bob and Edie Baker

HOURS: Noon to Closing Daily

HAPPY HOUR: No

GAMBLING: Video Poker/Keno

LIVE MUSIC: Informal Banjo Music

LOCATION: Kozy Korner Meadow

PHONE: 406-677-3030

BEER: Drafts; Domestics; Microbrews

AMUSEMENT: Horseshoes; Trap Shooting

FOOD: Full Menu Steak House

The Kozy Korner Steak house and Bar is in a place called Kozy Korner Meadow. You can get there by turning onto Woodworth Road from either Highway 200 (at mile post marker 38) or Highway 83 (at mile post marker 7). It's a four mile drive off Highway 83 or an eight mile drive off Highway 200. Either way you go, it's gravel road once you leave the highway. The bar and steak house are housed in a wood and log structure at the junction of Woodworth Road and Cottonwood Lake Road.

The Kozy Korner was built in 1934 to serve loggers who worked for the Anaconda Copper Company in a nearby community called Woodworth. The business consisted of a bar, grocery store, and service station at one time, but the grocery store and service station were closed several years ago. The steak house was added in 1979. The menu features everything from hamburgers to lobster, and the meals are excellent.

Some interesting characters have tended bar at the Kozy Korner over the years, but one in particular has reached legendary status. Warren Skillicorn is the legend, and he has resided in the area since 1910. Besides being the local historian, Warren is an excellent musician. He has played just about every musical instrument known to mankind since the 1920s, and he still plays the banjo at the Kozy Korner every weekend. Warren has witnessed everything from a public hanging in Ovando to a man getting a shot glass shot off his head in the Kozy Korner Bar. If you want to meet the living legend, stop at the Kozy Korner on any weekend evening.

Bob and Edie Baker bought the Kozy Korner in September, 1992. Being the avid hunters that they are, Bob and Edie installed an automated trap range outside the barroom. The traps are voice activated, and you can shoot for fun or competitively. If you're looking for a place to stay while in the area, the Kozy Kountry Bed and Breakfast is just next door. Year round accommodations are available, and they even have a 3200 foot grass airstrip if you prefer to fly in. The Kozy Korner Steak House and Bar in the heart of Kozy Korner Meadow has something for everyone.

LUMBERJACK LODGE AND SALOON

OWNERS: Rob and Molly Kuenzinger   **LOCATION:** Graves Creek Road, **Lolo**

HOURS: Noon to Closing Daily   **PHONE:** 406-273-2281

HAPPY HOUR: No   **BEER:** Drafts; Domestics

GAMBLING: Video Poker/Keno   **AMUSEMENT:** Pool; Darts; Volleyball; Horseshoes

LIVE MUSIC: Every Weekend   **FOOD:** Full Menu Grill

The Lumberjack Lodge and Saloon is 1-1/2 miles north of Highway 12 on Graves Creek Road (approximately 18 miles west of Lolo). The building's walls consist of four cedar logs that, when stacked on top of each other, rise to over ten feet in height. The interior is very roughly finished, creating a rustic appearance. High back log stools that were carved with chainsaws provide seating at the log bar facing the west wall. One of the bar stools is suspended with rope from a ceiling beam, so you can swing back and forth while you drink. A huge stone fireplace rises from the concrete floor against the south wall, and a wood burning stove stands in the northeast corner of the room. Numerous pieces of logger's art, including old boots, chainsaws, and a stuffed beaver wearing suspenders and a wool hat, hang from the log posts and ceiling beams. This only begins to describe the characteristics of the Lumberjack Saloon; it's a place you have to experience to appreciate.

The saloon was built by a group of local loggers. The men spent two years gathering building materials from the surrounding national forests and piecing the place together. In January, 1974, the Lumberjack Saloon was finally finished. Each of the eight log barstools was carved by a different person who worked on the building. If you look at the back of the stools, you will see the name of the man who carved out the chair.

Rob and Molly Kuenzinger bought the Lumberjack Saloon in early 1997. Rob and Molly weren't even running the business when I last visited the Lumberjack, but they have no plans to discontinue the traditional parties. 4X4 races, sand drag races, pig roasts, and the Logger's Day Celebration are just some of the annual festivities held at the Lumberjack Saloon. There's also live music every weekend, and weddings and private parties are held throughout the year. You can camp overnight on the property for free, and cabin rentals are available if you prefer indoor lodging. Although it's a little off the beaten path, the Lumberjack Lodge and Saloon is a one-of-a-kind place that everyone should experience. Believe me, you won't be disappointed.

LOLO HOT SPRINGS RESORT

OWNER: Don Stoen

LOCATION: Lolo Hot Springs

HOURS: 8:00 a.m. to 2:00 a.m. Daily

PHONE: 406-273-2290

HAPPY HOUR: No

BEER: Drafts; Domestics; Imports; Microbrews

GAMBLING: Video Poker/Keno

AMUSEMENT: Pool; Darts; Horseshoes; Volleyball

LIVE MUSIC: Occasionally

FOOD: Full Menu Restaurant

Lolo Hot Springs Resort is twenty-five miles west of Lolo on Highway 12. The saloon and restaurant are housed in a large wooden structure on the north side of the highway, just west of the pool area. The spacious barroom has a straight wooden bar facing the west wall, and several tables are spread throughout the room. The hand-crafted bar was fashioned from black walnut and bird'seye maple wood, and the wall coverings in the west end of the room match the beautiful woodwork of the bar. The entire building has undergone extensive renovations in recent years, so the facility is very modern and well-maintained.

The history of Lolo Hot Springs dates back hundreds, if not thousands, of years. The hot springs served as a meeting place and bathing area for Native Americans, and early explorers, trappers, and prospectors used the mineralized springs as a landmark and rendezvous point. The first saloon at the hot springs probably opened around 1885. The building was destroyed by fire, but a photograph (dated 1910) hanging from the wall in the dining room shows the original log structure. In the early years, gambling and prostitution were commonplace at the saloon. Allegedly, these activities continued on into the early 1980s when federal authorities also uncovered a rather sophisticated counterfeiting operation at the resort.

Don Stoen bought the saloon, restaurant, pools, and campground in 1988. Don doesn't own the motel, but lodging is available. During the summer months, tourists by the truckload come to the area for hiking and horseback riding. Visiting hunters provide a good share of the business in the fall, and snowmobilers keep things busy during the winter. Over 200 miles of trails are available, and horses and snowmobiles are rented at the resort. Don sponsors snowmobile grass drag races and pond riding events a couple of times during the summer and fall, so you snowmobilers don't have to wait until the ground turns white to get your machines out. There's always a friendly crowd on hand at the bar, so no matter what time of year it is, Lolo Hot Springs Resort is a great place to visit.

HAROLD'S CLUB

OWNER: Karen Keely

LOCATION: 11 Main Street, **Milltown**

HOURS: 10:00 a.m. to Closing Daily

PHONE: 406-258-6932

HAPPY HOUR: No

BEER: Drafts; Domestics; Microbrews

GAMBLING: Video Poker/Keno; Shake-A-Day

AMUSEMENT: Pool; Darts

LIVE MUSIC: Every Weekend

FOOD: Full Menu Cafe

Harold's Club is about one block south of Highway 200 on Main Street in Milltown. Their slogan "We cheat the other guy and pass the savings on to you" shouldn't be taken literally, but it provides a good indication that the folks at Harold's Club are fun-loving people with a sense of humor. The bar, pool tables, and gambling machines are in the front portion of the barroom, and a dining area and dance floor are in the rear. The oil paintings hanging from the barroom walls were done by Vic Solander, a local artist who recently passed away. I don't know who created the masterpiece that stands on top of the cooler behind the bar, but I'm told the kettle-looking device is an authentic moonshine still that came from the Great Falls area.

The history of the tavern dates back to 1896 when the Union Bar first opened. The business has gone through several owners and several names since then, but it's still a neighborhood bar where working class people gather. There's no formal happy hour, but a different drink special is available every day of the week. Canned and bottled beer is kept behind the bar in open coolers filled with ice, so you know you won't be served a warm beer. It's the little things like this that make Harold's Club such a special place.

Karen Keely bought Harold's Club in January, 1996. Aside from a lot of cleaning, Karen hasn't changed much about the place since she took over. The cafe is now leased out as a separate business, but you can still order food directly from the bar. Harold's Club typically has karaoke-style music on Friday nights and a live band on Saturday nights. Every year in September, the bar hosts a big family gathering, complete with live music, games, food, and raffles. Harold's Club is also a scheduled stop for local bikers who participate in the annual motorcycle run on January 1. No matter how bad the weather gets, you will see upwards of seventy-five motorcycles pulling into the parking lot at the bar between 1:00 p.m. and 2:00 p.m. on January 1. I guess it's better than sitting at home complaining about the snow.

MARVIN'S

OWNER: KC La Flesch

HOURS: 10:00 a.m. to 2:00 a.m. Daily

HAPPY HOUR: No

GAMBLING: Video Poker/Keno; Live Poker; Shake-A-Day

LIVE MUSIC: No

LOCATION: The "Y", **Missoula**

PHONE: 406-549-4468

BEER: Domestics

AMUSEMENT: Pool; Darts; Horseshoes

FOOD: Burgers; Soup; Frozen Pizza

Marvin's Tavern is at 7995 Highway 10, approximately seven miles west of Missoula. The locals refer to the junction in the road as The Y, but I find it easier to tell people who are unfamiliar with the area that the tavern is at the southwest corner of the interchange where Highway 200/93 and Interstate 90 cross (exit 96 off Interstate 90). The structure was built with lodgepole pine logs, so both the interior and exterior have a rustic appearance. An L-shaped wooden bar and an antique wooden back bar reside in the middle portion of the building. A stone fireplace rises from the floor in the southwest corner of the barroom, and an antique piano stands against the east wall. The piano still gets plenty of use by a few of the regular customers.

Marvin's was named after the man who built the place. At one time, it was the only commercial building between The Y and Missoula. The business started out as a gas station, grocery store, and cafe. Bootlegged booze was sold out of the store during the prohibition years, and alcohol sales were so good that the store and gas station became a licensed tavern when prohibition ended. Johnny La Flesch bought Marvin's in 1948. Johnny spent the next forty-six years behind the bar while his wife spent that time at the grill frying some of the best cheeseburgers ever made. Johnny's son, KC, took over the business in the fall of 1994.

Marvin's has always been a working class bar where local residents gather to drink and socialize. KC grew up around the bar, and he works hard to ensure the friendly atmosphere and home town environment continue on. The barroom today looks much the same as it did when Johnny La Flesch bought the business in 1948. Even the cheeseburgers haven't changed since the first one was served up nearly fifty years ago. The wooden tables and booths are still in the barroom, old photographs, snowshoes, paintings, and a bearskin rug hang from the walls, and the people are as friendly as you will find anywhere. If you miss the way things were in the good old days, take a drive to Marvin's at the Y west of Missoula. You'll be glad you made the trip.

NINE MILE HOUSE

OWNERS: Doug and Barbara Gaut

HOURS: 10:00 a.m. to Closing Mon-Sat
1:00 p.m. to 9:30 p.m. Sunday

HAPPY HOUR: No

GAMBLING: Video Poker/Keno

LIVE MUSIC: Occasionally

LOCATION: Nine Mile

PHONE: 406-626-5668

BEER: Drafts; Domestics;
Imports; Microbrews

AMUSEMENT: Pool; Video Games

FOOD: Full Menu Restaurant

The Nine Mile House is 1-1/2 miles north of Interstate 90 on Nine Mile Road (exit 82). A moderate-sized barroom and a small dining area reside in the middle portion of the building, and there's a separate dining room on each end of the building. The barroom has a straight wooden bar built in two sections. The wooden bar tops are made from thick planks that were cut from the center of a tree trunk. If you don't like sitting on a barstool, plenty of tables are available in the smaller area toward the back of the barroom. If you do choose to sit on a barstool, be careful where you put your glass. The bar top is warped in one place, and your drink may slide off into your lap if you're not careful.

George H. Brown built the original Nine Mile House in 1893. The two story structure housed a hotel, restaurant, and dance hall. The building also served as a stage stop between Frenchtown and the gold mines in the surrounding mountains. A photograph of the first Nine Mile House, along with the old two story outhouse that was used by the hotel guests, hangs from the wall in the west dining room of the existing building. The present-day structure was built across the road from the original building in 1946-47. Most of the lumber used to build the new Nine Mile House came from the original building. The only significant change that's been made to the new building was the addition of a second dining room in 1992.

Doug and Barbara Gaut have owned the Nine Mile House since 1971. They promote a very friendly atmosphere at the bar, and that attitude is definitely reflected by their employees and their customers. The local customer base consists of people who live as far away as Missoula, and they get plenty of business from tourists and hunters who visit the area. The dinner menu features steaks and seafood, and prime rib is the house specialty. Daily lunch specials are available, and all-you-can-eat barbecue ribs are served every Monday. The dining room opens at 5:00 p.m. Monday through Saturday and 2:00 p.m. on Sundays. The Nine Mile House may be a little off the beaten path, but the food, atmosphere, and people make the short detour off Interstate 90 well worth the time.

ROCK CREEK LODGE

OWNER: Rod Lincoln

HOURS: 8:00 a.m. to Closing Daily

HAPPY HOUR: No

GAMBLING: Video Poker/Keno

LIVE MUSIC: Occasionally

LOCATION: Rock Creek

PHONE: 406-825-4868

BEER: Drafts; Domestics; Microbrews

AMUSEMENT: Pool; Darts; Foosball; Horseshoes; Volleyball

FOOD: Full Menu Cafe

The Rock Creek Lodge, home of Montana's original Testicle Festival, is just south of the Rock Creek Interchange (exit 126) off Interstate 90. The 10,000 square foot building houses a barroom, restaurant, motel, and gift shop. There's also a Wild West Museum which houses several mounted big game animals. The barroom has a long wooden bar, several tables, and plenty of open floor space. Over 1,300 hats hang from the ceiling, and several autographed pictures of celebrities who have been to the lodge are displayed on the north wall of the barroom.

The Rock Creek Lodge was built in 1946 from timber and rocks gathered from the 100 acre parcel of property surrounding the building. The only significant changes that have been made to the original structure occurred in 1975 when the gift shop and museum were added. The nationally-renowned Testicle Festival began in 1982. Several hundred people gathered for the inaugural event to dine on a meal of Rocky Mountain Oysters, and the Testicle Festival has steadily gained in popularity ever since. In 1996, over 10,000 people consumed 5,000 pounds of bull testicles at the three day Testicle Festival.

Rod Lincoln bought the Rock Creek Lodge in 1984. His bar patrons range anywhere from bikers to businessmen, but there's never any problems between customers. A steady local and regional clientele keep the place going throughout the year, and tourists provide a boost to the business during the summer. To help promote the Testicle Festival, Rod created Ol Testy, a full-size wooden sculpture of a bull that nervously stares backward hoping nobody comes to castrate him. Ol Testy really has nothing to worry about, because the customers at the Rock Creek Lodge treat him as a sacred shrine. The Testicle Festival is always held in September, but the dates vary from year to year. If you plan on attending, it's best to call the lodge prior to September so you don't miss the event where "everyone has a ball". Rod allows people to camp overnight on his property for free, so you might as well spend the entire weekend.

**The Rock Creek Lodge, home to Montana's original
Testicle Festival.**

**Top Photo: A souvenir stand outside the Rock Creek Lodge
advertises the Testicle Festival.**

**Bottom Photo: Ol' Testy, the sacred shrine at the
Rock Creek Lodge.**

POTOMAC COUNTRY STORE AND BAR

OWNERS: Loretta Hayes

LOCATION: Highway 200, **Potomac**

HOURS: 7:00 a.m. to Closing Daily

PHONE: 406-244-5577

HAPPY HOUR: 5:30 to 6:30 Mon - Thurs

BEER: Drafts; Domestics; Microbrews

GAMBLING: Video Poker/Keno

AMUSEMENT: Pool; Video Games

LIVE MUSIC: Occasionally

FOOD: Full Menu Restaurant

The Potomac Country Store and Bar, home of the Awful Burger and Awful Pizza, is housed in a wooden structure on the north side of Highway 200 in Potomac. The bar is only part of the entire business, which includes a convenience store, a restaurant, and self-service gas. The convenience store is in the west side of the building, and the bar-room and dining area share an open room under the vaulted ceiling in the east side. A river rock fireplace and a wooden stairway leading to the loft above the dining area provide some separation between the bar and dining room. Large plate glass windows make up the south wall of the building. The windows provide the customers with an excellent view of the tree covered mountains in the Blackfoot River Valley. A wooden deck is just outside the barroom for those who want to more fully appreciate the outdoor splendor the area has to offer.

The business was established as the Valley Tavern in 1946, but the name was changed to the Potomac Bar in 1947. The original bar oper-ated out of a wooden building that was moved to Potomac from a nearby logging camp. The man who owned the bar served hamburg-ers he cooked on a grill, and for some reason, the customers started referring to them as Awful Burgers. The name stuck, and you can still get a home-grown Awful Burger at the Potomac Country Store and Bar today. Home-grown Awful Pizzas are now available as well. In 1981, a grocery store opened in a building behind the old bar. The store, barroom, and restaurant were all moved when construction on the new building was completed in July, 1991.

Loretta Hayes has owned the Potomac Country Store and Bar since 1978. A steady local clientele keeps the place going throughout the year, and visiting tourists, bicyclists, hunters, fishermen, and snow-mobilers stop in as well. There's typically a very friendly crowd at the bar, even during the annual Saint Patrick's Day party when the tradi-tional feast of corned beef and cabbage is served. Restaurant hours are 7:00 a.m. until 9:00 p.m. (10:00 p.m. in the summer), and everything from gas to groceries is available in the convenience store

HUNGRY BEAR STEAK HOUSE

OWNERS: Fred Styler & Tom Camp

LOCATION: Highway 83, **Swan Valley**

HOURS: 4:00 p.m. to Closing Daily
Winter Hours Vary

PHONE: 406-754-2240

HAPPY HOUR: Sometimes

BEER: Drafts; Domestics; Imports; Microbrews

GAMBLING: Video Poker/Keno

AMUSEMENT: Pool; Video Games

LIVE MUSIC: Occasionally

FOOD: Full Menu Steak House

The Hungry Bear Steak House is seven miles south of Condon (between mile post markers 38 and 39) on Highway 83. The modern log structure houses a spacious barroom and a separate dining room. The interior walls and ceiling supports are made from hand-peeled logs, and the vaulted ceilings are finished with tongue-and-groove pine boards. Several trophy-sized big game mounts hang from the walls in both the barroom and dining room. A long wooden bar, three buddy bars, and a wood burning stove reside in the north side of the barroom, and several tables, a hardwood dance floor, and an elevated bandstand occupy the floor space in the opposite side. A wooden deck is accessible through the sliding glass doors in the barroom, and a concrete patio is just off the dining room.

The Hungry Bear Steak House was established by Jim Busch in 1977. The business began as a restaurant with a retail beer and wine license. The original building was only about half the size it is now. The south side of the existing structure wasn't added until after a full liquor license was obtained in 1979. Fred Stryker and Tom Camp bought the Hungry Bear Steak House in 1993, and they continue to operate it today.

The Hungry Bear is noted as more of a dining establishment than a drinking establishment, but the barroom sees plenty of activity. The specialty drink of the house is a huckleberry daiquiri. The fruit flavored beverage has become very popular among the regular customers, and even the tourists have discovered the daiquiris are a great source of refreshment. The Hungry Bear holds an outdoor concert every summer, and they occasionally have live music in the barroom. The summer concerts showcase several excellent musicians who play throughout the day and evening. With its location in the beautiful Swan Valley, the Hungry Bear obviously gets more business during the summer months than the winter, but the bar and steak house are open year-round. It really doesn't matter what time of year it is, because the people are very friendly, the food is excellent, and the daiquiris are available any time.

233

WILDERNESS B&R

OWNER: Kathy Frisby

HOURS: Noon to 2:00 a.m. (Summer)
4:00 p.m. to Closing (Winter)

HAPPY HOUR: 6:00 to 7:00 Mon - Fri

GAMBLING: Video Poker/Keno;
Shake-A-Day

LIVE MUSIC: Every Other Week (Summer)

LOCATION: Hwy. 83, **Swan Valley**

PHONE: 406-754-2229

BEER: Drafts; Domestics;
Imports; Microbrews

AMUSEMENT: Pool; Darts

FOOD: Full Menu Restaurant

The Wilderness B&R (B&R stands for Bar and Restaurant) is housed in a wooden structure that stands on the east side of Highway 83, nine miles south of Condon. A spacious barroom is in the north side of the building, and a smaller dining room is in the south side. The Wilderness B&R has a rustic appearance and a very inviting atmosphere. A covered boardwalk spans the length of the front side of the building, and the interior walls are covered with log slats. Heavy log timbers support the ceiling, and the original wood flooring is still intact. Mounted moose, elk, and deer heads hang above a thick log shelf on the wall behind the bar. An antique upright piano stands beside the stone fireplace on the east wall of the barroom, and a wooden bandstand is against the south wall.

The business started out as an automobile service station in the late 1950s. All there was to the building at that time was the very north side of the existing structure where the raised portion of the floor is. A liquor license was obtained in 1971. A kitchen was built in the part of the building that now houses the dining room, and a corridor was added to connect the barroom with the kitchen. Interestingly enough, the middle portion of the existing structure was the last section to be completed.

Kathy Frisby bought the Wilderness B&R in April, 1996. Although Kathy and her husband, George, are relatively new to the bar business, they seem to be doing just fine in their new careers. The Wilderness B&R offers half price beer and well drinks during happy hour, and they serve excellent margaritas and huckleberry daiquiris throughout the day. The restaurant has a complete dinner menu featuring authentic Mexican dishes and steaks marinated in a special house sauce. Live music is played in the barroom every other week during the summer, and they have karaoke every Friday night. Kathy and George also host two pig roasts every summer; one as a community fund raising event and one as a customer appreciation party. There's three full RV hookups available on the property, so spending the night in your motor home is no problem.

THE OTHER PLACE

OWNERS: June and Tim Marek

HOURS: 3:00 p.m. to 2:00 a.m (Summer)
5:00 p.m. to 11:00 p.m. (Winter)

HAPPY HOUR: 4:00 to 6:00 (Summer Only)

GAMBLING: Video Poker/Keno

LIVE MUSIC: Occasionally

LOCATION: 12120 Hwy. 10 E., **Turah**

PHONE: 406-258-6882

BEER: Drafts; Domestics; Imports

AMUSEMENT: Video Games

FOOD: Full Menu Supper Club

The Other Place is on Old Highway 10, just north of the Turah Interchange on Interstate 90 (exit 113). The main barroom resides in the south side of the building. A spacious dining room with a separate walk-up bar is in the north side, and a small lounge area sits off to the east of the main barroom. A raised wooden deck that can seat approximately eighty people is off the northeast corner of the building. The outdoor deck is a popular dining and drinking spot when the weather is warm; however, its use becomes limited from October through May.

The business was established during the 1920s. The present-day building is actually two separate farm houses that were moved to the property and joined together. Several additions and renovations have taken place over the years, so the existing structure looks nothing like what the original building did. I'm told food and drinks weren't the only things served at the bar during the early years of operation. Allegedly, call girls "worked" in the small buildings behind the bar.

The call girls are long gone, and in recent years, the Other Place has evolved into more of a dining establishment than a drinking establishment. Dining room hours are 5:00 p.m. to 11:00 p.m. during the summer and 6:00 p.m. until 10:00 p.m. in the winter. Steaks are the house specialty, but the extensive dinner menu features seafood, chicken, pasta dishes, and hot sandwiches as well. Daily dinner specials are available throughout the year.

The Other Place has a steady local clientele, but a lot of tourists wander into the bar and restaurant during the summer months. A public campground is close by, so plenty of business comes in the form of travelers who stop over for the night. The dining is the big draw at the Other Place, so they enjoy a quiet, family-oriented atmosphere. The barroom should not be overlooked, however, because they offer an extensive selection of liquors and beers.

TURAH PINES BAR AND CASINO

OWNERS: Cyclone and Peggy Bjornberg   **LOCATION:** 12360 Hwy. 10 E., **Turah**

HOURS: Noon to 2:00 a.m. Daily   **PHONE:** 406-258-9924

HAPPY HOUR: No   **BEER:** Drafts; Domestics

GAMBLING: Video Poker/Keno   **AMUSEMENT:** Pool; Darts; Pinball; Video Games

LIVE MUSIC: Occasionally   **FOOD:** Full Menu Grill

The Turah Pines Bar and Casino is on Old Highway 10 in Turah. The wooden structure stands approximately 1/4 mile east of the Turah Interchange (exit 113) off Interstate 90. A wooden bar runs lengthwise through the narrow west end of the building. The barroom opens up considerably on the east side, with plenty of room for a dance floor, an elevated wooden bandstand, and several tables. There's also an antique coin-operated bowling game in the barroom that is very popular among the customers. I'm told the bowling game is one of a very few such devices in the United States that are still operable.

The history of the Turah Pines Bar and Casino dates back to 1951 when a gas station and convenience store called Johnson's Service Station obtained a retail beer license. The name of the business changed to the Turah Pines in 1971, just prior to the time the bar was issued a full liquor license. The original building was only a fraction of the size it is today. Several additions have been made to the east side of the building over the years.

Cyclone and Peggy Bjornberg have owned the Turah Pines since 1973. Cyclone and Peggy promote a friendly atmosphere at the bar, and they do their best to make sure their guests are treated well. Every summer, the Turah Pines hosts a customer appreciation party with activities ranging from river races to volleyball games. Although the bar is just off a major interstate highway, the Turah Pines is not a tourist stop. The place is basically a working man's tavern where local loggers and sawmill workers gather to relax and unwind. Hunters, fishermen, and snowmobilers also stop in occasionally, but the business lives and dies by its local trade. The bartenders are always courteous and quick to serve you, and the customers are friendly as well. The Turah Pines Bar and Casino is not the type of place where you have to worry about fights breaking out. With its easy access and small town environment, the Turah Pines Bar and Casino is one stop you shouldn't miss.

MELSTONE BAR AND CAFE

OWNERS: Mel and Judy Metzger	**LOCATION:**	109 2nd Ave. W, **Melstone**
HOURS: 10:00 a.m. to Closing Daily	**PHONE:**	406-358-2355
HAPPY HOUR: 5:00 to 6:00 Mon - Fri	**BEER:**	Drafts; Domestics
GAMBLING: Video Poker/Keno	**AMUSEMENT:**	Pool; Darts
LIVE MUSIC: Occasionally	**FOOD:**	Full Menu Cafe

The Melstone Bar and Cafe is housed in a steel sided-structure on 2nd Avenue in Melstone. You can see the building on the north side of Highway 12 as you pass through town. The barroom resides in the west side of the building, and the cafe is in the east side. Eight stools stand in front of the straight bar along the north wall, and a half dozen or so tables are spread across the floor. The signatures on the wall near the pool table are from local musicians who have played at the bar.

The Melstone Bar and Cafe was established in the mid 1980's. The business initially operated with only a beer and wine license, but a full liquor license became available when Melstone's Antler Bar and Grill closed. Mel and Judy Metzger bought the Melstone Bar and Cafe in 1991. Mel and Judy also operate a catering business from the building. They enjoy catering to wagon trains, brandings, cattle drives, and various other private parties so much that they've decided to get out of the bar business altogether. The Melstone Bar and Cafe was for sale the last I heard, so don't be surprised if someone other than Mel or Judy greets you when you walk through the door.

The majority of the people you will meet at the Melstone Bar and Cafe are residents of Melstone and the surrounding communities. Business is steady most of the year, but it picks up considerably when visiting hunters swarm to the area in the fall. You will typically find a fairly quiet, friendly crowd on hand. The cafe is open from 6:00 a.m. to 8:00 p.m. daily, except during hunting season when breakfast is served at 5:00 a.m. Daily meal specials are offered throughout the week, and a buffet is served every Sunday.

There's usually some locally-crafted artwork on display in the cafe. The artwork ranges anywhere from wood carvings to jewelry, and Mel and Judy sell the pieces on consignment. They sometimes have Schwabaur bronze statuettes for sale. Wildlife artist Lyle Schwabaur creates his masterpieces in Elliston, and Mel and Judy will be glad to show you his catalog if you want to order something special.

TRACY'S MECCA BAR

OWNER: Tracy Newland

HOURS: 1:00 p.m. to Closing Daily

HAPPY HOUR: No

GAMBLING: Video Poker

LIVE MUSIC: Occasionally

LOCATION: Hwy. 87, **Old Roundup**

PHONE: 406-323-9990

BEER: Drafts; Domestics

AMUSEMENT: Pool

FOOD: Microwave Foods

Tracy's Mecca Bar is on Highway 87 in a community known locally as Old Roundup. If you don't know where Old Roundup is, just follow Highway 87 south out of Roundup approximately 1-1/2 miles and you will see the bar on the right-hand side of the road. If you get to Klein, you've gone too far. Tracy Newland has been associated with the business since the early 1940's when her brother opened the Mecca Bar in Roundup. In 1953, Tracy bought the liquor license and moved the business to its present location. The 24 x 24 foot room that makes up the front part of the existing building was all there was when Tracy started out. The structure was originally a coal mine company house at the Klein #2 Mine. Over the years, Tracy made additions to the building as money allowed. Priorities being what they are, indoor toilets were not available until the early 1980's.

If there's one thing that sets Tracy's Mecca Bar apart, it's got to be Tracy Newland. This remarkable lady has virtually run the business singlehandedly since she bought the bar in 1953. Tracy used to stay open from 8:00 a.m. until 2:00 a.m. seven days a week. She now keeps more reasonable hours of 1:00 p.m. until closing. There's no formal happy hour, but seven ounce glasses of beer sell for 40 cents, twelve ounce mugs of beer are 75 cents, pitchers cost $3.50, and several brands of canned beer are sold for $1.00. With these prices, who needs a happy hour.

Tracy fondly recalls many memorable events that have taken place at the Mecca Bar over the years. Her stories range from streakers on busy dance nights to riders mounted on horseback during the Montana Centennial Cattle Drive party that was held in 1989. Although indoor toilets are now available, the outhouses come in handy during the many outdoor barbecues Tracy hosts during the summer. A lot of tourists stop and take pictures of the outhouses and the neighboring cabin where Tracy's father lived for several years. For some strange reason, some of the tourists actually prefer to use the outhouses instead of the indoor toilets. I guess some people who have never had to use an outhouse just want to find out what it's like. Whether you prefer indoor plumbing or privys, it's well worth your time to stop at Tracy's Mecca Bar in Old Roundup.

BRANDIN' IRON SALOON

OWNERS: Caroline Shupe

LOCATION: Highway 87, 12 Miles
South of **Roundup**

HOURS: 10:00 to Closing (Summer)
Noon to Closing (Winter)

PHONE: 406-323-3449

HAPPY HOUR: 5:30 to 6:30 Mon - Fri

BEER: Drafts; Domestics

GAMBLING: Video Poker/Keno;
Shake-A-Day

AMUSEMENT: Pool; Horseshoes;
Volleyball

LIVE MUSIC: Approximately Monthly

FOOD: Grill Items

The Brandin' Iron Saloon is twelve miles south of Roundup on Highway 87. The structure was built with hand-peeled logs, and natural wood trim was used to finish the interior. The ceiling is supported by log beams, and the L-shaped wooden bar has a log front. Plenty of tables are spread throughout the spacious barroom, and a large patio is just off the back side of the building.

The Brandin' Iron Saloon was established in June, 1992. The bar was built on the assumption that most of the business would come from workers at a coal mine that was scheduled to open in the area, but the owners soon discovered people who already lived locally provided plenty of business. Caroline Shupe bought the Brandin' Iron in July, 1996, and she operates the business as a service to the local community. Caroline hosts several barbecues during the summer, and benefits for local charities are held at the bar throughout the year. The Brandin' Iron also has some of the best singers in the state perform during the many karaoke style dances held at the saloon. In fact, two of the people who regularly sing at the Brandin' Iron have been invited to sing at Nashville's Grand Ole Opry. You're guaranteed to hear some great music on scheduled dance nights, but don't be surprised if you're at the bar some weekday evening and the bartender or one of the customers starts singing to the sound of the karaoke machine. Everybody is welcome to sing at any time at the Brandin' Iron. At least one Sunday each month, an informal jam session is held. The people who come to play are known as the Bull Mountain Jamboree.

With ten acres surrounding the building, Caroline hosts plenty of outdoor activities. A horseless rodeo is held at least once each summer, complete with mechanical bull riding, sheep riding, and other horseless events. Caroline plans on installing a roping arena in the spring of 1997, and sanctioned rodeos will be held at the bar. There's also plenty of room if you want to park your rig and spend the night. Free overnight parking is available, so you don't have to drive home after drinking.

239

TUMBLEWEED SALOON

OWNERS: Dennis and Rusty Anderson

HOURS: 10:00 a.m. to Closing (Mon-Sat)
Noon - Midnight (Sunday)

HAPPY HOUR: No

GAMBLING: Video Poker/Keno;
Shake-A-Day

LIVE MUSIC: Occasionally

LOCATION: Tumbleweed

PHONE: 406-323-1025

BEER: Drafts; Domestics;
Imports; Microbrews

AMUSEMENT: Pool; Darts; Pinball;
Horseshoes

FOOD: Grilled/Broiled Foods

The Tumbleweed Saloon is in the community of Tumbleweed, which is twenty-four miles north of Billings on Highway 87. A Tumbleweed Saloon sign near mile post marker 30 points the way to the bar. When you see the wood sided building with a penguin-shaped weather vane on the roof, you know you've arrived. The saloon was established in 1977 in a building that formerly housed a rabbit slaughter house. Although the official name of the business has always been the Tumbleweed Saloon, a lot of the locals affectionate-ly refer to the place as the Dead Rabbit. The original barroom has been expanded several times since the bar first opened. Although labor charges were never paid in the form of money, it's alleged the workers were paid off in booze. That helps explain the various types of materials used to finish the interior walls, floors, and ceiling.

The history and physical appearance of the Tumbleweed Saloon are unique, but the people are what make the place special. Dennis and Rusty Anderson bought the business in 1984, and they go out of their way to make sure their customers enjoy themselves. Several special events are held at the bar throughout the year, none more popular than the three day Tumbleweed Days celebration during the last weekend in July. Over the years, goat roping, mud wrestling, and var-ious other competitive events have been held during Tumbleweed Days, but the latest craze has become timed team toilet races. Three person teams compete against each other to see who can pull, push, and ride a toilet mounted on a piece of plywood with four bicycle wheels across the finish line the fastest.

If you're at the Tumbleweed Saloon and hear someone scream out "Polish The Penguin", be prepared to climb onto the roof and rub the weather vane. It's become a local tradition here, and you should take advantage of the opportunity to join in. And speaking of polished, don't take a chance by driving home if you've had too much to drink. Dennis and Rusty don't mind if you spend the night outside the bar in your vehicle, so there's no sense in risking the drive home.

240

CLYDE PARK TAVERN

OWNERS: Babe and Vicki Hager

LOCATION: 311 Miles St, **Clyde Park**

HOURS: 10:00 a.m. to Closing Daily

PHONE: 406-686-4778

HAPPY HOUR: No

BEER: Drafts; Domestics; Imports; Microbrews

GAMBLING: Video Poker/Keno; Shake-A-Day

AMUSEMENT: Pool; Darts

LIVE MUSIC: Occasionally

FOOD: Full Menu Cafe

The Clyde Park Tavern is at 311 Miles Street in Clyde Park. The barroom is housed in the north side of the building, and a dining room is in the south side. The interior walls are beautifully finished with tongue-and-groove woodwork, and the original hardwood floor in the dining room is still intact. The thick wooden top on the bar is made from a plank that was cut from the middle of a tree trunk. A polyurethane coating was applied before placing the chunk of log on top of the bar.

The existing dining room was once a grocery store, and the area where the barroom presently resides was originally a bank. The walk-in cooler behind the bar was built inside the old bank vault when the tavern first opened in 1944. There have been some interesting moments at the Clyde Park Tavern the years, but not all of them can be explained. One of the former owners once discovered several bullet holes in the ceiling above the false ceiling tiles, but nobody seems to know how they got there. The bullet holes were easy enough to cover with the false ceiling, but some unplanned structural repairs had to be made to the front of the building during the 1960s. It seems an unnamed individual inadvertently drove his vehicle through the wall.

Babe and Vicki Hager bought the Clyde Park Tavern in December, 1994. They serve excellent 1/2 pound burgers, and people commonly drive from as far away as Livingston and Bozeman for the broasted chicken and broasted pork chops. Local residents provide a steady business throughout the year, and tourists and hunters frequent the bar during the summer and fall. Other visitors to the tavern have included a full grown black bear, a wolverine, and a snow leopard. A local man trains these critters for television shows and movies, and he occasionally brings one of the animals into the bar with him. Photographs on the wall behind the bar show a black bear eating M&M's out of a customer's mouth and a wolverine standing on top of the bar. If you happen to be at the Clyde Park Tavern and see what you think is a very hairy man out the corner of your eye, look again; it may be a bear begging for candy.

SHIELDS RIVER INN

OWNER: Elsie Gregovich

HOURS: 10:00 a.m. to Closing Daily

HAPPY HOUR: No

GAMBLING: Video Poker/Keno

LIVE MUSIC: Occasionally

LOCATION: Highway 89, **Clyde Park**

PHONE: 406-686-4754

BEER: Drafts; Domestics; Imports

AMUSEMENT: Pool; Darts

FOOD: Sandwiches; Frozen Pizza

The Shields River Inn is on the east side of Highway 89 in Clyde Park. The spacious barroom has a long L-shaped bar, ample floor space, and about a half dozen tables spread throughout the room. A dance floor and a small bandstand are in the north end of the barroom. The building is relatively new, and it's kept very clean and well-maintained.

Dahl Evans established the Shields River Inn in 1979. The name of the business comes from the Shields River, which runs past Clyde Park on the west side of Highway 89. Dahl built the wood-framed structure and obtained a liquor license that previously belonged to Red's Bar, a tavern that stood across the highway. I'm told Red's Bar had quite a reputation, but fortunately, the reputation didn't follow the liquor license to the Shields River Inn. Dahl sold the business in the early 1980's. The new owner built an addition onto the north side of the building and extended the bar along the west wall. If you look at the ceiling above the north end of the bar, you can see the wooden beam where the addition started.

Current owner Elsie Gregovich bought the Shields River Inn in 1987. Elsie runs a friendly establishment where people gather to relax and unwind. Most of her business comes in the form of local trade, but tourists and hunters stop in during the summer and fall. Elsie primarily caters to adults, so you don't often see kids in the barroom. Of the two bars in Clyde Park, the Shields River Inn draws more of the older crowd.

As a bonus to her customers, Elsie holds a weekly cash drawing on Friday evenings. At least $50.00 is awarded to the lucky person whose name is drawn at random. Customers can enter their name for the drawing once a day throughout the week at no cost. On Friday evening, Elsie draws one name from all the entries and announces the winner. You must be present to win, so the pot increases by $50.00 a week until the person whose name is drawn personally claims their money. Elsie says the barroom is very busy on Friday evenings, especially when the pot gets over $100.00.

THE OLD SALOON

OWNERS: Bob and Shirley Fjelsted

HOURS: 7:00 a.m. to 2:00 a.m. Daily

HAPPY HOUR: No

GAMBLING: Video Poker/Keno

LIVE MUSIC: Occasionally

LOCATION: Highway 89, **Emigrant**

PHONE: 406-333-4482

BEER: Drafts; Domestics; Imports; Microbrews

AMUSEMENT: Pool; Horseshoes

Food: Full Menu Restaurant

Emigrant's Old Saloon is about as close as you will find to an authentic old west bar. The building today looks much the same as it did when the Old Saloon, Pool Hall, and Hotel was established in 1902. The original oak bar, back bar, liquor cabinet, and cigar case that were installed when the saloon first opened are still in use and still in excellent condition. Wooden stools stand in front of the bar, and a half dozen wooden tables are spread throughout the room. Antique firearms, framed photographs, and big game head mounts hang from the walls, and old spurs and saddles are suspended from the ceiling. Several dollar bills tacked to the ceiling above the bar spell out "OLD SALOON, EST 1902".

The Old Saloon has a very colorful history. One of the more popular stories involves a man known as Kickin' Horse George, who in 1910, won $10,000.00 in a poker game that lasted four days and three nights. The saloon tried to make it as a soft drink parlor during prohibition, but it soon became obvious the demand for soft drinks wasn't near as high as the demand for alcohol. The Old Saloon closed in 1921, and due to prohibition and various other circumstances, it remained closed until 1962. Although the barroom sat idle for forty-one years, nothing was ever removed from the building. Electrical upgrades have been made and indoor plumbing was added, but the place basically looks the same as it did in 1902.

Tourists and sportsmen who visit the area frequent the Old Saloon, but the locals keep the place going throughout the year. Breakfast and lunch are served in the barroom from 7:00 a.m. until 4:40 p.m. daily. Complete dinners are served in the Livery Stable Restaurant, which is housed in an old livery stable next door to the saloon, from 5:30 p.m. to 9:30 p.m. The Old Saloon hosts a pig roast every spring, and bed races are the big attraction in the fall. Minor rule changes go into effect for the bed races from year to year, but the basic rules require four people to carry a bed frame with a mattress and one rider across the parking lot and back. You may have to chug a beer or blow up a balloon somewhere along the route, but it's nothing a top-notch bed racer can't handle.

CHICO HOT SPRINGS SALOON

OWNERS: Mike and Eve Art

LOCATION: Pray

HOURS: 11:00 a.m. to Closing (Summer)
4:00 p.m. to Closing Mon-Thurs (Winter)
11:00 a.m. to Closing Fri-Sun (Winter)

PHONE: 406-333-4933

BEER: Drafts; Domestics; Imports; Microbrews

HAPPY HOUR: No

GAMBLING: Video Poker/Keno

AMUSEMENT: Pool; Pinball; Swimming

LIVE MUSIC: Every Weekend

FOOD: Full Menu Restaurant

The Chico Hot Springs Saloon is at Chico Hot Springs Resort, just off Route 540 near Pray. The resort has lodging facilities, a restaurant, poolside grill, natural hot water mineral pools, and of course, the saloon. The barroom is relatively large, with a wooden dance floor and a bandstand in the north end, a long bar that spans almost the entire length of the east wall, and a game room and casino area in the south side. The bar top is made from a thick plank cut from the center of a tree trunk. Wooden barstools and a wood burning stove add to the bar's rustic appearance. Hundreds of hats hang from a string suspended from the ceiling; a sample of the gifts donated by past customers.

The first known written description of Chico Hot Springs was in 1865. White settlers used the springs for bathing, washing clothes, and even as a moisture and heat supply for garden hothouses. The first building on the property was probably erected in 1888. It housed a wooden tub about five feet deep. William and Percie Knowles bought the property in 1900, the same year the first hotel opened. The first saloon at the hot springs opened in 1901, much to the chagrin of Mrs. Knowles. Prostitution was also part of the business, and Percie didn't care for that either. After William's death in 1910, Percie closed the saloon and evicted the prostitutes. Percie remained at the hot springs until 1936 when she was sent to the state hospital at Warm Springs. She died 4-1/2 years later, but it's rumored her ghost still inhabits Chico Hot Springs Resort.

Prostitution would not return to Chico Hot Springs, but the saloon reopened in 1948. Mike and Eve Art now own the business. The resort is open 365 days a year. Locals stop in throughout the year to eat, drink, and swim, and tourists by the thousands infiltrate the place during the warm weather months. There's plenty of activities for people of all ages at Chico Hot Springs. And who knows, you may even encounter the ghost of Percie Knowles after a rough night in the saloon.

BANK BAR

OWNERS: C. Lynn and Shirley Compton

HOURS: 10:00 a.m. to Closing Daily

HAPPY HOUR: No

GAMBLING: Video Poker/Keno; Shake-A-Day

LIVE MUSIC: Occasionally

LOCATION: Highway 89, **Wilsall**

PHONE: 406-578-2157

BEER: Drafts; Domestics; Microbrews

AMUSEMENT: Pool; Darts

FOOD: Frozen Pizza; Bar Snacks

The Bank Bar is housed in a stone and mortar structure on the west side of Highway 89 in Wilsall. The barroom has a straight wooden bar along the south wall, and a couple of tables are available if you can't find an empty barstool. An enclosed deck has recently been added, so you can always step out for some fresh air if things get too crowded inside. If you're a first time visitor, be sure to check out the life-sized wooden cowboy that stands inside the front entrance. You should also be sure to take a look at the mounted badger, bobcat, and authentic Indian arrowheads on display in the glass-enclosed display case on the east wall.

The Bank Bar was established in 1947. A bank operated out of the building prior to the bar moving in, so it's rather obvious how the business got its name. The old bank vault is still in use, but it now doubles as a walk-in beer cooler. A compressor was installed to keep the beer cold, but the lock and tumbler were left in place. The old bank vault now serves a convenient and secure storage area for extra beer, cash, and other valuable items.

Lynn and Shirley Compton have owned the Bank Bar since October, 1993. They run a friendly establishment where people of all ages are welcome. The Bank Bar is a place where you will occasionally see horses tied up in front of the building patiently waiting to take their owners home. Some of the locals mount up and ride to the bar when the weather is nice instead of burning their gasoline. Local trade keeps the Bank Bar going throughout the year, but tourists and visiting hunters provide a boost to the business during the summer and fall.

Shirley said she occasionally gets a good laugh when a tourist walks in and momentarily mistakes the wooden cowboy for a real person. It usually doesn't take people long to figure out it's just a wood carving, but there was one occasion when a very drunk man put his arm around the cowboy and talked to it for several minutes. The guy never did realize the cowboy was made of wood, and he staggered out the door before anyone tried to tell him he was talking to a statue.

245

WILSALL BAR AND CAFE

OWNER: Chuck Burdette

LOCATION: Highway 89, **Wilsall**

HOURS: 8:00 a.m. to Closing Mon-Sat
10:00 a.m. to Closing Sunday

PHONE: 406-578-2106

HAPPY HOUR: None

BEER: Drafts; Domestics

GAMBLING: Video Poker/Keno

AMUSEMENT: None

LIVE MUSIC: Occasionally

FOOD: Full Menu Cafe

The Wilsall Bar and Cafe is on the west side of Highway 89 in Wilsall. The barroom occupies the south side of the building, and a dining area is in the north side. The building's interior walls and ceiling are covered mostly with wood, but the type of wood varies depending on which part of the building you're in. Everything from tongue-and-groove woodwork to flakeboard has been installed. The interior decor primarily consists of beer signs, three mounted deer heads, and a wild boar's head. Seating in the barroom is limited to the fifteen or so stools at the bar, but plenty of tables are available in the dining area if you're entertaining guests.

The history of the Wilsall Bar and Cafe dates back to 1935 when a retail beer license was issued to the Brukert Hotel. The business was called Bill's Place in 1939 when the bar moved into a building that stood on the now-vacant lot to the south of the existing building. The bar became Fleck's Bar in 1946, and the name was changed again to the Wilsall Bar when the business moved to its current location in 1948. Chuck Burdette has owned the Wilsall Bar and Cafe since 1989, but the business was for sale the last time I visited the bar in the fall of 1996.

The Wilsall Bar and Cafe is operated as a family-oriented business, so you don't have to worry about encountering rude or obnoxious customers. There have been a few horses and motorcycles ridden through the barroom over the years, but there's usually a relatively calm and quiet crowd on hand. Residents of Wilsall and the surrounding communities are the regular customers, but visiting tourists and hunters provide a boost to the business from March through November. Local ranchers fill the barroom during cattle shipping season, and people from just about everywhere pack the house during the annual Wilsall Rodeo. The cafe is open from 8:00 a.m. to 8:00 p.m. daily. Lunch specials are available Monday through Friday, and dinner specials are offered every Friday evening. The ribeye steak and prime rib are the most popular dinner choices, but all the food is good. If you have a sweet tooth, ice cream, malts, shakes, sundaes, and floats are served at the bar.

KOZY KORNER BAR AND CAFE

OWNERS: Buck and Ellen Wood

HOURS: 2:00 a.m. to Closing Daily

HAPPY HOUR: At Bartender's Discretion

GAMBLING: Video Poker/Keno

LIVE MUSIC: No

LOCATION: 1 S. Broadway, **Winnett**

PHONE: 406-429-2621

BEER: Domestics

AMUSEMENT: Pool

FOOD: Full Menu Cafe

The Kozy Korner Bar and Cafe is at the intersection of First and Broadway Streets in Winnett. The barroom is relatively small, and the atmosphere is relaxed. Approximately ten people can be seated at the bar, and a couple of tables are available if you can't find an empty barstool. The deer and antelope mounts on the barroom wall are from animals taken locally. I'm told the large whitetail deer was big enough to make the Boone and Crockett Record Book.

The bar has a relatively short history, dating back to 1981. I don't know when the cafe first opened, but it resides in a building that had previously housed an automobile service station. The portion of the building where the bar now resides is an addition that was made to the original structure. Instead of building the addition from the ground up, a modular building that was formerly used as a home on a nearby ranch was moved to Winnett and tacked onto the cafe.

Buck and Ellen Wood bought the Kozy Korner Bar and Cafe in July, 1994. Most of their customers are local residents, but travelers passing through the area also stop by. Cafe hours are 6:00 a.m. to 9:00 p.m. The food is excellent since everything served is homemade. Daily lunch specials are available, and the Indian Tacos come very highly recommended. The cafe gets a lot of repeat business from people who occasionally travel through the area. The great food is what keeps people coming back. Buck said there's a couple from Seattle who stop by every time they are in the area just to have a piece of pie.

Although the official bar hours are 2:00 p.m. to whenever there's nobody left to serve, the hours drastically expand during hunting season. Don't worry if you get there a little early, because Buck will usually open the bar for you if he's there. Whereas most taverns either have a happy hour or don't have a happy hour, you never know at the Kozy Korner. Buck informed me they leave happy hour to the discretion of the bartender on duty, so sometimes they have one and sometimes they don't. It's a slightly different approach, but it seems to work just fine.

WINNETT BAR

OWNER: Lillian Moore   **LOCATION:** 13 East Main, **Winnett**

HOURS: 11:00 a.m. to 2:00 a.m. Daily   **PHONE:** 406-429-2029

HAPPY HOUR: 6:00 to 7:00 Friday   **BEER:** Drafts; Domestics

GAMBLING: Video Poker/Keno; Shake-A-Day   **AMUSEMENT:** Pool; Foosball

LIVE MUSIC: Occasionally   **FOOD:** Grill Items

The Winnett Bar is on Main Street in Winnett. As you enter town from Highway 200, turn left at the first stop sign and you will see the bar on your left. The barroom is relatively large, with plenty of open floor space. And speaking of floors, the building's original hardwood flooring is still intact. A straight wooden bar with a brass foot rail faces the east wall, and three tables are lined against the west wall. The interior decor primarily consists of a few beer signs, mirrors, and posters.

The Winnett Bar was established in 1980. A roller skating rink had operated out of the building prior to the bar moving in, so that helps explain the hardwood floor. Arthur and Lillian Moore ran the business together until Art's death in 1993. Lillian sold the bar and carried the mortgage over the next three years, but she ended up taking the bar back in May of 1996. The Winnett Bar reopened in July, 1996, and it's been going strong ever since. Gerri Chamberlain now manages the business.

The Winnett Bar is a friendly place where people kick up their heels. A lot of shipping parties are held at the Winnett Bar during the fall, and the local Jaycee's always hold their annual costume Halloween party and hunter's ball here on the weekend prior to Halloween. It doesn't take a party to get things going, however. Unlike the Kozy Korner down the street, things get very lively at the Winnett Bar. The customers are basically harmless, but they tend to get a little crazy at times. It's not uncommon for the juke box to be blaring out songs while people dance around the barroom. Male customers usually outnumber the females, so unattended ladies are always in high demand.

Even with the lively crowd, the Winnett Bar is not a place where you have to worry about your safety. Loud music and dancing are common, but fights are relatively rare. If you arrive with an appetite, there's no reason for you to go away hungry. Excellent steaks and burgers are served fresh from the grill throughout the day. Good food, cold beer, and a very lively crowd make the Winnett Bar a great place to visit. Be sure to say hello to Gerri the next time you stop by.

COWBOY BAR

OWNERS: Bud and Ellis Phillips

HOURS: 8:00 a.m. to Closing Daily

HAPPY HOUR: No

GAMBLING: Video Poker/Keno

LIVE MUSIC: No

LOCATION: Highway 2, **Dodson**

PHONE: 406-383-4337

BEER: Domestics

AMUSEMENT: Pool

FOOD: Chili; Stew

The Cowboy Bar is on Highway 2 in Dodson. The bar has no unusual physical characteristics, but the place has seen plenty of action since Bud Phillips bought business in 1946. Bud cowboyed and bartended around Dodson for 16 years prior to buying the bar, and it just may have been during his cowboy days when he acquired the tolerance needed to withstand fifty years of unruly bar patrons. Bud says the crowds aren't as rowdy as they once were, but things still turn crazy on occasion.

In the spring of 1995, Bud was knocked unconscious and robbed by two men who had been playing pool and drinking at the bar. One of the men hit Bud over the head with a pool stick, and the other guy raided the cash register while Bud was trying to regain consciousness. The felons made a clean get-a-way from town, but they were eventually apprehended, tried, and sentenced to prison. Bud didn't mention how long it took for the knot on his head to subside, but I'm sure it didn't go away overnight.

Bud still gets a little excited when he talks about the big shootout that occurred at the Cowboy Bar in the early 1970's. It was a dance night, and after the music ended, a brawl broke out in the barroom. One thing led to another, and a full-blown shootout erupted. One group of people started shooting into the barroom from behind their vehicles in the street, and another group began returning the gunfire from the roof of the building. Miraculously, only one person ended up with a minor bullet wound during the entire ordeal. Damages to the building, however, were much more extensive. The barroom was full of bullet holes, and every window in the front of the building was shot out. Some of the people involved in the incident stopped by a few days later and offered to help pay for the damages, but Bud ended up footing the entire bill. Everything was repaired except the bullet hole in the mirror, which can still be seen today.

I can't promise you a shootout, but you should certainly enjoy your visit to the Cowboy Bar. If Bud hasn't sold the business by the time you arrive, take the opportunity to talk with him if he's not too busy. The walls can't talk, but Bud can sure tell you a lot of stories about the place. It's definitely one of the more interesting bars I've ever visited.

HI-WAY BAR

OWNERS: Skip and Sue Cole

LOCATION: Highway 2, **Dodson**

HOURS: Noon to 1:00 a.m. Daily

PHONE: 406-383-9991

HAPPY HOUR: 5:00 to 7:00 Mon - Fri

BEER: Drafts; Domestics; Microbrews

GAMBLING: Video Poker/Keno

AMUSEMENT: Pool

LIVE MUSIC: Occasionally

FOOD: Burgers; Soup; Frozen Pizza

The Hi-Way Bar is housed in a two story cinder block building on the south side of Highway 2 in Dodson. The spacious barroom has a straight bar along the east wall, a few tables spread throughout the room, and a wood burning stove against the south wall. Even with two pool tables in the middle of the barroom, there's plenty of open floor space if you get the urge to wander around. A sign posted above the main exit warns customers to "Watch Your Step, You Are 2300 Feet Above Sea Level".

The Hi-Way Bar was established as G I Joe's Place in 1946. G I Joe's stood about a block away from where the Hi-Way Bar now stands. The name was changed to the Hi-Way Bar in 1947, and the business moved to its present location in 1957. The second floor of the existing building was an addition that was made during the 1970s. Current owners Skip and Sue Cole bought the business in October, 1996.

Of the two drinking establishments in Dodson, the Hi-Way Bar is the more peaceful place to drink. Skip and Sue promote an atmosphere where people of all ages can gather to enjoy an evening out with friends and family without having to worry about rude or obnoxious behavior from other customers. Residents of Dodson and the neighboring Fort Belknap Indian Reservation make up the regular crowd at the Hi-Way Bar, and a few travelers stop in throughout the year. The place gets very busy during the first week of August when the Phillips County Fair is in full swing, but other than that, you never know when a crowd will be on hand.

Skip and Sue were just getting started in the business when I last visited Dodson, but they planned on managing the bar in the same friendly manner as it has been operated in the past. They've added a happy hour Monday through Friday from 5:00 p.m. until 7:00 p.m. wherein all drink prices are reduced twenty-five cents. As a community service, Skip and Sue keep a selection of video rentals on hand. Guns, ammunition, and hunting and fishing licenses will also be sold from the bar as soon as Skip and Sue obtain the required licenses.

LORING CLUB

OWNERS: Mike and Chris Henderson

HOURS: 8:00 a.m. to Closing Daily

HAPPY HOUR: No

GAMBLING: Video Poker

LIVE MUSIC: No

LOCATION: Route 242, **Loring**

PHONE: 406-674-5224

BEER: Domestics

AMUSEMENT: Pool; Darts

FOOD: Grill Items; Frozen Pizza

The Loring Club is housed in a wooden structure on Route 242 in Loring. A straight wooden bar faces the south wall in the front portion of the building, and several tables are spread throughout the remainder of the room. It's certainly not a fancy place, but the atmosphere is pleasant and the people are very friendly.

The bar's history dates back to 1928 when a barber shop opened in the building. The structure was one of several buildings that had recently been moved to Loring from a nearby community called Lovejoy. Lovejoy was quickly becoming a ghost town because the railroad had just come through Northern Montana at Loring. Prohibition was in effect at the time, but the barber shop sold bootlegged liquor on the side. The barber shop closed when prohibition ended, and the building became a legitimate saloon.

Tragedy struck the Loring Club in 1978. The couple who ran the bar and the bartender on duty were shot to death by four men who entered the building late one evening to rob the place. Allegedly, the gunmen killed the people for fear of being identified in the robbery. The men were eventually apprehended in California, tried, and sentenced to prison.

Shootings are certainly not common at the Loring Club. The bar basically functions as the town's community center, and you will typically find a very friendly crowd on hand. A lot of local celebrations are hosted at the bar, and it's not uncommon for kids to wait for the school bus from inside the barroom when the weather turns bad. Over the years, Sunday School classes and church meetings have even been held at the Loring Club. It's a great place to meet nice people and have a good time.

Mike and Chris Henderson have owned the Loring Club since 1987. Most of their customers are local residents, but a lot of Canadians stop in and tack a signed Canadian currency bill to the ceiling above the bar. The 2,000 or so Canadian bills have been multiplying since about 1978. It's rumored among the Canadians that you always have a drink coming at the Loring Club as long as you have a signed bill posted on the ceiling, even if you walk into the bar flat broke.

JAKE'S BAR

OWNER: Linda Beadle

HOURS: 10:00 a.m. to 2:00 a.m. Mon-Sat
1:00 p.m. to 2:00 a.m. Sunday

HAPPY HOUR: No

GAMBLING: Video Poker/Keno

LIVE MUSIC: Occasionally

LOCATION: Highway 2, **Saco**

PHONE: 406-527-3322

BEER: Drafts; Domestics

AMUSEMENT: Pool; Darts; Video Game

FOOD: Microwave Sandwiches;
Frozen Pizza

Jake's Bar is housed in a brick structure on the north side of Highway 2 in Saco. The barroom is relatively large, with a straight bar along the west wall. Most of the floor space in the east side of the room is occupied by a game room, several tables, and a small bandstand. If you've had a few drinks and think you might be seeing letters of the alphabet on the barroom floor, don't be alarmed. The light-colored tile flooring behind the barstools has been customized with dark tiles that spell out "JAKES". Even the sober people see them.

The building that presently houses Jake's Bar was originally a hardware store. The bar initially operated out of the Big Dome Hotel in Saco. Knute Jacobson moved the bar to its present location and changed the name of the business to Jakes in 1969. Linda Beadle bought the business in 1975, and she continues to operate it today.

The majority of the customers at Jake's are residents of Saco and the surrounding communities. The bar enjoys a steady business throughout the year, but the place gets very busy during the fall when visiting hunters come to town. Linda promotes a family-oriented atmosphere at Jake's. People of all ages gather here to unwind and converse with friends. There's a great selection of music on the CD juke box, which satisfies customers from all age groups. Linda supports a lot of community events such as the town's Labor Day celebration, the local basketball league, and community softball teams. Jake's Bar is also a popular gathering place after scholastic sporting events.

The painted animal bones hanging above the doorway leading to the rest rooms were created by a local artist. It may not seem like a big deal to you, but I've always found it fascinating that someone can take a dead animal carcass and turn it into a beautiful work of art. I don't know who designed the artwork on the Jake's Bar souvenir sats that are sold from the bar, but you may want to pick one up for your spouse or kids. That way, they will know you were thinking of them while you were out boozing. I've been told spouses and kids appreciate that sort of thing.

OB'S BAR

OWNERS: Tami and Jason Plouffe

LOCATION: Highway 2, **Saco**

HOURS: 10:00 a.m. to 2:00 a.m. Mon-Sat
1:00 p.m. to 2:00 a.m. Sunday

PHONE: 406-527-3373

HAPPY HOUR: No

BEER: Drafts; Domestics; Imports

GAMBLING: Video Poker/Keno

AMUSEMENT: Pool; Darts; Horseshoes

LIVE MUSIC: Occasionally

FOOD: Homemade Pizza

OB's Bar is on the north side of Highway 2 in Saco. You will recognize the place by the building's false wooden front and the green and white OB's Bar Sign above the door. Once inside, you can't help but notice a striking contrast in appearance between the front and rear portions of the barroom. The front half of the room has rough cut boards covering the walls, and the decorative tin ceiling that was installed when the building was constructed is still in place. The back half of the barroom has painted plasterboard walls and a false ceiling.

OB's history dates all the way back to 1914 when a saloon and bowling alley opened in the building. The antique back bar that's in the building today is the original back bar that was installed in the saloon in 1914. During prohibition, the saloon officially became a pool hall. The saloon reopened as a licensed tavern in the early 1930s.

Tami and Jason Plouffe bought the business in May, 1985. They promote a friendly atmosphere at the bar, and their customers are fun-loving people. Several years ago, Tami and Jason returned to the bar after being away for the day and discovered half the false ceiling had been removed. Some of the customers wanted the original tin ceiling back, so they started ripping out the drop ceiling. Jason admits the people told him they were going to do it, and his response was "yea, right--go ahead". Go ahead they did, but interest in the project apparently diminished about half way through. Jason and Tami had to quickly devise a scheme to make the place look respectable, so they restored the exposed tin ceiling to its original condition and covered the walls beneath it with rough cut boards. The back half of the barroom was basically left as it was; thus, we have a logical explanation for the contrast in appearance between the front and back portions of the barroom at OB's Bar.

OB's sells excellent homemade pizzas, and Tami's Bloody Mary's have gained notoriety as an effective hangover cure (or cause). As for the bar's logo, a huge mosquito drinking from a mug of beer, you'll have to get the explanation from Tami or Jason when you stop in.

253

SLEEPING BUFFALO RESORT

OWNER: Roger Ereaux

LOCATION: Highway 2, 10 Miles West of **Saco**

HOURS: 9:00 a.m. to Closing Daily

PHONE: 406-527-3370

HAPPY HOUR: No

BEER: Domestics

GAMBLING: Video Poker/Keno;

AMUSEMENT: Pool; Darts; Golf; Horseshoes; Volleyball

LIVE MUSIC: Weekly

FOOD: Full Menu Restaurant

The Sleeping Buffalo Resort is ten miles west of Saco on Highway 2. There are two separate bars at the resort along with a nine hole golf course, natural hot water health pools, water slides, rustic lodging facilities, camping facilities, a cafe, supper club, and a convenience store. The Big Barn is the name of the building that houses one of the barrooms, the supper club, and a dance hall. The Big Barn is the more formal of the two bars, with banquet facilities that can accommodate up to 300 people. The Little Bar has a more traditional saloon look.

The history of the business dates back to 1923 when natural hot water was accidentally discovered while drilling for oil. The water surfaced from a depth of over 3,000 feet beneath the ground, forming hot water ponds. The first wooden swim tank on the property was built in 1927, and local American Legion Posts raised money and built the first public pool in 1932. The American Legion Health Pools were eventually purchased by a private company, and the name was changed to the Sleeping Buffalo Resort. The name comes from an enshrined stone landmark that now stands along Highway 2 at the entrance to the resort. The stone was taken from a rock formation on a nearby ridge that, from a distance, resembled a herd of sleeping buffalo. The Sleeping Buffalo Rock has great religious and cultural importance to Native Americans throughout the region. In 1987, the stone was listed on the National Register of Historic Places.

The Sleeping Buffalo is a full service resort where you can stop for one beer or stay for an entire month. There are plenty of activities, and they even have a church on the grounds where Sunday services are held in the summer. The Little Bar is open daily throughout the year. It's a popular spot among visiting hunters, fishermen, and residents of the surrounding communities. The area has exceptional upland bird and water foul hunting, and the fishing and boating on nearby Nelson Reservoir brings a lot of outdoors enthusiasts to the region. There's always a friendly crowd on hand at the bar, which makes it a great place to stop.

NORTH 40 BAR AND CAFE

OWNERS: Mark and Mary Lageson

HOURS: 10:00 a.m. to 2:00 a.m. Fri-Sun
10:00 a.m. to 10:00 p.m. Mon-Thurs

HAPPY HOUR: No

GAMBLING: Video Poker/Keno;
Shake-A-Day

LIVE MUSIC: Occasionally

LOCATION: Main Street, **Whitewater**

PHONE: 406-674-8220

BEER: Domestics

AMUSEMENT: Pool; Darts; Foosball;
Video Games

FOOD: Full Menu Cafe

The North 40 Bar and Cafe is housed in a steel-sided structure on Main Street in Whitewater. Getting to Whitewater requires traveling a minimum of nine miles on gravel roads, but the people at the North 40 make the trip worth while. A game room and dining room reside in the east side of the building, and the barroom is in the west side. The antique wooden back bar against the east wall of the barroom was moved to Whitewater from a pharmacy in Saco in 1953. The original woodwork, embedded stained glass, and large mirrors are still in excellent condition. The brands on the barroom walls are authentic brands from local ranches. A branding party was held at the North 40 in July, 1995 to help raise money to paint the interior of the building.

The North 40 had its humble beginnings in 1940 when a beer parlor opened in a small house just south of where the bar and cafe stand today. It's said the owner of the business had just enough money to buy the beer license and one case of beer when he first started. A full liquor license was obtained about a year after the beer parlor opened, and after another year, the bar moved out of the house and into a garage across the street. The bar operated from the old garage until 1984 when a new building was put up by a group of local ranchers who called themselves the Whitewater Development Corporation. Vic and Mary Lefdahl operated the bar and cafe until July, 1995 when Mark and Mary Lageson bought the business.

The North 40 is a neighborhood bar and cafe where local residents gather to eat, drink, and socialize. An excellent brunch is served every Sunday from noon to 1:30 p.m., and excellent steaks and burgers are available any time. Like many small town taverns, the North 40 serves as a community social center. Several local organizations hold their meetings at the North 40, and spectators at scholastic sporting events commonly stop at the bar after the final buzzer sounds. You will forget all about the nine mile drive on gravel roads once you experience the good food, great people, and wonderful atmosphere at the North 40 Bar and Cafe.

MINER'S CLUB BAR AND CAFE

OWNER: Roger Ereaux

HOURS: Noon to 2:00 a.m. Daily

HAPPY HOUR: 5:00 to 6:30 Mon - Fri

GAMBLING: Video Poker/Keno

LIVE MUSIC: Approximately Twice Monthly

LOCATION: Whitcomb St., **Zortman**

PHONE: 406-673-9456

BEER: Domestics

AMUSEMENT: Pool

OOD: Full Menu Cafe

The Miner's Club is housed in a log structure on Whitcomb Street in Zortman. The main part of the barroom has a straight bar with a log front, a lone wooden booth against the wall, and a wood burning stove in one corner. A spacious dance floor and a wooden bandstand occupy the back part of the barroom, and a cafe resides in the adjacent room.

The history of the Miner's Club dates back to the early days of Zortman, which was settled as a mining camp in 1884. Like many mining town saloons, the Miner's Club has seen its share of unruly customers. It's a friendly establishment these days, but numerous fights and even a few shootings have taken place at the bar over the years. The last fatal shooting I'm aware of occurred in March, 1974. The bar owner and a customer got into an argument, and the argument erupted into a barroom brawl. The bar owner ended up shooting the man because he was about to beat the bar owner's son in the face with a belt buckle. Charges were filed, but the jury found the bar owner innocent of all charges.

Lloyd and Juanita Malmend were in the process of buying the bar when I last visited Zortman in November, 1996. Lloyd and Juanita were already managing the cafe, and they intend to continue operating the Miner's Club as a community-minded business. A free Thanksgiving Dinner and a costume Halloween Party are just two of the community events held at the Miner's Club each year. The cafe is open daily from 6:00 a.m until 8:00 p.m. Lunch and dinner specials are available, and everything is made fresh from scratch. If you've got a big appetite, I'd recommend the Miner Burger.

There were still a few holes in the men's room door and the adjacent wall the last time I visited the Miner's Club; remnants of the bar's rough and rowdy past. Fortunately, the holes are just remnants and not an indication of the type of behavior you will witness from the customers today. The Miner's Club is now a family-owned, family-operated business. In fact, it's become the unofficial social center of Zortman. About the only trouble you might experience at the Miner's Club these days is trying to figure out how to beat a local eleven year old pool shark at the billiard table.

DUSTY'S BAR AND GRILL

OWNER: Mark Stephens **LOCATION:** Central Street, **Brady**

HOURS: 9:00 a.m. to 2:00 a.m. Daily **PHONE:** 406-753-2292

HAPPY HOUR: 6:00 to 7:00 Mon - Sat **BEER:** Drafts; Domestics; Imports

GAMBLING: Video Poker/Keno; Shake-A-Day **AMUSEMENT:** Pool; Darts

LIVE MUSIC: Occasionally **FOOD:** Full Menu Grill

Dusty's Bar and Grill is housed in a two story brick structure on Central Avenue in Brady. A moderate-sized barroom resides in the ground-level floor, and a dance hall is in the second story. An L-shaped bar faces the west wall of the barroom, and a wooden awning with a six inch strip of lighted stained glass hangs directly above the bar. The interior walls are covered with rough cut wood, which creates a rustic appearance. The dance hall has its own bar, a hardwood dance floor with running lights, and mirrored walls. The dance hall is a great place to hold parties and celebrations without interfering with the business downstairs.

A bank operated out of the building from 1923 until it crashed in the early 1930s. The building sat vacant until 1941 when the Brady Tavern opened in the basement. The name of the business became Dusty's Bar in 1946. I'm told a barber shop once operated out of the building along with the bar, but I don't know when the barber was evicted. The barroom eventually moved from the basement to the first floor, and the second floor was renovated into a dance hall.

Mark Stephens has owned the business since May, 1995. Of the two bars in Brady, Dusty's is the more family-oriented establishment. Daily lunch specials are offered on weekdays, an all-you-can-eat spaghetti dinner is served on Saturdays, and the Wednesday lunch special is Mexican food. Dusty's hosts a great Cinco de Mayo celebration every year, complete with authentic Mexican foods, karaoke, a pinata, and innovative contests such as a tortilla toss and jalapeno relay race. They also have a great costume Halloween costume party every year, and the customers have an on-going contest amongst themselves involving Christmas lights. Three strings of twenty-five colored light bulbs are hung behind the bar, and one customer stakes his or her claim to one of the bulbs. The owner of the first bulb to burn out is proclaimed a preliminary winner, and the owner of the last bulb left burning is proclaimed the grand prize winner. It sounds like fun, but I'd hate to be the guy who has to sit there and watch all the lights until there's only one bulb left burning.

LOG CABIN BAR

OWNER: Silver Pelka

LOCATION: Central Street, **Brady**

HOURS: 10:00 a.m. to 2:00 p.m. Daily

PHONE: 406-753-2235

HAPPY HOUR: 5:00 to 6:00 Mon - Sat

BEER: Drafts; Domestics; Imports

GAMBLING: Video Poker/Keno; Shake-A-Day

AMUSEMENT: Pool; Pinball; Foosball Horseshoes

LIVE MUSIC: Occasionally

FOOD: Lunches; Frozen Pizza

The Log Cabin Bar is on Central Avenue in Brady. An L-shaped bar spans nearly the entire length of the west wall of the barroom, and a couple of small tables are spread throughout the room. A high tech CD sound system is usually in use whenever the juke box isn't being played, so you will always hear quality music at the bar. If you start to feel confined inside the barroom, there's a fairly large lawn outside with horseshoe pits, a barbecue pit, and plenty of space to roam around.

The business was established as the Brady Beer Parlor in 1933. The beer parlor became the Log Cabin Bar in 1935 when the bar moved into a hotel that previously stood on the lot. The hotel was destroyed by fire in the 1940s, so the log building was erected and the bar reopened. Although the building is approximately fifty years old, recent upgrades have been made to make the facility totally accessible to the handicapped.

Mike "Silver" Pelka has owned the Log Cabin Bar since December, 1989. Silver promotes a fun atmosphere where just about anything goes. The only local rule is you have to keep your clothes on. Surprisingly, there's not many fights, but people have been known to ride horses and motorcycles through the barroom. With its inviting atmosphere, the Log Cabin has become a favorite stop for Canadian travelers. There always seems to be something going on such as a horseshoe tournament, karaoke, or even sumo wrestling, complete with the rubber sumo suits.

The Log Cabin Bar is heavily involved in community service efforts, and Silver is a big supporter of the Muscular Dystrophy and Multiple Sclerosis Foundations. The bar has also served as an ABATE (American Bikers Aiming Toward Education) hospitality stop, and they host an annual Thanksgiving dinner for people in the community who have nowhere else to go. Male customers should enjoy their visit to the Log Cabin Bar because there's always a very pretty female bartender on duty. Even if you don't care much for the lively atmosphere, you will certainly enjoy being served while sitting at the bar.

RANGER BAR

OWNER: Carolyn Murphy   **LOCATION:** Highway 89, **Dupuyer**

HOURS: 10:00 a.m. to 2:00 a.m. Daily   **PHONE:** 406-472-3296

HAPPY HOUR: No   **BEER:** Drafts; Domestics

GAMBLING: Video Poker/Keno   **AMUSEMENT:** Pool

LIVE MUSIC: Occasionally   **FOOD:** Frozen Pizza; Bar Snacks

The Ranger Bar is housed in a wood-sided structure on the east side of Highway 89 in Dupuyer. The front portion of the barroom has a straight bar facing the north wall and a couple of booths lined against the south wall. The back part of the building is basically home to a lone pool table and the rest rooms. The interior decor is certainly not elaborate, but a large chunk of wood with the words *Love Club* written across it hangs from the wall behind the bar. I'm told this innovative peace-keeping device really has no practical application because the customers are always friendly and well-mannered.

The history of the Ranger Bar is somewhat vague, but I'm told the business has been in Dupuyer since about 1900. The name of the bar was the Mountain View Tavern when the first liquor license was issued in 1939. Allegedly, the bar has been destroyed by fire and rebuilt at least three different times. The present-day structure is an old army barracks that was moved to Dupuyer and renovated into a tavern after the latest fire swept through. Hopefully, the fires will be kept under control and they won't need to rebuild for at least a few more years.

Carolyn Murphy has owned the Ranger Bar since 1988. She runs the business as a simple country bar where you can get a shot, a beer, and some basic mixed drinks. This is not a cocktail lounge, so don't be surprised if you get a blank stare from the bartender when you order a White Russian or some other fancy mixed drink. If you absolutely have to have something fancy, they will try to mix it for you as long as you can tell them what to put in it and they have the ingredients on hand.

The Ranger Bar is pretty much a local hang out where people gather to relax and socialize. The customers are fairly mellow these days, but I'm told there have been some gunshots fired inside the barroom over the years. The rowdy days have long since passed, however, and all the bullet holes have been repaired. The Ranger Bar hosts a party on New Years Eve, Valentine's Day, and Saint Patrick's Day, but other than that, it's business as usual. This is not the type of place that attracts business through special promotions.

STONER'S LAST CHANCE SALOON

OWNERS: Guy and Mary Jo Stoner

LOCATION: Highway 12, **Elliston**

HOURS: 10:00 a.m. to 2:00 a.m. Daily

PHONE: 406-492-8596

HAPPY HOUR: No

BEER: Domestics

GAMBLING: Video Poker/Keno

AMUSEMENT: Pool; Video Games

LIVE MUSIC: Occasionally

FOOD: Grill Items; Broasted Chicken; Frozen Pizza

Stoner's Last Chance Saloon is housed in a wooden structure on Highway 12 in Elliston. The moderate-sized barroom has a horseshoe-shaped bar in the middle of the floor, and a couple of wooden buddy bars stand along the east wall. A life-sized wooden cowboy holding a guitar stands near the bar in the east side of the room.

Stoner's Last Chance Saloon is actually the product of an evolution process wherein an automobile service station transformed into a bar. Dougherty Service was the name of the business when the first retail beer license was issued in 1934. I'm told the original bar was so small that only four people could be seated without bumping elbows with each other. The barroom eventually displaced the service station altogether. Ownership has changed hands several times since the bar first opened, but the business is still going strong today.

Guy and Mary Jo Stoner have owned the Last Chance Saloon since 1987. They operate a friendly establishment, and they also sell a lot of 1/2 pound cheeseburgers off the grill. There always seems to be something just a little out of the ordinary going on at the bar. Every year in March, Stoner's holds their annual Bigfoot Hunt on the Saturday closest to the full moon. Over 100 grown men and women show up at the bar to wander through twenty acres of wooded property stalking Bigfoot, a creature that is hiding somewhere amongst the trees. Two Wild Rainiers also hide on the property, and cash prizes are awarded to people who spot Bigfoot and one of the Rainiers with a flashlight. Of course, a huge party is held at the bar after the hunt. Stoner's also holds a Best Legs contest on Super Bowl Eve in conjunction with the local volunteer fire department's annual snowmobile run. A chili cookoff is the main attraction in February, and duck races are held in June. Contestants in the duck races reel plastic ducks across a track with fishing rods. Another big event is the annual cow pasture golf tournament that's held every summer. The entire course consists of one hole that's a mile long. The people at Stoner's may be a little out of the ordinary, but they sure know how to have fun.

JJ'S ROUGH COUNTRY STEAK HOUSE & LOUNGE

OWNERS: Jerry and Jonnie Teets

LOCATION: Frontage Road, **Garrison**

HOURS: Noon to Closing Daily (Summer)
Noon to Closing Wed-Sun (Winter)

PHONE: 406-846-3267

HAPPY HOUR: None

BEER: Drafts; Domestics

GAMBLING: Video Poker/Keno;
Shake-A-Day

AMUSEMENT: Horseshoes

LIVE MUSIC: Occasionally

FOOD: Full Menu Steak House

JJ's Rough Country Steak House and Lounge is just west of Garrison on the Frontage Road that parallels Interstate 90. A small motel (three units), an RV park, and the steak house and lounge are all on one parcel of property on the banks of the Clark Fork River. The dining room occupies most of the floor space inside the building. The lounge basically consists of a small wooden bar in the northwest corner of the room.

JJ's Rough Country Steak House and Lounge started out as the Silver Star Bar in 1951. At that time, the barroom was in the east side of the building and a dance hall and poker room were in the west side. The name of the business eventually changed to Pat's Place and then to the Rough Country. A restaurant was added to the business in 1987, and the bar was moved to the west end of the building to make space for the dining room.

Jerry and Jonnie Teets bought the Rough Country Restaurant and Lounge in March, 1996. Jerry and Jonnie added the initials JJ's to the name of the business, but it's still the same friendly place it was before they took over. A steady local clientele keeps the place going throughout the year, and visiting sportsmen and travelers stop in for food and drinks during the summer and fall. Lunch and dinner are served daily in the dining room, and the menu features steaks, seafood, and chicken.

Besides being a great place to eat and drink, JJ's Rough Country Steak House and Lounge is the world wide headquarters for Assholes International, an organization that was established in 1987 by Jerry and Jean Westlund. Assholes International currently has over 4500 active members from all over the world. To become a member, all you have to do is fill out an application, submit a $5.00 fee, and hope your check doesn't bounce. New members are awarded an official Assholes International Membership Certificate, and your name is maintained on the membership roster at the bar. Jerry and Jonnie even host an annual Asshole Reunion so the members of this prestigious organization can catch up on what all the other assholes have been doing for the past year.

261

COPPER QUEEN SALOON

OWNERS: Jim and Mary Ward

HOURS: 9:00 a.m. to Closing Daily

HAPPY HOUR: 5:00 to 6:00 Mon - Fri

GAMBLING: Video Poker/Keno; Live Poker (Occasionally)

LIVE MUSIC: Occasionally

LOCATION: 11 W. Main, **Helmville**

PHONE: 406-793-9612

BEER: Drafts; Domestics

AMUSEMENT: Pool; Pinball; Horseshoes

FOOD: Broiled Burgers; Bar Snacks

The Copper Queen Saloon is at 11 West Main Street in Helmville. The structure is actually a double-wide trailer, but the building's false wooden front and covered boardwalk give the place a more traditional western appearance. The barroom has a straight wooden bar along the south wall, and a couple of tables are spread throughout the room. A small room in the west end of the building is used for occasional poker games and as a video rental display area. The barroom ceiling is covered with brief messages and the names of people who have been to the Copper Queen Saloon in past years. You've already missed your chance to add your own name and message, however, because all the available space has been used. A covered wooden deck is just off the east side of the building if you prefer drinking outdoors. There's also a wooden bandstand and a couple of wooden picnic tables on the lawn.

The Copper Queen Saloon was established 1975. The liquor license came from the old McCormick's Bar in Helmville. The building was destroyed by fire in 1980, so the double-wide trailer was moved in and the bar reopened. The practice of writing on the ceiling dates back to 1983. I'm told the bar owner planned on painting the ceiling anyhow, so he allowed a customer to write her name on it, thinking the name would soon be covered with paint. When other customers saw the name, they demanded equal space, and things progressed from there.

Jim and Mary Ward have owned the Copper Queen Saloon since 1988. The bar is the social center of Helmville since they sell the only gasoline and prepared food in town. Most of the customers are local residents, but visiting hunters and fishermen also frequent the saloon during the summer and fall. Weekends are usually busy, but weekdays, especially during the summer months, can be very slow. The bar is always crowded on Labor Day weekend during the Helmville Rodeo. The Copper Queen Saloon also hosts a great Saint Patrick's Day party, so be sure to stop by if you happen to be in the area on March 17. Better yet, stop in anytime.

TRIXIE'S ANTLER SALOON

OWNERS: Leo and Verla Bush

HOURS: 10:00 a.m. to Closing Daily

HAPPY HOUR: 5:00 to 6:00 Mon - Fri

GAMBLING: Video Poker/Keno

LIVE MUSIC: Monthly During Summer

LOCATION: Highway 200, **Ovando**

PHONE: 406-793-9611

BEER: Drafts; Domestics; Imports; Microbrews

AMUSEMENT: Pool; Foosball; Video Games

FOOD: Full Menu Restaurant

Trixie's Antler Saloon is on the south side of Highway 200 in Ovando. The wooden structure houses a spacious barroom that occupies over 2/3 of the available floor space. A semi-formal dining room known as the Weeping Willow Room resides in the west end of the building. An L-shaped bar stands just inside the front entrance. The front panel of the bar is covered with red upholstery and decorative silver tacks, and the wooden elbow rail has brands from local ranches burned into it. Two decorative collages fashioned from rocks, wood, adhesive, and model-sized plastic people and animals are on display in the barroom. One collage has been assembled on top of the wooden awning behind the bar, and the second is in the corner near the antique wooden organ.

Trixie's McCormack established Trixie's Antler Saloon in 1960. Trixie was a professional trick roper who had performed at rodeos, in vaudeville acts, and on television, but she eventually ended up in Ovando where she leased a bar for a few years before opening her own business. Trixie was a very creative lady who decorated the barroom in a most unique fashion. She had an interesting collection of antiques on display, and she personally created the wood and rock collages, upholstered bar front, and several other pieces of handiwork that are no longer in the building. Trixie was also very well known for her phenomenal meals and no-nonsense management style. I'm told the gal wasn't shy about firing her pistol inside the barroom if the customers got too far out of line.

Trixie sold the saloon to Leo Bush in 1978. Leo and his wife, Verla, now operate the bar. They manage the business in a family-oriented manner, and they still serve outstanding meals at reasonable prices. Breakfast, lunch, and dinner are served daily, and specials on prime rib and barbecue beef rib are offered on weekends. Hunting season is always a busy time at Trixie's, and the bar hosts a free Thanksgiving Day dinner for the hunters. Although you won't find Trixie at her beloved Antler Saloon, you can still feel her presence when you enter the barroom.

GEM BAR AND STORE

OWNERS: Elmer McGhee, Laurie McGhee, and Linda Quilling

LOCATION: 871 South Frontage Road, **Racetrack**

HOURS: 9:00 a.m. to Closing Daily

PHONE: 406-846-2852

HAPPY HOUR: 6:00 to 7:00 Daily

BEER: Domestics; Microbrews

GAMBLING: Video Poker/Keno; Shake-A-Day

AMUSEMENT: Pinball

LIVE MUSIC: No

FOOD: Frozen Pizza; Snacks

The GEM Bar and Store is on the Frontage Road approximately 1/4 mile north of the Racetrack Interchange (exit 195) off Interstate 90. The barroom resides in the south side of the building, and a convenience store is in the north side. The barroom is relatively small, and seating is limited to the eight barstools at the straight bar facing the north wall. The barroom decor basically consists of a mounted deer's rear end hanging above the door between the barroom and convenience store, but there are some nice pieces of Black Hills Gold jewelry and Montana Silversmith gift items in the glass display case near the main entrance.

The history of the GEM Bar and Store dates back to the 1930s when Bill Fisher opened a grocery store in an old schoolhouse. Bill sold the store to Harriet Geil and her daughters, Carmilita Evans and Frances McGhee, in 1948, and the business has been in the same family ever since. The three ladies combined the first initial from each of their last names (GEM) to come up with the new name for the business. The bar opened in 1950 in the milled log addition that was built onto the south side of the store. Frances McGhee's son and daughters, Elmer McGhee, Laurie McGhee, and Linda Quilling, now own the GEM Bar and Store; however, Elmer basically operates the business solo.

The GEM Bar and Store is a friendly establishment where people of all ages are welcome. The business is operated in a community-minded manner for the benefit of local residents. Besides being a full time bartender and store keeper, Elmer is the dispatcher and fire truck driver for the Racetrack Valley Volunteer Fire District. Local emergency fire calls are received directly at the GEM Bar and Store, and Elmer is responsible for notifying the other volunteers and driving them to the scene of the fire. I don't know whether Elmer benefits from this arrangement, but I'm sure the other volunteers don't mind having Elmer drive them back to the bar after a fire. A few cold beers are probably just what the volunteers need after fighting a hot blaze.

LOG CABIN BAR

OWNER: Mary Harrington

LOCATION: Racetrack Rd., **Racetrack**

HOURS: 10:00 a.m. to Closing Daily

PHONE: 406-693-2437

HAPPY HOUR: No

BEER: Drafts; Domestics; Microbrews

GAMBLING: Video Poker/Keno; Shake-A-Day

AMUSEMENT: Pool

LIVE MUSIC: Occasionally

FOOD: Fresh Sandwiches

The Log Cabin Bar is at 931 Racetrack Road in Racetrack. If you exit Interstate 90 at the Racetrack Interchange (exit 195), you can't miss it. The barroom resides in the west side of the log structure, and a spacious dance hall is in the east side. An L-shaped wooden bar stands along the west wall in front of an antique back bar that was handcrafted from maple and oak. The beautiful back bar originally stood in Swede's Bar in Deer Lodge, but it was moved to the Log Cabin Bar in 1984. The dance hall has a hardwood floor, a raised bandstand, and a separate bar.

The history of the Log Cabin Bar dates back to 1928. The bar opened in an old train station and ticket office that was built by the Burlington Northern Railroad Company in 1889. The dance hall was added in 1935. Although the existing bar and back bar appear to be a matching set, they were not built at the same time. Both pieces were installed during a renovation project that was completed in 1984, but the bar was custom built at that time and stained to match the finish on the back bar.

Mary Harrington has owned the Log Cabin Bar since 1979. Mary operates a friendly tavern where people gather to relax and socialize with friends. The Log Cabin Bar is a community-minded business. The local chapter of ABATE (American Bikers Aiming Toward Education) and the Log Cabin Bar co-sponsor an annual costume Halloween party for children who live in the area, and the bar has also hosted several benefits to raise money for local people in need.

The big event of the year at the Log Cabin Bar is the annual turkey races on the first Saturday of October. Live turkeys run in heat races to qualify for the final race, and the winner of the final race is proclaimed the overall champion. You can rent or buy a turkey at the bar on the day of the big race, or you can bring your own turkey from home. There's even a human turkey mascot to help cheer on the contestants. After the races, the bar has a roasted turkey dinner and live music. Don't be alarmed; the losing turkeys don't end up on the roaster. The turkey races are always a great time, and the event gets more popular each year.

LAZY JD BAR AND CAFE

OWNER: Sue Dukart

HOURS: 10:00 a.m. to 10:00 p.m. Daily

HAPPY HOUR: No

GAMBLING: Video Poker/Keno

LIVE MUSIC: Occasionally

LOCATION: Railroad Ave., **Fallon**

PHONE: 406-486-5400

BEER: Domestics

AMUSEMENT: Pool; Darts

FOOD: Full Menu Cafe

The Lazy JD Bar and Cafe is on Railroad Avenue in Fallon. To get there from Interstate 94, turn off at the Fallon Interchange (exit 185) and drive south into town. The Lazy JD is in a large wooden building on the left-hand side of the road. The moderate-sized barroom has a straight wooden bar that can seat about ten people, and a few tables are available if you can't find an empty barstool. A separate dining room is in the east side of the building, and the kitchen is just off the south side of the barroom. The framed photographs on the barroom walls are pictures of rodeo champions from 1913 through 1927. These photos were originally on display in the Range Rider Bar in Miles City. The Prairie County Old Timers photographs on the wall in the dining room came from the Yellowstone Bar and Cafe in Terry.

The business has been housed in the same building since at least the early 1920's. Several owners have operated the bar under several different names over the years, but its reputation for outstanding food began when Johnny Johnson bought the business in 1963. Mr. Johnson was a truck driver who drove west with his wife from Michigan in search of a bar business to buy. I'm told Johnny even brought a beer can collection with him to decorate the bar he would eventually purchase. The Johnson's bought the bar in Fallon and renamed it the Fallon Feedlot. They quickly gained a reputation for outstanding food, and that reputation lives on today at the Lazy JD Bar and Cafe.

Sue Dukart has owned the business since 1989. She has done a lot of work on the building, and her efforts show. The dining room was completely renovated in 1993, the barroom was remodeled in 1995. A small game room was added in 1996. Needless to say, the interior of the building is now very modern. The cafe specializes in steaks and seafood, and a smorgasbord is available every Sunday from 11:00 a.m. until 2:00 p.m. A steady local clientele provides most of the business at the Lazy JD; however, local is a relative term, depending on what day of the week it is. "Local" gets a lot larger during the weekends when people from all over Eastern Montana drive to the Lazy JD Bar and Cafe for dinner.

OUTPOST

OWNERS: Mark and Martin Strandberg

LOCATION: Highway 93 S., **Conner**

HOURS: 11:00 a.m. to Closing Daily

PHONE: 406-821-3388

HAPPY HOUR: 4:30 to 6:30 Daily

BEER: Drafts; Domestics; Imports; Microbrews

GAMBLING: Video Poker/Keno; Shake-A-Day

AMUSEMENT: Pool; Darts; Horseshoes; Volleyball

LIVE MUSIC: Occasionally

FOOD: Full Menu Restaurant

The Outpost is south of Conner on Highway 93. The 8,000 square foot peeled log structure stands on the east side of the road at mile post marker 21. The interior of the building is completely finished in logs and natural wood, creating a rustic appearance and a comfortable atmosphere. A spacious barroom resides in the north side of the building, and two separate dining rooms are in the south side. The small loft in the south dining room and vaulted wooden ceilings throughout the facility enhance the building's rustic charm. Log stools surround the wooden bar in the southeast corner of the barroom, and several wooden tables are available for additional seating. The bar has a sturdy top that was fashioned from a plank cut from the middle of a tree trunk.

Mark and Martin Strandberg built the Outpost in 1992. There was only one dining room at that time, but the owners soon discovered their food was drawing more customers than they could seat. A second dining room was added in 1994, and the restaurant continues to flourish. All the big game taxidermy mounts and animal skins hanging throughout the barroom are from animals taken locally. There are also numerous numbered prints of western outdoor scene paintings on display in both dining rooms. The prints are from a collection Mark and Martin's mother owns.

Any place that has to add another dining room after being in business for only two years obviously serves great food, and the Outpost is no exception. Their dinner menu features hand-selected cuts of beef, including an excellent prime rib. Baby back pork ribs and fresh pizzas are two of the more popular menu items, and a Mexican menu is offered every Monday during the summer. The restaurant isn't the only attraction, however; the barroom does a brisk business as well. Horseshoe tournaments are held throughout the summer, and a great costume Halloween party is held at the bar each year. Whether you're looking for a fun place to drink or a great place to eat, the Outpost has what you're looking for. You will definitely enjoy your visit.

ROCKY KNOB

MANAGER: Diana Davis

LOCATION: 6065 Hwy. 93 S., **Conner**

HOURS: 11:30 a.m. to Closing Daily

PHONE: 406-821-3520

HAPPY HOUR: 4:00 to 6:00 Daily

BEER: Drafts; Domestics; Imports; Microbrews

GAMBLING: Video Poker/Keno; Shake-A-Day

AMUSEMENT: Pool; Darts

LIVE MUSIC: Occasionally

FOOD: Full Menu Restaurant

The Rocky Knob is housed in a log building that stands on the west side of Highway 93 between mile post markers 17 and 18 near Conner. The barroom, a dining room, and a banquet room are all housed in the ground-level floor of the two story structure. The building's interior is finished with logs and tongue-and-groove woodwork. Wooden furniture and stone fireplaces add to the rustic charm. Five motel rooms are available in a separate building if you're in need of overnight lodging.

The business was established as Joe's Bitterroot Ranch by Jesse "Ptomaine Joe" White in 1946. Ptomaine Joe was a legendary woman who is rumored to have paid off the loggers who built the lodge with free use of her "girls". If you look closely at the fireplace in the dining room, you will see the words Joe's Ranch spelled out in white rocks. The Bitterroot Ranch was a very popular saloon, gambling parlor, and brothel until 1950 when the Montana Liquor Division finally suspended Joe's liquor license. Joe left the area and eventually passed away, but her legacy lives on.

Ptomaine Joe's spirit allegedly still inhabits the building, and her presence is sometimes felt by the guests and employees. The sounds of coins falling into the metal tray of a slot machine and the low voice of a woman have been heard at the Rocky Knob on more than one occasion since Joe's departure from the Bitterroot Valley. Diana Davis has been the manager at the Rocky Knob since 1993. Diana didn't mention the ghost by name, but she too claims to have experienced the presence of a spirit in the building. Diana swears she sometimes hears a woman's voice and sounds like footsteps coming from the second story

Ghost or no ghost, the Rocky Knob is a wonderful place. The people are friendly, and the atmosphere is relaxed. First time visitors always feel at home at the Rocky Knob, especially if they've stopped by for a meal. The dinner menu features steaks, seafood, and chicken entrees. Hickory smoked pork ribs are the house specialty, and homemade desserts are prepared daily. Be sure to stop at the bar before leaving, because you never know when Joe's ghost will appear for an encore performance.

CORVALLIS TAVERN

OWNER: Cal McOmber

LOCATION: 1015 Main, **Corvallis**

HOURS: 10:00 a.m. to 2:00 a.m. Mon-Fri
9:00 a.m. to 2:00 a.m. Sat-Sun

PHONE: 406-961-3591

HAPPY HOUR: 5:30 to 6:30 Mon - Fri

BEER: Drafts; Domestics

GAMBLING: Video Poker/Keno

AMUSEMENT: Pool; Darts

LIVE MUSIC: No

FOOD: Burgers; Frozen Pizza

The Corvallis Tavern, "Where Friends Meet", is at 1015 Main Street in Corvallis. The barroom is relatively large, but the atmosphere is definitely one of a friendly, small town bar. The barroom has an antique mahogany bar and a matching back bar with a large leaded-glass mirror. An extension has been added to the original bar, and a wooden liquor cabinet stands beside the back bar against the wall. The bar and back bar were initially sent to England, but they were eventually shipped back to the United States around Cape Horn to Oregon. From the Oregon Coast, the pieces were hauled overland by team and wagon to Corvallis. Although barrooms can't talk (and most of us are truly grateful for this), the photographs on the walls in the Corvallis Tavern provide a glimpse into the rural lifestyle of the residents of this beautiful Bitterroot Valley community. Past hunting and fishing trips, rodeo events, and 4-H entries in local fairs are just some of the memories captured in the photographs.

Nobody I spoke with knew exactly when the business was established, but it's believed the tavern first opened around 1900. The bar operated out of a building that stood about a block north on Main Street until it moved to its present location in 1933. At least part of the building that presently houses the bar was a blacksmith shop during the early 1900s. The business operated under the names Blue Goose and Corvallis Pool Hall and Tavern before becoming the Corvallis Tavern. Cal McOmber bought the business in 1982, and he continues to operate it today.

The Corvallis Tavern (CT) is a neighborhood bar where working class people gather to relax and unwind. The CT has gained a reputation as one of the friendliest bars in Montana, so you know you'll be treated well. As a community service, the CT participates in the Home Free program, wherein the bar owner provides a coupon for a free cab ride home to customers who may not be able to safely drive. Another service offered at the CT is special prices on Bloody Marys every Sunday. I suppose anyone who needs a cab ride home on Saturday night probably needs something to help take the edge off a vicious hangover on Sunday morning.

PORTER'S PLACE

OWNER: Dean Porter

HOURS: 10:00 a.m. to Closing Daily

HAPPY HOUR: 5:00 to 6:00 Daily

GAMBLING: Video Poker/Keno

LIVE MUSIC: Every Weekend

LOCATION: 2nd & Market, **Corvallis**

PHONE: 406-961-4471

BEER: Drafts; Domestics

AMUSEMENT: Pool; Darts

FOOD: Full Menu Restaurant

Porter's Place is on the corner of Second and Market Streets in Corvallis. A spacious barroom is housed in the west side of the building, and a restaurant is in the east side. A drive-up food service window has recently been installed on the south side of the building, so you can grab something and run if you're in a hurry. The barroom is very modern, and the facility is clean and well-maintained. A horseshoe-shaped bar stands in the southeast corner of the barroom, several tables are spread across the floor, and a dance floor and bandstand are in the west side.

Cherry's Ranch House was the name of the business when the first liquor license was issued in 1981. The Happy Hour Bar operated out of the building prior to Cherry's Ranch House moving in, but the Happy Hour only had a retail beer and wine license. When the liquor license was obtained, a small barroom was built in the west side of the building. Cherry's Ranch House remained in operation until November, 1994 when Dean Porter bought the bar and renamed it Porter's Place. Dean had owned the Riverside Inn near Hamilton for ten years during the 1970s, so he was no newcomer to the tavern business. In 1995, Dean made a large addition to the west side of the building which quadrupled the size of the old barroom.

Dean Porter's Good Old Boys Band plays at the bar every Friday and Saturday night. Dean is a songwriter and musician, and his band plays an older style of country music that attracts mostly middle-aged and older people. The music of yesteryear is apparently still popular, because the barroom is packed on Saturday nights. Dean also has karaoke music occasionally, and he recently started having motorized shopping cart races during the week just to keep things interesting.

Regardless of the day of the week or the time of the day, the customers at Porter's Place are always friendly and well-mannered. The bar doesn't open until 10:00 a.m., but the restaurant opens at 6:00 every morning. An extensive breakfast, lunch, and dinner menu is offered, and some of the best prime rib in the Bitterroot Valley is served on Friday and Saturday evenings. Porter's Place also offers an excellent smorgasbord from noon to 8:00 p.m. every Sunday.

270

WEST FORK LODGE

OWNERS: Raddatz Family

HOURS: 8:00 a.m. to 2:00 a.m. Daily

HAPPY HOUR: 5:30 to 7:30 Daily

GAMBLING: Video Poker/Keno; Live Poker; Shake-A-Day

LIVE MUSIC: Occasionally

LOCATION: West Fork Road, **Darby**

PHONE: 406-821-3069

BEER: Drafts; Domestics; Imports; Microbrews

AMUSEMENT: Pool; Darts; Horseshoes; Volleyball

FOOD: Full Menu Restaurant

The West Fork Lodge is south of Darby at 5857 West Fork Road. The barroom, a restaurant, and a general store are housed in a 6,000 square foot log structure on the north side of the road. Self-service gas, a motel, campground, cabin rentals, and laundromat are also available. The main lodge is rustic in appearance, with thick wooden ceiling supports, wooden floors, and rough cut boards covering the walls and ceiling. The barroom has a long wooden bar with a thick top that was made by cutting a plank from the center of a tree trunk. A wood burning stove stands along one wall, and a huge wooden deck is off the north side of the building.

The business was established in 1952. The original lodge was relatively small, but several additions and improvements have been made to the building and the property over the years. Guests now have a variety of lodging options ranging from tepees and tent sites to modern motel rooms.

The West Fork Lodge promotes a very relaxed atmosphere. Peanuts in the shell are provided to bar customers at no charge, and people are encouraged to throw the shells on the floor. Alcohol isn't served until 8:00 a.m., but the restaurant opens at 6:00 every morning through the summer. Daily lunch and dinner specials are also available during the summer months. If you have a big appetite, the West Fork Burger comes highly recommended. A full Philippino menu is offered, but the lodge also serves a wide assortment of traditional American dishes.

The West Fork Lodge attracts business from local residents as well as tourists and outdoors enthusiasts. The lodge is in a premier outdoor recreation area, so they see plenty of outdoors enthusiasts. Mountain bike and snowmobile rentals are available if you enjoy these activities. Even if you're not an outdoors fanatic, the West Fork Lodge's remote location provides an excellent opportunity for people to get away from their problems. If you hate driving, you can always fly in. An FAA-approved 2,500 foot landing strip is on the property, so you really have no excuse for not visiting the West Fork Lodge.

BUM STEER CASINO AND SALOON

OWNER: Cheryl McKinney

HOURS: 10:00 a.m. to 2:00 a.m. Daily

HAPPY HOUR: 5:00 to 7:00 Mon - Fri

GAMBLING: Video Poker/Keno; Shake-A-Day

LIVE MUSIC: Monthly

LOCATION: 5739 Hwy. 93 S, **Florence**

PHONE: 406-273-3884

BEER: Drafts; Domestics; Imports; Microbrews

AMUSEMENT: Pool; Darts

FOOD: Pizza; Burgers

The Bum Steer Casino and Saloon is on Highway 93 in Florence. The barroom is housed in the north side of the building, and a restaurant is in the south side. The restaurant is currently managed as a separate business, but you can order food directly from the bar and have your meal brought to you. The north side of the barroom has a straight bar facing the west wall. Brands from local ranches were burned into the wooden bar top before the polyurethane coating was applied. Several tables are spread throughout the room, and a beautiful stone fireplace rises from the floor against the west wall. The old piano in the corner is still in tune, but it doesn't get much use anymore. Only on rare occasions will a customer drink enough courage to get up from the bar and play a song.

I'm told the bar was originally part of a hotel that stood on the property, but the hotel was destroyed by fire. The bar and restaurant reopened when construction on the new building was completed; however, the hotel was lost forever. The business operated under the name Florence Bar from 1947 until 1974 when it became the Bum Steer. Cheryl McKinney bought the Bum Steer in October, 1994. Cheryl decided to concentrate solely on the saloon portion of the business, so she now leases out the restaurant, which operates under the name Wagon Wheel Pizza.

The Bum Steer is a fun place where working class people gather to relax and unwind. A lot of the customers are avid pool and dart players, so Cheryl sponsors several teams in the local leagues. Cheryl also promotes the business with karaoke every Wednesday and Saturday, and live bands perform on a monthly basis. The Bum Steer hosts several annual parties for their customers. Cheryl has pot luck dinners on every major holiday, and she hosts an anniversary party in October and a golf tournament at the end of April. Parties with a 1950s theme are also held whenever Cheryl gets the urge. The Bum Steer has even hosted a couple of funeral wakes. I realize nobody wants to die, but you might as well have your send off party at a bar if you have to go.

DYNA-MART

MANAGER: Janet Knapp

HOURS: 8:00 a.m. to 1:00 a.m. Daily

HAPPY HOUR: No

GAMBLING: Video Poker/Keno; Shake-A-Day

LIVE MUSIC: No

LOCATION: 5323 Hwy. 93 S, **Florence**

PHONE: 406-273-9993

BEER: Domestics

AMUSEMENT: Video Games; Pinball

FOOD: Deli Foods

The Dyna-Mart is on the west side of Highway 93 in Florence. If you're wondering why someone would name a bar the Dyna-Mart, all you have to do is visit the place to find out. The bar is only one part of the entire business. The Dyna-Mart is a convenience store, delicatessen, self service gas station, laundromat, RV dump, mechanic's shop, car wash, and saloon all rolled into one neat little package. In other words, you can have your vehicle repaired, do your laundry, eat a sandwich, wash your car, buy gas, and get gassed without ever leaving the property. What a splendid idea! On the single person's convenience scale of one to ten, the Dyna-Mart is a definite ten.

The Dyna-Mart was established in 1988. I'll never know what possessed the owners to open a bar inside a convenience store, but the business has been very successful. The barroom is in the north side of the building, but it's not in a separate room from the delicatessen and convenience store. There is enough of a partition to allow some privacy, however. Once you get situated at the horseshoe-shaped bar, it doesn't take long to realize there's a genuine barroom atmosphere at the Dyna-Mart. The familiar sounds of the video gambling machines, beer cans snapping open, and conversations at the bar make you aware the Dyna-Mart is more than just a convenience store.

Janet Knapp manages the bar, and she basically operates it like a neighborhood tavern. Locals gather at the Dyna-Mart after work to relax and unwind, and a lot of motorists traveling along Highway 93 stop by for the other services. The deli makes great sandwiches, so many of the people who drink at the bar in the evening stop at the deli on their way to work to get something for lunch. There's usually a very friendly crowd on hand. On those rare occasions when someone gets out of line, they're quickly escorted out the door by the bartender or other customers. The Dyna-Mart is the closest thing I've found to complete one stop shopping. If you can't get what you're looking for here, you probably didn't really need it in the first place.

RUSTIC HUT

OWNER: Fred Peters		**LOCATION:**	5341 Hwy. 93 S, **Florence**
HOURS: Noon to 2:00 a.m. Daily		**PHONE:**	406-273-9992
HAPPY HOUR: 4:00 to 6:00 Mon - Fri		**BEER:**	Drafts; Domestics; Imports
GAMBLING: Video Poker/Keno		**AMUSEMENT:**	Pool; Darts; Pinball; Video Games
LIVE MUSIC: DJ Music Thurs/Fri/Sat		**FOOD:**	Frozen Pizza

The Rustic Hut is a bar and dance club on the east side of Highway 93 in Florence. The main barroom is housed in the east side of the building, and a spacious dance hall resides in a separate room in the west side. The barroom is relatively large, with a curved bar facing the west wall. The dance hall has its own bar, a sunken dance floor, and a new CD sound system with a laser disk video hookup for karaoke. Contrary to popular opinion, the carpeting throughout the barroom and dance hall was not installed because there was a good deal on carpet when the place was built. It turns out the carpet has exceptional acoustical properties that enhance the building's sound system.

Fred Peters established the business on Mother's Day in 1973. The Rustic Hut was one of the first discotheques to open in Montana, and it quickly became the most popular night club in the Missoula area. During the week, the Rustic Hut was nothing more than a neighborhood tavern. On the weekends, however, the disco ducks from Missoula infiltrated the place and things got crazy. The DJ played a mix of country and rock music, so there were all kinds of people in the bar. There were also plenty of fights between the rock and roll fanatics and the cowboys. When business started dropping off in 1985, the discotheque was closed. The west side of the building sat vacant until October 18, 1996 when the old discotheque reopened as a modern dance club.

Pool tables and dart boards replaced the discotheque as the main source of entertainment during the years when the dance hall was closed, and the bar still sponsors several pool and dart tournaments throughout the year. On Thursday, Friday, and Saturday evenings, however, people come to dance. Country music is the theme on Thursday nights, and top 40 music is played on Friday and Saturday. When they don't have a dance scheduled, the dance hall can be rented out for wedding receptions or other private parties. The Rustic Hut is once again the hottest night club in the Bitterroot Valley, so why not head on out and kick up your heels.

LOST HORSE CREEK LODGE

OWNER: Robert Embesi

LOCATION: 1000 Lost Horse Road, south of **Hamilton**

HOURS: Noon to Closing Daily

PHONE: 406-363-1460

HAPPY HOUR: No

BEER: Drafts; Domestics

GAMBLING: Video Poker/Keno; Live Poker

AMUSEMENT: Horseshoes; Volleyball

LIVE MUSIC: Occasionally

FOOD: Full Menu Restaurant

The Lost Horse Creek Lodge is five miles west of Highway 93 on the Lost Horse Road between Hamilton and Darby. The entire business includes primitive and modern lodging facilities, a restaurant, campground, gift shop, and one of the most interesting saloons I've ever seen. Describing the barroom as rustic would be an enormous understatement. The building and practically every fixture in it are made completely from logs and rough cut lumber. Pine slats cover the front of the bar, and the thick bar top is a plank cut from the middle of a tree trunk. Virtually every square inch of the walls and ceiling are covered with some sort of object. Signed dollar bills, old license plates, antique tools and farm implements, animal skins, antlers, and an array of other items have been used for decoration. This is one place you really have to see to appreciate.

The business was established in 1971. The existing saloon building and three other cabins were moved to the property from Virginia City. One of the original cabins was destroyed by fire, but the remaining buildings have historical significance since they were built in Virginia City in the 1800s. The building that now houses the formal dining room and gift shop was built in the 1970s. The addition was originally a dance hall, but it also served as living quarters before being renovated into a dining room. Robert Embesi bought the lodge in November, 1996. He has done a lot of work since buying the business, so things are only getting better.

The Lost Horse Creek Lodge is a wonderful place to get away from your worries. Mountain bikes and horses are rented from the lodge in the summer, and snowmobiles are rented in the winter. Guided fishing and hunting trips are even available, as are guided tours of historic Virginia City. If you aren't an ambitious type, you can simply kick back and relax with a few drinks. The resort borders the Bitterroot/Selway National Forest, so you're not far from the middle of nowhere. Both fine and casual dining are available, and a variety of lodging options are offered. People who stay in the hot tub suites get a free bottle of champagne, and all lodging guests receive a complimentary continental breakfast.

275

LOST TRAIL HOT SPRINGS RESORT

OWNERS: Ray, Mary Dell, Stann, and Lisa Honey

LOCATION: 8321 Hwy. 93 S., **Sula**

HOURS: 8:00 a.m. to Closing Daily
Closed Mon & Tues During the Winter

PHONE: 406-821-3574

HAPPY HOUR: 4:00 to 6:00 Daily

BEER: Drafts; Domestics; Imports; Microbrews

GAMBLING: Video Poker/Keno

AMUSEMENT: Horseshoes; Basketball

LIVE MUSIC: Occasionally

FOOD: Full Menu Restaurant

Lost Trail Hot Springs Resort is six miles south of Sula on Highway 93. The barroom and dining room are housed in one open area in the second floor of the main lodge. A vaulted wooden ceiling and a beautiful river rock fireplace enhance the building's rustic charm. A relatively small bar stands in the northwest corner of the room, and several hand-crafted log tables and chairs are spread across the floor. A large wooden deck overlooks the main pool off the west side of the building. The augured wooden pipes hanging from the rafters were manufactured during the late 1800s. These are the original pipes that were used to transport water from the hot springs when the area was first being developed.

Development on the natural hot water springs began in the early 1890s. A two story, fourteen room house and hotel building was built around 1895. James Gallogly bought the property and the building in 1897, and he started improving the grounds. Mr. Gallogly began rebuilding the springs in 1935 when construction on the new highway began. The existing lodge was completed in 1941. The pool is actually the foundation of the original hotel building. James Gallogly died soon after he rebuilt the springs, and the pool was closed to the public until the 1970s.

Ray, Mary Dell, Stann, and Lisa Honey have owned the business since February, 1992. The lodge is located in a heavily forested setting consisting of large ponderosa pines. The hot springs were a wintering area for Native Americans, and a lot of the trees have historic markings on them. The Honey's have developed the area into a family resort specializing in large group parties. Cabin rentals, motel rooms, and a full-service campground are now available along with the outdoor pool, indoor hot tub, and sauna. The resort has become a popular place for social gatherings such as wedding ceremonies, receptions, and family reunions. The lodge is also serves as an outdoor recreation headquarters for every season. Hunters, hikers, skiers, snowmobilers, and fishermen flock to the region for the outstanding recreational opportunities.

CANTINA LA COCINA

OWNER: Carole Dickson	**LOCATION:** 2359 Hwy. 93 S., **Victor**
HOURS: 4:00 p.m. to 9:00 p.m. Sun-Fri 4:00 p.m. to 10:00 p.m. Sat	**PHONE:** 406-642-3192
HAPPY HOUR: 5:00 to 6:00 Mon - Fri	**BEER:** Drafts; Domestics; Imports
GAMBLING: Video Poker/Keno	**AMUSEMENT:** No
LIVE MUSIC: No	**FOOD:** Full Menu Restaurant

The Cantina La Cocina, home of the Almost Famous Margarita, is at 2359 Highway 93 South in Victor. A spacious dining room resides in the south side of the building, the lounge is in the middle, and a casino room is in the north side. A covered wooden walkway spans the length of the front side of the building, and a wooden deck enclosed in white lattice woodwork is off the west side. An L-shaped bar faces the west wall of the lounge, and a few small tables and two booths are available if you prefer sitting away from the bar. Three television sets are available if you get bored with your date.

The Cantina La Cocina was established in 1982. I'm told things weren't going all that well when Carole Dickson bought the business in 1988, but Carole has done an exceptional job at turning things around. Carole worked as a waitress in the restaurant prior to buying the business, so she had a good idea what needed to be done. Her hard work has certainly paid off, because the Cantina La Cocina is now a very popular dining and drinking establishment.

The Cantina La Cocina is a friendly place with a family-oriented atmosphere. People waiting to be seated in the dining room commonly wait in the lounge or casino, so the customers are expected to behave themselves accordingly. Smoking is not permitted in the dining room, but you can still light up in the lounge and casino areas. They do their best to accommodate everyone at the Cantina La Cocina.

A complete dinner menu featuring both Mexican and traditional American dishes is offered. The Fiesta Tostadas and Burrito Colorados are two of the more popular menu items, but all the food is good. The restaurant is what keeps the place in business, but they also get plenty of customers in the lounge and casino. A wide array of blended drinks are served, including the house specialty Almost Famous Margaritas. Two for the price of one margaritas are the featured drink on Tuesdays and Wednesdays, and happy hour prices feature two for the price of one on draft beer and mixed drinks.

THE HAMILTON A PUBLIC HOUSE

OWNERS: John and Mary Hamilton

HOURS: 12:30 a.m. to Closing Mon-Fri
Noon to Closing Saturday

HAPPY HOUR: No

GAMBLING: No

LIVE MUSIC: Occasionally

LOCATION: 104 Main Street, **Victor**

PHONE: 406-642-6644

BEER: Drafts; Domestics;
Imports; Microbrews

AMUSEMENT: Darts; Board Games

FOOD: Full Menu Restaurant

The Hamilton A Public House is at 104 Main Street in Victor. Several flags hang from the front of the brick structure, so you shouldn't have any trouble recognizing the place. The Hamilton was fashioned in the tradition of an authentic Scottish pub. Old world charm was combined with modern day influences to create an atmosphere unlike any I've seen in Montana. The wooden bar was hand-crafted locally to match the tables, chairs, and pews that were imported from England. Items such as knights helmets, swords, and Scottish drums are displayed from the top of the wooden back bar. The visible features create a very pub-like atmosphere, but the mood is enhanced with Celtic and classical music played over the stereo system.

John and Mary Hamilton established the Hamilton A Public House on March 17, 1994. The building was originally an automobile service station, but it had become an office building prior to the pub moving in. John and Mary did a magnificent job putting the place together, and it seems only appropriate that their grand opening occurred on St. Patrick's Day. The grand opening celebration was a smashing success, and the business has thrived since that time.

John and Mary have made the St. Patrick's Day party an annual event, but the Hamilton is a great place to visit any time of the year. The lunch and dinner menus feature a variety of items, including English style fish and chips and calamari. The Hamilton also stocks over thirty different brands of imported and microbrewed beers, so you're bound to find at least one kind you like. If you happen to over-indulge and think you're hallucinating about a Scotsman walking around the barroom playing the bagpipes, you're probably not hallucinating at all. John normally wears his traditional Scottish kilt when he's at the pub, and he sometimes plays the bagpipes to entertain his guests. The Hamilton A Public House was voted the best out of town bar in Missoula in 1996. Mary says they must be doing something right, because a lot of English tourists stop by the Hamilton to get a taste of home while vacationing in the area.

LONGBRANCH SALOON

OWNERS: Perry and Chris Jasper

HOURS: 9:00 a.m. to 2:00 a.m. Daily

HAPPY HOUR: 5:30 to 6:30 Mon - Fri

GAMBLING: Video Poker/Keno

LIVE MUSIC: Occasionally

LOCATION: Highway 93, **Victor**

PHONE: 406-642-9988

BEER: Domestics; Microbrews

AMUSEMENT: Pool; Foosball; Pinball; Ping Pong; Golf Putting

FOOD: No

The Longbranch Saloon is housed in a wooden structure on the east side of Highway 93 in Victor. Log posts support the wooden ceiling, the interior walls are covered with rough cut boards, and the floor is made of wood planks. A long bar stands in front of the antique wooden back bar against the east wall. The bar has a thick wooden top made from massive planks that were cut from the center of a tree trunk. Horseshoes have been welded together to form the legs on the barstools, providing a sturdy base for even the heftiest of customers. The stone fireplace against the west wall has a wood burning insert at the base and a handsome moose head hanging midway between the floor and ceiling. An elevated bandstand is in the northwest corner of the room, and three picnic tables are spread across the middle of the floor.

The business was established as Maggie's Fine Food Restaurant in 1976. The building originally had a sunken floor that was at the same elevation as the base of the existing fireplace, but a raised wooden floor was installed a few years after the restaurant opened. Perry and Chris Jasper bought Maggie's in 1981, but they decided to operate the business solely as a saloon. The restaurant was eliminated altogether, and the new owners changed the name of the business to the Longbranch Saloon.

The Longbranch is a fun bar with a friendly clientele. It's the type of place where people commonly buy rounds of drinks, so be prepared to hoist a few and buy an occasional round when you visit. Most of the customers are residents of Victor and the surrounding communities, but fishermen, skiers, and a few tourists wander in every so often. An entire rugby team from Pocatello, Idaho also stops by every year after the annual Maggot Fest Rugby Tournament in Missoula. The arrival of the rugby team is always the start of an interesting evening. The Longbranch sponsors several annual events, including the Longbranch (Barroom Games) Olympics in March, a golf tournament in June, and a pig roast in early fall. There's no need to worry if you can't make it to one of the special events, because the Longbranch Saloon is a fun place to visit any time.

279

MARTIN'S INN

OWNERS: Phyllis Lambert and Frank Riitano

HOURS: 11:00 a.m. to Closing Daily

HAPPY HOUR: 4:30 to 6:30 Fridays

GAMBLING: Video Poker/Keno

LIVE MUSIC: Karaoke Every Friday

LOCATION: 1 Main Street, **Victor**

PHONE: 406-642-3412

BEER: Drafts; Domestics; Imports; Microbrews

AMUSEMENT: Pool; Darts; Video Game

FOOD: Fresh Sandwiches

Martin's Inn is at the junction of Highway 93 and Main Street in Victor. The front part of the barroom houses a straight bar along the west wall, a big-screen TV in one corner, and an open brick fireplace in the center of the floor. The south side of the barroom is basically reserved as a dining and seating area.

The building was built in 1917, making it one of the oldest remaining structures in the Bitterroot Valley. The building was initially used as a train depot for the Northern Pacific Railroad Company. Victor was once an important shipping point in the Bitterroot Valley; so important, in fact, that it almost became the county seat. Apparently, Marcus Daly was able to use his powerful political influence to defeat A. B. Hammond's attempts to make Victor the county seat, and Hamilton was eventually selected for this role.

When the railroad depot closed in 1927, the building was moved to its present location and renovated into a soda fountain and dance hall. A retail beer license was obtained after prohibition ended, but there's rumor the soda fountain had sold beer all along. The bar was called the Oasis because it was the only bar along Highway 93 between Hamilton and Missoula. Bill and Carol Martin bought the business in 1960, but they didn't change the name to Martin's Inn until 1979. The Martins did some minor renovations during the late 1970s, but the building still basically looks the same as it did when it was built. Phyllis Lambert and Frank Riitano have owned Martin's Inn since 1984. Phyllis and Frank operated the business as a bar and restaurant until 1994, but they decided to take the kitchen out and concentrate solely bar portion of the business.

Martin's Inn is a friendly tavern with a family-oriented atmosphere. Although the full menu restaurant is no longer open, fresh sandwiches are still served. The majority of the customers come from Victor and the surrounding communities, so you're certain to meet some great people. Martin's Inn may be in one of the oldest buildings in the valley, but it's also one of the best bars in the valley.

STUMBLE INN

OWNERS: Lynn and Tye Payne

HOURS: 11:00 a.m to 2:00 a.m. Daily

HAPPY HOUR: 4:30 to 6:00 Mon - Fri

GAMBLING: Video Poker/Keno; Shake-A-Day

LIVE MUSIC: Occasionally

LOCATION: Highway 93, **Victor**

PHONE: 406-642-9991

BEER: Drafts; Domestics

AMUSEMENT: Pool; Darts; Horseshoes

FOOD: Grill Items
Broasted Chicken

The Stumble Inn is at the junction of Highway 93 and Railroad Avenue in Victor. The straight bar facing the east wall of the barroom has a steel foot rail and padded elbow rests. Several tables are spread throughout the room, and a brick fireplace with a wood burning insert rises from the floor against the south wall. There's nothing elaborate about the place, but the beer is cold and the people are friendly.

The business was established in 1973. There's not a lot in the way of unusual history to report, but I'm told one of the former owners of the bar was noted for pulling out a gun and shooting up the barroom whenever he got drunk. This annoying little habit drove away so many customers that the man eventually lost the business. Most of the bullet holes have since been repaired, but if you look closely at the ceiling in the northwest corner of the room, you can still see some of the man's handiwork.

Lynn and Tye Payne have owned the Stumble Inn since October, 1991. They haven't shot up the barroom even once since they took over. Lynn and Tye promote a friendly atmosphere, and there's rarely any trouble at the bar these days. Excellent broasted chicken is served, and the Stumble Inn features a delicious beef patty with ham and cheese called the Almost Famous Stumble Burger. An great ribeye steak is now available, and prime rib is served on occasion. As a change of pace, Lynn and Tye always have a flea market in the parking lot on Chief Victor Day, which is the second Saturday in July. They also host dart tournaments on occasion, and a pig roast is held once a year as a show of appreciation for the customers.

The Stumble Inn started gaining notoriety in 1995 when country music star Daryle Singletary released his hit song "Too Much Fun". A verse from the song has two men getting thrown out of the Stumble Inn for fighting, so they end up going to the Longbranch for the rest of the night. It turns out Victor's Longbranch Saloon is next door to the Stumble Inn, and many people believe the song writer had these two establishments in mind when he wrote the verse. An informed source assured me that was not the case, but the unexpected publicity certainly hasn't hurt the business.

281

CQ BAR

OWNERS: Paula and Dave Roberts

HOURS: 10:00 a.m. to 2:00 a.m. Daily

HAPPY HOUR: Wednesdays, 6:00 to 7:00
(7:00 to 8:00 in Winter)

GAMBLING: Video Poker/Keno;
Shake-A-Day

LIVE MUSIC: Occasionally

LOCATION: Main Street, **Lambert**

PHONE: 406-774-3477

BEER: Domestics

AMUSEMENT: Pool; Darts; Foosball;
Video Games; Volleyball

FOOD: Grill Items; Bar Snacks

The CQ Bar is on Main Street in Lambert. The spacious barroom has a long bar and plenty tables, so finding a place to park your butt should be no problem. If you decide to sit at one of the wooden buddy bars, you can't help but notice the branding marks that have been burned into the wood. All the markings are authentic brands from local ranches. There's also a very unique brand on the men's room wall, but I doubt you'll find a local rancher who will claim the mark.

The business was established in a building on an adjacent lot in 1944. The bar moved to it's present location when construction on a new building was completed in 1971. The name changed from Mickey's Bar to CQ's Bar in 1976. The rationale behind the name change was explained to me, but I don't remember all the details because my mind started wandering into my beer mug as the story unfolded. From what I can recall, the man who had just bought the bar had a particular fondness for a place called the CQ Lake in Washington State. Apparently, he named the bar after the lake.

Paula and Dave Roberts bought the CQ Bar in April, 1994. They spent endless hours making improvements to the building, and their efforts show. Paula and Dave run a friendly bar, and the customers are fun-loving people who dream up interesting forms of entertainment. The long slice in the formica bar top is evidence of one of those entertaining moments. Several years ago, one of the customers tried to impress the other bar patrons by cutting a beer can in half with a machete. I'm told the beer can escaped injury, but the bar top was permanently damaged.

There have been some rowdy times at the CQ Bar, but not since the oil boom days of the late 1970s. It was during this time when a roughneck from Oklahoma shot out one of the mirrors behind the bar. Nobody seems to know whether the shooting was accidental or intentional, but the only damage done was to the mirror. It's a more mellow scene at the CQ Bar these days, but you still never know when someone will try to assault an innocent beer can with a machete.

282

BURNS CREEK INN

OWNERS: Joanne Hagler

HOURS: 1:00 p.m. to 2:00 a.m. Daily

HAPPY HOUR: No

GAMBLING: Video Poker/Keno

LIVE MUSIC: No

LOCATION: 76 Main Street, **Savage**

PHONE: 406-776-2323

BEER: Domestics

AMUSEMENT: Pool; Video Games

FOOD: Grill Items; Pizza

The Burns Creek Inn is on Main Street in Savage. The barroom is housed in the original wood-framed building, and a spacious dance hall resides in the steel-sided addition on the west end. Although the bar was built in the early 1900's, it doesn't seem like you're inside an old musty room when you step through the front door. The interior was completely renovated during the early 1980's, and it's been maintained in excellent condition ever since. The walls are trimmed with tongue-and-groove wood, and the hardwood floor has been refinished to near original condition. A long bar spans the length of one wall, and beautiful antique back bar fashioned from oak stands against the wall behind the bar.

The business was established as the Star Bar, but name was changed to the Burns Creek Inn in 1974. Don and Joanne Hagler bought the bar in 1988. Don passed away in 1996, but Joanne still operates the business. Like many small town taverns in Montana, the Burns Creek Inn is as much a community center as it is a bar. Don and Joanne have always promoted a family-oriented atmosphere, and it's doubtful that will ever change. The busiest time of the year at the Burns Creek Inn is during the fall. Local sugar beet farmers hold informal after-harvest parties in the barroom, and visiting hunters stop in during the evenings. It's not uncommon for the hunters and farmers to spontaneously join forces and party until the proverbial cows come home. New friends are made this way, and old friendships are often rekindled during the parties.

They no longer have live music at the Burns Creek Inn, but the dance hall gets plenty of use as a meeting room. It also makes a great overflow seating area when the barroom is full. One practice that hasn't been discontinued is dumping ice in the urinals. If you're like most men and enjoy watching ice cubes crumble while emptying your bladder, the Burns Creek Inn still affords this simple pleasure. Before leaving the bar, be sure to check out the special Snout Trout souvenir T-shirts. Snout Trout is local terminology for Paddlefish, which are abundant in the nearby Yellowstone River.

BAINVILLE BAR

OWNER: Donnie Miller

HOURS: 11:00 a.m. to 2:00 a.m. Daily

HAPPY HOUR: 5:00 to 6:00 Mon - Fri

GAMBLING: Video Poker/Keno; Shake-A-Day

LIVE MUSIC: Occasionally

LOCATION: Highway 2, **Bainville**

PHONE: 406-769-9441

BEER: Drafts; Domestics

AMUSEMENT: Pool; Darts

FOOD: Homemade Pizza; Burgers; Sandwiches

The Bainville Bar is on the south side of Highway 2 in Bainville. There are actually two separate buildings interconnected by an enclosed walkway, but they are both part of the same business. The barroom resides in the building on the east side of the property, and a dance hall is housed in the building to the west. A bar and a couple of tables occupy the floor space in the north side of the barroom, and a game room and casino area reside in the south side.

The business was established as the Town Pump Beer Parlor in 1934. The Town Pump originally stood on the corner of Clinton Street and Wilson Avenue in Bainville, but it was later moved to a building on Main Street. Wylie's Bar was the name of the business in 1961 when the building on Main Street was destroyed by fire. The bar was rebuilt along Highway 2, and it's been operating there ever since. The existing dance hall was added in 1979. Like most taverns in this part of the state, there were some wild times during the oil boom days of the late 1970s and early 1980s. Things have settled down since then, and the customers now have fun in less threatening ways.

Donnie Miller bought the business in 1991. He hosts several parties each year, complete with free food and live music. Annual events include a fish feed on Good Friday, a bratwurst feed the last weekend in August, and a wild game feed at the end of November. In 1994, Donnie hosted a Nerd Party on Halloween weekend. The guests dressed as nerds, drank themselves silly, and ended up dancing on everything except the floor by the end of the evening. During an outdoor dance in 1993, the field to the west of the bar was inadvertently set on fire. Fortunately, one of the customers brought the blaze under control by beating it out with a carpet before the voluntary fire department arrived on the scene.

The parties are great, but Donnie has a good day-to-day business as well. He serves excellent ham and cheese sandwiches, and you can still get a fourteen ounce mug of draft beer for $1.00. If you're ever in the area, be sure to stop at the Bainville Bar and say hello to Donnie and the gang.

SMOKEY'S

OWNER: Doris Lambert

HOURS: 9:00 a.m. to 2:00 a.m. Mon-Sat
1:00 p.m. to 2:00 a.m. Sundays

HAPPY HOUR: Change of Shift Drink

GAMBLING: Video Poker/Keno;
Shake-A-Day

LIVE MUSIC: Karaoke on Request

LOCATION: 114 Clinton, **Bainville**

PHONE: 406-769-2871

BEER: Domestics

AMUSEMENT: Pool; Darts

FOOD: Microwave Sandwiches;
Frozen Pizza

Smokey's is housed in a steel-sided structure at 114 Clinton Street in Bainville. You can't see the bar from Highway 2, but it's only a couple of blocks south of the highway on the left-hand side of the street. A spacious barroom resides in the west side of the building, and a smaller casino area is in a partitioned-off room in the east side. A straight bar runs along the south wall in the main part of the barroom, and several tables are spread across the carpeted area in the north side of the room.

Doris Lambert has owned Smokey's since 1972. The business was formerly called the Club Bar, but the name was changed when the bar was moved a short distance to its present location in 1981. During the summer of 1994, the interior of the building sustained extensive damage from a fire that started in one of the video gambling machines after hours. Renovations were completed in July of that same year, and Smokey's reopened for business with a new look.

Back in the oil boom days of the late 1970s and early 1980s, you never knew what to expect from the roughnecks, pipeline workers, and other transients who visited the bar. Excitement was abundant in those days, but things have pretty much returned to normal over the past several years. The regular crowd now consists primarily of local farmers and ranchers. Of the two bars in town, Smokey's caters more to the older crowd. A lot of North Dakotan residents also come to Smokey's to play the video gambling machines and buy lottery tickets. Smokey's is only eight miles from the Montana-North Dakota border, and it's the closest place via Highway 2 that North Dakotans can go to play the Powerball, Triwest, and Montana Cash lotteries.

Smokey's doesn't offer a traditional happy hour, but they provide a free change of shift drink to their customers at 5:00 p.m. Monday through Friday. The approach is slightly different, but one free drink usually equates to the same amount of savings as offering reduced prices on drinks over an hour's time.

LOG CABIN BAR (HEY JOHN'S BAR)

OWNER: Ellis John Nordwick

HOURS: 9:00 a.m. to 2:00 a.m. Daily

HAPPY HOUR: No

GAMBLING: Video Poker/Keno

LIVE MUSIC: Occasionally

LOCATION: Highway 2, **Brockton**

PHONE: No Phone

BEER: Domestics

AMUSEMENT: Pool

FOOD: Deep Fried Foods

The Log Cabin Bar is housed in a steel-sided building on the north side of Highway 2 in Brockton, which is the northern-most point on the Missouri River. The name of the business is a bit deceiving because nothing on the exterior of the building resembles a log cabin. In fact, the words *HEY JOHNS BAR* are painted above the main entrance, which further adds to the confusion. The interior of the building does, in fact, have some features that remind you of a log cabin. The back bar is constructed of painted logs, and rough cut log slats cover the north wall.

The Log Cabin Bar has been in Brockton since the end of Prohibition, but it hasn't always been where it is today. Ellis John Nordwick, known affectionately as Hey John to his customers, bought the business in 1961. The bar originally stood about twelve miles east of where it is today. The building was moved to its present location in 1985 because, in John's own words, it was about to fall over. The bar and large coolers stayed in the building when it was moved, but the back bar was moved separately.

The regular customers at the Log Cabin are local farmers, ranchers, and Native Americans from the Fort Peck Reservation. A lot of pheasant hunters and Canadians who are visiting or passing through the area also frequent the tavern. Friday and Saturday nights are always action packed, and even Sunday mornings can be a little wild. The customers are typically well-behaved, but things can get a little out of hand on occasion. John has a blackball list posted behind the bar, but he is usually reluctant to put any names on it. Realistically, the list would never have been posted if it weren't requested by one of the local peace officers.

Cherry bombs (cherries soaked in grain alcohol) are sold at the bar for 25 cents each, and there's usually a mystery drink, which is a bottle of liquor wrapped in a brown paper bag, available for $1.00 a shot. The contents of the bottle, which are known only by God and the bartender, change when someone guesses what the drink is or the bottle runs dry. The objective is to take a drink and guess what kind of liquor it is. If you guess correctly, you get a free shot. Be careful, though, because people have been known to drink most of a bottle trying to guess what it is.

286

ANNEX BAR

OWNERS: Jim O'Toole & Liana Peters

HOURS: 4:00 p.m. to 1:00 a.m. Wed-Sat
1:00 p.m. to 1:00 a.m. Sundays
Closed Monday and Tuesday

HAPPY HOUR: Change of Shift Drink

GAMBLING: Shake-A-Day

LIVE MUSIC: Occasionally

LOCATION: Main Street, **Froid**

PHONE: 406-766-2270

BEER: Domestics

AMUSEMENT: Pool; Darts

FOOD: Broasted Chicken; Fresh
Pizza; Deep Fried Foods

The Annex Bar is on Main Street in Froid. The spacious barroom has a straight bar along the east wall, several tables spread throughout the room, and a bandstand in the southwest corner. Although the building is relatively old, the facility is very clean and well-maintained.

The business was established in 1934 as a beer parlor in the old Froid Hotel Annex. The hotel was about two blocks west on Main Street from where the bar is today. The business moved to its present location in 1945. Jim O'Toole & Liana Peters bought the Annex Bar in March, 1995. The bar had been closed for several months prior to that time, so Jim and Liana teamed up and got things rolling again. New flooring was installed, a fresh coat of paint was applied, and a lot of general cleaning was performed before the doors were opened. Jim and Liana now have the old bar looking as good as new.

Jim and Liana promote a friendly atmosphere at the Annex Bar. They cater primarily to residents of Froid, but visiting hunters frequent the bar in the fall, and motorists traveling through the area occasionally stop in. The barroom environment is very comfortable, and the locals go out of their way to make strangers feel welcome. The broasted chicken and pizzas served at the Annex are terrific, and a free change of shift drink is provided for the bar patrons at 6:00 p.m. daily.

The Annex Bar and Froid's other tavern, the Mint Bar, are separate businesses; however, there is not a competition for customers between the two. The bars often team up to promote community events such as the annual hunters and landowners feast. The bars, in conjunction with the local rod and gun club, sponsor a steak dinner to bring together hunters and landowners prior to the opening day of pheasant season. The objective of the gathering is for the hunters to meet the landowners and get permission to hunt on private property prior to the season opening. This benefits both parties because the hunter doesn't have to wake up the landowner at 6:00 in the morning to get permission to hunt.

MINT BAR AND CAFE

OWNER: Jan Peters   **LOCATION:** Main Street, **Froid**

HOURS: 9:00 a.m. to 1:00 a.m. Mon-Sat   **PHONE:** 406-766-9955
1:00 p.m. to 1:00 a.m. Sundays

HAPPY HOUR: Change of Shift Drink   **BEER:** Domestics

GAMBLING: Video Poker/Keno   **AMUSEMENT:** No

LIVE MUSIC: No   **FOOD:** Full Menu Cafe

The Mint Bar and Cafe is on Main Street in Froid. The barroom resides in the east side of the building, and a cafe is in the west side. The north end of the barroom has a straight bar that can comfortably seat about ten people, and a few tables are available for additional seating. A small casino area is in the south end of the room.

Pat's Place was the name of the bar when it first opened in 1910. When prohibition went into effect, Pat's Place closed down and the building was renovated into the First National Bank of Froid. The old walk-in bank vault is still in the basement. A grocery store replaced the bank in 1926, and sometime between then and 1945, a bowling alley took over occupancy. The Mint Bar opened in 1945, and it's been going strong ever since.

Jan Peters has owned the Mint Bar since 1980. If I were to compare the Mint to Froid's other tavern, the Annex Bar, I would say the Mint seems to be more of a no-frills tavern. There's no pool table in the barroom; just plenty to drink and a very friendly crowd. The barroom and cafe are physically separated, so you normally don't see kids at the bar. If you arrive at the Mint with an appetite, the cafe hours are 7:00 a.m. to 7:00 p.m. Dinner specials are offered on a daily basis, and the prime rib comes highly recommended when it's available.

Local farmers, ranchers, business people, and oil field workers are the regular customers at the Mint Bar. After a hard day's work, people gather here to relax and visit with friends. It's common for customers to buy each other drinks or buy a round of drinks for everyone in the bar. In fact, the beers sometimes come so fast that they seem to multiply in front of you. You can't help but make friends at the Mint, especially when it's your turn to buy. I've not seen the issue, but one of the customers told me Life Magazine published an article in 1947 that stated more alcohol was consumed per capita in Froid, Montana than any other town in the Unites States. Perhaps this isn't what some people would consider good publicity for their home town, but sometimes it's just nice to be recognized.

STATE LINE CASINO

OWNER: Sharon Turbiville

LOCATION: Hwy. 2, **MT/ND Border**

HOURS: 11:00 a.m. to 2:00 a.m. Daily

PHONE: 701-875-4353

HAPPY HOUR: None

BEER: Domestics

GAMBLING: Video Poker/Keno; Live Poker; Shake-A-Day

AMUSEMENT: Pool; Darts; Video Games

LIVE MUSIC: Occasionally

FOOD: Full Dinner Menu

The State Line Casino is just west of the Montana/North Dakota border on Highway 2. The building is in Montana, but it's so close to North Dakota that the phone number for the business has a North Dakota area code. The barroom is relatively large, with a wooden bar that's over fifty feet long. Approximately twenty video gambling machines are available, and live poker is played Friday through Monday in the smaller room off the north side of the barroom. The building also houses a formal dining room and two separate dance halls.

The business was established in the early 1930s. The original building was destroyed by fire in 1936, so the existing structure was built and the bar reopened. Prize fights were held in a boxing arena in the second floor during the early years of operation, and it's also rumored a brothel once operated out of the building. For better or worse, both the boxing and the brothel are gone. Sharon Turbiville has owned the State Line Casino since 1981. Sharon primarily runs the business as a casino to attract gamblers from the Williston, North Dakota area.

The dinner menu at the State Line Casino features steaks and seafood, and a prime rib dinner is offered every day of the week for $4.95. Dining room hours are 4:00 p.m. until 9:00 p.m. daily. Live dinner shows are occasionally held at the casino to entertain the guests. Aside from the gambling and the restaurant, the State Line Casino also sponsors mud races and demolition derbies during the summer on a mud track that shares the property with the casino.

It may have been purely coincidental, but during my first visit to the State Line Casino, it seemed like the video gambling machines were very liberal in paying off. I only spent a little over an hour in the place, but an unusually high percentage of the people playing the machines brought printed receipts to the bar to cash out on their winnings. I happened to benefit from other people's luck, because a couple of the customers who won larger sums of money bought a round of drinks for the house. I certainly didn't object to their generosity.

CLUB BUFFET BAR

OWNER: Margaret Howard

HOURS: 11:00 a.m. to Closing Daily

HAPPY HOUR: 4:30 to 5:30 Wednesdays

GAMBLING: Video Poker/Keno; Shake-A-Day

LIVE MUSIC: 2-3 Times a Month

LOCATION: Highway 212, **Ashland**

PHONE: 406-784-2166

BEER: Domestics

AMUSEMENT: Pool; Darts

FOOD: Frozen Pizza

The Club Buffet Bar is on Highway 212 in Ashland. What appears from the street to be two partially dressed ladies in the second story windows are actually murals painted on the building's false front. The ladies aren't real, but they sure get the attention of passing motorists who often stop to take pictures. The barroom has a long wooden bar, part of which makes a matching set with the antique mahogany back bar and liquor cabinet. The hand-crafted back bar was slightly damaged by a fire, but the exquisite woodwork and three arched mirrors are still intact.

I wasn't able to find out exactly when the business was established, but the people I spoke with indicated it has been around since at least the 1920s. At one time, a two story outhouse stood just outside the bar. The ladies did their business in the ground-level outhouse, but the men had to climb the steps to the second floor. Unfortunately, this unique structure went up in flames when the motel next door burned down several years ago. Dub and Margaret Howard bought the Club Buffet Bar in 1973. They sold the business in 1980 but ended up repossessing it in 1992. The bar was closed during the three year court battle that ensued. Dub passed away in 1993, so Margaret began managing the business on her own when the bar reopened in November, 1995.

Things are pretty mellow at the Club Buffet Bar these days, but there have been some wild times over the years. It was once common for people to ride their horses into the barroom, shoot holes in the ceiling, and throw coins on top of the back bar. The coins would fall into the hollow columns, and as far as anyone knows, they're still in there today. There are plenty of bullet holes in the original ceiling above the new drop ceiling, but I know of only one person ever being shot in the barroom. During the 1970s, the bartender pulled a gun out from behind the bar and fired two shots at a man who allegedly had been harassing him. One bullet struck the man in the forehead, killing him on the spot, and the other bullet went through the large painting that hangs from the west wall. The bullet hole is still in the painting if you care to see it.

OFFICE BAR

OWNERS: Debbie and Jan Rukavina

LOCATION: Highway 212, **Ashland**

HOURS: 9:00 a.m. to 1:00 a.m. Mon-Sat
10:00 a.m. to 10:00 p.m. Sunday

PHONE: 406-784-2340

HAPPY HOUR: No

BEER: Domestics

GAMBLING: Video Poker/Keno

AMUSEMENT: Pool; Horseshoes

LIVE MUSIC: No

FOOD: Grill Items; Frozen Pizza

The Office Bar is on the north side of Highway 212 in Ashland. The moderate-sized barroom has a straight wooden bar along the east wall, two buddy bars in the middle of the floor, and a stone fireplace against the west wall. The wood burning stove is fully functional, as it is the only source of heat used for the building during the winter months.

The history of the Office Bar is somewhat vague. Nobody I talked to knew exactly when the bar first opened, but there seemed to be a consensus opinion that it's been around since at least 1920. Debbie and Jan Rukavina bought the business in 1987. They changed the name from the Ashland Bar to the Office Bar, but that's about all the history I was able to obtain. Debbie and Jan may or may not still be operating the bar when you arrive. When I last spoke with them in September, 1996, they indicated the business was in the process of being sold.

Although it's nothing of great historical significance, the Office Bar did play a role in the Great American Drive of 1995. The Great American Drive was an actual cattle drive from Texas to Miles City, Montana that was inspired, at least in part, by the movie Lonesome Dove. During a stretch of inclement weather the week before Labor Day in 1995, the people taking part in the cattle drive had a huge party at the Office Bar. When the weather finally broke, a lot of hungover people rode out of town with some great memories of Ashland and the Office Bar.

The regular customers consist of local ranchers, farmers, loggers, and Native Americans from the North Cheyenne Indian Reservation. A lot of the tourists who stop in during the summer mention they heard about the place from friends or relatives. The Office Bar is also a popular stop for bikers on their way to or from the annual bikers rally in Sturgis, South Dakota. Visiting deer and antelope hunters find the atmosphere appealing as well. There's typically a very friendly crowd on hand, and those who get out of line find their names on the 86 list posted behind the bar. There may be new owners when you arrive, but I doubt the fun atmosphere at Ashland's Office Bar will ever change.

JERSEY LILLY BAR AND CAFE

OWNER: Jerry J. Brown		**LOCATION:**	**Ingomar**
HOURS: 7:00 a.m. to 2:00 p.m. Daily		**PHONE:**	406-358-2278
HAPPY HOUR: 7:00 to 7:00 Mon - Fri		**BEER:**	Domestics
GAMBLING: Video Poker		**AMUSEMENT:**	Video Game; Horseshoes; Volleyball
LIVE MUSIC: Occasionally		**FOOD:**	Full Menu Cafe

The Jersey Lilly is on the west side of the gravel street leading into Ingomar from Highway 12. You shouldn't have any trouble recognizing the place, because there's not another one like it in Montana. Just a few of the unique features about the Jersey Lilly include the wooden hitching posts out front, the wood slat awning that covers the boardwalk on the east and south sides of the building, the piece of rope that serves as the door handle, and the open air toilets. If nature calls while you're at the Jersey Lil', don't look for rest rooms inside the building. They still use outhouses here, so just follow the wooden sidewalk to the appropriate privy (Bull Pen for the men and Heifer Pen for the gals) and get on with your business. Things can get a bit drafty in the winter, but it beats squeezing your legs together until you reach the nearest rest area.

The bar first opened in an old bank building in 1933. Bob Seward bought the business in 1948 and renamed it the Jersey Lilly after Judge Roy Bean's Jersey Lilly Saloon in Texas. Bob's son, Bill, took over in 1958, and over the next thirty-three years, Bill Seward and the Jersey Lilly became almost legendary. Bill's secret bean recipe and his colorful anecdotes are known across Montana. Jerry Brown bought the business in August of 1995, but the legacy of Bill Seward and the Jersey Lilly live on. Bill still comes in, but he tells his stories from the other side of the bar now.

The Jersey Lilly is one of Montana's most famous and most loved taverns. It is truly something you have to experience to appreciate. The famous bean soup is still served, and you will be treated to some of the most interesting stories you've ever heard if Bill happens to be at the bar when you visit. If you don't get a chance to talk to Bill, articles explaining such things as how the bar got its name, Bill's boxing career, the cigarette in the moose's mouth, and the best beans in the west are posted on a glass-encased bulletin board in the large room adjoining the barroom. If you've never been to the Jersey Lilly, it's worth going 100 miles out of your way to spend some time there. Enjoy your visit, and be sure to tell all your friends about the Jersey Lilly in Ingomar, Montana.

Ingomar's Jersey Lilly Bar and Cafe

Top Photo: A wood slat awning covers the wooden walkway on the east and south sides of the building.

Bottom Photo: The open air toilets at the Jersey Lilly.

HATHAWAY BAR

OWNER: Jim Patrick

LOCATION: Hathaway

HOURS: 8:00 a.m. to 10:00 p.m. Mon-Sat
Closed Sunday

PHONE: 406-347-5525

HAPPY HOUR: None

BEER: Domestics

GAMBLING: Video Poker

AMUSEMENT: Pool; Darts;
Video Games

LIVE MUSIC: No

FOOD: Frozen Pizza

The Hathaway Bar is housed in a wooden structure that stands approximately 1/8 of a mile northeast of the Hathaway Interchange (exit 117) off Interstate 94. The barroom is relatively small, but additional seating is available in the adjacent game room. The beautiful antique cash register behind the bar is still in use. The till was made in 1908, but it's still in perfect working condition. The cash register isn't the only antique in the building. Extra beer is stored in an oak cooler that stands in the small room past the rest rooms. Nobody knows how old the cooler is, but Jim Patrick, the owner of the bar, remembers seeing it in a store in Miles City in 1936.

Jim Patrick is a decorated World War II veteran. Jim bought the Hathaway General Store and Post Office in 1946, and he ran the store and served as Postmaster of Hathaway until 1991 when the U.S. Postal Service started providing mail service to the area from Miles City. The part of the building where the barroom now resides originally served as a warehouse for the store. Jim converted the warehouse into a barroom in 1948, but only beer was served for the first nine years. A full liquor license was issued in 1957. Jim added a dance hall onto the west end of the building in 1972, but the old dance hall is used primarily as a game room today. There's no longer enough business to support live music at the Hathaway Bar.

Jim runs a quiet establishment where local farmers and ranchers gather to drink and socialize. Business picks up during the summer tourist season, and visiting hunters and snowmobilers frequent the bar in the winter and fall. Jim said a lot of people running for public office have been to the bar to meet the voters and try to persuade a few votes out of them. A lot of first time visitors show great interest in the replica Calamity Jane outhouse that sits on top of the ice cream freezer in the barroom. This locally-crafted piece of artwork can be most appreciated by opening the door and looking inside. There's nothing that will harm you, but be ready for a good laugh when you open the door.

JIMTOWN BAR

OWNER: Mary and Dean Dillon

LOCATION: Rte. 39, **Jimtown**
(4 Miles N. of Lame Deer)

HOURS: 9:30 a.m. to 2:00 a.m. Daily

PHONE: 406-477-6459

HAPPY HOUR: 6:00 to 7:00 Mon - Fri

BEER: Domestics

GAMBLING: Video Poker/Keno;
Shake-A-Day

AMUSEMENT: Pool; Rodeo; Bump-N-
Run Auto Races

LIVE MUSIC: Occasionally

FOOD: Frozen Pizza; Sandwiches

The Jimtown Bar is four miles north of Lame Deer on Route 39—
just 200 yards north of the Cheyenne Indian Reservation. You
shouldn't have any trouble recognizing the place because the parking
lot is typically filled with hundreds of empty beer cans. There's also
what's been referred to by National Geographic Magazine as the
world's largest pile of beer cans behind the bar. So many cans have
accumulated over the years that the pile has grown higher than the
roof of the building. Don't get too concerned if you see what appears
to be dead bodies laying on the logs in the parking lot. People commonly sleep on the logs, both day and night, regardless of the weather conditions. Needless to say, the Jimtown Bar has an atmosphere all
its own. Even the original barstools, which are nothing more than
tree stumps bolted to the floor, are still used for seating.

The business was established by Jim Allison in 1934, and over the
next sixty years, the Jimtown Bar gained a reputation as the toughest
saloon in Montana. Numerous shootings, stabbings, and brawls have
occurred at the Jimtown Bar. The bar once had such a bad reputation
that most people wouldn't even go near the place for fear of being
killed. The rowdy days at Jimtown continued until Mary and Dean
Dillon bought the business in February, 1986. Mary and Dean are
consistently strict but fair with their customers, and they've gotten
things to the point where you don't have to fear for your life when
you walk through the front door. These days, nobody will generally
bother you unless you're looking for trouble.

Since Mary and Dean took over, they have added a pawn shop, a
rodeo arena, and a bump-n-run dirt track to the business. The bump-
n-run track is used for automobile races in the summer and snowmobile races in the winter. The new attractions and the new management style proved to be very positive changes. In 1987,
Hollywood film makers were impressed enough to shoot the opening
scene for the movie Pow Wow Highway in the barroom. If you're
looking for an old west experience, look no further than the Jimtown
Bar. It's definitely an experience you won't soon forget.

LONGHORN BAR AND STEAK HOUSE

OWNERS: Gary and Glenna Holm

HOURS: 10:00 a.m. to Closing Daily

HAPPY HOUR: No

GAMBLING: Video Poker/Keno

LIVE MUSIC: No

LOCATION: Rosebud

PHONE: 406-347-5393

BEER: Drafts; Domestics

AMUSEMENT: Pool; Shuffleboard; Video Games

FOOD: Full Menu Steak House

The Longhorn Bar and Steak House is on the main drag in Rosebud. A spacious barroom with a long L-shaped bar resides in the front portion of the building, and a smaller dining room is in the rear. Over 800 hats that were donated by customers over the past several years cover the barroom walls. The "celebrity status" hats hanging from the wall behind the bar include three commemorative caps from recent space shuttle launches, one genuine green beret hat, and an antique trainsman hat.

The history of the Longhorn Bar dates back to around the turn of the 20th century. The building originally housed a mercantile and liquor store. Prohibition didn't stop the sale of liquor at the mercantile, it merely drove it under ground. The Longhorn Bar was issued a liquor license after the infamous 18th Amendment was repealed, and it's been a legitimate saloon ever since. Gary and Glenna Holm bought the business in 1981. They keep the bar open seven days a week, but the dining room is only open Wednesday through Sunday from 5:00 p.m. until 10:00 p.m.

Most of the bar business comes from people who live in and around Rosebud, but the quality of food has become so renowned that people from all over the world have stopped in to eat. Some people stop by chance, and others stop because of recommendations made by friends or relatives. Because of the excellent food and comfortable atmosphere, the Longhorn gets great word-of-mouth advertising. The relatively small dining room promotes conversation among strangers, so people often make new friends while dining.

First time visitors at the Longhorn commonly sign a dollar bill and leave it for Gary to post on the barroom wall. A few years ago, a young man dressed in cowboy garb asked Gary if he could donate a dollar and have it posted with all the others. Gary said "sure", so the man signed the bill, handed it to Gary, and left with some friends. Gary didn't realize he had just been talking to Garth Brooks until he took a moment to read the signature. Garth's dollar bill is still hanging amongst the hundreds of other signed bills on the wall at the Longhorn Bar and Steak House.

DIXON BAR

OWNER: Joanne Schmauch

HOURS: 1:00 p.m. to Closing Daily

HAPPY HOUR: No

GAMBLING: No

LIVE MUSIC: Once a Year

LOCATION: Highway 200, **Dixon**

PHONE: 406-246-3518

BEER: Domestics; Imports

AMUSEMENT: Horseshoes

FOOD: Grill Items

The Dixon Bar is on the south side of Highway 200 in Dixon. The building is relatively old and the barroom is relatively small, but the Dixon Bar is probably the most popular tavern within a fifty mile radius. A straight wooden bar and an antique back bar stand along the east wall, and two small tables and a wooden bench are against the north wall. That's really about all there is to the place except for the rest rooms.

The business was established as Bob's Place in 1944. The bar initially operated out of another building in town, but a staunch supporter of prohibition bought the building in 1947 and evicted both bar owner and saloon. The existing structure was built in 1910. A blacksmith shop operated from the building until the people of Dixon found themselves in need of a home for their bar. The blacksmith shop moved out, the bar moved in, and everyone lived happily ever after.

Joanne Schmauch has owned the Dixon Bar since 1951. Joanne says there have been some real characters in the barroom over the years, and there's also been some interesting moments. The customers are typically friendly and well-behaved, but Joanne recalls one time during the 1960s when a man announced his presence outside the front entrance by shooting out the window in the door. The barroom customers all ran for the side door as the guy walked in and shot holes in the refrigerator and the door to the women's rest room. Fortunately, nobody got hurt during the ordeal.

Joanne hosts several outdoor keg parties and barbecues during the summer months, but entertainment at the Dixon Bar usually consists of juke box music and conversations between the customers. There's always a steady crowd on hand, but rarely a big crowd. There's no one reason why the bar is so popular, but Joanne is doing something right because the New Yorker Magazine published three poems about the Dixon Bar in 1971. Perhaps it's Joanne's famous Dixon Burger, a hamburger with a fried egg on top of it, that keeps people coming back. Joanne says first time visitors usually have so much fun they end up staying much longer than they had planned. I can't pinpoint exactly why this is, but I often find myself wanting to return to the friendly confines of the Dixon Bar.

COWBOY BAR

OWNERS: Bill Beckner & Mike Blake

HOURS: 9:00 a.m. to 2:00 a.m. Mon-Sat
10:00 a.m. to 2:00 a.m Sunday

HAPPY HOUR: 6:00 to 7:00 Mon - Fri

GAMBLING: No

LIVE MUSIC: Every Friday Evening

LOCATION: Main Street, **Hot Springs**

PHONE: 406-741-2900

BEER: Drafts; Domestics; Imports

AMUSEMENT: Pool; Darts; Pinball; Video Game; Volleyball; Horseshoes

FOOD: Delivery Available

The Cowboy Bar is on Main Street in Hot Springs. The barroom has recently been refurbished, so the facility is very modern except for the area immediately around the bar. An antique wooden bar and back bar stand along the east wall toward the front of the room, and a nice collection of beer steins and porcelain liquor decanters is on display on the wooden shelves behind the bar. The ten barstools more closely resemble the seating you would find at a soda fountain than a bar. The padded seats swivel, but they have no back rest. The single metal posts supporting the seats are permanently affixed to the floor, so you can't move the stools around the room. The lawn behind the building has a patio, a wooden deck, and a barbecue pit to accommodate outdoor festivities.

The Cowboy Bar is the oldest of Hot Springs' three saloons, having been in business since 1910. "Wild" Bill Beckner and Mike "Blazing" Blake bought the business in January, 1996. Bill says he got his nickname while serving in the military because he was sometimes rude to the officers, and Mike was dubbed Blazing Blake after he inadvertently shot a hole through the door of Bill's pickup truck. Mike is more of a silent partner, so Bill and his mother, "Calamity" Jean, run the bar. I didn't ask how the nickname Calamity came about, but I'm sure there's a story behind it.

Bill says the Cowboy Bar had its share of rowdy customers before he and Mike bought the place, but they have gradually gotten things under control. It took a lot of work to get the customers to behave themselves and finish renovating the barroom, but Bill has been successful at both. There's typically a friendly crowd these days, and Bill is quick to intervene if trouble starts. The Cowboy Bar has live music every Friday, and a special event is held once a month with music, contests and cash prizes. You probably won't get to meet the man who shot an innocent pickup truck, but you can always stop in and say hello to Wild Bill and Calamity Jean at the Cowboy Bar.

MONTANA BAR

OWNER: Lorre King

HOURS: 12:00 a.m. to 2:00 a.m. Daily

HAPPY HOUR: 5:00 to 6:00 Mon - Fri

GAMBLING: No

LIVE MUSIC: Occasionally

LOCATION: Main Street, **Hot Springs**

PHONE: 406-741-9694

BEER: Drafts; Domestics

AMUSEMENT: Pool; Darts

FOOD: Grill Items

The Montana Bar is on the corner of Main and Arlee Streets in Hot Springs. The barroom houses one of the longest single-piece bars in Montana at a whopping fifty-five feet in length. With a bar that long, it's unlikely all the barstools will be occupied when you arrive; however, they've installed five booths along the west wall just in case. A wooden back bar stands behind the bar against the east wall. A fairly extensive collection of old beer bottles and several antique kerosene lamps line the top of the back bar. Some of the bottles have been in the barroom since the 1960s.

The Montana Bar was established in 1937. Like many other taverns in the area, murals with old west scenes have been painted on the barroom walls. The murals were done in the 1950s by an Idaho artist named Joe Breckenridge. I'm told Mr. Breckenridge used unconventional methods to paint his murals, such as sponges and two inch brushes commonly used for painting houses. His methods were effective, however, and they earned him enough money to continue on with his profession. By the time Mr. Breckenridge left Western Montana, he had left his mark on many of the barroom walls in this region of the state.

Lorre King has owned the Montana Bar since 1983; however, the business has been in her family since 1966. Lorre operates a family-oriented establishment where people of all ages gather to eat, drink, and socialize. The customers at the Montana Bar are locals, for the most part, and everyone is friendly and well-mannered. There have been a few occasions where horses and motorcycles were ridden through the barroom, but these antics were all done in fun.

Lorre is very customer-oriented. She sponsors a dart team in the local league, and she keeps her drink prices at a very reasonable level. The last time I checked, you could still get a twelve ounce can of beer for $1.25, and draft beer was 75 cents. Reduced prices on drinks go into effect during happy hour, which runs from 5:00 p.m. until 6:00 p.m. Monday through Friday. Lorre also serves exceptional hamburgers, which is the main reason entire families commonly stop by for meals.

PIONEER BAR

OWNERS: Beau and Todd Sanders

HOURS: 8:30 a.m. to 2:00 a.m. Daily

HAPPY HOUR: 5:00 to 6:00 Mon - Fri

GAMBLING: No

LIVE MUSIC: Approximately Monthly

LOCATION: 413 Main, **Hot Springs**

PHONE: 406-741-2416

BEER: Drafts; Domestics; Imports

AMUSEMENT: Pool; Darts

FOOD: Fried Chicken

The Pioneer Bar is at 413 Main Street in Hot Springs. The barroom has a straight wooden bar facing the east wall, and a beautiful antique liquor cabinet stands behind the bar. The interior walls are mostly covered with rough cut boards, providing a rustic appearance and a comfortable atmosphere. Several hand-painted murals cover the top of the walls in the east and center portions of the room. An Idaho artist named Joe Breckenridge painted the murals in the 1950s.

The business was established in 1935 as The Club Beer Parlor. It also operated under the names Log Cabin Tavern and Ted's Place before becoming the Pioneer Bar in 1947. The original barroom was relatively small compared to the size it is today, but I'm told the area immediately around the bar really hasn't changed much since the business first opened. The center portion of the existing barroom was once a barber shop, and the west side previously housed a cafe. The barroom first expanded into the old barber shop, and it took over occupancy of the entire building after the cafe went out of business.

The Pioneer Bar has had several owners over the years, and the bar owners have always taken a personal interest in their customers and the community. The people of Hot Springs are very compassionate and quick to lend a helping hand. The bar gets most of its business from local residents, but visitors who come to town to soak in the natural hot spring pools stop in occasionally. It doesn't matter where you're from, because everyone gets treated in the same friendly manner at the Pioneer Bar.

Beau and Todd Sanders have owned the Pioneer Bar since 1984. Like their predecessors, Beau and Todd treat their customers well and strongly support community events. There's not a wide selection of food items at the Pioneer, but the fried chicken and jo jo's are some of the best you will find anywhere. The busiest time of year at the Pioneer Bar is during the annual Hot Springs Homesteader Days celebration on the 2nd weekend in June. The bar also gets busy during a community street dance that's held at the end of the summer.

HEREFORD BAR AND RESTAURANT

OWNERS: Don and Beverly Sharp

HOURS: 3:00 p.m. to Closing Daily

HAPPY HOUR: No

GAMBLING: Video Poker/Keno; Shake-A-Day

LIVE MUSIC: Occasionally

LOCATION: Highway 200 W, **Noxon**

PHONE: 406-847-2635

BEER: Drafts; Domestics; Imports; Microbrews

AMUSEMENT: Pool; Darts; Volleyball; Horseshoes

FOOD: Full Menu Restaurant

The Hereford Bar and Restaurant is approximately four miles west of Noxon on Highway 200. The barroom in the middle of the building is flanked on the west by a dining room and on the east by a dance hall and game room. The large stone fireplace in the dining room creates a comfortable environment for the dinner guests, and the wooden deck off the west side of the building enables customers to be served outdoors during the summer. The barroom has a straight wooden bar that's separated into two sections. If you can't find an empty barstool, a couple of wooden booths are available along the north wall. Numerous framed photographs of successful hunting and fishing trips cover the barroom walls. After looking at the pictures, I concluded the people around Noxon have bagged just about everything except a sasquatch.

The history of the bar dates back to 1947 when Weare's Service Station obtained a retail beer license to serve construction workers who were building the Noxon Rapids Dam. The original building was a small bar that occupied only the center portion of the existing building. The dining room and the dance hall weren't added until the early 1970s.

Don and Beverly Sharp bought the Hereford Bar and Restaurant in 1986. They promote a family-oriented atmosphere, and the customers are typically friendly and well-mannered. There was a night several years ago when a customer took a couple of shots at another man in the parking lot, but that was only after the guy caught his wife and the other man together in the rest room performing unmentionable acts. Fortunately, nobody got shot during the confrontation.

These days, the Hereford does more restaurant business than bar business. Excellent homemade pizzas are available for dining in or taking out, and dinner specials are offered on weekends. The bar stocks a wide assortment of beers, including several different microbrews and imports. Cabin rentals and RV hookups are also part of the business, which makes it convenient for travelers and visiting outdoors enthusiasts.

BOAR'S BREATH

OWNER: Don and Gail Peterson

HOURS: 11:00 a.m. to 2:00 a.m. Daily

HAPPY HOUR: No

GAMBLING: Plastic Pigs Shake-A-Day

LIVE MUSIC: No

LOCATION: 890 Highway 200, **Noxon**

PHONE: 406-847-2082

BEER: Drafts; Domestics; Imports; Microbrews

AMUSEMENT: Horseshoes

FOOD: Full Menu Restaurant

The Boar's Breath is on Highway 200 between Noxon and Heron. The relatively small barroom is completely finished in natural wood, with the exception of the concrete floor which is normally covered with crushed peanut shells. The rustic atmosphere in the barroom is enhanced by the vaulted wooden ceiling and a stone fireplace. Seating space is limited to the twenty or so stools at the horseshoe-shaped bar and three wooden picnic tables in the north side of the room.

Don and Gail Peterson established the Boar's Breath in July, 1995. The business was named for their pet potbellied pig and mascot of the bar, Sudsarella. The pig became a popular attraction at the Boar's Breath because she used to roam about the barroom foraging through the empty shells for peanuts. Suds eventually grew to a weight of 300 pounds on her steady diet of nuts, but she got to be such a nuisance that she is now banned from the barroom altogether. Suds still occasionally sneaks through the front door, and it can be quite a trick to persuade her to leave. Although Suds loves the peanuts, she now spends most of her time foraging for food around the yard outside the bar.

The Boar's Breath is a popular bar and restaurant among residents of the surrounding communities, and people from all over the country have stopped in just to see Suds. Sudsarella is probably the most photographed pig in Montana. Don and Gail don't allow the pig in the barroom anymore, but they keep their customers happy with excellent food, cold beer, and free peanuts. The Boar's Breath gives away an average of fifty pounds of peanuts every day. All-you-can-eat dinner specials are offered three nights a week, and ladies can get any drink they choose for 99 cents on Saturdays. Hog Heaven and Hog Spit Shooters are the names of the specialty drinks of the house, and Don uses plastic pigs instead of dice for his shake-a-day to ensure the pig theme stays alive. Beer is kept on ice in an open stainless steel tub behind the bar, so you know your beer won't be warm. The pig's been banned from the barroom, but you can still stop by and see Suds in her turbo-heated pig condo outside the bar.

**Sudsarella, the official mascot of the
Boar's Breath near Noxon.**

TOBY'S TAVERN

OWNER: Toby Therrian   **LOCATION:** Railroad Street, **Noxon**

HOURS: Variable   **PHONE:** 406-847-2351

HAPPY HOUR: None   **BEER:** Drafts; Domestics

GAMBLING: Video Poker/Keno   **AMUSEMENT:** Pool; Video Games

LIVE MUSIC: No   **FOOD:** Grill Items

Toby's Tavern is on Railroad Street in Noxon. The barroom might best be described as half tavern and half museum because just about every trinket imaginable is on display inside the building. For starters, hundreds of wooden beer steins hang above and behind the bar. A plexiglass display case near the front entrance holds several porcelain liquor decanters, and numerous beer tap handles are mounted to the top of the display case. Various hats, photographs, big game head mounts, signs, and items you wouldn't envision in your wildest dreams cover every square inch of the walls. To top it all off, 10,171 Susan B. Anthony (SBA) dollar coins are embedded in the walls and the wooden bar top.

The business was established as the Noxon Beer Parlor in 1934. Toby Therrian bought the bar in August, 1969 and changed the name to Toby's Tavern. The only decorative items in the building when Toby bought the place were the two large paintings on the west wall. Things certainly have changed over the years. Toby began collecting the SBA coins in 1979, and by 1987, he was ready to put them on display. 1,618 coins were embedded in the wooden bar top, and 8,553 are embedded in the walls. Most of the other items were donated by customers, but Toby buys at least one interesting piece to add to his collection every year.

Toby and his daughter, Gail, run the bar in a very informal manner. They have no set hours of operation, but the tavern is usually open by noon. Even with all the stuff hanging around, the place is kept very clean and organized. Space limitations now prevent people from bringing items in for display on the walls, but there is some unoccupied space on the ceiling. Customers are encouraged to put a tack through a signed dollar bill, wrap a 50 cent piece in the dollar, and throw the whole mess toward the ceiling. If, on the first try, the dollar bill sticks and you catch the coin as it drops, you win a free drink. Special parties aren't a common occurrence at the tavern, but there's already an "Everything Free but What You See" party planned to celebrate Toby's 30th anniversary at the bar. If you're anywhere near Noxon on January 1, 2000, be sure to stop and join in on the festivities.

WAUNEGAN BAR AND CAFE

OWNERS: Larry and Sharon Larkin

HOURS: Noon to Closing Daily

HAPPY HOUR: No

GAMBLING: Video Poker/Keno

LIVE MUSIC: Rarely

LOCATION: Railroad St., **Noxon**

PHONE: 406-847-2248

BEER: Drafts; Domestics; Imports; Microbrews

AMUSEMENT: Darts; Shuffleboard

FOOD: Full Menu Cafe

The Waunegan Bar and Cafe is on Railroad Street in Noxon. The barroom has a long L-shaped bar and a wooden back bar along the west wall toward the front of the room. Several collectors item liquor decanters line the top of the back bar, and four collectors series Hamm's Beer mirrors hang from the east wall. An antique piano stands against the wall at the back of the room. The piano was manufactured in the late 1800s, but it's kept in tune for those rare occasions when someone drinks enough courage to play for the other guests. The western outdoor scenes depicted in the murals on the barroom wall were done by a local artist in 1981. The murals are nice, but customers can experience an even nicer western outdoor scene in the enclosed yard off the east side of the building.

The Waunegan Bar was established in 1951 during the construction phase of the Cabinet Gorge Dam. The Dam is west of Noxon on the Clark Fork River near the Montana-Idaho Border. Photographs of the construction site before, during, and after the dam was built are on top of the back bar. A couple of interesting pictures of the Cabinet Gorge area have also been built into the back bar. The photographs were placed behind glass plates that are illuminated from within the wooden back bar. Light projects through the pictures, creating an image similar to a slide projector.

Larry and Sharon Larkin have owned the Waunegan Bar since 1980. They operate a friendly establishment where people gather to socialize with friends. A variety of items are available from the grill, but the broasted chicken and homemade pizzas are the big sellers at the Waunegan. The bar also stocks a large assortment of beers to help you wash down your meal.

The Waunegan Bar is managed as a community-minded business. The bar takes part in Noxon's annual Easter Egg Hunt, 4th of July Parade, and Invitational Basketball Tournament. A Christmas Party is held at the Waunegan each year, complete with gift exchanges and a visit from Santa Claus, and they also sponsor a co-ed Snow Bowl football game on Super Bowl Sunday. After the Snow Bowl, the players gather at the Waunegan Bar to warm up and watch the professional teams play.

PAIR-A-DICE BAR

OWNERS: Doug and LeeAnn Overman

LOCATION: Highway 200, **Paradise**

HOURS: Noon to 2:00 a.m. Daily

PHONE: 406-826-3413

HAPPY HOUR: 5:30 to 7:30 Daily

BEER: Drafts; Domestics; Imports; Microbrews

GAMBLING: Video Poker/Keno; Shake-A-Day

AMUSEMENT: Pool; Darts; Snooker; Foosball; Horseshoes; Volleyball

LIVE MUSIC: Occasionally

FOOD: Full Menu Steak House

The Pair-A-Dice Bar is on the north side of Highway 200 in Paradise. The barroom resides in the front part of the building, and a dance hall/dining area is housed in the adjoining room. The barroom decor is rustic, with rough cut boards covering the walls and ceiling. Two wagon wheel chandeliers provide illumination, and heat is supplied by a wood burning stove. A straight wooden bar faces the north wall, and a few tables are spread across the floor. The sliding partition between the barroom and dining room is opened during the evening hours, providing ample seating space for the dinner guests.

The history of the business dates back to 1924 when the Green Shingle first opened. There were no saloons in Paradise at that time, so a local railroad worker decided to build a small bar just outside the city limits. I'm not certain why Paradise had no saloons at the time, but I assume it was because prohibition was in effect. Regardless of the infamous 18th Amendment, the Green Shingle was a prosperous business. Paradise was a dividing point for railroad crews, and the railroad hands were anxious to boost their spirits with alcohol when they arrived in town. The Green Shingle provided just the boost they needed. The bar went through several owners and several name changes through the years. It finally became the Pair-A-Dice Bar in 1967.

Doug and LeeAnn Overman bought the business in 1989. They keep a large selection of domestic, microbrewed, and imported beers on hand, including the very popular Guiness and Harp on tap. Doug and LeeAnn also serve exceptional meals. Homemade soups are available throughout the day, and the Big Hurt, a forty-eight ounce steak with all the trimmings, is the featured dinner item. Parties of up to six people can feast on a single Big Hurt. Doug informed me nobody has ever eaten an entire Big Hurt at one sitting, and he has a standing offer of $100.00 to the person who can finish off the entire meal.

QUINN'S HOT SPRINGS

OWNERS: John & Michele Hayder and John & Johnnie Leinan

LOCATION: Highway 135, 5 Miles South of **Paradise**

HOURS: 8:00 a.m. to Closing Daily

PHONE: 406-826-3150

HAPPY HOUR: No

BEER: Drafts; Domestics; Imports; Microbrews

GAMBLING: Video Poker/Keno

AMUSEMENT: Pool; Horseshoes

LIVE MUSIC: Approximately Monthly

FOOD: Full Menu Restaurant

Quinn's Hot Springs is five miles south of Paradise on Highway 135. The entire business consists of the bar, restaurant, campground, cabin rentals, general store, public laundry and shower facilities, and naturally fed hot pools. The bar and restaurant are housed in a log structure that stands approximately 100 yards off the highway. The barroom has a rustic appearance and a comfortable atmosphere. The vaulted wooden ceiling is supported by wooden rafters, and the sections of the walls that aren't made from logs are finished in natural wood. A J-shaped bar is in the west side of the room, and several tables are spread across the floor. There's also a spacious dance hall attached to the east side of the barroom. A wooden deck surrounds the large outdoor pool that's accessible through the door in the south wall of the barroom.

Quinn's Hot Springs was established in 1885 by Martin Quinn, an Irish Immigrant and miner. Mr. Quinn discovered the springs while conducting a survey in the area, and he quickly staked his claim to the property and established a residence. People soon started coming to the hot springs to be cured of "various afflictions" in the mineral baths, and Mr. Quinn soon became known as Dr. Quinn. A bar and restaurant were built on the property by Martin Quinn's grandsons in 1948. The original barroom was in the part of the building that now houses the restaurant. The present-day barroom was built in the 1970s, and the dance hall was added in the late 1980s.

John and Michele Hayder and John and Johnnie Leinan now own Quinn's Hot Springs. The restaurant is open for breakfast, lunch, and dinner daily, and dinner specials are available seven nights a week. Prime rib is the specialty of the house, and the bar stocks an extensive selection of domestic and microbrewed beers. People from all over the world have visited Quinn's Hot Springs, but locals frequent the bar and restaurant as well. It's a beautiful place in a beautiful setting, but Quinn's Hot Springs is not a resort that caters solely to the wealthy.

NAUGHTY PINE SALOON

OWNER: Audie Hanley

LOCATION: Hwy. 200, **Trout Creek**

HOURS: Noon to Closing Daily

PHONE: 406-827-3282

HAPPY HOUR: 5:00 to 6:00 Mon - Fri

BEER: Drafts; Domestics; Imports; Microbrews

GAMBLING: Video Poker/Keno; Shake-A-Day

AMUSEMENT: Pool; Darts; Horseshoes; Volleyball

LIVE MUSIC: At Least Monthly

FOOD: Grilled, Char-Broiled, & Deep Fried Foods

The Naughty Pine Saloon is on the north side of Highway 200 in Trout Creek. The barroom has a high vaulted ceiling, and a mezzanine surrounds the floor on three sides. Several trophy-sized big game head mounts hang from the walls. I'm told a couple of the deer and elk mounts made the Boone and Crockett Record Book. A horseshoe-shaped bar stands along the east wall, and several booths line the wall on the north side of the barroom. An outdoor deck leads to a spacious back yard on the south shore of Noxon Rapids reservoir.

The building that houses the saloon was previously used as a mechanic's shop. In 1983, the mechanic's shop was renovated into a tavern, and the Naughty Pine Saloon was born. Over the years, the back yard has become an integral part of the business. Boaters often tie their boats off at the dock on the shoreline and follow the lighted stairway and boardwalk through the back yard to the bar. Once inside, the boaters kick back and relax with a drink. There's also a barbecue pit, volleyball court, and horseshoe pits in the yard to entertain people during the many outdoor festivities held at the Naughty Pine.

Audie Hanley bought the Naughty Pine Saloon in May, 1996. Audie completely renovated the barroom, and he also started serving meals. The seating capacity was expanded with the addition of the mezzanine and the horseshoe-shaped bar. It turns out the extra chairs were needed, because it didn't take long for word to spread about Audie's char-broiled New York and Ribeye steaks. People from all over Western Montana and Northern Idaho now stop in for the steaks. Besides being a great place to eat and drink, the Naughty Pine serves as the headquarters for local and regional bass fishing tournaments on the Noxon Rapids Reservoir. With the dock in the back yard and the outdoor facilities on the shore of the lake, the Naughty Pine Saloon is a favorite stop for professional and amateur fishermen. It's also a great stop for the average Joe off the street.

WAYSIDE BAR

OWNERS: Dave and Sheryl Schopp

LOCATION: Hwy. 200, **Trout Creek**

HOURS: Noon to 2:00 a.m. Daily

PHONE: 406-827-9996

HAPPY HOUR: 5:00 to 6:00 Mon - Fri

BEER: Drafts; Domestics; Imports; Microbrews

GAMBLING: Video Poker/Keno; Shake-A-Day

AMUSEMENT: Pool; Darts

LIVE MUSIC: No

FOOD: Full Menu Cafe

The Wayside Bar is on Highway 200 in Trout Creek. The barroom has a vaulted ceiling covered with hand-split cedar boards. A long L-shaped bar stands along the south wall, and several small tables are spread throughout the room. A large set of moose antlers hang from the wall above the front entrance, several sets of deer and elk antlers project out from the ceiling beams, and there's even a couple of mounted deer's butts amongst the antlers. Outdoor facilities include a wooden gazebo and an unsheltered wooden deck.

The Wayside Bar was established in 1956 during the construction phase of the Noxon Rapids Dam. The bar originally operated out of a small building that stood just west of the present-day structure. A framed photograph of the original bar is on the south wall near the entrance to the men's room. Construction on the existing building was completed in 1972. Dave and Sheryl Schopp bought the business in July, 1981. They added the cedar ceiling, a new kitchen, the gazebo, and the wooden deck during a major renovation project that began in 1983.

Dave and Sheryl promote a family-oriented atmosphere at the Wayside Bar. A steady local clientele keeps the place going throughout the year, and tourists, hunters, and fishermen provide a boost to the business during the summer and fall. The customers are always friendly, and it's common for entire families to be at the bar during the afternoon and evening hours. The menu features 1/2 pound hamburgers, and the hot pepper cheeseburger has become a very popular menu item. As an added benefit, Dave and Sheryl serve free coffee with every meal.

Friday nights are the normally the busiest times at the Wayside Bar. Things also get pretty hectic during the town's annual Huckleberry Festival on the 3rd weekend in August and during local bass fishing tournaments. The nearby Noxon Rapids Reservoir has some of the best bass fishing in Montana, but I get the feeling the fishermen would sometimes rather be at the Wayside Bar than on the lake.

ANTELOPE TAVERN

OWNER: Barbie Ueland

LOCATION: Main Street, **Antelope**

HOURS: 8:00 a.m. to 2:00 a.m. Daily

PHONE: 406-286-9231

HAPPY HOUR: No

BEER: Domestics

GAMBLING: Video Poker/Keno

AMUSEMENT: Darts

LIVE MUSIC: No

FOOD: Full Menu Grill

The Antelope Tavern is on Main Street in Antelope. You can see the building as you pass by the town on Route 16. A relatively small barroom resides in the west side of the building, and for lack of a better term, a "banquet room" is housed in the addition on the east side. An antique wooden bar and matching back bar stand along the west wall of the barroom. The long rectangular mirror in the hand-crafted back bar has rounded corners at the top of each end that follow the arch of the woodwork. The bar and back bar were shipped to Northeastern Montana via steamboat up the Missouri River. I'm told both pieces resided in a bar in Bainville for fourteen years before being moved to Antelope by team and wagon.

The history of the Antelope Tavern dates back to 1911 when the Gold Dollar Saloon first opened. The saloon was forced to close during prohibition, so a meat market, grocery store, and farm implement dealership operated out of the building for at least the next fourteen years. After prohibition ended, the building once again became a saloon. The bar has changed hands several times over the past half century. Barbie Ueland bought the business in July, 1994, and she continues to operate it today.

The Antelope Tavern is a friendly place where local residents gather for coffee in the mornings and for drinks after work. It's also a popular place for people to have lunch. The grill is open from 9:00 a.m. to 1:00 a.m. daily. Breakfast is served throughout the day, and lunch specials are offered during the week. The omelets have become known as somewhat of a house specialty, but all the food is good.

Some of the older residents in the area fondly recall a local gal known as Pistol Packing Mama who tended bar at the Antelope Tavern during the 1940's. During her tenure as bartender, Pistol Packing Mama occasionally discharged her firearm inside the barroom to get the attention of those who had temporarily lost their manners. Apparently, this innovative approach to peace-keeping was effective. I'm told nobody ever got shot, but plenty of people changed their behavior. The bullet holes in the ceiling have all been repaired, but Pistol Packing Mama's legacy lives on at the Antelope Tavern.

CLUB BAR

OWNER: Marilyn Smith

HOURS: 11:00 a.m. to 2:00 a.m. Daily

HAPPY HOUR: 11:00 to 6:00 Mon - Fri

GAMBLING: Video Poker/Keno; Live Poker; Shake-A-Day

LIVE MUSIC: Occasionally

LOCATION: Main St., **Medicine Lake**

PHONE: 406-789-2208

BEER: Domestics

AMUSEMENT: Pool; Darts; Foosball; Shuffleboard; Pinball

FOOD: Fresh Pizza; Grill Items

The Club Bar is housed in the ground-level floor of a two story structure on Main Street in Medicine Lake. The barroom and three adjoining game rooms now occupy the entire lobby-level of an old hotel. Eight hotel rooms are in the second story, but the rooms were in the process of being renovated the last time I stopped in. An antique wooden bar stands near the west wall in the main barroom, and a few tables are available for additional seating. An outdoor beer garden is off the east side of the barroom through the sliding glass doors. The beer garden is actually a concrete slab with a couple of picnic tables on it, but it makes a fine beer garden nonetheless.

The building was originally a hotel that was built in a nearby community known as Flanders. When the railroad came through Northeastern Montana in 1911, the hotel was physically moved so it would be close to the tracks. The building was jacked up from its foundation and placed on a flatbed trailer that was built with heavy timbers and steel wheels. A steam-powered tractor pulled the trailer to Medicine Lake, where the hotel was off-loaded and placed on a new foundation.

Marilyn Smith bought the Club Bar in November, 1993. The building still has much of its original character, and Marilyn plans on having the hotel rooms ready for occupancy in the near future. The decorative tin ceiling that was installed when the hotel was built is still intact in the four rooms on the ground-level floor. The layout of the place reminds me of the hotel lobbies I've seen in western movies.

The bar seems to draw more of an older crowd, but people of all ages stop in for the delicious pizza. There's always plenty of cold beer on hand to help you wash down your meal, and there's occasionally a bottle wrapped in a brown paper bag behind the bar that's labeled *Mystery Shot.* You can buy a mystery shot for 50 cents. It's not bad booze, it's just a brand of liquor that hasn't sold well recently. The Club Bar is the only place I know of where you can get a shot of anything for 50 cents.

311

EIGHT BALL INN

OWNERS: Gerald and Elsie Jensen

LOCATION: Main St., **Medicine Lake**

HOURS: 9:00 a.m. to 2:00 a.m. Mon-Sat
1:00 p.m. to 2:00 a.m. Sunday

PHONE: 406-789-2252

HAPPY HOUR: 2:00 to 6:00 Mon - Fri

BEER: Domestics

GAMBLING: Video Poker/Keno;
Live Poker

AMUSEMENT: Pool; Darts

LIVE MUSIC: Occasionally

FOOD: Full Menu Grill

The Eight Ball Inn is housed in a wooden structure on the south side of Main Street in Medicine Lake. You won't have any trouble recognizing the place, because it's the only blue building in town with the words Eight Ball Inn painted in large white letters above the entrance. The barroom has ample seating space. About a dozen people can be seated at the bar, and plenty of tables are available in the north side of the room. An open dance floor and an elevated bandstand are in the southwest corner of the barroom. The Eight Ball Inn is one of the few taverns I've been to that has two men's rest rooms. You have to be somewhat selective in choosing which one to use, however, because one of the men's rooms has two urinals but no toilet.

The business was established in 1934 as a beer parlor in the old Lake Hotel. In 1938, the bar moved to its present location and operated under the name Hub Bar. The name became the Eight Ball Inn in 1944. Elsie Jensen has been part owner of the Eight Ball Inn since 1981. She and her son, Gerald, now own the business.

Elsie and Gerald operate the business in a community-minded manner. Entire families often gather at the bar for meals, and visiting high school athletic teams and their fans frequently stop by to eat after scholastic sporting events. Sports fanatics can always get current information about their favorite professional teams at the Eight Ball Inn. Each team's win-loss record, standings in their division, and the number of games they stand ahead or behind their competition are updated daily on cardboard signs posted behind the bar.

The Eight Ball Inn serves a variety of items off the grill. Daily lunch specials are offered during the week, and an excellent roasted turkey dinner is served every third Thursday of the month. The roasted turkey is actually served at noon, but they call it a dinner anyhow. You can even get some breaded chicken gizzards if you're looking for something a little out of the ordinary.

HUB BAR

OWNER: Harold Benson

LOCATION: Main Street, **Outlook**

HOURS: 3:00 p.m. to 2:00 a.m. Mon-Sat
1:00 p.m. to 2:00 a.m. Sundays

PHONE: 406-895-2473

HAPPY HOUR: No

BEER: Domestics

GAMBLING: Video Poker/Keno;
Shake-A-Day

AMUSEMENT: Pool; Darts

LIVE MUSIC: No

FOOD: Bar Snacks

The Hub Bar is on Main Street in Outlook. You need to keep in mind the old saying *don't judge a book by its cover* when you first see the place from the outside, because the building's pale green exterior is in no way indicative of what you'll find inside. The barroom is very modern, immaculately clean, and quite organized. A straight bar stands along the south wall in the front portion of the room, and several padded booths are lined against the north wall. A smaller game room and the cleanest public rest rooms I've ever seen in my life are in the rear of the building. The barroom walls are covered with beautifully-finished pine and cedar boards, the linoleum floor is spotless, and the glass brick windows on either side of the front door look like they're brand new. I honestly can't remember ever being in a cleaner barroom.

The Hub Bar was established in 1944. Herbert E. Benson bought the Hub in 1949. Herbert and his son, Harold, operated the bar together for many years, but Harold now runs the bar on his own. The barroom was completely renovated in 1982, but the place is so well-maintained that you would swear the renovations were just completed yesterday.

The Hub Bar serves as the focal point of Outlook. The customers all know each other, and an assumed trust exists among the people that you rarely find these days. If Harold is momentarily away from the bar, the customers feel comfortable serving themselves. They just settle up with Harold when he returns. Most of the bar patrons are volunteer fire fighters, so the place empties out in a hurry when the fire whistle goes off. In fact, they've installed a special "fire phone" in the bar because this is the one place in town where someone is usually available to answer emergency calls. The town fire alarm can be activated from the barroom, so no time is lost if there doesn't happen to be anybody at the fire station. Of course, if the volunteer fire fighters have been in the bar too long, their response time may be somewhat hindered. No need to worry, though; they will eventually find the fire and bring the situation under control.

RESERVE BAR

OWNERS: Loren and Beanie Lee   **LOCATION:**   411 Central Ave, **Reserve**

HOURS: 8:30 a.m. to 2:00 a.m. Daily   **PHONE:**   406-286-5416

HAPPY HOUR: 4:00 to 6:00 Daily   **BEER:**   Drafts; Domestics

GAMBLING: Video Poker/Keno;   **AMUSEMENT:**   Darts
Shake-A-Day

LIVE MUSIC: No   **FOOD:**   Full Menu Cafe

The Reserve Bar is on Central Avenue in Reserve, which is just west of Route 16 on the northeastern point of the Fort Peck Indian Reservation. A relatively small bar stands just inside the front entrance, and several tables are available if you can't find an empty barstool. A cafe also operates out of the building, so it can be a very busy place.

The Reserve Bar was established in 1956. Loren and Beanie Lee bought the business in December, 1994, and they pretty much operate the business by themselves. The Reserve Bar is the only place in town that serves prepared food, but Loren and Beanie don't take advantage of the situation. Noon lunch specials are offered Monday through Friday for the nominal fee of $3.00. The Reserve Bar also sells excellent broasted chicken for dining in or taking out, and homemade soups are available seven days a week during the winter months. As an added service to their customers, Loren and Beanie sell milk and bread at the bar.

The barroom is typically crowded with people who stop by for coffee and sweet rolls in the mornings. Children accompanied by their mothers or grandmothers often stop in for lunch, and entire families wander in during the evenings for dinner. No matter what time of day it is, the customers are always friendly and courteous. Pay no attention to the sign behind the bar that reads "Any Unattended Children Will Be Sold As Slaves". Even though I've only spent a short amount of time at the Reserve Bar, I have a comforting feeling that anyone is welcome, even unattended book writers.

The Reserve Bar serves as a community gathering place and a banquet facility for local parties and celebrations. The bar's motto, "We'll serve 10,000 people...30 at a time", puts into perspective their desire to provide quality service. If you happen to stop by during the winter months, be prepared for flying darts. Dart leagues are popular in this region of the state, and the two electronic boards in the barroom see plenty of action throughout the season. No need for alarm, however, because the folks here are accurate. Even if you do get struck with a stray dart, the tips are made of plastic these days.

CHARLIE'S PLACE

OWNER: Gene Kavon

HOURS: Noon to 2:00 a.m. Daily

HAPPY HOUR: No

GAMBLING: Video Poker/Keno; Shake-A-Day

LIVE MUSIC: No

LOCATION: Main Street, **Westby**

PHONE: 406-385-7405

BEER: Domestics

AMUSEMENT: Pool; Darts; Foosball; Video Games

FOOD: Homemade Pizza; Grilled Foods

Charlie's Place is housed in a wooden structure on Main Street in Westby. A three-sided bar stands in the center of the floor near the front entrance, and plenty of tables are scattered throughout the room. The facility is very modern, and it's kept clean and well-maintained.

Charlie's Place was established in 1982 when Gene Kavon renovated a former bank building into a tavern. In 1984, Gene expanded the barroom to twice its original size by knocking out a wall and incorporating the floor space in the old City Hall Building next door. Things ran smoothly over the first several years, but a fatal shooting occurred at the bar during the late 1980s. The incident involved two men who had been involved in a confrontation earlier in the day at another bar. To make a long story short, one of the men entered the barroom holding a rifle, and the other man stood up from his barstool and approached the guy with the gun in an aggressive manner. A struggle ensued, shots were fired, and the man who had gotten up from his barstool ended up dead on the floor. Fortunately, no other customers were injured during the ordeal. The excitement from the shooting quickly faded, and the atmosphere soon returned to the friendly environment people had become accustomed to.

Gene has always taken a personal interest in his customers. He sponsors teams in local softball, bowling, and basketball leagues, and you can tell by the size and number of trophies on the barroom walls that his teams do well. Since Westby is within ten miles of the Canadian border and just west of North Dakota, Gene gets a lot of business from Canadians and North Dakotans. Residents of Westby provide a steady business throughout the year, but the Canadians come for a change of pace, and North Dakotans are attracted by the gambling and later operating hours. North Dakota law requires bars to close at 1:00 a.m., whereas Montana bars stay open until 2:00 a.m. Also, the time zone changes at the Montana/North Dakota border, so die hard North Dakotan's can get in two extra hours of drinking by driving to Montana. Those North Dakotan's aren't so dumb after all!

315

CRYSTAL BAR

OWNER: Louise Johanson

HOURS: 11:00 a.m. to 2:00 a.m. Mon-Sat
Noon to 2:00 a.m. Sundays
Winter Hours Vary

HAPPY HOUR: 5:00 to 7:00 Mon - Thur

GAMBLING: Video Poker/Keno;
Shake-A-Day

LIVE MUSIC: No

LOCATION: 206 Main St., **Westby**

PHONE: 406-385-7402

BEER: Drafts; Domestics

AMUSEMENT: Pool; Darts;
Shuffleboard

FOOD: Full Menu Cafe

The Crystal Bar is housed in a cinder block and brick building at 206 Main Street in Westby. A straight wooden bar faces the south wall of the barroom, and several tables are spread throughout the room if you prefer sitting away from the bar. The main part of the barroom is fairly spacious, and a separate casino area is housed in a small room off the east side of the bar.

The Crystal Bar is the older of the two taverns in Westby. I don't know when the town was founded, but I'm told the Crystal Bar has been there since the beginning. Louise Johanson has owned the business since 1985. Although this is an older establishment, the place is kept very clean and well-maintained. Attitude Adjustment Period (Happy Hour) at the Crystal Bar runs from 5:00 p.m. to 7:00 p.m. Monday through Thursday. Homemade pizza, burgers, and chicken are available seven days a week, and formal dinners are served on Saturday and Sunday evenings. Steaks and seafood are featured on the dinner menu. The Crystal Bar also serves a great prime rib dinner, but it's only available on an occasional basis.

The regular crowd at the Crystal Bar consists of local residents of the Westby area as well as people from nearby communities in North Dakota and Canada. The customers are friendly and fun-loving. It's not all that uncommon for someone to ride a horse or motorcycle into the barroom, but it's just people having a good time. Perhaps the most interesting event to ever take place at the Crystal Bar was the time a man drove a nail into the top of the bar with his bare hand. As the story was told to me, a man who was passing through town stopped in to have a few drinks, and for some strange reason, the guy decided to drive a nail into the solid wood bar top with his bare hand. It's hard to imagine this actually happening, but the locals will swear to it. Unfortunately, the original bar top has been covered with formica, so you can't see the nail hole.

316

BLUE MOON SALOON

OWNERS: Philip and Lillian Lillegard   **LOCATION:** Route 43, **Divide**

HOURS: 8:30 a.m. to Closing Daily   **PHONE:** 406-267-3339

HAPPY HOUR: None   **BEER:** Domestics

GAMBLING: Video Poker/Keno   **AMUSEMENT:** Pool

LIVE MUSIC: Karaoke Occasionally   **FOOD:** Frozen Pizza

The Blue Moon Saloon is on Route 43 in Divide. The barroom has a straight wooden bar that spans the length of the west wall, and a small dance floor is in the east side. If you need a padded seat, there's a sofa in front of the wood burning stove near the rest rooms. The murals on the barroom walls were painted by Lillian Lillegard, who owns and operates the bar with her husband, Phil.

The history of the bar is somewhat vague, but it is known that the east side of the existing building was once a storage shed for supplies destined for a mine in Idaho. Receipts for items that were purchased as far back as 1893 have been found in the attic. Somewhere along the line, the storage shed was renovated into a bar. An addition was built onto the west side of the building in the early 1940s, and a kitchen and dining room operated out of the addition. The food business apparently wasn't profitable, because the barroom eventually expanded into the west end of the building. The kitchen and dining room were eliminated altogether.

Philip and Lillian Lillegard have owned the Blue Moon Saloon since 1970. Phil was held up at gunpoint and robbed in 1973, but that was the only time he's ever had any real problems at the bar. Phil and Lil are an intriguing couple who keep plenty of interesting gadgets on hand to entertain their customers. I've seen dancing beer cans, a plastic eyeball that rolls around on the bar, and talking puzzles at the Blue Moon Saloon. And that all occurred before I had my first beer of the day.

Celebrations aren't commonly held at the bar, but Phil and Lil usually host the Blue Moon Festival every year in late July or early August. Karaoke music and a barbecue are the big events at the festival, and it typically draws a pretty good crowd. A different Blue Moon Saloon souvenir T-shirt comes out every year, and Phil says people from all over the country stop in to pick up the current year's model. People have been known to drive hundreds of miles out of their way just to buy a shirt. There's really nothing elaborate about the Blue Moon Saloon, but it's a great place to relax and unwind, especially if you've been on the road for a while. They even sell gas if you're running on empty.

D CLUB BAR

OWNERS: Rod and Shirley Archer

LOCATION: Highway 91, **Melrose**

HOURS: 8:00 a.m. to 2:00 a.m (Summer)
11:00 a.m. to Closing (Winter)

PHONE: 406-835-2100

HAPPY HOUR: No

BEER: Drafts; Domestics; Imports; Microbrews

GAMBLING: Video Poker/Keno

AMUSEMENT: Pool; Pinball; Video Games

LIVE MUSIC: Occasionally

FOOD: Frozen Pizza

The D Club Bar is housed in the ground-level floor of a two story wooden structure on the east side of Highway 91 in Melrose. An L-shaped bar stands along the north wall of the barroom, and a game room and dance floor are in the south side of the building. There's nothing fancy about the place, but you can always get a cold beer.

The D Club Bar is in the oldest remaining building in Melrose. The history of the business dates back to the late 1800s when the Melrose Hotel and Saloon first opened. The oldest known photograph of the Melrose Hotel and Saloon is dated 1890, but I wasn't able to find out the exact year it was established. The hotel lobby and a restaurant originally occupied the portion of the building that now houses the barroom. The original barroom was in the small building to the north where a fly shop now resides. At one time, there was a round dance hall called the Snow Shed just north of the hotel building, but the structure was destroyed by fire several decades ago. The hotel stayed in business until the late 1950s. The second floor of the building was used as living quarters for a while, but it is now utilized only as a storage area.

Rod and Shirley Archer bought the D Club Bar in 1992. They have a steady local clientele throughout the year, and visiting sportsmen provide a boost to the business during the summer and fall. The famed Bighole River is only a couple of hundred yards away from the bar, and big game is abundant in the mountains surrounding the community. There's always a friendly crowd on hand at the bar, and the atmosphere is relaxed and comfortable. Several outdoor barbecues are held at the D Club throughout the summer, and impromptu parties seem to get going all the time. The bar is a big supporter of the town's Sewer Days Celebration, which is an annual event commemorating the installation of a sewage system in Melrose. The D Club Bar has live music on the weekend of Sewer Days, and they usually sponsor a Sewer Days Queen candidate. How much more involved in the community can you get than that?

LIVELY'S MELROSE BAR AND GRILL

OWNERS: Burr and Connie Lively   **LOCATION:** Highway 91, **Melrose**

HOURS: 8:00 a.m. to Closing Daily   **PHONE:** 406-835-2711

HAPPY HOUR: No   **BEER:** Domestics; Imports

GAMBLING: Video Poker/Keno; Shake-A-Day   **AMUSEMENT:** Pool; Horseshoes

LIVE MUSIC: Occasionally   **FOOD:** Full Menu Cafe

Lively's Melrose Bar and Grill is on the east side of Highway 91 in Melrose. A moderate-sized barroom resides in the south side of the building, and a cafe is in the north side. The barroom has a Z-shaped wooden bar that either zigs or zags (I'm not sure which is the correct technical term) across the room. The barroom walls and ceiling are finished in wood, and a beautiful river rock fireplace covers the entire wall on the north side of the dining room.

Leonard and Clara Lively established a general store in Melrose in 1939. The store was converted into the Melrose Bar in 1946, and the business has been in the Lively family ever since. The original building was destroyed by fire in 1949, but rebuilding efforts quickly commenced and the bar was soon back in business. Leonard and Clara had both passed away by the time their son, Burr, and his wife, Connie, assumed complete ownership of the business in 1990.

Lively's Melrose Bar and Grill is a friendly place where people of all ages are welcome. A steady local crowd keeps the place going throughout the year, but visiting hunters and fishermen swarm to the area during the summer and fall. Excellent big game hunting and blue ribbon trout fishing are within a stone's throw from Melrose, and people from all over the world converge on the area to test their skills in the great outdoors. Gasoline, diesel fuel, fishing licenses, and fishing tackle are sold at the bar, and a fly shop adjoins the building.

The biggest weekend of the year in Melrose is the annual Sewer Days Celebration when the townsfolk all gather to commemorate the installation of Melrose's sewage system. Lively's Melrose Bar and Grill actively participates in "Montana's Shittiest Weekend", which usually occurs during the first weekend of August. Live music, the crowning of the Sewer Queen, and the traditional burning of an outhouse ceremony are all part of the festivities, and Lively's Melrose Bar and Grill is right in the middle of it all. Sewer Days is something everyone should experience at least once in their lifetime, and so is Lively's Melrose Bar and Grill.

STILLWATER SALOON

OWNERS: Jack and Ross Hanna

HOURS: 11:00 a.m. to Closing Daily

HAPPY HOUR: 4:00 to 7:00 Mon - Thurs

GAMBLING: Video Poker/Keno

LIVE MUSIC: At Least Monthly

LOCATION: Route 419, **Dean**

PHONE: 406-328-6780

BEER: Drafts; Domestics; Imports; Microbrews

AMUSEMENT: Pool; Video Game

FOOD: Full Menu Restaurant

The Stillwater Saloon is housed in a wooden building with a stone foundation on Route 419 in Dean, a small community approximately ten miles west of Fishtail. The saloon is part of a larger business incorporated under the name Montana Hanna's. The Trouthole Restaurant and Fish Montana Fly Shop are also part of Montana Hanna's. The barroom has a huge stone fireplace in the middle of the floor. A long bar with a stone front and a wooden top spans the length of one wall, and large mirrors framed in logs hang behind the bar. The interior walls are finished in rough cut wood, which accentuates the barroom's rustic appearance.

The history of the saloon dates back to the 1940s when the Y Lodge opened in the building where the Trouthole Restaurant now resides. The bar moved to its present location some years later when a new building was constructed. Fire has damaged the barroom on two separate occasions, but the original stone foundation has held up rather well over the years. It's rumored a whorehouse once operated out of the small building between the saloon and restaurant, but that part of the business was closed years ago.

Jack and Ross Hanna have owned Montana Hanna's since 1991. Jeni Guckenberger manages the business for Jack and Ross. Although the saloon may, at first, appear to be in business solely for the tourists who flock to this part of the state, residents of Dean and the surrounding communities provide a steady customer base throughout the year. Dean has its own unofficially elected mayor, vice mayor, and sheriff. Elections are held every two years, and I'm told the population of Dean is so small that nearly every permanent resident holds one of the elected offices. Of course, summer brings tons of tourists to the area, and many of them visit Montana Hanna's. The barroom has live entertainment about twice a month during the summer and once a month during the winter. The restaurant serves lunch and dinner from 11:00 a.m. to 8:00 p.m. during the week and 11:00 a.m. to 9:00 p.m. on the weekends. Although there has been one incident where a man nearly got his nose bit off in a fight outside the barroom, you will normally find a friendly crowd at the Stillwater Saloon.

COWBOY BAR AND SUPPER CLUB

OWNERS: Al Walker and Jim Wallace

HOURS: 10:00 a.m. to Closing Daily

HAPPY HOUR: No

GAMBLING: Video Poker/Keno

LIVE MUSIC: Occasionally

LOCATION: Route 419, **Fishtail**

PHONE: 406-328-4288

BEER: Drafts; Domestics; Imports; Microbrews

AMUSEMENT: Pool; Darts; Video Game

FOOD: Full Menu Supper Club

The Cowboy Bar and Supper Club is on Route 419 in Fishtail. As you walk through the main entrance, the bar is to your right and the supper club is to your left. The building's exterior is your basic metal siding, but the interior is beautifully finished with natural woodwork. The spacious barroom has a long bar that spans the entire length of one wall, and there are plenty of tables and open floor space. Several brands have been burned into the pine boards covering the barroom walls, and an amusing sketch of a cowboy on horseback has been burned into the wooden door.

The business was established as a stage stop and hotel in the early 1900s. Bootlegged booze was sold at the hotel during prohibition, and it's more than just rumored a brothel once operated out of the hotel. The Cowboy Bar began operating as a legitimate saloon after prohibition ended. The barroom had no barstools during the early years, so the customers had to lean over the brass spittoons to reach the bar and drink while standing up. In 1979, the structure that housed the original bar and hotel was destroyed by a fire that burned so hot it blew the plate glass windows out of the building next door. Another building was quickly erected, and the Cowboy Bar reopened in its new home in 1980.

Al Walker and Jim Wallace bought the business in May, 1996. Their customers are mostly local residents through the winter, but tourists by the truckload visit the Cowboy Bar and Supper Club during the summer months. The influx of summer tourists is probably the reason the bar's motto has become "Bring In Your Old Friends And Trade Them In For New Ones". There's indoor plumbing in the building, but they still put ice in the urinal at the Cowboy Bar and Supper Club. Contrary to what some of the locals might tell you, the ice in the urinal is not the same ice they use to mix the drinks. It just so happens the male customers have grown accustomed to watching ice cubes melt while they pee, and complaints are lodged if the supply runs low. It's one of life's simple pleasures, but obviously an important one. I guess the customer is always right.

CARTER'S CAMP TAVERN

OWNERS: Fran and Gordon Curran

HOURS: 8:00 a.m. to 2:00 a.m. Daily

HAPPY HOUR: No

GAMBLING: Video Poker/Keno; Shake-A-Day

LIVE MUSIC: Occasionally

LOCATION: Route 419, **Nye**

PHONE: 406-328-6186

BEER: Domestics; Imports; Microbrews

AMUSEMENT: Pool; Darts; Pinball; Video Game

FOOD: Grill; Fresh Pizza

Carter's Camp Tavern is on the south side of Route 119 in Nye. 1-1/2 story barrooms aren't very common, but Carter's Camp has just that. The bar stands in the back portion of the barroom, where the ceiling is eighteen feet high. The front part of the room has a second story loft above the ground-level floor, making it a 1-1/2 story barroom. It's a unique design, but very functional.

The tavern's history dates back to 1953 when the Corral Bar opened in the building that stands behind the present-day tavern. A couple named Carter bought the bar in the mid 1960s and changed the name to Carter's Camp. When the business moved to it's present location, the building only consisted of the small portion of the barroom where the bar now stands, minus about half of the vertical rise. The building was expanded both horizontally and vertically in 1982. An addition was built onto the east end of the barroom, the roof was raised, and the loft was added.

Fran and Gordon Curran bought Carter's Camp in 1974. Gordon says the customer base averages about 60% local residents and 40% tourists, depending on the time of year. Everyone from TV and movie personalities to local miners have been in the barroom, but they all get treated the same at Carter's Camp. It's a fun place where people go to relax and unwind.

The people at Carter's Camp are great, but there are several other noteworthy aspects about the place. An extensive collection of beer cans and beer bottles, many from companies I've never heard of, lines the barroom walls. Carter's Camp also has a fully functional L-shaped pool table. There's a regular table upstairs, but the one on the main level was built in an "L" shape. Gordon said it was one of only three such pool tables west of the Mississippi when he bought it in 1994. If you don't care for beer can collections or pocket billiards, try tacking a dollar bill to the ceiling above the bar. The ceiling is eighteen feet high, but there's a way to tack a dollar to it without ever getting off your stool. The regular customers or the bartender can tell you how it's done.

BOOMER'S BAR AND CAFE

OWNERS: In Transition

HOURS: 11:00 a.m. to 2:00 p.m. Daily

HAPPY HOUR: 5:00 to 7:00 Mon - Thur

GAMBLING: Video Poker/Keno

LIVE MUSIC: Occasionally

LOCATION: 5 1st Ave SE, **Park City**

PHONE: 406-633-2206

BEER: Drafts; Domestics; Imports

AMUSEMENT: Pool; Darts; Horseshoes

FOOD: Full Menu Cafe

Boomer's Bar and Cafe is on 1st Avenue in Park City. To get there from Interstate 90, take exit 426 and drive into Park City. You will see the bar and cafe on your left just as you reach 1st Avenue. The barroom resides in the east side of the building, and the cafe is in the west side. Both the barroom and cafe are spacious and modern. A large L-shaped bar runs along the north and west walls of the barroom, and several tables are available if prefer some privacy. If you really want some privacy, there's a concrete deck just off the north side of the building.

Boomer's Bar and Cafe opened on Super Bowl Sunday in 1993, shortly after construction of the building was completed. The Valley Creek Bar formerly stood on the property, but it was destroyed by fire in the early 1990's. When I last visited Park City in December, 1996, Boomer's Bar and Cafe was in the process of being sold. Unfortunately, I wasn't able to speak with the new owner prior to the time this book went to print. I don't know what, if any, changes will be made. The bar will still be there, but it may be operating under a different name.

Under the circumstances, it's impossible to know whether the business will be managed as it has been in the past. About all I can do is encourage you to visit the bar and find out for yourself. Traditionally, Boomer's has been a neighborhood tavern where people gather to socialize with friends. The crowds are typically quiet and friendly, so you don't have to worry about fights breaking out every five minutes. Besides the locals, a couple of more famous personalities have visited Boomer's Bar and Cafe. Actor Jeff Kober was born and raised in Park City, and he stops by the bar occasionally. Actor Kevin Bacon also stopped in during the summer of 1994 while he was in the area performing research for a movie.

One thing that I doubt will ever change about Boomer's is the chicken fried steaks. They are so exceptional that in 1994, a publication that rated restaurants named Boomer's chicken fried steaks the best in a three state region. If you're hungry, be sure to stop in and try one.

POP'S INN

OWNER: Jack Wandler

HOURS: 10:00 a.m. to 2:00 a.m. Daily

HAPPY HOUR: 5:00 to 7:00 Mon - Fri

GAMBLING: Video Poker/Keno

LIVE MUSIC: Occasionally

LOCATION: 117 1st Av SW, **Park City**

PHONE: 406-633-2740

BEER: Drafts; Domestics

AMUSEMENT: Pool; Darts; Foosball

FOOD: Bar Snacks

Pop's Inn is at 117 1st Avenue SW in Park City. To get there from Interstate 90, turn off at the Park City Interchange (exit 426), drive into town, and turn right on First Avenue. The bar is on the left-hand side of the street in a cinder block building. The sign above the doorway reads *Pop's Inn...Where the Sidewalk Ends and the West Begins.* As you enter the building from 1st Avenue, it looks like you are about to walk into a small barroom. Once inside, however, you quickly realize the depth of the room is at least three times the width. I would estimate the dimensions of the barroom are about thirty feet wide by ninety feet long. A long bar runs north and south through the front portion of the building, and a game room is in the rear. The interior walls are your basic painted cinder block, but the place is very clean and well-maintained.

The bar got its name from a man affectionately known as Pops, who established the business in an old church building in 1967. I'm told Pops would gladly loan money to anyone who asked for it, and he never had any problem collecting on the loans. This was partly because of the loyalty between Pops and his customers, and partly because people knew damn well that Pops would come looking for them if they didn't pay him back when promised. The church building was destroyed by fire, so another building was constructed and the bar reopened. Unfortunately, this building was also destroyed by fire. The latest rebuilding effort resulted in the flame-resistant cinder block structure that houses the bar today.

Jack Wandler bought the business in May, 1996. Of the two bars in Park City, I would describe Pop's Inn as the basic drinking man's (and woman's) tavern. Jack doesn't serve prepared food, so he doesn't get children in the bar. A few travelers passing through the area occasionally stop by, but the vast majority of Jack's business comes from residents of Park City and the surrounding communities. Pop's Inn is basically a friendly, home town bar where people gather to drink and socialize with friends and neighbors. If you're ever in Park City, it's a great place to stop for a drink.

324

STOCKMAN BAR AND GRILL

OWNERS: Ron and Vicki Thueson

HOURS: 8:00 a.m. to Closing Mon-Sat
10:00 a.m. to Closing Sunday

HAPPY HOUR: No

GAMBLING: Video Poker/Keno

LIVE MUSIC: Occasionally

LOCATION: Fourth & Main, **Rapelje**

PHONE: 406-663-2156

BEER: Drafts; Domestics;
Microbrews

AMUSEMENT: Pool

FOOD: Full Menu Cafe

The Stockman Bar and Grill is housed in a steel-sided building on the corner of Fourth and Main Streets in Rapelje. The barroom has an L-shaped bar, several tables, and plenty of open floor space. The building is relatively new, so everything very modern.

The Stockman Bar opened in 1946. The business originally resided in a two story structure on the south side of Fourth Street, but fire destroyed the building in 1989. In the old bar, dances were held in the second story. On busy nights, the dance floor swayed up and down so much that a person could get motion sickness if they stayed too long. That's not the case anymore, because the floor in the new bar is concrete. The bar was out of business for two years until the former Cenex Station across the street was renovated into the new Stockman Bar and Cafe.

Ron and Vicki Thueson bought the Stockman Bar and Cafe in July, 1995. Like many small town taverns in Montana, the Stockman serves as a community center for the local residents. Adults and kids alike come here since it's the only place in town where you can get a prepared meal. The cafe is open until 10:00 p.m. daily, and lunch specials are offered Monday through Friday. Fresh pizzas are available, and excellent prime rib specials are served on dance nights.

Probably the most interesting thing about the Stockman Bar and Cafe is the rattlesnake rattle collection on the barroom wall. Every year, people bring in the rattles from snakes they have killed and enter them in the weekly, monthly, and annual Biggest Rattle Contests. Weekly winners are awarded a free six pack of their choice, and the biggest rattle of the month and the biggest rattle of the year entitle the proud snake slayer to a free case of beer. At the end of the snake season, which varies depending on the weather, all the rattles that have been brought in are affixed to a piece of cardboard and hung on the barroom wall. This tradition started at the old Stockman Bar in 1975, but the first fourteen years worth of rattles were lost in the fire. The current collection only dates back as far as 1991.

WATERHOLE SALOON

OWNERS: Chris and Diana Hahn

HOURS: 10:00 a.m. to 2:00 a.m. Summer
Noon to 2:00 a.m. Winter

HAPPY HOUR: Varies

GAMBLING: Video Poker/Keno;
Shake-A-Day

LIVE MUSIC: At Least Monthly

LOCATION: Main Street, **Reedpoint**

PHONE: 406-326-9911

BEER: Drafts; Domestics

AMUSEMENT: Pool; Darts; Video Games

FOOD: Grill Items; Pizza;
Chester Fried Chicken

The world famous Waterhole Saloon is on Main Street in Reedpoint. You will easily recognize the place by the sign out front that reads "Waterhole Saloon, Indians and Mountain Men Welcome". Chris and Diana Hahn opened the Waterhole Saloon in 1975, and their slogan "Ain't No City Bar" is an accurate description of the place. Chris and Diana intentionally built the bar to resemble the typical 1860s western saloon. The exterior of the building is log, and the interior is entirely finished in rough cut lumber and logs. The customers are allowed, if not encouraged, to sit back, relax, and put their feet up on whatever piece of furniture they so desire. In a nutshell, there's nothing formal about the Waterhole Saloon.

As you enter town, you'll note a sign proclaiming Reedpoint as the Sheep Drive Capitol of the World. This prestigious title was bestowed upon the community in 1989 when the Waterhole Saloon organized Reedpoint's first annual sheep drive. The event was intended to draw people to town on the same day the Montana Centennial Cattle Drive was scheduled to start. Word of the sheep drive quickly spread, and over 14,000 people showed up to watch 2000 sheep get herded down Main Street. The major TV networks provided national coverage of the event, a picture and three-column story appeared on the next day's edition of the Wall Street Journal, and the media rated the sheep drive as the best one day State Centennial event of the year. The sheep drive is now an annual event that draws an average of 9,000 people to Reedpoint on the Sunday of Labor Day Weekend.

Chris said he and Diana originally planned on running the bar for about five years and then moving on, but they've had so much fun they don't want to leave. One indication of the saloon's popularity among the customers is the thousands Eisenhower and Susan B. Anthony coins that have been pounded into the wooden beams throughout the barroom. People are encouraged to have a good time at the Waterhole Saloon, and those that don't have no one to blame but themselves. The Waterhole Saloon is an absolute must stop if you're traveling between Billings and Bozeman.

Top Photo: The road sign welcoming people to Reedpoint.

Bottom Photo: The world famous Waterhole Saloon.

327

FOUR WINDS INN

OWNERS: Todd and Beth Killen

HOURS: 5:00 a.m. to 2:00 a.m. Daily

HAPPY HOUR: No

GAMBLING: Video Poker/Keno

LIVE MUSIC: Every Sunday Evening
Karaoke Every Friday

LOCATION: Old Hwy. 10, **Greycliff**

PHONE: 406-932-6576

BEER: Drafts; Domestics; Microbrews

AMUSEMENT: Pool; Darts; Horseshoes

FOOD: Ranch House Cooking

The Four Winds Inn is on Old Highway 10 in Greycliff. To get there from Interstate 90, take exit 377 and drive west on the frontage road until you see the bar and cafe on your left. The bar is in the south side of the building, and a cafe is in the north end. The entire facility has recently undergone extensive renovations, so everything is very modern. A straight bar faces the west wall of the barroom, and a spacious dance floor and an elevated bandstand are in the south end of the room. The large black and white photographs of the white-faced steers on the front of the bar were taken when the business first opened in 1946. The photographs formerly hung from the wall in the dance hall.

The business was established under the name Eaton's Inn. Eaton's was a popular truck stop along Highway 10, a major east-west route across Montana before Interstate 90 was built. Over the years, the truck stop gained quite a reputation for prostitution. I've heard from a reliable source that a lot of truckers have been overheard on the telephone at the Four Winds Inn lying to their wives about where they were calling from. For better or worse, the prostitution was phased out during the 1970s.

Todd and Beth Killen bought the business in July, 1996. They spent a lot of time and money renovating the facility, and their efforts show. Both the barroom and dining room were recently expanded, and everything from the carpeting to the wall coverings was replaced. Todd and Beth weren't quite finished with the remodeling when I last visited the Four Winds Inn. Plans were in place to renovate the five cabins on the property during the summer of 1997 and rent them out as lodging facilities.

If you're tired of fast food, you should stop at the Four Winds Inn. Everything prepared in the kitchen is fresh, never frozen, and the beef is hand-cut on the premises. Three different meal specials are offered every day through the summer, and at least two daily meal specials are available at other times. The steaks and roasts at the Four Winds Inn are exceptional. If you like to dance, the Four Winds Inn has live music every Sunday and karaoke-style music on Friday evenings.

MCLEOD BAR

OWNERS: Bob and Claire Bryan

HOURS: No Set Hours

HAPPY HOUR: No

GAMBLING: Video Poker/Keno; Shake-A-Day

LIVE MUSIC: Occasionally

LOCATION: Route 298, **Mcleod**

PHONE: 406-932-6174

BEER: Drafts; Domestics; Imports; Microbrews

AMUSEMENT: Pool; Darts; Video Games

FOOD: Grill; Sandwich Bar

The McLeod Bar, home of the infamous *Silva Devil* (a shot of tequi-la and peppermint schnapps), is on Route 298 in McLeod. It's hard to drive past the place without noticing the large Road Kill Cafe sign above the front entrance. A long curved bar faces the north wall in the front portion of the barroom. The back part of the room houses a hardwood dance floor, an elevated bandstand, and a few wooden booths. A huge bear skin rug hangs from the wall behind the band-stand. The brick fireplace against the south wall and cedar boards covering the ceiling create a rustic appearance and a comfortable atmosphere for the barroom guests.

The McLeod Bar was established in 1945. The bar originally stood about 1/2 mile south in the town of McLeod, but the building was moved in 1958. Bob and Claire Bryan have owned the McLeod Bar since 1989, but the business was for sale as of December, 1996. The bar was operating on limited hours from Noon to closing on Friday, Saturday, and Sunday, but I suspect the hours will be expanded as soon as the business sells.

McLeod is located in the heart of the beautiful Boulder River Valley near the Absaroka-Beartooth Wilderness. Local residents provide a fairly steady business throughout the year, but visiting tourists and outdoors enthusiasts pack the barroom during the summer months. You will see dude ranch guests, hikers, hunters, fishermen, and just everyone else who loves the great outdoors at the McLeod Bar during the summer months. If you're there at the right time, you may even see a few celebrities.

The McLeod Bar sponsors an annual team relay triathalon where people ride bicycles, float down the Boulder River on innertubes, and walk or run to the finish line on an eight mile course. The event is held just for fun, so it's nothing serious. There bar also sells Mcleod Bar/Road Kill Cafe souvenir shirts if you're looking for a unique gift. And speaking of the Road Kill Cafe, they've become famous for their highly delicious hoagies. Excellent burgers and blooming onions (a batter-dipped, deep fried onion) are also served. They don't actually kill it and grill it here, but the food is good nonetheless.

KATY'S WILDLIFE SANCTUARY

OWNER: Katy Resh   **LOCATION:** Highway 89, **Bynum**

HOURS: Noon to 2:00 a.m. Wed-Mon   **PHONE:** 406-469-9231
Closed Tuesday

HAPPY HOUR: No   **BEER:** Domestics

GAMBLING: Video Poker/Keno   **AMUSEMENT:** Pool; Foosball;
                                         Video Games

LIVE MUSIC: Occasionally   **FOOD:** Frozen Pizza

Katy's Wildlife Sanctuary is housed in the old Bynum Bank building on Highway 87 in Bynum. The main barroom has an L-shaped wooden bar that partially extends into the adjoining game room. The floor is made of hardwood slats, and the interior walls are mostly wooden. It's not a fancy joint, but it's a great place to visit.

The Bynum Bank occupied the building from the time it was built in 1911 until the business went under in the early 1930's. The structure sat vacant until 1946 when the Bynum Bar moved in. Katy Resh, a native of the Gulf Coast of Texas, took over the business in August, 1986. It's a long story, but Katy claims she never would have gone to Bynum in the first place if she hadn't consumed an extensive amount of Wild Turkey one night at a bar she ran in Texas. You can hear the complete story the next time you stop by the Wildlife Sanctuary, but to this day, Katy refuses to stock Wild Turkey at her bar. Katy adopted the name Wildlife Sanctuary because of a Moe Bandy song about an imaginary bar with the same name in South Texas. The first few months in Bynum were not easy for Katy. A musician that she had recently fired walked into the barroom one day, pulled out a gun, and took a shot at Katy. Fortunately, Katy ducked out of the way. Unfortunately, the bullet blew the pinky finger off a man who was standing behind her. That's been the only real trouble Katy has ever had at the bar, but it took her a long time to live it down.

Katy is a self proclaimed bullshitter and somewhat of a natural entertainer. She used to sell live bait at the bar, but Katy said she got tired of handling live leaches. It's quite common for Katy and the regular customers to bad-mouth each other and even throw objects at each other. These antics are all done in the name of fun, so don't panic if you happen to see such behavior when you stop in. Katy's is such a fun place that people from all over the world have visited the bar to see for themselves the things they've heard about from friends and relatives. You can hear Moe Bandy's Wildlife Sanctuary song on the juke box at Katy's Wildlife Sanctuary, but you can't get a shot of Wild Turkey.

MIKE'S CLUB TAVERN

OWNERS: Mike and Pat Bayala

LOCATION: Main Street, **Dutton**

HOURS: 11:00 a.m. to 2:00 p.m.
Closed Every Other Sun and Mon

PHONE: 406-476-3422

HAPPY HOUR: 5:00 to 6:00 Fridays

BEER: Drafts; Domestics

GAMBLING: Video Poker/Keno

AMUSEMENT: Pool; Darts; Foosball

LIVE MUSIC: Occasionally

FOOD: Grill Items;
Frozen Pizza

Mike's Club Tavern is housed in a wooden structure on the north side of Main Street in Dutton. To get there from Interstate 15, simply drive into Dutton and look for the bar on your right as you pass through town. The main part of the barroom is in the east side of the building, and a smaller room with a pool table and electronic dart boards is in the west side. A long L-shaped bar partially extends out of the main barroom into the adjoining game room, and additional seating is available at the tables against the east wall. The barroom isn't elaborately decorated, but there's a nice collection of porcelain liquor decanters in the glass display case behind the bar.

The structure that houses Mike's Club Tavern was built in 1935. A grocery store operated out of the building for several years, but sometime during the 1940s, a pharmacy moved into the west side of the building and a bar opened in the east side. The bar survived, but the pharmacy was eventually replaced by a restaurant. Sometime around 1980, the restaurant was closed and the barroom expanded westward.

Mike and Pat Bayala have owned the tavern since 1987. They operate the business in a very informal manner, and their customers appreciate the relaxed environment. Most of the people you will meet at Mike's Club Tavern are residents of Dutton and the neighboring communities, but the bar also does a fair trade with Canadians traveling to and from Great Falls. Visiting hunters and custom cutters also frequent Mike's Club Tavern during the fall. The bar basically serves as a community center for Dutton. Adults, families, and kids are all welcome here, and there's always a friendly crowd on hand.

Mike's Club Tavern does a steady business throughout the week, but the place gets even livelier on the weekends. Perhaps the busiest time of the year occurs during Dutton's Fun Days Celebration, which is always held on the weekend following the Fourth of July. When or why you show up really doesn't matter, because you will always find friendly people, a relaxed atmosphere, and plenty of cold beer.

HEGLAND'S GIBSON LAKE LODGE

OWNERS: Betty, Pat, & Kathy Hegland

LOCATION: Sun River Canyon Road, **Mortimer Gulch**

HOURS: 10:00 a.m. to Closing Daily

PHONE: 406-562-3500

HAPPY HOUR: No

BEER: Drafts; Domestics; Microbrews

GAMBLING: Video Poker

AMUSEMENT: Pool; Video Games

LIVE MUSIC: No

FOOD: Grill Items

Hegland's Gibson Lake Lodge is at Mortimer Gulch in the Sun River Canyon. The best directions I can offer are to follow the Willow Creek Road west out of Augusta, veer right at the Y in the road, and follow the Sun River Canyon Road. Just before you come to the dam, turn right and cross the bridge over the Sun River. Go past the Gibson Reservoir Overlook, and keep driving until you see the lodge on your right. The barroom has a straight wooden bar with a thick top made from planks cut from the center of a tree trunk. A wood burning stove, log bar stools, and log slats covering the front of the bar and the bottom half of the walls create a rustic appearance and a comfortable atmosphere.

Ed and Betty Hegland established Hegland's Gibson Lake Lodge in 1969. Prior to opening the lodge, Ed and Betty lived in the former C. M. Russell house in Great Falls, where Betty was the curator at the C. M. Russell Studio. The Heglands were the last people to live in the house before it became the Russell Museum.

Instead of building the lodge from the ground up, Ed and Betty moved the building that formerly housed the Gopher Bar in Great Falls to Mortimer Gulch. A dance hall was added a few years later, but Ed passed away before the addition was completed. Pat and Kathy Hegland now operate the business, and Kathy tells me they plan on expanding the bar into the addition and finishing it off. The room won't actually be used as a dance hall, but they may finish part of it into lodging facilities.

Hegland's Gibson Lake Lodge is a family-owned, family-operated business. People from around the world have visited the lodge, and the customers are always friendly. If you arrive with an appetite, the Gibson Lake Lodge serves some of the best chicken and beef fajitas you will find anywhere. The meat is barbecued over mesquite coals, providing a flavor second to none. Even if you're not hungry, you're sure to enjoy the relaxing atmosphere, friendly people, and beautiful surroundings at Hegland's Gibson Lake Lodge.

ROSE ROOM

OWNERS: Bob and Dorene Sheeler   **LOCATION:** Main Street, **Pendroy**

HOURS: 5:00 p.m. to Closing Daily   **PHONE:** 406-469-2205

HAPPY HOUR: No   **BEER:** Domestics

GAMBLING: Video Poker/Keno   **AMUSEMENT:** Pool; Video Game

LIVE MUSIC: No   **FOOD:** Full Menu Supper Club

The Rose Room is housed in a brick structure on the south side of Main Street in Pendroy. A moderate-sized barroom resides in the north side of the building, and a smaller dining room is in the south side. If you're interested in antique tools (and who isn't these days), there's a fairly extensive collection hanging from a peg board just inside the front entrance. The original purpose for most of the devices has already been identified, but people still argue over the intended use of a couple of the items hanging from the board.

The building that houses the Rose Room was built in 1917. A bank initially operated out of the building, but it closed in 1933. The old bank vault is still in the building; however, it's been renovated into a kitchen. A gas station and ice cream parlor operated out of the building after the bank closed, and in 1947, a bar called the Bank Inn took over occupancy. Paul Rose bought the bar in 1950 and renamed it the Rose Room. I'm told Paul was a rugged, self sufficient type who once pulled his own tooth while he was bartending. Apparently, the tooth had been bothering Paul for some time, so he slugged down a few shots of whiskey and yanked the tooth with a pair of pliers. The dining room and rest rooms weren't added until 1966. Since that time, the Rose Room has become "Downtown Pendroy's Finest Dining".

Bob and Dorene Sheeler bought the Rose Room in June, 1974. They promote a friendly, family-oriented atmosphere at the bar, and the food draws people from all over Montana. Their dinner menu features steaks and seafood, and the shrimp is some of the best you'll find anywhere. In fact, the food is so good that people have actually landed their private airplanes in the fields around Pendroy just to eat at the Rose Room before continuing on to their final destination. The Rose Room is a very popular spot for formal gatherings such as wedding rehearsal dinners, private parties, and meals prior to high school proms. Weekends are always busy in the dining room, so it's advisable to make reservations. That way, you won't have to wait until a bunch of people who just jumped off a plane finish eating before you can be seated.

LES' BAR

OWNERS: Dick and Susan Snellman

LOCATION: Central & Main, **Power**

HOURS: 8:00 a.m. to 2:00 a.m. Daily

PHONE: 406-463-2461

HAPPY HOUR: 4:00 to 6:00 Daily

BEER: Drafts; Domestics

GAMBLING: Video Poker/Keno; Shake-A-Day

AMUSEMENT: Pool; Darts; Pinball; Video Games

LIVE MUSIC: Karaoke Music Monthly

FOOD: Full Menu Cafe

Les' Bar is housed in a cinder block building on the corner of Main Street and Central Street in Power. A straight bar faces the north wall of the barroom, and about a half dozen tables are spread across the floor. A small room in the middle of the building is used as a grocery store and video rental display area, and two game rooms are in the west end of the building. The larger game room has a pool table, a dart board, and a few small tables, whereas the smaller game room has just enough floor space for a pinball machine and three video games.

Les and Madge Giese established Les' Bar in 1947. Les and Madge used the back part of the building as living quarters, so they didn't have far to travel to get to work. The Giese's operated the business in a very community-minded manner. The environment has always been very friendly, and people of all ages have always been welcome. This philosophy continued after current owners Dick and Susan Snellman bought the bar, and I doubt it will ever change. Susan now organizes Power's Touchdown Football Club, which is an organization devoted to raising money to buy equipment for the high school football team. Local residents join the club by pledging money for every touchdown scored by the home team at home games. A party is held at the bar after every home game, and the players and spectators alike gather for the festivities.

Les' Bar basically serves as the community center of Power. Private gatherings such as birthday parties, anniversary parties, and wedding dances are commonly held at the bar, and several community events are held here throughout the year. The annual community events including a Cinco de Mayo celebration, a Rocky Mountain Oyster feed, and a Christmas Party. Les' Bar enjoys a relatively steady business throughout the year. You can always expect a big crowd during the special events mentioned above and also during the town's annual Harvest Festival in the fall. Probably the greatest thing about Les' Bar is the family-oriented atmosphere. It's definitely a fun place where you can take your entire family for a good time.

334

POWER POLE BAR

OWNERS: Charles and Peggy Pulst

HOURS: 11:00 a.m. to Closing Daily

HAPPY HOUR: 5:00 to 7:00 Daily

GAMBLING: Video Poker/Keno

LIVE MUSIC: Occasionally

LOCATION: 303 Main Street, **Power**

PHONE: 406-463-2350

BEER: Drafts; Domestics

AMUSEMENT: Pool; Darts; Foosball

FOOD: Frozen Pizza

The Power Pole Bar is housed in a cinder block building at 303 Main Street in Power. Assuming you can find Main Street, you shouldn't have any trouble finding the bar. Just look for the building with the Power Pole Bar sign on the roof and you can't miss it. The moderate-sized barroom has a straight wooden bar facing the south wall, and a few tables are lined against the north wall. Rough cut wood and paneling cover the interior walls, and a wood burning stove stands toward the back of the room. There's nothing elaborate about the place, but the facility is maintained in excellent condition.

The business was established in 1929. The original building had a barroom, barber shop, and the only ice cream and public telephone available in Power. Leo's Place was the name of the bar when the first retail beer license was issued in 1933. The name of the business was changed to the H&V Bar in 1954, Bill's Place in 1956, Scottie's Bar in 1963, Our Place in 1971, the Power House Bar in 1976, and finally to the Power Pole Bar in 1977. The business has always been at the same location, but the original building was destroyed by fire in 1972. The cinder block building that now houses the bar was built later that same year, and the bar reopened. Charles and Peggy Pulst bought the Power Pole Bar in 1994, and they continue to operate it today.

The Power Pole Bar is basically a neighborhood tavern where people gather to relax and unwind. Unlike Power's other bar, children are a rare sight in the Power Pole Bar. Pool and darts are popular forms of entertainment among the customers, and the bar sponsors teams for the local leagues. The regular customers are residents of Power and the surrounding communities. Travelers passing through the area occasionally stop by, and visiting hunters and custom cutters provide a boost to the business during the fall. Regardless of who happens to be in the barroom, the customers are always friendly. The Power Pole Bar is not the type of place where you have to worry about people creating problems.

FRONTIER BAR AND SUPPER CLUB

OWNERS: MH, Inc.   **LOCATION:** Highway 2, **Dunkirk**

HOURS: 11:00 a.m to 11:00 p.m. Wed-Mon   **PHONE:** 406-432-3600
Closed Tuesday Except By Special Arrangement

HAPPY HOUR: 3:00 to 6:00 Daily   **BEER:** Drafts; Domestics

GAMBLING: Video Poker/Keno;   **AMUSEMENT:** Pool; Video Games
Shake-A-Day

LIVE MUSIC: Occasionally   **FOOD:** Full Menu Supper Club

The Frontier Bar and Supper Club, home of the *Half-A-Heifer Challenge*, is on the south side of Highway 2 in Dunkirk. The barroom resides in the west side of the building, and a separate dining room is in the east side. The barroom is relatively large, with a straight bar facing the east wall, an elevated bandstand against the west wall, and the largest dance floor in a three county area in the middle of the room.

The Frontier Bar was established in 1948. In its earlier years, the place was quite a road house, complete with big name entertainment, gambling, and prostitution. The customers were a rowdy bunch of characters who sometimes resorted to gunplay to settle their disputes. I'm told a man once tried to shoot his own brother in the stomach during an argument they were having in the barroom. Fortunately, the first shot misfired, and the unarmed brother was able to dodge the second bullet, which went through the bar. Nobody got shot during the ordeal, but the concept of brotherly love took on whole new meaning.

Thankfully, the rowdy days are long gone. Today's customers are mellow and friendly. Seven course meals are served in the dining room from 5:00 p.m. until 10:00 p.m. daily, but any item on the dinner menu can be ordered from the bar throughout the day. The menu features steaks and seafood, and the Taiwan Shrimp is just one of the house specialties. A twenty-four ounce porterhouse steak is on the menu for those with a big appetite, and people with an enormous appetite are encouraged to take on the Half-a-Heifer Challenge. The meal consists of a full pound of ground beef with cheese and all the fixin's on a homemade sourdough bun. A pound of fries accompanies the burger. If you can eat the entire meal in 1/2 hour or less without leaving your chair, you receive the meal and a souvenir T-shirt for free. If you fail in your quest, you pay double the normal price for the Half-A-Heifer Meal. The regular price is only $9.95, so you really don't lose. As of January, 1997, over fifty people had taken the Half-A-Heifer Challenge, and nobody was able to finish the entire meal.

CECIL'S PUB

OWNERS: Cecil and Diane Lazenby

HOURS: 8:00 a.m. to Closing Daily

HAPPY HOUR: No

GAMBLING: Video Poker/Keno

LIVE MUSIC: No

LOCATION: Front Street, **Kevin**

PHONE: 406-337-2495

BEER: Drafts; Domestics

AMUSEMENT: Pool; Video Games; Horseshoes

FOOD: Broasted & Grilled Foods

Cecil's Pub is housed in the ground-level floor of a two story wooden structure at the junction of Route 215 and Front Street in Kevin. A moderate-sized barroom is in the front part of the building, and a seating area and kitchen are in the back. A straight wooden bar faces the north wall of the barroom, and a lone wooden buddy bar stands alongside the pool table in the middle of the floor. The smaller room in the back of the building is a seating area and storage room.

The business was established as Bert's Place by Alberta (Bert) Farris in 1946. The bar is still referred to as Bert's Place by a lot of the local residents. In the early days, there were two propane-heated outhouses behind the bar. I'm told a local man who had been evicted from his apartment took up residence in an outhouse one winter, and he may never have been discovered if Bert hadn't investigated her unusually high heating bill. I never did find out where the man went after Bert evicted him from the outhouse. The name of the business was changed to the Oil Patch Junction in the late 1980s, and finally to Cecil's Pub when Cecil and Diane Lazenby bought the business in September, 1994.

Cecil's Pub is a friendly place where the customers aren't shy about buying a round of drinks for the house. Strangers are always included in the rounds, so be prepared to hoist a few and buy a round occasionally if you plan on visiting. Besides the local crowd, the bar gets some business from travelers and visiting hunters in the summer and fall. Diane says a surprisingly high number of people named Cecil and Kevin stop in because of the name of the business and the name of the town (even though the name of the town is pronounced "Keevin").

As a service to the community, Cecil and Diane sell gasoline and consumable goods at the bar. Cecil's Pub also serves breakfast, lunch, and dinner daily. All the food is good, and their Philly Steak Sandwich has become a very popular menu item. Every Friday, shrimp cocktails are available for $1.50 apiece. The bar also sells some very hot salsa and stuffed olives if you're brave enough to try them.

DERRICK BAR

OWNER: Jane Postma

HOURS: 8:00 a.m. to Closing Daily

HAPPY HOUR: Change of Shift Drink

GAMBLING: Video Poker/Keno

LIVE MUSIC: No

LOCATION: Front Street, **Kevin**

PHONE: 406-337-2691

BEER: Drafts; Domestics

AMUSEMENT: Pool; Darts

FOOD: Full Menu Cafe

The Derrick Bar is housed in a stucco building on Front Street in Kevin. The barroom is relatively large, with a straight wooden bar facing the south wall and a few booths against the north wall. A small convenience store is in the back part of the barroom.

The business has been in Kevin longer than anyone I spoke with could remember, but it's likely the bar opened in the early 1900's. Jane Postma bought the bar in the fall of 1993. Jane has a very close relationship with the people of Kevin. She basically treats her customers like family, and when she's not at the bar, Jane can often be found running errands for Kevin's senior citizens.

The Derrick Bar is a place where you get your money's worth. They serve large portions of good food at reasonable prices, and they always offer a daily lunch special which includes soup and free coffee. All the meats are fresh, never frozen, and the french fries are hand-cut as you order them. If you have a craving for something that's not on the menu, just tell them what you want and they will try to make it for you. The drinks are also reasonably priced. Draft beer is only 75 cents, and mixed drinks are $1.50. Be careful with the mixed drinks, because they're made with two shots instead of one. They even sell milkshakes at the Derrick Bar, which goes over very well with the kids.

The vast majority of the customers at the Derrick Bar are locals. They're all very friendly, and everyone takes a personal interest in everyone else's well being. The bar is a popular gathering place for morning coffee, and a lot of parties and celebrations are held there. People go to the Derrick Bar to cash checks, buy their newspapers, and even borrow a cup of sugar. There's usually a pitch game going on in the barroom on Thursday evenings and Sunday afternoons. If you're an accurate shot with a beer tab, you can participate in the local ritual of trying to toss the tab off your beer can into a kerosine lamp shade behind the bar. It's a difficult shot, but you win a free beer if the tab goes into the lamp shade. It doesn't cost you anything to try, so why not take a chance the next time you're at the Derrick Bar.

FOUR CORNERS BAR AND CAFE

OWNER: Roxy Peltier

LOCATION: Oilmont

HOURS: 7:30 a.m. to 2:00 a.m. Daily

PHONE: 406-337-2955

HAPPY HOUR: No

BEER: Drafts; Domestics

GAMBLING: Video Poker/Keno

AMUSEMENT: Pool; Foosball

LIVE MUSIC: Occasionally

FOOD: Full Menu Cafe

The Four Corners Bar and Cafe is just west of the Kevin/Oilmont Interchange (exit 379) off Interstate 15. The barroom is housed in the front (west) side of the building, and a separate dining room is in the rear. An L-shaped wooden bar faces the north wall of the barroom, and a few tables are available if you can't find an empty barstool. The facility is relatively new, so everything is modern.

The bar first opened under the name Jules Place in 1927. I'm told a "softening shop" operated out of the building along with the bar for several years. If you've never heard of a softening shop, don't feel alone. I hadn't either until I visited the Four Corners Bar and Cafe. Apparently, "softening shop" is local terminology for whorehouse. The original building was destroyed by fire in 1989, but that may have been more of a blessing than a tragedy. From what I've been told, the building was about to fall over anyhow. The bar was rebuilt that same year, and the Four Corners Bar and Cafe was back in business.

Roxy Peltier has owned the Four Corners Bar and Cafe since 1985. Roxy promotes a friendly atmosphere where adults and kids alike gather to socialize with friends. The majority of the customers are local residents, but travelers going to and from Canada frequent the bar, as do visiting hunters during the fall. The Four Corners Bar and Cafe is basically the social hub for family gatherings around Oilmont. A lot of local celebrations are held at the Four Corners, and Roxy commonly sponsors auctions to raise money for people in need. Roxy also hosts a great Halloween Party, complete with costumes and prizes.

The cafe hours are 7:30 a.m. until 10:00 p.m. daily. Although the bar can't start serving alcohol until 8:00 a.m., the doors are open at 7:30 every morning to serve coffee. Daily lunch specials are offered Monday through Friday, and dinner specials are available on the weekends. Broasted chicken is a house specialty, but those with a large appetite may want to try the Four Corners Burger, which is a double beef patty with a slice of ham. Even if you're not hungry, be sure to stop in to say hello. The people are friendly, and the beer's always cold.

MINT BAR

OWNERS: Gene and Kim Luckenbill

HOURS: 10:00 a.m. to Closing Daily

HAPPY HOUR: No

GAMBLING: Video Poker/Keno

LIVE MUSIC: No

LOCATION: Railroad Ave., **Sunburst**

PHONE: 406-937-2675

BEER: Drafts; Domestics

AMUSEMENT: Pool

FOOD: Frozen Pizza

The Mint Bar is on the north side of Railroad Avenue in Sunburst. You shouldn't have any trouble recognizing the place because the bar is housed in the old Sunburst Lutheran Church building. The appearance of the building is basically the same as it was when people gathered for Sunday services. The wood siding is coated with white paint, and a vaulted roof towers above the front entrance. Looking at the building from the street reminds me of a scene from "Little House on the Prairie". As you pass through the front door, the cathedral ceilings and tall wooden archways reinforce the thought that the place was once inhabited by God, himself (or herself, depending on what your beliefs are and how much you've had to drink). Aside from the wooden bar, tap system, bear skin rug, and beer signs, not much has changed since the building became a bar.

The business was established as Tuck's Place in 1937, but the name was changed to the Mint Bar one year later. The original bar was destroyed by fire in 1979, and the owner chose to move another building onto the property instead of rebuilding from the ground up. As luck would have it, a new Lutheran Church had recently been built, and the old church building was on the market. The timing seemed right, so the vacant church building was purchased and moved to the lot where the original bar stood. Minor renovations were soon completed, and the Mint Bar was back in business. Of course, a few people in town weren't too keen on the idea of turning their beloved church into a bar. They would have rather remembered the building as the place where they got married and their children got baptized rather than a place where people guzzle beer.

Gene and Kim Luckenbill now run the Mint. The business has been in Gene's family since the mid 1980's. Most of the customers are local residents, but a few travelers, especially the Canadians, like to stop at the bar when they're in the area. Visiting hunters also frequent the bar during the fall. The customers at the Mint Bar treat each other like family. Everyone knows each other, and they're quick to offer assistance to someone in need. With its church-like appearance, the Mint Bar is a great place to go for Sunday services. Just be careful what you pray for.

**Sunburst's Mint Bar. The Building was the Sunburst
Lutheran Church before becoming the Mint Bar in 1979.**

NORMA'S NORTHWAY BAR

OWNER: Norma Smith

LOCATION: 1st St. N., **Sunburst**

HOURS: 8:00 a.m. to Closing Daily

PHONE: 406-937-6240

HAPPY HOUR: Buy 1, Get 1 Free Specials

BEER: Drafts; Domestics

GAMBLING: No

AMUSEMENT: Pool

LIVE MUSIC: No

FOOD: No

Norma's Northway Bar, home of the only Free Bed and Breakfast I know of in Montana, is across from the post office on 1st Street North in Sunburst. The front portion of the building houses a relatively small barroom, and the back part is used as living quarters. A straight bar stands along the west wall of the barroom, and a lone wood burning stove is in one corner. One of the more interesting physical features about the place is the barroom floor, which slopes away from the middle of the room toward the east wall at a rather drastic grade. The slope is so steep that the legs on one side of the pool table have to be elevated with 2 x 4 boards to keep the table level. The grade is such that you could sled ride on the floor if there were snow on it.

The business was established as Mac's Place in 1938. The name was changed to Dutch's Bar in 1954, and it may still be called Dutch's Bar if a former owner of the business hadn't been caught stealing pigs from a local farm. After the felony "swine theft" conviction, the man changed the to the Northway Bar and transferred ownership over to his wife. That way, he didn't have to sell the bar (convicted felons are not allowed to hold a liquor license in Montana).

Norma Smith has owned Norma's Northway Bar since 1978. If there's one thing you can always count on from Norma, it's the fact that she goes out of her way to ensure her customers are treated well. Norma doesn't sell prepared food at the bar, but she usually has something on the stove that she serves at no cost. With this approach, Norma doesn't have to deal with the bureaucrats at the Health Department. Norma also takes Canadian money at par, meaning she doesn't factor in the U.S./Canadian currency exchange rate. A Canadian dollar is always worth an American Dollar at the Northway Bar. Perhaps the most surprising incentive Norma offers is the free bed and breakfast. Like most tavern owners, Norma has discovered people often leave the bar early because of today's stiff DUI penalties. To combat that problem, Norma has four bedrooms where her customers can spend the night if they've had too much to drink to safely drive home. Norma will even fix you a free breakfast in the morning before you leave.

VET'S CLUB

MANAGERS: Nyle and Ellavon Snell

HOURS: 12:30 p.m. to Closing Daily

HAPPY HOUR: No

GAMBLING: Video Poker/Keno

LIVE MUSIC: No

LOCATION: Railroad Ave., **Sunburst**

PHONE: 406-937-3933

BEER: Drafts; Domestics

AMUSEMENT: Pool; Video Games

FOOD: Frozen Pizza

Sunburst's Vet's Club is a chartered member of the national Veterans of Foreign Wars (VFW) organization. Sunburst doesn't have a large enough population to support the bar on private memberships alone, so they've opened the doors to the general public. The barroom is housed in the ground-level floor of a two story structure on the corner of First Street and Railroad Avenue.

The building that houses the Vet's Club was originally a boarding house. The Sunburst VFW operated out of the west side of the building for several years, and a laundromat was in the west side. The barroom moved into the east side of the building after the laundromat vacated. Although the barroom occupies only part of the ground-level floor (the rest of the building basically sits vacant), it is relatively large. A straight wooden bar stands in front of a wooden back bar just inside the main entrance, and the room opens up toward the rear of the building. There's plenty of tables and open floor space to handle large crowds.

Nyle and Ellavon Snell have managed the Vets Club since 1986. Nyle indicated they have ninety-seven members, sixty-two of whom are lifetime members. The club serves as a banquet room for organized parties and celebrations, and they have been a steady sponsor of local youth boxing over the years. Unfortunately, there hasn't been a local boxing team in the past couple of years to add to the trophies in the display case.

Most of the business at the Vet's Club comes in the form of local trade. A few travelers and hunters wander in throughout the year, but you will normally find residents of Sunburst and the surrounding communities at the bar. Although the Vets Club is one of three bars in Sunburst, they basically get the same customers as the other two bars in town. Like most small towns in Montana, the same people patronize different bars, so everyone always knows what's going on at the other places in town. When the Vet's Club does get crowded, you can bet there will be a very friendly crowd on hand. This is not the type of place where you will find a bunch of rowdy customers creating problems.

343

GLOCCA MORRA INN

OWNERS: Companian Family

HOURS: 10:00 a.m. to 2:00 a.m. Daily

HAPPY HOUR: No

GAMBLING: Video Poker/Keno; Live Poker

LIVE MUSIC: Occasionally

LOCATION: Main Street, **Sweetgrass**

PHONE: 406-335-2850

BEER: Domestics

AMUSEMENT: Pool; Video Games

FOOD: Full Menu Cafe

The Glocca Morra Inn is on Main Street in Sweetgrass. The bar and a cafe occupy the ground-level floor of the building, and nine motel rooms are in the second story. The spacious barroom has an L-shaped wooden bar along the east wall, several tables in the middle of the room, and plenty of open floor space. If you stop in during the winter, you will probably see a Harley Davidson motorcycle parked in the corner of the barroom. The bike belongs to Danny Companian, who now manages the bar and motel. The business has been in Danny's family since 1947, but Danny is the first to use the barroom as a storage area for his Harley.

The Glocca Morra has been in Sweetgrass since the 1920's. It first opened in a building a few blocks north on Main Street. When the highway came through, a business decision was made to move the bar next to the new road. The Glocca Morra operated from this building until 1963 when the U.S. Government decided to build a new customs office where the bar was. After Uncle Sam issued the Glocca Morra an eviction notice, a vacant building that was previously used as a hospital at a petroleum refinery in Sunburst was purchased and moved to Sweetgrass. The old hospital was renovated into a bar and motel, and a cafe was built on the south end.

Sweetgrass is a border town, so it's obviously the first and last stop for Canadian travelers entering and leaving the United States. It's not uncommon for the Canadians to outnumber the Americans in the barroom. The Glocca Morra is a place where people of all ages and all types gather to have a good time. Cowboys, bikers, Americans, and Canadians all frequent the bar, but things don't get out of hand too often. The bar hosts a great St. Patrick's Day party each year, and a motorcycle rodeo is held during the last part of August. It's basically a fun place where everyone is welcome. Although the cafe is managed separately from the bar, it's just through the south door of the barroom. Cafe hours are 7:00 a.m. to 10:00 p.m. (9:00 p.m. in the winter), and they serve excellent food. Daily lunch specials are available, and the Gloc Burger (a double beef patty with ham and cheese, loaded) will appease even the largest appetite.

344

PAPER DOLLAR BAR AND CAFE

MANAGER: Melva Cooper

LOCATION: Main Street, **Sweetgrass**

HOURS: Noon to 2:00 a.m. Sat-Sun
10:00 a.m. to 2:00 a.m. Mon-Fri

PHONE: 406-335-2881

HAPPY HOUR: No

BEER: Domestics

GAMBLING: Video Poker/Keno

AMUSEMENT: Pool; Darts; Pinball; Video Games

LIVE MUSIC: Occasionally

FOOD: Full Menu Cafe

The Paper Dollar Bar and Cafe is on Main Street in Sweetgrass. The bar and cafe reside in the north side of a facility that also houses a convenience store and gas station. The huge barroom has two L-shaped bars, a whole bunch of tables, several wooden booths, and an elevated bandstand. The dining room adjoins the barroom, but there's a sectioned-off area along the east wall if you prefer dining where you can't see the bar. The tops of both bars and the wooden booths are covered with paper currency under the polyurethane coating. The bills are mostly from Canada and the United States, but there's a few bills from over-seas mixed in. All the bills are signed by the person who left them and most have a short message written on them.

The first bar to operate in the building was a business called Vince's Bar, which moved from Main Street is Sweetgrass in 1981. Prior to becoming a bar, the north side of the building was part of a large truck stop. A pizza parlor and a laundromat also operated out of the building at one time. The bar and cafe have a steady business today, but the place was a lot busier in past years. Canadians by the truck load used to come to the Paper Dollar to party, especially on Sundays, but they seem to stay home more these days. The decrease in business is likely due to a combination of factors, including the unfavorable currency exchange rate for Canadians, stiff Canadian DUI laws, the recent legalization of some forms of gambling in Canada, and a change in the Canadian Law that allows bars to be open on Sundays.

The Paper Dollar Bar and Cafe is a friendly place where entire families gather to eat, drink, and socialize. There's plenty of video gambling for the adults and lots of video games for the kids. The Paper Dollar has a steady local clientele, and travelers passing through the area stop in as well. The bar is a popular spot for holiday parties, local celebrations, and family gatherings. The cafe serves lunch and dinner daily. All the food is good, and the prime rib is excellent when available.

345

BRUNSWICK BAR

OWNERS: Steve Kerr and Janet Dennet

HOURS: 10:00 a.m. to 2:00 a.m. Daily

HAPPY HOUR: Thursdays 6:00-7:30

GAMBLING: Video Poker/Keno;
Shake-A-Day

LIVE MUSIC: Occasionally

LOCATION: Main Street, **Hysham**

PHONE: 406-342-5880

BEER: Drafts; Domestics

AMUSEMENT: Pool; Horseshoes;
Video Game

FOOD: Full Menu Grill

The Brunswick Bar is on Main Street in Hysham. The spacious bar-room has a straight bar along the south wall, and plenty of tables are spread throughout the room. A screened-in patio is just off the east end of the building, so you can drink outdoors without having to worry about bugs dive bombing your beer.

Early in the 20th century, a saloon was built on the property where the Brunswick Bar now stands. After several years of operation, the saloon became Treasure County's first courthouse, site of the only two hangings to ever take place in Treasure County. In 1923, two men were hanged at the old courthouse for murdering a deputy sheriff. After the first hanging was over, the next man scheduled to be exe-cuted admitted he made false statements about the other defendant during the trial. The prosecuting attorney, who was present at the hangings, determined the false testimony was the reason the other defendant was sentenced to die. The problem was the man was already dead, and there was nothing that could be done to correct the mistake. A new courthouse was built after the hangings took place, so the building once again became a saloon. Irv's Bar was the name of the tavern when the building was destroyed by fire in 1987. When the bar was rebuilt, it opened under the name Brunswick Bar. Steve Kerr and Janet Dennet are now the owners of the business.

The Brunswick Bar has a definite local crowd atmosphere. It's a place where friends meet to drink, swap stories, and enjoy the free coffee, iced tea, and popcorn served at various times throughout the day. Local legend has it the bar is now haunted by the restless ghost of the man who was wrongfully hanged at the old courthouse. The ghost is not believed to be wicked or revengeful because he hasn't harmed anyone thus far. Some say the man is unable to rest in peace because of the manner in which his life was taken, so his ghost inhab-its the grounds where he was put to death. Occasionally, unex-plained shadows move about the building, small items in the bar seem to vanish from existence, and mysterious noises are heard inside the barroom by people walking past the building on the street.

TOWN AND COUNTRY LOUNGE

OWNERS: Mel and Bonnie Hert

HOURS: 8:00 a.m. to 2:00 a.m. Daily

HAPPY HOUR: Thursdays 6:00 to 8:00

GAMBLING: Video Poker/Keno

LIVE MUSIC: Occasionally

LOCATION: Main Street, **Hysham**

PHONE: 406-342-5657

BEER: Drafts; Domestics

AMUSEMENT: No

FOOD: Full Menu Restaurant

The Town and Country Lounge is on Main Street in Hysham. Getting to Hysham is relatively easy, but I discovered it's not advisable to drive directly from Ingomar on the unimproved route shown on the road atlas, especially if the ground is even the slightest bit wet. If you choose to take this "shortcut", be prepared for twenty-five miles of wet, sticky clay and several hundred cows standing on the road. Regardless of the route you take to the Town and Country Lounge, you will undoubtedly notice the top of the bar is covered with Montana agates set in polyurethane. Behind the bar is a beautiful antique back bar that's been maintained in excellent condition. A very large rattlesnake skin is mounted on a board hanging over the barroom. Don't be afraid to walk around outside, however, because the snakes don't get that big in this part of the country. This particular skin came from a snake killed in Mexico.

The history of the business dates back to 1933 when the Silver Dollar Bar opened. The owner of the Silver Dollar died in 1934, so Joe Ferkovich moved his beer parlor into the building in 1935. Joe continued to run the bar until his death in 1957. The name became the Town and Country Lounge in 1974. Mel and Bonnie Hert bought the bar in 1980 and added the Hysham Hills Supper Club in the building adjoining the lounge in 1990. The supper club offers a full menu for breakfast, lunch, and dinner seven days a week. Mel claims the biggest chicken fried steak in eastern Montana is served here, and it draws customers from within a fifty mile radius. Every Sunday, a smorgasbord is served along with the regular menu items.

Most of the people you will meet at the Town and Country Lounge are residents of the Hysham area. Visiting hunters also stop in, especially during goose season. The pale-colored goose on the wall in the supper club was shot outside of Hysham in 1991. As of September, 1996, nobody who had seen the bird was able to identify the exact species it belonged to. If you know anything about ornithology, you may want to stop by and try to identify the origin of this peculiar creature. Even if you don't really give a damn about the bird, you can always stop in for a few drinks.

GATEWAY INN AND SUPPER CLUB

OWNERS: John and Joy Johnson

LOCATION: Route 24, **Fort Peck**

HOURS: 11:00 a.m. to 2:00 a.m. Daily

PHONE: 406-526-9988

HAPPY HOUR: 4:30 to 6:00 Mon - Fri

BEER: Drafts; Domestics; Microbrews

GAMBLING: Video Poker/Keno; Shake-A-Day

AMUSEMENT: Pool; Darts; Pinball; Video Games; Volleyball

LIVE MUSIC: Occasionally

FOOD: Full Menu Restaurant

The Gateway Inn and Supper Club stands atop a hill approximately two miles west of Fort Peck on Route 24. The building houses a horseshoe-shaped bar, a spacious hardwood dance floor, and a separate dining area. A wooden deck overlooks the Fort Peck Reservoir. The man-made lake was formed during the 1930's when the world's largest earthen dam was built on the Missouri River.

The Gateway Inn is the last remaining bar that was established during the early construction days of the Fort Peck Dam. Dam construction began in 1933, and the bar was built one year later. At one time, over 10,000 people were employed in construction activities associated with the dam. The Inn originally opened under the name B&F's. The name of the business later became Ernie's and finally changed to the Gateway Inn in the early 1960's. John and Joy Johnson bought the business in May, 1984. They added the words "and Supper Club" to the name in 1991 so people visiting the area would be aware food was available at the bar. Extensive remodeling was completed on the interior of the building in the spring of 1994; however, the original hardwood dance floor and the lighted glass brick embedded in the dance floor were not disturbed. These features have been in place since the business first opened, and John didn't want to change them. The old piano on the bandstand has its own unique history. It was originally played for waiting customers in Ruby's Place, a former house of ill repute in the nearby community of Wheeler.

With its proximity to Fort Peck Lake, the Gateway Inn has become a favorite detour for hunters and fishermen. A lot of local residents also frequent the Gateway Inn, making it very busy year round. The beer selection is always good, but it increases during the summer season when tourists and college students come to the area. If you need a warmer-upper, try a Bloody Dudley, one of the specialty drinks at the bar. The restaurant serves excellent lunches and dinners daily. Specialties include thirty-two ounce ribeye steaks, fresh walleye, and barbecued ribs.

BABY LONNIE'S BEER MUG

OWNERS: Lonnie and Marilyn Steele

HOURS: Noon to Closing Daily

HAPPY HOUR: No

GAMBLING: No

LIVE MUSIC: Occasionally

LOCATION: Main Street, **Frazier**

PHONE: 406-695-9900

BEER: Drafts; Domestics

AMUSEMENT: Pool; Horseshoes

FOOD: Frozen Pizza; Bar Snacks

Baby Lonnie's Beer Mug is on Main Street in Frazier. If you're looking for a unique place to drink, Baby Lonnie's won't disappoint you. The barroom walls are bright blue, and the walls in the small area where the rest rooms are located are hot pink. It may take a while for your eyes to adjust to the decor, but it won't take you long to notice how big the barroom is. There's plenty of open floor space, even with the three pool tables, a long bar, and several tables.

The building that houses the bar was formerly the Frazier Post Office. In 1987, Lonnie and Marilyn Steele opened a beer parlor in the building. Baby Lonnie's was selected as part of the name for the business because Lonnie and Marilyn had a newborn son named Lonnie when they opened the bar. The Beer Mug part of the name reflects the fact that they didn't have a full liquor license at the time, and beer was all they sold. The bar was issued a liquor license in 1992, but Lonnie and Marilyn decided not to create confusion by changing the name.

Because Frazier is on the Fort Peck Indian Reservation, most of the customers at Baby Lonnie's Beer Mug are Native Americans. There's usually a friendly crowd on hand, but occasionally someone will misbehave and end up on the 86 List posted behind the bar. The bar used to run three different happy hours during the day, but they have discontinued this practice. Horseshoe tournaments are still held during the summer, however, and pool tournaments are common in the winter. Free barbecues are usually held concurrent with these events.

According to local lore, Baby Lonnie's is haunted by a mischievous ghost that enjoys playing pranks and shooting pool. Over the years, pool balls have mysteriously moved during pool games, cards have disappeared during card games, unexplained shadows have been cast across the barroom, and the cracking of billiard balls has been heard in the barroom hours after the bar has closed. The noises have been heard by an individual who lives in an apartment that adjoins the barroom. Some people believe the culprit is the friendly ghost of a postal worker who didn't want to leave when the post office moved. It sounds logical to me.

RAINBOW ROOM

OWNERS: Bob and Linda Olson

HOURS: 8:00 a.m. to 2:00 a.m. Daily

HAPPY HOUR: 6:00 to 7:00 Mon - Fri

GAMBLING: Video Poker/Keno

LIVE MUSIC: Occasionally

LOCATION: Montana St, **Hinsdale**

PHONE: 406-364-9954

BEER: Drafts; Domestics

AMUSEMENT: Pool; Darts; Horseshoes

FOOD: Full Menu Grill

The Rainbow Room is housed in a brick structure at 200 Montana Street in Hinsdale. The barroom has an L-shaped wooden bar along the north wall, and a few tables are spread throughout the room if you can't find an empty barstool. Every ceiling tile in the barroom has some sort of markings on it. Most of the tiles are marked with brands from local ranches, but a few have the names of individuals who have visited the bar over the past several years. The names of some out-of-state hunting clubs are also painted on a few tiles.

The Rainbow Room was established in 1946 in an old bank building. I don't know how long the bank had been closed prior to the bar moving in, but the walk-in bank vault has never been removed from the basement. The basement has been renovated into living quarters, and a bedroom now resides inside the old bank vault. Nobody currently lives downstairs, but visiting hunters occasionally stay here as guests of the owners.

Bob and Linda Olson started managing the Rainbow Room in 1989, and they eventually bought the business. Bob and Linda are very customer oriented, and they try to provide whatever services their customers request. Hunting and fishing licenses are sold at the bar, and the regular menu is supplemented with homemade soups and chili through the fall and winter. Shelled peanuts are sold, and people are encouraged to forget their manners and throw the peanut shells on the floor. Linda says they make a great sweeping compound, so why waste them.

A lot of gambling and a little bit of gunfire have occurred at the Rainbow Room over the years. During the bar's early days, customers often played poker from the time the bar opened until they got thrown out at closing time. Unfortunately, the gambling went away when the state started enforcing stricter gambling laws and insisting on a larger share of the profits. The gunfire has also died down, but I was told a man who owned the business in the early 1970s occasionally got downright ornery and filled the walls and ceiling with bullet holes. This annoying habit usually flared up whenever he and his wife got into a fight. I don't think anyone ever got shot, but I suspect it drove away a few paying customers.

RAWHIDE SALOON

OWNER: Jon A. Blockhus

HOURS: 10:00 a.m. to 2:00 a.m. Daily

HAPPY HOUR: No

GAMBLING: Video Poker/Keno; Shake-A-Day

LIVE MUSIC: Occasionally

LOCATION: Montana St, **Hinsdale**

PHONE: 406-364-9952

BEER: Drafts; Domestics

AMUSEMENT: Pool; Darts; Video Games

FOOD: Grill Items; Homemade Pizza

The Rawhide Saloon is at 220 Montana Street in Hinsdale. The wooden structure houses a spacious barroom with a long L-shaped bar, a couple of tables, and plenty of open floor space. The interior walls are tastefully decorated with antique guns, tools, and farm implements, and numerous brands have been burned into the front of the bar. The brands were made by local ranchers who came equipped with their branding irons during a grand opening party on June 22, 1996.

The saloon was originally part of the Northern Hotel, which stood on the lot just south of the bar. The hotel was built around 1918, and the bar opened a few years later. A cafe was also part of the business at one time, but it hasn't been in operation since the 1960's. The barroom is the only part of the original business that remains today. The few tables that are now in the barroom were the original tables from the old Northern Cafe. The hotel building was torn down in the mid 1970's.

The bar officially became a pool hall during prohibition; however, it was common knowledge that bootlegged liquor was sold out the back door. Most of the whiskey was driven in from Canada, and local moonshiners supplied their own brand of homebrew. When the bar "reopened" after prohibition ended, it became a popular spot for local gamblers. Poker games commonly ran from opening until closing time, and maybe even a little past closing time on occasion.

The business has changed hands several times over the years, but it was always called the Northern Bar until Jon Blockhus bought it in the fall of 1995. Jon indicated he felt a name change was in order because the bar had not been maintained to the high standards people had become accustomed to when it was part of the Northern Hotel business. Jon made some much-needed upgrades and repairs when he took over, and business has been steadily improving. Whereas the Northern Bar had traditionally drawn the older crowd in town, people of all ages now come to the Rawhide Saloon for the great food, friendly atmosphere, and relaxing environment.

VICK'S BAR

OWNERS: Larry and Judy Boyum

HOURS: Noon to 2:00 a.m. Daily

HAPPY HOUR: 6:00 to 7:00 Mon - Fri

GAMBLING: Video Poker/Keno; Shake-A-Day

LIVE MUSIC: Occasionally

LOCATION: Main Street, **Nashua**

PHONE: 406-746-3272

BEER: Drafts; Domestics

AMUSEMENT: Pool; Darts

FOOD: Homemade Sandwiches; Frozen Pizza

Vick's Bar is on Main Street in Nashua. If you're entering town from Highway 2, turn south on Route 117 and drive approximately 1/4 mile. Route 117 becomes Main Street for a couple of blocks, and the bar is on the left-hand side of the road. If you're coming into Nashua from the south on Route 117, just watch for the bar on your right as you drive through town. Vick's Bar is next door to Vick's Bowling Alley, so you should be able to spot at least one of the two businesses as you motor through Nashua. The spacious barroom has a high ceiling, a long bar that can comfortably seat about twenty people, plenty of floor space, and a row of tables lining one wall. The interior walls are finished in your basic wood paneling, and a few beer signs and mirrors are used as decorations. It's nothing elaborate, but you'll find all the luxuries required for a relaxing evening away from home.

Vick's Bar was established in 1944. The bowling alley next door was originally part of the business, but the bar and bowling alley were sold separately in 1984. In all the years of operation, there have only been two owners of Vick's Bar. The original owner and his wife ran the bar for the first forty years, and Larry and Judy Boyum have owned it since 1984.

For the most part, the customers at Vic's Bar are local residents. There's usually a steady crowd on hand, but things pick up considerably late in the evenings after the neighboring bowling alley closes for the night. Apparently, the bowlers in Nashua like to hoist a few drinks after a stressful evening of throwing a heavy ball at ten little pins across the room, and Vick's Bar is a convenient place to do just that. Visiting hunters often stop at the bar, especially those who have been to Vick's during past hunting trips. It seems the same hunters stop here year after year to renew old friendships. Boaters and fishermen passing through town on their way to or from Fort Peck Lake also stop in on occasion, and a few tourists find their way to Vick's during the summer months. The friendly, comfortable atmosphere makes it a very nice rest stop.

WAGON WHEEL BAR

OWNERS: Ron, Rick, and Cindy Ost		**LOCATION:**	Highway 2, **Nashua**
HOURS: 2:00 p.m. to 2:00 a.m. Daily		**PHONE:**	406-746-3239
HAPPY HOUR: No		**BEER:**	Drafts; Domestics
GAMBLING: Video Poker/Keno		**AMUSEMENT:**	Pool; Darts
LIVE MUSIC: Occasionally		**FOOD:**	Delicatessen

The Wagon Wheel Bar is on the south side of Highway 2 in Nashua. The bar is part of a larger business consisting of a convenience store, self-service gas station, and delicatessen. A large horseshoe-shaped bar with a padded elbow rail stands in the middle of the barroom floor. The upholstery on both the elbow rail and the barstools is embroidered with the names of other local businesses. This unusual practice began in 1987 as a means of generating revenue for the bar while promoting other businesses in the area. It's obviously become quite popular, because every barstool has the name of some local company embroidered on it, and every available inch of space on the elbow rail is covered as well.

The business was established in 1942 during the latter phases of the Fort Peck Dam construction era. The bar was initially housed in a building just two doors down from Vick's Bar, Nashua's other tavern. The Wagon Wheel moved to its present location in 1992. Ron, Rick, and Cindy Ost bought the business in 1994, and Ron says the coldest beer in town and the best chicken in the area are sold at the Wagon Wheel Bar.

The Wagon Wheel is a friendly establishment where people go to have fun. There's usually a local crowd on hand, but people traveling along Highway 2, especially the Canadian travelers, are starting to discover the bar. The Wagon Wheel is a popular place for people to hold private gatherings such as holiday parties, wedding receptions, and class reunion dinners. Meals are prepared on request for these functions, and just about any type of food will be served.

Sanctioned arm wrestling tournaments, pool and dart tournaments, and dances are held at the Wagon Wheel Bar at various times throughout the year. It's not uncommon for impromptu jam sessions to break out, so you may end up hearing live music on a night when there's no dance scheduled. The photographs on the barroom wall are evidence that the people of Nashua know how to enjoy themselves, especially during wet T-shirt contests. Ron, Rick, and Cindy host so many special events at the Wagon Wheel that any time is a good time to visit. You won't always find a party, but you will always see people having a great time at the Wagon Wheel bar.

BAR 80

OWNERS: Sue Nyquist/Dorothy Crandell

HOURS: 10:00 a.m. to 2:00 a.m. Mon-Sat
1:00 p.m. to 2:00 a.m. Sunday

HAPPY HOUR: 5:30 to 6:30 Mon - Fri

GAMBLING: Video Poker/Keno;
Shake-A-Shift

LIVE MUSIC: No

LOCATION: Main Street, **Opheim**

PHONE: 406-762-9993

BEER: Domestics

AMUSEMENT: Pool; Darts; Foosball

FOOD: Broiled Foods;
Frozen Pizza

The Bar 80 is on Main Street in Opheim. The old Turk's Tavern sign still hangs above the front entrance, but the name of the business was officially changed in 1992. The old sign has remained simply because the new owners are in no particular hurry to replace it. A moderate-sized barroom resides in the south side of the building, and a smaller game room is in the north side. A straight bar runs along the south wall, and a couple of tables are available if you prefer sitting away from the bar.

A meat market, grocery store, and cafe opened in the building in 1926. A beer parlor was added when prohibition ended, and some years later, a full liquor license was obtained. Walter "Turk" Williams bought the business in July, 1946. He got rid of the store and meat market and turned the cafe into a lunch counter. Turk married in 1948, and his wife, Alma, ran the lunch counter while Turk managed the bar. The lunch counter closed a few years later, so Alma helped run the bar until Turk's death in 1973. Alma continued operating Turk's Tavern until August, 1992 when she sold the business to Sue Nyquist and Dorothy Crandell. Sue and Dorothy changed the name to the Bar 80, but they proudly admit the business will probably always be referred to as Turk's by the older residents of Opheim. That helps explain why they're in no hurry to change the old sign.

Alma has many fond memories of her forty-four years at Turk's. During the winter of 1950-51, the snow was so deep that Turk had to cut steps into an eight foot deep snowbank so his customers could walk down to the barroom door. The snow eventually piled up so high that heavy equipment had to be brought in from the Opheim air base radar site to move the snow away from the buildings. Alma also remembers the time hockey hall of famer Bobby Hull was in Turk's. It was nice to see a celebrity, but Alma says what she misses most about the tavern business is the wonderful people she saw on a daily basis. Those same wonderful people still frequent the Bar 80, but Dorothy and Sue now serve the drinks.

354

MINT BAR

OWNERS: Dave, Deb, and Doug Baily

HOURS: 10:00 a.m. to 2:00 a.m. Mon-Sat
1:00 p.m. to 2:00 a.m. Sunday

HAPPY HOUR: 6:00 to 7:00 Mon - Fri

GAMBLING: Video Poker/Keno;
Shake-A-Day

LIVE MUSIC: Occasionally

LOCATION: Main Street, **Opheim**

PHONE: 406-762-3299

BEER: Domestics

AMUSEMENT: Pool; Darts; Video Games

FOOD: Microwave Sandwiches;
Frozen Pizza

The Mint Bar is on Main Street in Opheim. The barroom has a long bar that spans over half the length of the north wall, and several tables are spread across the hardwood floor. The high ceiling is covered with the original decorative tin that was installed when the structure was built in 1926. The antique wooden bar, back bar, and liquor cabinet are believed to have come from a tavern in Wyoming, but nobody I spoke with knew when, why, or how they found their way to Opheim.

Fred Whittle established the business as Fred's Place in 1940. Fred operated the business solo until 1945 when he took on a partner. Fred and his partner chose the Mint Bar as the new name for their business, and they moved the bar across Main Street into the old pool hall building. The Mint Bar has been operating out of the building ever since.

Dave, Deb, and Doug Baily bought the Mint Bar in 1986. They operate a friendly tavern where local residents gather to drink and socialize. There's nothing elaborate about the building, but the people are friendly and honest. It's very common for customers to buy rounds of drinks, so be prepared to down a few and buy an occasional round if you ever stop by. During my first visit to the Mint Bar, I quickly discovered how fast the drinks can pile up. While trying to keep pace with the people buying rounds, I overheard a lady commenting to her husband that every time they stop after work for one beer, they end up staying for several hours and staggering out the door with six full beers in their pockets. I laughed to myself and then watched the two of them stagger out the door with six full beers in their pockets.

Several times a year, the Mint hosts parties for their customers. A wild game feed, Rocky Mountain Oyster feed, and pig roast are three of the annual festivities. Most of the customers are from Opheim and the surrounding communities, but travelers on their way to and from Canada occasionally stop in, as do visiting hunters. It's a great place to stop because you'll start making friends the minute you enter the door.

HORSESHOE BAR

OWNERS: Lowell and Irene Standing

HOURS: 10:00 a.m. to 2:00 a.m. Daily

HAPPY HOUR: No

GAMBLING: Video Poker/Keno; Shake-A-Day

LIVE MUSIC: Occasionally

LOCATION: Highway 2, **Oswego**

PHONE: 406-695-9915

BEER: Domestics

AMUSEMENT: Pool; Darts; Pinball; Video Games; Horseshoes

FOOD: Grill Items

The Horseshoe Bar is on the south side of Highway 2 in Oswego. The main part of the barroom is housed in the north side of the metal-sided building. A straight bar faces the beer coolers against the north wall, and a separate bar faces the grill against the east wall. Both bars get plenty of use, as do the three pool tables in the room. The south side of the building houses a dance hall/auxiliary area that can be accessed by opening a sliding partition. This end of the building is normally blocked off, but the partition is opened from time to time to make room for dances and pool tournaments.

The history of the Horseshoe Bar dates back to 1948 when Jensen's Bar first opened in Oswego. The name was changed to Buck's Bar in 1953. I'm told Buck's survived three separate fires, but the building finally deteriorated to the point where it was about to collapse. In 1982, the liquor license was transferred to the new bar that was built along Highway 2. The business operated under the name Flynn's Bar until 1985 when Lowell and Irene Standing bought it. Lowell and Irene changed the name to the Horseshoe Bar, and they've been hard at work ever since.

The Horseshoe Bar is a basic shot-and-a-beer place. There's nothing elaborate about the bar, but the people are very friendly. Lowell and Irene don't tolerate rude behavior from their customers, so you never have to worry about problems erupting. You may want to be selective about who you shoot pool against, however, because the Horseshoe Bar sponsors ten different teams in the local pool leagues. The bar also hosts several pool tournaments throughout the year, and they occasionally hold horseshoe tournaments during the summer.

Every August, Lowell and Irene treat their regular bar patrons to a free customer appreciation dinner. Unlike most places that have a pot luck dinner, all the food is supplied by the Horseshoe Bar. They also invite everyone who participates on their pool teams to an end-of-the-season party in May. The pool shooters get to blow off some steam at the bar while listening to the sounds of a live band.

PARK GROVE BAR AND CAFE

OWNER: Larry DeBeau   **LOCATION:** Route 117, **Park Grove**

HOURS: 10:00 a.m. to 2:00 a.m. Daily   **PHONE:** 406-526-9997

HAPPY HOUR: 6:00 to 7:00 Mon - Fri   **BEER:** Drafts; Domestics

GAMBLING: Video Poker/Keno;   **AMUSEMENT:** Pool; Darts;
Shake-A-Day   Shuffleboard

LIVE MUSIC: Occasionally   **FOOD:** Full Menu Cafe

The Park Grove Bar and Cafe is on the west side of Route 117 in Park Grove, a small community that you probably won't find on your road map. Park Grove is only two miles north of the town of Fort Peck, so you shouldn't have any trouble finding the place. An L-shaped bar stands in the southwest corner of the barroom. The kitchen and a small lunch counter are just north of the wall behind the bar, and a seating area and game room reside in the east side of the building. The old red piano that resides in the northeast corner still gets played occasionally, but not as much as it used to. Every so often, one of the customers will drink enough courage to get up and play a song or two, but it's not a common occurrence.

I'm told the Park Grove Bar opened in the late 1940s during the latter phases of construction on the Fort Peck Dam. The business originally operated out of a building that stood beside the existing structure, but it was destroyed by fire sometime in the early 1950s. The house next door was selected as the new site for the bar. Renovations quickly commenced, and the former house became the present-day bar. The property where the old bar stood was transformed into a parking lot, and the Park Grove Bar was back in business.

The Park Grove Bar and Cafe has only had only four owners since it first opened. Larry DeBeau has owned the bar since 1981, and he runs a very friendly establishment. Local residents, tourists, and outdoors enthusiasts make up the clientele. Summers bring a lot of boaters and swimmers to the area, hunters flock to the region in the fall, and fishermen are on Fort Peck Lake year round. There's always plenty of cold beer on hand, and the prices are very reasonable. This is one place where you can still get a twelve ounce can of Pabst Blue Ribbon for $1.00. The cafe serves terrific 1/2 pound hamburgers, and noon lunch specials are offered Monday through Friday. The Park Grove Bar and Cafe is a friendly place with cold beer and good food. If you're ever near Fort Peck, it's worth your time to stop by and say hello Larry and the gang.

SILVER DOLLAR BAR AND CAFE

OWNERS: Albert & Virginia Gundermann

LOCATION: Main Street, **Richland**

HOURS: 9:00 a.m. to Closing Mon-Fri
10:00 a.m. to Closing Saturday
1:00 p.m. to Closing Sunday

PHONE: 406-724-9467

HAPPY HOUR: No

BEER: Domestics

GAMBLING: Video Poker/Keno;
Shake-A-Day

AMUSEMENT: None

LIVE MUSIC: Occasionally

FOOD: Full Menu Cafe

The Silver Dollar Bar and Cafe is housed in the ground-level floor of a two story building on Main Street in Richland. You will recognize the place by the sign out front which proclaims "Silver Dollar Bar, Cafe, Grocery...Something Superior for Your Interior". The sign is a bit outdated, because the grocery store part of the business has been gone for several years. The barroom has an L-shaped bar that doubles as a lunch counter, and several tables are spread throughout the room. The room adjacent to the barroom is used for everything from meetings to quilting.

The bar first opened in the Richland Hotel in 1933. A beer parlor occupied the first floor of the building, and ten hotel rooms were in the second story. A full liquor license was issued in 1939. During the early years of operation, it wasn't all that uncommon for a horse and rider to pass through the barroom, but with barroom etiquette being what it is today, you just don't see horses in the Silver Dollar anymore. The building has undergone several renovations since the beer parlor and hotel first opened. Doorways have changed locations, the bar has moved more than once, and the old hotel rooms upstairs are now a single living quarters. One thing has remained constant; there's still good food and cold beer at the Silver Dollar Bar and Cafe.

Albert and Virginia Gundermann bought the business in June, 1992. They have a steady local clientele, but business usually picks up during hunting season. Breakfast, lunch, and dinner are served daily, and lunch specials are offered Monday through Friday. The Silver Dollar is basically the community center of Richland. Various social groups meet here, local celebrations are held at the bar, and people commonly gather informally to catch up on the latest news or talk to their neighbors. They also have quite a selection of videos for rent. It's a quiet place with a friendly atmosphere, and that's how the people of Richland like it.

358

BAR 100

OWNERS: Richard and Rita Swartz   **LOCATION:** Hwy. 191, **Judith Gap**

HOURS: 10:00 a.m. to Closing Daily   **PHONE:** 406-473-9906

HAPPY HOUR: No   **BEER:** Drafts; Domestics

GAMBLING: Video Poker/Keno   **AMUSEMENT:** Pool; Video Games

LIVE MUSIC: Karaoke Music Occasionally   **FOOD:** Full Menu Grill

The Bar 100 is on Highway 191 at the south end of Judith Gap. A small L-shaped bar faces the north and west walls toward the back of the barroom, and a few small tables share the floor space with the pool table and video gambling machines in the front part of the room. The barroom is relatively small, but it's comfortable and clean.

The history of the Bar 100 dates back to 1934 when the Midway Cafe was issued a retail beer license. The bar moved into a hotel and cafe on Main Street in 1937. In 1954, the Midway Bar moved to its present location. An old boxcar that had previously been used as housing for railroad hands was moved to the property and renovated into a small tavern. Over the next several years, three small additions were made to the north side of the building. Today, the bar and kitchen occupy the area where the additions were made, and the pool table and gambling machines are in the old boxcar. The name of the business was changed to the Bar 100 in 1970. Bar 100 was the brand from the owner's ranch, and she decided it would also make a fine name for the business.

Richard and Rita Swartz bought the bar in October, 1994. They didn't change the name of the business, but they did finally fix the roof that had leaked for the past forty years. Fixing the roof seemed like a good idea at the time, but some of the customers were a little upset because they could no longer place bets on where the first drop of water would come through the ceiling when it started to rain. All bets are off now, but at least you don't have to worry about getting rain water in your beer.

You will usually find a local crowd at the Bar 100. Kids gather at the bar to play video games and pool earlier in the day, but the adults take over in the evening. Things are usually quiet, but there have been a few gunshots fired inside the barroom over the years. A man once shot a 38 caliber bullet through the wall above the door while attempting to shoot out a light. Another man once exterminated a mouse with his pistol and then placed the dead mouse on another customer's hamburger when he wasn't looking. You don't have to worry about being shot when you're in the Bar 100, but you may want to inspect your food before you eat it.

HITCHING POST BAR

OWNERS: Dennis and Charlene Fyler

LOCATION: Hwy. 191, **Judith Gap**

HOURS: 11:30 a.m. to Closing Tue-Sun
Closed Monday

PHONE: 406-473-9993

HAPPY HOUR: 5:00 to 6:00 Tue - Fri

BEER: Domestics; Imports

GAMBLING: Video Poker

AMUSEMENT: No

LIVE MUSIC: Occasional Informal Jam Sessions

FOOD: Fresh Pizza;
Tacos; Sandwiches

The Hitching Post Bar is on the west side of Highway 191 in Judith Gap. True to the name of the business, two wooden hitching posts stand near the front entrance in case you need a spot to tie your horse. The small barroom is just big enough for a sectioned bar, four small tables, and a few square feet of standing room. If you need a place to camp for the night, six full RV hookups are available outside.

The history of the Hitching Post Bar dates back to 1945 when the Tavern Bar and Cafe opened on Main Street in Judith Gap. The name was changed to the Judith Gap Tavern when the business moved to its present location in 1949. The Judith Gap Tavern operated out of an old schoolhouse that was moved from Hyde Creek; however, the building was destroyed by fire in March, 1972. Unfortunately, the bar owner was asleep in the second floor when the fire started, and he died in the blaze. It was either later that same year or the following year (there's a local argument over the date) that the present structure was moved to the property. Ironically, this building was also originally a schoolhouse, but it had been used as a home on the DeBuff Ranch prior to becoming the Hitching Post Bar.

Dennis and Charlene (Charlie) Fyler bought the Hitching Post in January, 1995. Since taking over, they have gained an excellent reputation for their homemade pizza. Dennis and Charlie serve free pizza and soda to local scholastic basketball players after the games, and the players are commonly accompanied by their parents for the feast. Needless to say, the barroom gets very crowded after the gym lets out.

There's usually a friendly crowd on hand at the bar. The last real excitement to occur was during the 1970's when a jealous boyfriend entered the building and shot his girlfriend, who happened to own the place and was working behind the bar at the time. The 22 caliber bullet went completely through the lady's shoulder and lodged in the wall behind the bar. The bullet hole remains today, but the bullet was extracted for evidence. It turns out the wound was not life threatening, but I have serious doubts the relationship was able to survive the shooting.

TWO DOT BAR

OWNERS: Susan Musgrove

HOURS: 10:00 a.m. to Closing Daily

HAPPY HOUR: No

GAMBLING: Video Poker/Keno; Shake-A-Day

LIVE MUSIC: Occasionally

LOCATION: Wilson Ave., **Twodot**

PHONE: 406-632-9992

BEER: Domestics; Microbrews

AMUSEMENT: Pool; Darts; Video Game

FOOD: Full Menu Grill

The world famous Two Dot Bar is on the west side of Wilson Avenue, the main street running north and south through Twodot. The barroom is fairly long and narrow. The main part of the barroom is in the front portion of the building, and a game room resides in the smaller room in the rear. A glass-encased candy counter and a wooden bar stand along the north wall, and three buddy bars are lined against the south wall. An extensive beer can collection containing many brands I've never heard of is on display on shelves throughout the main barroom.

The Two Dot Bar has been around since the early 1900s. It's known that the first structure in the town of Twodot was a saloon, but nobody I spoke with seemed to know whether the Two Dot Bar was this structure. The local history book is full of information about the early days of Twodot, but it doesn't provide much information on the history of the Two Dot Bar. I do know that Susan Musgrove bought the bar in October, 1993. I'm not sure when or how the Two Dot Bar became world famous, but several foreign travelers stop by every year, and Hank Williams, Jr. even has a song entitled "Twodot, Montana" on his Strong Stuff Album. Perhaps the fact that there's actually a town named Twodot is reason enough for the bar to be world famous.

If you happen to be in the neighborhood and decide to stop in, you can expect to find a friendly crowd. Local residents provide a steady business throughout the year, and visiting tourists and hunters stop in during the summer and fall. On those rare occasions when trouble starts, it's either stopped immediately or settled outside so innocent people and property don't get hurt. The temperature inside the barroom cycles anywhere between too cold and too hot during the winter, but Susan says she is getting better at controlling the heat put out by the wood burning stove. If you want to pick up something for the people you left stranded while you went to the bar, souvenir shirts, hats, jackets, and posters are available. Just be sure to enjoy yourself while you're there, and sign the guest book before you leave.

ACTON BAR AND COW CAMP STEAK HOUSE

OWNERS: Lou and Duane Cowdin

LOCATION: Route 3, **Acton**

HOURS: 8:00 a.m. to Midnight Daily

PHONE: 406-652-9438

HAPPY HOUR: No

BEER: Draft; Domestics

GAMBLING: Video Poker/Keno; Shake-A-Day

AMUSEMENT: Pool; Darts; Video Game

LIVE MUSIC: One Night Per Weekend

FOOD: Full Menu Restaurant

The Acton Bar and Cow Camp Steak House is housed in a modern log structure on Route 3 in Acton. This is one place you really can't miss because the bar basically **IS** the town of Acton. A long wooden bar faces the east wall in the south end of the building, and plenty of tables are available in the dining area. Locally-crafted artwork is on display throughout the building, some of which is sold at the bar.

The Acton Bar has been in operation since at least the 1930's. At one time, a post office and convenience store operated out of the building along with the bar. The bar has always been on the same property, but fire destroyed the original building. The existing log structure was built in 1988. Lou and Duane Cowdin bought the business in November, 1993. They have done an admirable job with the interior decorating; not too cluttered, but not too plain. All the horsey-cowboy stuff, as Duane calls it, was donated by local residents.

Lou and Duane run a friendly establishment, so don't expect to find a rough bunch of characters when you visit the Acton Bar. Local residents make up the regular crowd; however, local includes people from Billings, which is fifteen miles away. Weekends get pretty busy. A band usually plays one night each weekend, and informal jam sessions are held on the last Sunday of each month. Besides the scheduled jam sessions, a guitar, banjo, and piano are available near the bandstand for anyone to play any time they want. Special events also attract people to the Acton Bar and Cow Camp Steak House. Dances, cowboy poets, and wagon rides take place on Acton Extravaganza Day, which is held on the Sunday prior to Memorial Day. The bar also sponsors its annual Harvest Bawl at the end of September.

Lunches and dinners are served daily from 11:00 a.m. until closing, which is whenever there's nobody left to serve and the kitchen shuts down. The prime rib and seafood served on weekends draw people from as far away as Malta. All the steaks are cut fresh daily on the premises, so you are assured a good cut of meat. If you're looking for something on the lighter side, Rocky Mountain Oysters are available for $2.75 a plate.

BOARDWALK BAR AND CAFE

OWNER: Jose Romero

HOURS: 11:00 a.m. to Closing Daily

HAPPY HOUR: 4:00 to 7:00 Daily

GAMBLING: Video Poker/Keno

LIVE MUSIC: No

LOCATION: 2nd St. W., **Ballantine**

PHONE: 406-967-6600

BEER: Domestics; Imports

AMUSEMENT: Pool; Darts; Foosball

FOOD: Full Menu Cafe

The Boardwalk Bar and Cafe is on 2nd Street West in Ballantine. To get there from Interstate 94, take exit 14 and drive north approximately 1/2 mile. Turn west (right) on Canal Road (also known as Ash Street) and drive three blocks to 2nd Street West. Turn north (left) on 2nd Street West and look for the bar on the left-hand side of the street. There's a covered wooden sidewalk in front of the building, so the name Boardwalk Bar and Cafe is appropriate. A spacious barroom is in the south side of the building, and a smaller cafe is in the north side.

The building was built in 1918. The original decorative tin ceiling is still in place, although it's in need of repair. A post office and grocery store occupied the building until 1973 when a bar and cafe named the El Sombrero opened. The name of the business was changed to the El Chaparral in 1976, and it finally became the Boardwalk Bar and Cafe in 1991. Jose Romero most recently bought the business in May, 1994.

The cafe is open Wednesday through Friday from 5:00 p.m. until 10:00 p.m. and Saturday and Sunday from 9:00 a.m. until 10:00 p.m. The cafe offers daily specials, with Mexican food featured every Thursday. Excellent broasted chicken is available daily for dining in or taking out. If the cafe doesn't happen to be open when you arrive, frozen pizzas are always available in the bar.

Most of the customers at the Boardwalk Bar and Cafe are residents of the Ballantine area. A few travelers find their way to the bar during the summer as do visiting hunters in the fall. The barroom customers seem to enjoy themselves, at least from what I could gather when I first visited the place. Besides myself and the bartender, there were only three other people at the bar, and they were the three drunkest men I've ever seen in one place at one time. The guys weren't rude or threatening, but their slurred speech and awkward movements made it obvious they had long ago forgotten whatever it was they came in to drink off their minds. It's unlikely I'll ever witness such a sight again, but it's nice to see people still know how to have a good time.

LONGBRANCH CASINO

OWNER: Greg and Becky Pekovich

HOURS: 6:00 a.m. to 2:00 a.m. Daily

HAPPY HOUR: No

GAMBLING: Video Poker/Keno; Shake-A-Day

LIVE MUSIC: Occasionally

LOCATION: Ballantine

PHONE: 406-967-3855

BEER: Drafts; Domestics; Microbrews

AMUSEMENT: Volleyball; Horseshoes

FOOD: Full Menu Cafe

The Longbranch Casino is just south of the Ballantine Interchange (exit 14) off Interstate 94. The barroom and casino are housed in the west side of the building, and a dining room is in the east side. The entire facility has recently undergone extensive renovations, so everything is very modern. A straight bar with a brass foot rail faces the west wall of the barroom. Two wooden buddy bars stand in the corner near the television set, and video gambling machines line the mirrored walls in the east side of the room. The dining room has a small coffee counter along the east wall, several new tables in the middle of the floor, and padded booths against the walls.

The business was established in 1972. Greg and Becky Pekovich bought the Longbranch in June, 1996, and they spent the next several months upgrading and renovating the building. On November 13, 1996, the Longbranch Casino reopened. Greg's sister, Stephanie Davies, manages the business. The renovations weren't quite finished when I last visited the Longbranch in December, 1996. Plans were in place to add an elevated deck off the north side of the casino and to reopen the truck stop next door. A refueling station, showers, and a truckers lounge will all be part of the truck stop, which is scheduled to open in 1997.

The Longbranch Casino had only been open for a couple of weeks the last time I was in Ballantine, but Stephanie seemed to have things well under control. She operates the business in a community-minded manner. Locals gather at the Longbranch for morning coffee, and visiting scholastic sports teams often stop in for meals before making the trip back home. Because of the casino's close proximity to Interstate 94, a lot of travelers stop by, especially during the summer months. The restaurant is open from 6:00 a.m. until 10:00 p.m. daily, and meal specials are offered throughout the week. Prime rib is the featured dinner item on Friday and Saturday, and a great chicken fried steak is served any time.

BROADVIEW BAR

OWNER: Ada Cassady

HOURS: 10:00 a.m. to Closing Daily

HAPPY HOUR: No

GAMBLING: Video Poker/Keno; Shake-A-Day

LIVE MUSIC: Occasionally

LOCATION: Route 3, **Broadview**

PHONE: 406-667-2267

BEER: Domestics

AMUSEMENT: Pool; Darts; Foosball

FOOD: Grill Items

The Broadview Bar is housed in a wooden structure on the west side of Route 3 in Broadview. A moderate-sized barroom resides in the south side of the building, and a small game room is in the northeast corner. The rest of the building is occupied by a private apartment. A straight wooden bar faces the north wall of the barroom, and a few tables are lined against the south wall.

The history of the Broadview Bar dates back to 1946 when the Golden West Bar opened. The building housed a grocery store prior to the bar moving in. The name of the business was changed to Greusing's Bar in 1949, Nalley's Bar in 1967, and the Sportsman Bar in 1969. Ada Cassady bought the business in 1992 and renamed it the Broadview Bar. Ada's son, Dan, now manages the business.

Lunches and dinners are served from 11:00 a.m. until 10:00 p.m. daily. Burgers and steaks are available off the grill, and if you're interested in pickled foods, there's quite a selection of pickled animal parts in jars behind the bar. I don't know what all they have, but you can probably choose from just about any part of any animal you want.

I'm hesitant to use the words "regular crowd" to describe the customers who routinely hang out at the Broadview Bar. They're great people, but they do uncommon things. In 1991, an informal contest was held to determine who had, shall we say, the biggest manhood. Measurement marks that were etched into the bar top during the contest are still visible near the corner of the bar. Although Dan is unable to produce a copy of the official rules used to govern the competition, he claims the guy who won the contest cheated. On another occasion, Dan exterminated a pesky mouse with a 22 caliber rifle. If you look closely under the middle table along the south wall of the barroom, you can still see the bullet hole in the carpet and floor. Many other noteworthy events have taken place at the Broadview Bar, but space restrictions limit what can be written here. The only way to truly discover what fun awaits you is to visit the Broadview Bar yourself.

HOMESTEAD INN

OWNER: Les Calder

HOURS: 10:00 a.m. to Closing Daily

HAPPY HOUR: No

GAMBLING: Video Poker/Keno; Shake-A-Day

LIVE MUSIC: Occasionally

LOCATION: Route 3, **Broadview**

PHONE: 406-667-2178

BEER: Drafts; Domestics

AMUSEMENT: Pool; Pinball; Video Games

FOOD: Full Menu Grill

The Homestead Inn is housed in a cinder block building on the east side of Route 3 in Broadview. The barroom is relatively large, with a long L-shaped bar near the south wall. Several tables are available if you prefer sitting away from the bar, and there's plenty of open floor space. The building's interior is modern, and it's kept clean and well-maintained. If you prefer the great outdoors, an enclosed deck with tables and a barbecue grill is just off the east side of the barroom.

The business was established in 1933 when the Lance Cigar Store was issued a retail beer license. I'm told it was one of the first such licenses issued in Montana. The name of the bar was changed from the Snuggle Inn to the Homestead Inn when the business moved to its present location in 1975. Les Calder, a former professional hockey player, coach, and scout with the Toronto organization, bought the Homestead Inn in 1991. In Les' first year at the helm, a fire that started in the kitchen caused extensive damage throughout the interior of the building. Renovations were completed in 1992, and Les was back in business.

The Homestead Inn is a friendly establishment where people of all ages gather to socialize with friends. Most of the customers are outgoing types who show a genuine interest in strangers who happen to be at the bar. Residents of Broadview and travelers along Route 3 provide a steady business throughout the year, and custom cutters frequent the Homestead Inn during the fall when they're not harvesting crops in the nearby fields. Occasionally, tour buses even stop so the passengers can stretch their legs and get something to eat or drink.

If you arrive at the Homestead Inn with an appetite, the grill is open throughout the day and evening. Les serves a 1/2 pound hamburger that not only tastes great, it's more filling. Les does the cooking; however, you will never see him in the kitchen wearing the souvenir apron he got from Skinny Dick's Bar and Grill in Alaska. If you're not the kind of person who's easily offended, ask Les to show you the apron he got from Skinny Dick's. After seeing it, you will probably want one of your own.

366

FORT CUSTER BAR AND RESTAURANT

OWNERS: John/Alice/Darren Sjostrom

HOURS: 8:00 a.m. to 2:00 a.m. Daily

HAPPY HOUR: 5:00 to 6:00 Mon - Fri

GAMBLING: Video Poker/Keno; Shake-A-Day

LIVE MUSIC: Occasionally

LOCATION: I-94, Exit 49, **Custer**

PHONE: 406-856-4191

BEER: Drafts; Domestics

AMUSEMENT: Pool

FOOD: Full Menu Restaurant

The Fort Custer Bar and Restaurant is two miles east of Custer at the junction of Interstate 94 and Route 47. The building houses a bar-room and dining room in one open area. A horseshoe-shaped bar stands just outside the kitchen in the north end of the building, several tables line the east wall, and a small dance floor occupies the southwest corner of the floor near the juke box. There's a small wooden deck off the south side of the building, and a campground with full RV hookups is outside.

The Prairie Diner originally stood on the property. The diner was torn down in 1987, and the Fort Custer Bar and Restaurant was built. Although the old diner has been gone for several years, a lot of the local residents still refer to the Fort Custer Bar and Restaurant as the Prairie Diner or just The Diner, so you may hear it called by the old name. Crews from a nearby farm gather at the bar for morning coffee before heading off to work. Don't be surprised if you're eating breakfast in a crowded room one minute, and the next minute you're the only customer there. A mass exodus occurs every day at 9:00 a.m. sharp.

John, Alice, and Darren Sjostrom have owned the Fort Custer Bar and Restaurant since September, 1995. Their regular customers are local residents, but a lot of tourists stop in during the summer. Visiting hunters also frequent the bar and restaurant during big game and bird seasons. The restaurant serves excellent meals at reasonable prices. The last time I checked, you could still get a twenty ounce T-Bone steak for less that $13.00. Everything prepared in the kitchen is made from scratch, including the soups and pies.

The bar hosts celebrations for special occasions such as birthday parties and the annual Labor Day Calcutta. The calcutta is a two day team roping contest held in Custer every Labor Day weekend. The party rotates annually between the Fort Custer Bar and Cafe and the Junction City Saloon. On the years the party is held at the Fort Custer Bar and Cafe, they make a bandstand on a flatbed trailer, set up an outdoor beer garden, and have a dance each night after the roping is over.

JUNCTION CITY SALOON

OWNER: Marian Evenson

HOURS: 10:00 a.m. to 2:00 a.m. Daily

HAPPY HOUR: No

GAMBLING: Video Poker/Keno; Bingo

LIVE MUSIC: Occasionally

LOCATION: 5th St & 2nd Ave, **Custer**

PHONE: 406-856-4888

BEER: Drafts; Domestics

AMUSEMENT: Pool; Video Games

FOOD: Full Menu Grill

The Junction City Saloon is housed in a cinder block building on the corner of 5th Street and 2nd Avenue in Custer. The barroom has a straight bar that stands along the north wall, and several tables are spread throughout the room. A beautiful stone fireplace has recently been added in the southeast corner of the barroom, and a barbecue pit and gas grill are available for outdoor festivities. Canned beer is served from behind the bar out of an old bathtub filled with ice, so you never have to worry about the beer not being adequately chilled.

The saloon gets its name from the old community of Junction City, which was a fur trading town at the junction of the Yellowstone and Bighorn Rivers. High water flooded Junction City in 1903, and the entire town was forced to move. Once things got settled after the move, the new community was named Custer, and Junction City was nothing but a memory.

The Junction City Saloon was built in 1985. Marian Evenson bought the bar in 1989, and she continues to operate it today. The regular customers are residents of Custer and the surrounding communities. Cribbage and card games are popular pastimes at the bar, and live bingo is played every Thursday night. A lot of the local senior citizens gather in the barroom in the mornings to drink coffee, discuss recent world events, and develop solutions for the nation's problems. People also gather to watch televised sporting events, and those who don't care to watch the game can always visit with friends. Unlike most taverns, it's more likely a crowd will be at the Junction City Saloon at 2:00 p.m. on a Tuesday than at 8:00 p.m. on a Saturday. The people in Custer show up at the bar when they feel like it, not when you expect them to.

Free popcorn is available for all customers, and prepared food is served throughout the day. The chili and broasted chicken are popular menu items throughout the week, and an all-you-can-eat buffet is served every Sunday for $5.00 a person. When you're done eating, be sure to take note of the 112 pound sailfish mounted in the glass display case on the west wall of the barroom. The sailfish was the prize catch of Marian's husband, Lehre, in 1991.

BLUE CAT

OWNER: Charlene Loveridge

HOURS: 11:00 a.m. to 2:00 a.m. Daily

HAPPY HOUR: 4:30 to 6:30 Daily

GAMBLING: Video Poker/Keno

LIVE MUSIC: Occasionally

LOCATION: Northern Avenue, **Huntley**

PHONE: 406-348-3517

BEER: Drafts; Domestics

AMUSEMENT: Pool

FOOD: Full Menu Grill

The Blue Cat is housed in a blue cinder block building at 139 Northern Avenue in Huntley. You will easily recognize the place by the sign out front and the stained glass window above the entrance to the barroom. The bar is to your right as you enter the front door, and several tables are available if you can't find an empty barstool. An interesting painting on the back wall depicts a barroom scene where a blue male cat is hustling a white female cat. A local artist did the painting, and he did an excellent job capturing the mood of this establishment.

The Blue Cat had its humble beginnings in 1938 when Dave Whitman opened the Huntley Beer Parlor and Dance Hall. Some fairly wild times are said to have taken place during dance nights at the old beer parlor. Perhaps it was due to the fact that Dave was trying to raise thirteen kids while he owned the business that the dance hall was moved to a place called the Hide-A-Way some years later. When Dave sold the bar, the name became the Huntley Bar. Fire destroyed the building in 1970, so a trailer house was moved onto the property and the bar operated out of the trailer. Fire destroyed the trailer in 1972, so the owners decided to rebuild with fire-resistant cinder blocks.

Charlene Loveridge has owned the business since 1984. Charlene promotes a friendly atmosphere where local folks come to have fun. Because of its location, the Blue Cat doesn't attract a lot of tourist traffic. It's a place where everyone seems to know each other and friends meet to drink and swap stories. Almost immediately upon entering the bar, I could tell the people are what makes the Blue Cat special. Even Bobby Knight, the legendary basketball coach at Indiana University, spent an evening here several years ago without as much as throwing a chair.

Christmas, Thanksgiving, and Easter are the three days of the year the bar is closed. I guess everybody is entitled to a day off. If you're hungry when you arrive, the grill is open anytime except during happy hour, which runs from 4:30 p.m. until 6:30 p.m. seven days a week. Apparently, nobody wants to be interrupted when the drinks are being served at a reduced price. With this crowd, who can blame them.

PRYOR CREEK BAR

OWNER: Keith Wolff   **LOCATION:** I-94, Exit 6, **Huntley**

HOURS: 10:00 a.m. to 2:00 a.m. Daily   **PHONE:** 406-348-9202

HAPPY HOUR: 4:00 to 7:00 Daily   **BEER:** Drafts; Domestics

GAMBLING: Video Poker/Keno; Shake-A-Day   **AMUSEMENT:** Pool

LIVE MUSIC: Occasionally   **FOOD:** Full Menu Cafe

The Pryor Creek Bar is housed in a wooden structure just north of the Huntley Interchange (exit 6) off Interstate 94. The building is visible from the highway, so finding the place shouldn't be a problem. The barroom walls and ceiling are finished with natural wood, providing a comfortable atmosphere. There's plenty of seating space at the horseshoe-shaped bar near the front entrance, and a couple of tables are available in the west side of the room if you prefer sitting away from the bar. A beautiful antique back bar stands against the south wall behind the bar. The hand-crafted piece was built around the turn of the 20th century. I'm told the back bar resided in the old Custer Bar in Custer before being moved to the Pryor Creek Bar.

The Pryor Creek Bar was established in 1978. Elmer Link built the bar and installed the gas pumps in front of the building, and he operated the business until 1982. Rose Lantz owned the business in the mid 1980s when the cafe was added to the north side of the building. Rose called the business the Pryor Creek Bar and Lounge, and she ran the place until Keith Wolff bought it in August, 1996. The cafe is still in operation, but it's currently leased out as a separate business. Meals are served from 6:00 a.m. to 9:00 p.m. daily. I don't know a whole lot about the cafe, but I do know they specialize in home cooking.

Keith was really just getting started when I last visited the Pryor Creek Bar, but he seemed to have things well under control. The bar has always been a friendly local tavern, and I don't expect things to change just because there's a new owner. People on a tight budget can still afford to drink at the Pryor Creek Bar. It's one of the few places I've found that still serves a twelve ounce mug of Old Milwaukee Beer for fifty cents. The draft beer even comes in a frosted mug, so you can't go wrong. Keith plans on having Rocky Mountain Oyster feeds several times a year, perhaps at the change of every season. That's about all the information he could provide when I last saw him, but I have the feeling Keith will do just fine with his new business.

LEWIS AND CLARK TAVERN

OWNER: Leo Miller

HOURS: 9:00 a.m. to 2:00 a.m. Daily

HAPPY HOUR: No

GAMBLING: Video Poker/Keno

LIVE MUSIC: No

LOCATION: Pompey's Pillar

PHONE: 406-875-2531

BEER: Domestics

AMUSEMENT: Pool; Darts

FOOD: Frozen Pizza

The Lewis and Clark Tavern is on the corner of 2nd and Cane streets in Pompey's Pillar. To get there from Interstate 94, take exit 23 and follow the Frontage Road east to the town of Pompey's Pillar. The tavern is inside an old wooden building on the left-hand side of the first, and as far as I know, the only intersection in town. The structure was originally a storage building in a lumber yard. In 1934, the building was renovated into a beer parlor called Eddie's Corner. Leo Miller bought the business in 1970, and although the official name of the bar is the Lewis and Clark Tavern, most people around the area refer to it simply as Leo's or Leo's Place. If you happen to get lost and nobody seems to know where the Lewis and Clark Tavern is, try asking where Leo's is.

Leo operates a basic small town tavern with few frills; a drinking man's bar, if you will. On damp days, a faint musty aroma infiltrates the barroom. A coal furnace on the floor near the front entrance provides heat for the building. The tile floor is kept clean; however, many of the tiles are broken. The front of the bar is well worn, and numerous dollar bills signed by visitors from years past cover the antique wooden back bar. The formica bar top and the paint on the walls match; however, their unique green/blue color is a bit outdated. Pictures and posters cover most of the walls, and porcelain liquor decanters line the top of the liquor cabinet. The barroom definitely has a character all it's own.

Leo very much portrays the laid back atmosphere of the tavern. When people ask if there's a happy hour, Leo simply replies "yes, from 9:00 a.m. until 2:00 a.m.". If you're in a hurry, you better think twice about stopping at Leo's. In an effort to provide quality service to his customers, Leo approaches his job very systematically, to say the least. You will get what you ask for, but it may take a bit longer than you expect. The regular customers don't seem to mind the wait, and about the only other people who come into the bar are lost tourists looking for Pompey's Pillar Landmark. If you happen to be one of those lost tourists, I'd recommend forgetting about the landmark and spending some quality time with Leo Miller at the Lewis and Clark Tavern. Trust me on this one.

RED ROOSTER

OWNERS: Joan and Wesly Fisk

HOURS: 11:00 a.m. to Closing Daily

HAPPY HOUR: 4:00 to 7:00 Mon - Fri

GAMBLING: Video Poker/Keno

LIVE MUSIC: Occasionally

LOCATION: Carey Avenue, **Shepherd**

PHONE: 406-373-5346

BEER: Domestics

AMUSEMENT: Pool

FOOD: Full Menu Grill

The Red Rooster is on the Shepherd-Acton Road, also known as Carey Avenue, in Shepherd. The barroom has a straight bar along the east wall, and plenty of tables are spread across the floor. The cinder block building is quite a fortress if you're trying to break in. The roof is made from 4 x 6 inch pine boards supported by a single wooden beam that runs the entire length of the ceiling.

The bar's origin dates back to 1916 when a business called the Wheeler Inn opened. The Wheeler Inn stood on the south side of Carey Avenue, a few blocks to the west of where the Red Rooster stands today. Allegedly, the bar received the second liquor license issued by the state of Montana. The name of the business was changed to the Red Rooster in 1939 when the bar moved into a building across the road from the present-day bank building. The bar moved to its present location in 1960.

Joan and Wesly Fisk bought the Red Rooster in April, 1990, and they run the business as a neighborhood tavern. There's no pattern to when a crowd may gather at the bar. If you show up on a Friday evening, the place may seem deserted. Likewise, you may find a packed house at 2:30 in the afternoon on a weekday. Years ago, the Red Rooster had a reputation as a place where rowdy characters went for wild times. The bar's reputation has changed considerably in recent years, especially since Joan and Wes took over. These days, the Red Rooster is a quiet, friendly bar where entire families gather to enjoy an evening out together.

The last real excitement to occur at the bar was in 1976 when the owner was robbed at knifepiont by two masked men. The men entered the building in the morning as the owner was making out bank deposit slips. They held a knife to her throat and got away with approximately $1,500 worth of cash and personal checks. Unfortunately, the bad guys were never apprehended. The cash was gone forever, but there was no attempt on the part of the robbers to cash the stolen checks. As a show of support, nearly every customer who had written a check that was stolen from the bar came back and made good on the money. I guess that goes to show that there is at least one advantage of accepting personal checks at a bar.

BEARTRAP BAR

OWNER: Arnold Miller

LOCATION: Main Street, **Worden**

HOURS: 10:00 a.m. to 2:00 a.m. Mon-Sat
Noon to 2:00 a.m. Sundays

PHONE: 406-967-2472

HAPPY HOUR: 5:00 to 7:00 Daily

BEER: Domestics

GAMBLING: Video Poker/Keno

AMUSEMENT: Pool; Darts

LIVE MUSIC: No

FOOD: Frozen Pizza

The Beartrap Bar is on Main Street in Worden. Of the three watering holes in town, the Beartrap might best be described as the no frills drinking establishment. While the other bars cater to families and offer a variety of food items, the Beartrap serves a lot of drinks and has frozen pizzas if you get the munchies. The interior of the barroom is somewhat plain, but why bother with fancy decorations when all the customers want is to drink and enjoy some company.

The bar first opened in 1944 when the building was transformed from a candy store and cafe into a bar and restaurant. The name of the bar has changed twice since then, but the people I spoke with didn't know the exact dates when the name changes occurred. Arnold Miller has owned the bar since 1994. Arnold likes his customers to enjoy themselves, and there's always a lively crowd on hand. Any time is a good time to be there (assuming they're open, of course), but things usually pick up during happy hour, which runs from 5:00 p.m. to 7:00 p.m. seven days a week. If it's cold outside, a Hot Damn Sam from the Beartrap Bar is sure to warm you up. Even if it's not cold outside, a Hot Damn Sam will put you in the right frame of mind for an evening at the Beartrap Bar.

A few tourists wander into the barroom during the summer, but most of the bar patrons are residents of the Worden area. There's a steady crowd throughout the year, but a substantial increase in business usually occurs during hunting season. It seems that visiting hunters come here to relax during the evenings, and local hunters use the bar as a make-shift base camp where they meet other members of their party both before and after a hunting trip. Occasionally, the morning planning stage of the hunt gets so involved that the fearless hunters don't get out of the bar until it's either too dark to hunt or their vision is impaired to the point where they can no longer safely shoot. It's likely that whoever posted the sign behind the bar that reads "Marriage Is The Main Cause Of Divorce" had just attended one of these all-day planning sessions before being evicted from their residence by an angry spouse.

DARK HORSE SALOON

OWNERS: Dixie and Dick Miller

LOCATION: Main Street, **Worden**

HOURS: 9:30 a.m. to 2:00 a.m. Daily

PHONE: 406-967-3050

HAPPY HOUR: 4:30 to 6:30 Mon - Fri

BEER: Drafts; Domestics; Imports; Microbrews

GAMBLING: Video Poker/Keno

AMUSEMENT: Pool; Darts; Horseshoes

LIVE MUSIC: Occasionally

FOOD: Full Menu Cafe

The Dark Horse Saloon is on Main Street in Worden. A spacious barroom resides in the front part of the building, and a dining room is in the rear. The barroom displays many of the early features of the building, such as the original decorative tin ceiling and a beautiful antique back bar and liquor cabinet. The back bar and liquor cabinet were hand-crafted from cherry wood in the late 1800s, transported by steamship up the Missouri and Yellowstone Rivers, and installed in the building when the saloon first opened. The original mirrors are still in the back bar, and both the back bar and liquor cabinet have recently been restored to their original condition.

A mercantile store operated out of the building during the early 1900s, but a saloon took over occupancy in 1913. During prohibition, the saloon officially became a pool hall and gambling parlor. A tavern called the Worden Bar opened in the building after prohibition ended. I'm told the original bar ran almost the entire length of the building. The bar was shortened in the 1950s, and the back half of the barroom was walled-off and renovated into apartments. The bar operated under the name Diamond Lil's from the 1950s through 1988. Dick and Arnold Miller bought the bar that year and changed the name to the Dark Horse Saloon. Dick and Arnold also started a series of renovation projects that finally ended in 1995. Dick and his wife, Dixie, now own the business.

Dixie and Dick promote a family-oriented atmosphere at the bar. Over the past few years, the Dark Horse has become noted for its exceptional seafood and char-broiled rib steaks. Lunches and dinners are served daily, and dinner specials are offered every weekend. The regular customers are mostly working class residents of the Worden area. The bar sponsors pool, bowling, softball, and flag football teams in the local leagues, and they are big supporters of scholastic sports teams. As if they weren't already busy enough, Dixie and Dick also operate a catering business out of the saloon. If you have a big enough party, Dick and Dixie will bring the fixins from the Dark Horse Saloon right to your door step.

DINTY'S

OWNER: Dave Reiner

HOURS: 11:30 a.m. to 2:00 a.m. Daily

HAPPY HOUR: No

GAMBLING: Video Poker/Keno

LIVE MUSIC: Occasionally

LOCATION: Main Street, Worden

PHONE: 406-967-3955

BEER: Drafts; Domestics

AMUSEMENT: Pool; Pinball; Video Games

FOOD: Full Menu Grill

Dinty's is on the east side of Main Street in Worden. Assuming you can find Worden, finding Dinty's is no problem at all. As you enter the front door, a straight bar stands off to your left, two pool tables are to your right, and the dining area is in the back of the building.

The business was established in 1939. The bar was originally called the Silver Wedge, but the name was changed to Dinty's in 1941. The Silver Wedge had a very small barroom, probably the size of the area where the bar alone now stands. Over the years, various owners have completed various renovations and expansions on the building.

Dave Reiner bought the business in 1991. Dave says the one thing that sets Dinty's apart from other bars in the area is the kitchen grill. Dave insists the old grill somehow makes whatever you cook on it taste better than it would if it were cooked on another grill. Science has not yet explained this phenomenon, but Dave's customers all seem to agree that the food cooked on the grill in Dinty's has a better flavor than similar foods they have eaten off other grills. The local explanation centers around the theory that the grill top has absorbed juices and vapors from the thousands of cuts of meat cooked on it over its many years of service. In turn, it is believed the grill somehow releases the special flavorings into the food as it heats it. I don't know if this is possible, but there's presently no other explanation.

Because Worden is somewhat off the beaten path, the vast majority of the bar customers reside in Worden and the surrounding communities. The dining room, on the other hand, draws people from all over the region. Burgers and hot sandwiches are served for lunch, and steaks, seafood, and Mexican foods are available for dinner. Excellent steak specials are offered on Thursday, Friday, and Saturday evenings. Every steak served at Dinty's is hand-cut fresh on the premises, which ensures you will always get a good cut of meat. If you're really hungry, the menu features a thirty-two ounce ribeye steak that's sure to quell your appetite, at least until you get home.

GLOSSARY

86'd - To have been permanently barred from entering an establishment. In other words, once you're 86'd from a saloon, you are never allowed back in.

Blind Pig - A building where alcohol is sold illegally, e.g., a speakeasy. The term is typically used in reference to places where bootlegged liquor and beer were sold during prohibition.

BYOB - Acronym for "Bring Your Own Bottle".

Prohibition - The period from January 29, 1920 to December 5, 1933, during which time it was illegal to manufacture, transport, or sell alcoholic beverages in the United States.

Pub Crawler - One who goes from bar to bar (as defined in Webster's Ninth Collegiate Dictionary)

Roughneck - A person who works on an oil rig.

Small Town - A community with 500 or fewer permanent residents, as reported in the 1990 census.

INDEX A

ALPHABETICAL LIST OF TOWNS

INDEX A

INDEX B

ALPHABETICAL LIST OF TAVERNS